Our Box Was Full

Richard Daly

Our Box Was Full:
An Ethnography for the
Delgamuukw Plaintiffs

UBCPress · Vancouver · Toronto

15 14 13 12 11 10 09 08 07 06 05   5 4 3 2 1

Printed in Canada on acid-free paper

Library and Archives Canada Cataloguing in Publication

Daly, Richard Heywood, 1942-
  Our box was full : an ethnography for the Delgamuukw plaintiffs / Richard Daly.

Includes bibliographical references and index.
ISBN 0-7748-1074-2 (bound); 0-7748-1075-0 (pbk.)

  1. Gitksan Indians – British Columbia – Social conditions. 2. Wet'suwet'en
Indians – British Columbia – Social conditions. 3. Gitksan Indians – British Columbia – Economic conditions. 4. Wet'suwet'en Indians – British Columbia – Economic
conditions. 5. Gitksan Indians – British Columbia – Kinship. 6. Wet'suwet'en
Indians – British Columbia – Kinship. 7. Gitksan Indians – British Columbia – Gifts.
8. Wet'suwet'en Indians – British Columbia – Gifts. I. Title.

E99.K55D34 2004   305.897'2   C2004-906057-0

Canadä

UBC Press gratefully acknowledges the financial support for our publishing
program of the Government of Canada through the Book Publishing Industry
Development Program (BPIDP), and of the Canada Council for the Arts, and
the British Columbia Arts Council.

This book has been published with the help of a grant from the Canadian Federation
for the Humanities and Social Sciences, through the Aid to Scholarly Publications
Programme, using funds provided by the Social Sciences and Humanities Research
Council of Canada, and with a grant from the International Council of Canadian
Studies.

Printed and bound in Canada by Friesens
Set in Stone by Artegraphica Design Co. Ltd.
Copy editor: Joanne Richardson
Proofreader: Deborah Kerr
Indexer: Noeline Bridge
Cartographer: Eric Leinberger

UBC Press
The University of British Columbia
2029 West Mall
Vancouver, BC V6T 1Z2
604-822-5959 / Fax: 604-822-6083
www.ubcpress.ca

To the coming Gitksan and Witsuwit'en generations
and in memory
of the lives and wisdom of those who went before

The people from the "Old World" cannot go back across the sea, nor should they. And the mixed people born of both worlds can have no other home. But the intruders and their offspring can at least make room for the American peoples who remain. They can offer true equality, not annihilations disguised as "integration" or *mestizaje*, nor the fictitious liberty of citizenship in Euro-American countries where the Indian will always be outnumbered and out-voted. They can accept the right of American Indians to be free, equal, and different.

The invaders can stop "conquering and discovering." And if they begin to treat America as a home in which to live, not a treasure house to ransack – a home for the First Nations as well as themselves – they may, unlike Christopher Columbus, discover where they are.

– Ronald Wright, 1992, *Stolen Continents*

Contents

Maps and Figures

Foreword

Michael Jackson

Law and anthropology ought to be on speaking terms. Anthropology, like law, builds upon an understanding of cultural, personal, and economic relationships within societies. Law, like anthropology, has assembled an impressive archive of case studies in the ordering of those relationships and the processes and laws by which conflicts are addressed and resolved. The most venerable centres of both law and anthropology are often the most illustrious and well-known architectural landmarks, be they the US Supreme Court and the Smithsonian Institution in Washington, or the Museum of Civilization and the Supreme Court of Canada in Ottawa. Indeed, in Vancouver, the Museum of Anthropology and the Vancouver Law Courts, centres not only of anthropology and law but also symbols of West Coast modernity, were designed by the same distinguished Canadian architect.

It is not, therefore, surprising when the hereditary chiefs of the Gitksan and Witsuwit'en Houses sought recognition from the Canadian courts of their rights to ownership and jurisdiction of their ancestral territories that they sought a collaboration of the best in both legal and anthropological scholarship. In *Our Box Was Full* Richard Daly aptly describes the role of the *Delgamuukw* case in the hereditary chiefs' pursuit of a legal and political settlement of their grievances and recognition of their rights:

> They envisioned a case based upon postcolonial governance according to long-standing principles of kinship and affinity – a form of reciprocal social life marked by the richness, complexity, and historical depth of their two traditions and culture. They entertained the possibility of establishing sets of overlapping rights and jurisdictions with federal and provincial governments. They hoped to push back the boundaries of what constituted admissible evidence. They hoped to call on Canada and British Columbia to redress some of the injustices of colonial and postcolonial practices by recognizing alternative Aboriginal ways of being human and the values to be found in Aboriginal stewardship and management practices on the land. (3)

Daly's expert evidence, the foundation for this splendid book, was tendered to Chief Justice McEachern at the *Delgamuukw* trial as an essential part of a dialogue between law and anthropology in search of the pathways to justice for the Gitksan and Witsuwit'en. That dialogue never occurred, because Daly's expert evidence, like the evidence of the two other anthropologists who prepared expert opinion reports – Antonia Mills and Hugh Brody – was given short shrift. The chief justice was concerned that Daly's research was based upon participant observation through living in Gitksan and Witsuwit'en territory for two years after the commencement of the litigation; that his research dealt almost exclusively with chiefs (the chief justice made no reference to the evidence that chiefs have the authority to speak for their Houses and are educated in the histories of their Houses); and that Daly was more an advocate than a witness, based on his subscribing to the Statement of Ethics of the American Anthropological Association, which, at that time, required that an anthropologist "must do everything within his power to protect the physical, social and psychological welfare of those studied and to honour their dignity and privacy." The chief justice also found Daly's report "exceedingly difficult to understand" because "it is highly theoretical and I think, detached from what happens 'on the ground.'" The implication seems to be that the field of law and its expert opinions have none of these problems, an implication my first-year students at UBC Law School would vociferously dispute.

For these reasons Daly's report, arguably the most comprehensive anthropological account of the nature of Gitksan and Witsuwit'en economy and society and their distinctive system of ownership and stewardship, was excluded from the factual matrix of the chief justice's judgment in *Delgamuukw*. Lest it be thought that anthropology was singled out for exclusion, it should be noted that the great majority of the legal scholarship that the hereditary chiefs' lawyers brought to bear on the case was also rejected and formed no part of the legal matrix of the chief justice's judgment.

Our Box Was Full therefore brings out of the archive of the *Delgamuukw* case Daly's evidence together with his own reflections on the nature of the dialogue between anthropology and law in Aboriginal rights cases, and the appropriate contribution that anthropologists can make "to the ongoing debate ... about justice and injustice as these issues pertain in that corner of society about which we have specialized knowledge" (5).

A central part of Daly's evidence – a centrality reflected in this book – is the nature of social interaction in gift-giving kinship societies such as those of the Gitksan and Witsuwit'en. Daly suggests that the metaphor of the gift enables us to understand what the Gitksan and Witsuwit'en hereditary chiefs brought to the courtroom and, in turn, what Daly hopes to bring to the attention of the Canadian public and the academy.

In the courtroom ... both the plaintiff witnesses and their so-called expert witnesses engaged in the risky business of gift-giving. They made contributions to a community in search of truth, offering public education about an ancient way of life ... They sought to gift the public with particular knowledge and information, and to give what is at the core of all gifts, namely, ideas and relationships ... The gifting of one another with ideas, counterideas, and something of the personality of their donor is essential to the well-being of any community. In this sense, academic and scientific communities are no different from kinship-based communities. Gifting provides structural strength to the community. However, it has little currency in those fields of human endeavour where gift relations have been superseded by contracts, as in the courts of law. The contents of *Our Box Was Full* were given to the court and returned unopened, but in order to avoid the breaking of the ring, this book has been prepared and given as a contribution to what, it is hoped, might become a future community of understanding. (46-7)

As Daly reflects later in the book, how we of the newcomer society respond to the gifts of knowledge extended by the Gitksan and Witsuwit'en "will determine the quality of the social fabric we weave into the increasingly global future" (98).

The contribution that Daly's work makes to the ethnographic literature will be assessed in due course by the anthropological academy. However, it is important to remember that Daly was not invited into the Gitksan and Witsuwit'en territories to write his doctoral dissertation; rather, he was charged with the task of applying his academic training and expertise towards providing the court with opinions relevant to the proof of Gitksan and Witsuwit'en Aboriginal rights. In an appropriate reversal of fortunes, the Supreme Court of Canada – in articulating the nature of Aboriginal title (recognized and affirmed by section 35 of the Constitution Act, 1982) and in establishing the necessary elements of proof of such title – over-ruled by Chief Justice McEachern. Consistent with the Supreme Court of Canada's judgment in *Delgamuukw,* Daly's analytical framework for understanding Gitksan and Witsuwit'en social and economic institutions – a framework rejected by Chief Justice McEachern – has now become one of the models for how anthropological evidence can fulfill its appropriate place (1) in the respectful dialogue with both Canadian and Aboriginal law in the proof of Aboriginal title and (2) in establishing a reconciliation between the preexisting rights of First Nations and the sovereignty of the Crown.

It may come as a surprise to many readers of *Our Box Was Full* that, at the time of the trial of Delgamuukw, some 140 years after the founding of the Colony of Vancouver Island and over 300 years after the British Crown first entered into treaties with Aboriginal nations in North America, the nature of Aboriginal title and its legal status in British Columbia were still unresolved by the courts. A large part of the challenge faced by the Gitksan and Witsuwit'en hereditary chiefs and their lawyers involved persuading the judiciary that a conceptualization of Aboriginal title as a non-proprietary interest that gave the right to use land only for traditional subsistence purposes, at the pleasure of the Crown, was inconsistent with the principles and practice upon which the Crown had concluded treaties with Aboriginal nations in other parts of North America – principles reflected in the Royal Proclamation of 1763, which had ripened into fundamental principles of the common law applicable to the relationships between Aboriginal peoples and the Crown in British Columbia. The Gitksan and Witsuwit'en argued before Chief Justice McEachern that the evidence of the hereditary chiefs and of their experts showed that the true character of their pre-existing rights reflected a proprietary relationship based on concepts and laws of ownership as well as a fully elaborated jurisdiction based on concepts and laws regarding land stewardship, all of which was grounded in the interlocking weave of a kinship society. Chief Justice McEachern, in rejecting this evidence and the legal argument upon which it was based, adopted a non-proprietary conception of Aboriginal title that was limited to subsistence use of the land. This was based on a Hobbesian view of Aboriginal society as having only a primitive economy and no real laws. Given such a conception of Aboriginal rights and Aboriginal society, it is not surprising that Daly's report, which contained a detailed elaboration of the sophisticated nature of Gitksan and Witsuwit'en social and economic life, fell on deaf ears.

The Supreme Court of Canada's judgment in *Delgamuukw,* while not embracing the language of ownership and jurisdiction, unambiguously rejected Chief Justice McEachern's narrow conception of Aboriginal title. In affirming that Aboriginal title was a property right encompassing the right to exclusive use and occupation of land, the court stated that its characteristics "must be understood by reference to both common law and Aboriginal perspectives." In articulating the content of Aboriginal title, Chief Justice Lamer stated:

> Aboriginal title arises from the prior occupation of Canada by Aboriginal peoples. That prior occupation is relevant in two different ways: first, because of the physical fact of occupation, and second, because Aboriginal title originates in part from pre-existing systems of Aboriginal law. However, the law of Aboriginal title does not only seek to determine the historic rights of Aboriginal peoples to land; it also seeks to afford legal protection to prior occupation in the present-day. Implicit in the protection of historic patterns of occupation is recognition of the importance of the continuity of the relationship of an Aboriginal community to its land over time.

I develop this point below with respect to the test for Aboriginal title. The relevance of the continuity of the relationship of an Aboriginal community with its land here is that it applies not only to the past, but to the future as well. That relationship should not be prevented from continuing into the future. As a result, uses of the lands that would threaten that future relationship are, by their very nature, excluded from the content of Aboriginal title. (*Delgamuukw* at para. 126-7)

As the reader of *Our Box Was Full* will assuredly find, Daly's expert report in the *Delgamuukw* trial fits comfortably within this conception of Aboriginal title and reveals in elegant detail the importance of "the continuity of the relationship" of the Gitksan and Witsuwit'en "to its land over time."

Daly's analytic framework is even more compellingly relevant to the Supreme Court's ruling on the test for the proof of Aboriginal title. That test requires the Aboriginal group asserting title to satisfy the following criteria: (1) The land must have been occupied prior to sovereignty (in British Columbia this is 1846); (2) if present occupation is relied on as proof of occupation pre-sovereignty, then there must be continuity between present and pre-sovereignty occupation; and (3) at sovereignty, that occupation must have been exclusive (*Delgamuukw* at para. 143). In proving occupancy, Chief Justice Lamer stated: "the Aboriginal perspective on the occupation of their lands can be gleaned, in part, but not exclusively, from their traditional laws, because those laws were elements of practices, customs and traditions of Aboriginal peoples. As a result, if at the time of sovereignty, an Aboriginal society had laws in relation to land, those laws would be relevant to establishing the occupation of lands which are the subject of a claim for Aboriginal title. Relevant laws might include, but are not limited to, a land tenure system or laws governing land use" (para. 148).

In proving the exclusivity of Aboriginal occupation, the Supreme Court also held that this must be assessed from the perspective of both the common law and Aboriginal law, placing equal weight on each. Chief Justice Lamer stated:

A consideration of the Aboriginal perspective may also lead to the conclusion that trespass by other Aboriginal groups does not undermine, and that presence of these groups by permission may reinforce, the exclusive occupation of the Aboriginal group asserting title. For example, the Aboriginal group asserting the claim to Aboriginal title may have trespass laws which are proof of exclusive occupation, such as that the presence of trespassers does not count as evidence against exclusivity. As well, Aboriginal laws under which permission may be granted to other Aboriginal groups to use or reside even temporarily on land would reinforce the finding of exclusive occupation. (para. 157)

Daly's finely woven and textured account of the Gitksan and Witsuwit'en land tenure system anticipates with remarkable symmetry the Supreme Court of Canada's judgment in *Delgamuukw*. In compiling the evidentiary proof of Gitksan and Witsuwit'en Aboriginal title, Daly appropriately focuses on indigenous concepts of exclusivity reflected in the crest system; identifies the complex set of laws governing access to and use of House territories, deeply embedded in concepts of kinship and reciprocity; and illustrates the well-defined laws of trespass that were once enforced with ultimate punishment but, as befits an evolving civilization, have been replaced with proportionate punishment.

In this important respect, the Supreme Court's judgment in *Delgamuukw* and Richard Daly's expert opinion evidence, as refined and explained in *Our Box Was Full*, open up the real possibility for the much-needed dialogue between law and anthropology in the ongoing collective pursuit of justice for Aboriginal peoples.

Michael Jackson, QC
Professor of Law
Vancouver

Foreword

Peter Grant

Richard Daly has had the singular experience of providing the most extensive ethnological opinion evidence heard before any Canadian court with respect to Aboriginal rights and title. His analysis and conclusions are finally being made available to the wider academic and legal communities and are a tribute to the Gitksan and Witsuwit'en elders who entrusted Dr. Daly with their histories.

This publication of Dr. Daly's evidence enriches the understanding of the antiquity of Canada's economic, social, and spiritual foundations and of what this country can be if Aboriginal peoples and their rights are recognized as an essential and distinctive part of Canada's history as well as its future. This work is not only for anthropologists, academics, and those with a keen interest in understanding the Gitksan and Witsuwit'en peoples. It is also an essential read for legal practitioners who want to understand the role of expert witnesses and, in particular, those whose evidence is of a type with which the courts are not generally familiar. It is also an essential read for any who want to understand the foundation for Aboriginal rights and title in what is now British Columbia.

In 1977, nine years before Richard Daly and Richard Lee arrived in Gitksan and Witsuwit'en territory, Canada's minister of Indian and northern affairs, Hugh Faulkner, accepted the Gitksan and Witsuwit'en claim over their traditional territory as a foundation for negotiating a "comprehensive claim" under the federal treaty-making process. Unfortunately, British Columbia refused to acknowledge Aboriginal rights or title in this province and would not participate in such negotiations. Canada had a policy of negotiating only six comprehensive claims at one time and only one in British Columbia.

By 1982 the Gitksan and Witsuwit'en chiefs had waited five years, and there was no sign of treaty negotiations in the foreseeable future. Many of those chiefs had been born in the late nineteenth or early twentieth centuries and were repositories of oral histories taught by their parents and grandparents. These oral histories went back to long before the arrival of the first white person within the Gitksan and Witsuwit'en territories. It was readily apparent that these chiefs would not live long enough to sit at a treaty negotiation table with Canada.

Many of these chiefs had travelled over their traditional House territories and those of their *wil'naat'ahl* (closely related Houses in their clans) and of their *wilksiwitxw* (father's side). As a result of this there was, across the community, a collective knowledge of the entire Gitksan and Witsuwit'en territories. If the Crown continued to delay treaty negotiations, then the strength of this collected knowledge and oral histories would not be a valued part of any treaty negotiations. Furthermore, unless it was forced to recognize Aboriginal rights and title, there was nothing to compel British Columbia to participate in treaty negotiations. Although it was not legally necessary for British Columbia to be at the treaty table, Canada refused to negotiate without it.

After many months of careful deliberation, the Gitksan chiefs and Witsuwit'en chiefs decided to take their claim to title to their land ("ownership" of the territory) and their system of governance over the lands and resources ("jurisdiction" over the territory and their peoples) to the Canadian courts to obtain the long-standing recognition denied them since 1860.

The Gitksan and Witsuwit'en made it very clear to their legal counsel and to the experts that they wished the case to be founded on their own evidence and their oral histories. This was unlike the method of presentation in previous well-known Aboriginal rights cases in Canada, including *Calder* and *Baker Lake,* in which the main evidence was presented by non-Aboriginal "experts." It was in this context that Richard Daly agreed to work with the Gitksan and Witsuwit'en in the preparation of their case. The integrity and strength of his evidence lies in the fact that he respected this decision of the Gitksan and Witsuwit'en.

Working from his own research, from the descriptions that they had provided to him, and on their testimony in court, Daly was able to articulate and describe in extensive detail the Gitksan and Witsuwit'en system. However, he was sensitive to their strategy, and he acknowledged that they were the experts with respect to their traditional system.

The author states in his introduction that he is "partisan," as indeed he is: in the sense that he respects the methodology by which the Gitksan and Witsuwit'en wished their evidence to be presented. As the legal counsel who introduced Dr. Daly's evidence at trial, I can positively state that he was an "expert" in the true sense of the word, as used by the courts. He neither overstated nor exaggerated the strengths of the Gitksan or Witsuwit'en systems, and he neither understated nor minimized the impacts of colonialism on these systems; rather, he used his expertise to put the Gitksan and Witsuwit'en evidence in context.

It was within the context of his own ethical standards – standards set by the American Anthropological Association – that Daly was criticized in the court. How absurd it would be to say that a medical doctor was biased due to her/his obligation under the Hippocratic Oath to safeguard her/his patient's well-being. This is what happened to Dr. Daly because Canadian courts were not familiar with a science whose method of analysis includes the methodological practice of "participant observation" – a standard anthropological method applied to the study of culture(s).

In this case, the trial judge effectively rejected Daly's evidence. Because the appellate courts in Canada rely on the trial judge's findings of fact, the succeeding five Court of Appeal judges and nine Supreme Court of Canada judges who considered this case did not have the opportunity to observe Dr. Daly's presentation of his evidence and refused to overturn (with two exceptions) the trial judge's rejection of Daly's evidence.

Dr. Daly's skill and his ability to translate his observations of the impact of colonialism on Aboriginal peoples is exemplified by his description of the "hypothetical elderly woman seated in the witness box." This description demonstrates how the courtroom might appear to an Aboriginal witness, and it should be required reading for any lawyer who intends to call Aboriginal evidence in a court. Daly's observation of the exceedingly difficult task of testifying before a court with respect to the nature of Aboriginal ownership and jurisdiction brings alive the enormous challenge of mounting such cases.

I distinctly recall 8 March 1991, the day upon which the trial judgment in *Delgamuukw* was handed down. One of the leading Witsuwit'en chiefs came to me that day in Smithers and asked me: "Why did the judge ask me questions when he wasn't listening to anything I had to say?" I had no answer for him. In *Our Box Was Full* Dr. Daly places the role of the court in context, with respect to the recognition of the rights of Canada's Aboriginal peoples, and, in doing so, provides the chief with an answer to his question.

Peter Grant
Co-counsel for the Plaintiffs, *Delgamuukw et al.* v. *The Queen*
Vancouver

MAP 1   Gitksan and Witsuwit'en territories
Source: Gitksan and Wet'suwet'en Chiefs (1988).

Preface

This book is based partly on opinion evidence offered to the Gitksan and Witsuwit'en peoples, whose territories lie within the boundaries of British Columbia. Research was undertaken in conjunction with the Aboriginal rights litigation known as *Delgamuukw et al. v. The Queen in the Right of the Province of British Columbia and the Attorney-General for Canada*. I arrived in Gitksan-Witsuwit'en territory together with fellow consultant, Professor Richard B. Lee of the University of Toronto, in April 1986.[1] We were greeted by the political leaders of what, at the time, was called the Gitksan-Wet'suwet'en Tribal Council. The leaders explained their aim of achieving public and official recognition of their rights to their lands and to self-governance. We learned that, unlike other cases in Canada at the time, such as *Bear Lake* in Ontario or *Baker Lake* in the Northwest Territories, which confined Aboriginal land rights to usufruct on lands not currently needed for other uses, the present case would stress rights that had to do with what the plaintiffs had decided to call "ownership and jurisdiction." In other words, they would stress the indigenous roots of Gitksan and Witsuwit'en Aboriginal tenure – roots that pre-dated European presence in the region. These First Nations would also be pressing for "non-frozen rights," or the recognition of the right to sustain themselves in a high-tech manner and not simply by "traditional" hunting and fishing (or what they sometimes referred to as "the buckskin and berries syndrome" of government officials).

We also learned that the plaintiffs' concept of landholding differed from that of the neighbouring Nisga'a. By 1986, when I began work in the region, the Nisga'a had been negotiating with the Government of Canada for thirteen years – since their land rights case (*Calder*) had emerged from the Supreme Court in 1973 – and still had another eleven years to go before an agreement was reached in 1997. The Nisga'a had constituted themselves as a corporate sole, wherein their chiefs *(simgigat)* and four clans *(pdeek)* pooled their lands and hereditary rights into "a common bowl," which was equated with the watershed of the Nass, or Lisiims, River. As a geopolitical entity, this also coincided rather closely with the Department of Indian Affairs' administrative territorial boundaries and the band council structure that had been imposed on the Nisga'a (and most other First Nations peoples) in the nineteenth century. This, in the eyes of the Gitksan (and the Witsuwit'en), was injurious to Gitksan interests (particularly to the villages of Gitanyow and Kispiox), whose residents had House territories within the watershed of the upper Nass River.

Lee and I were told that the Nisga'a had adopted a new form of organization that conflicted with that based on long-standing ties of kinship and marriage, which was formerly in place all across this inter-ethnic region. According to this long-standing indigenous arrangement, the Nisga'a were clan brothers and sisters, and often cousins, rather than strangers from a different administrative district. We were informed that the newer, Euro-influenced system ignored both historical and sociological truth (Sterritt et al. 1998 make a considerable case for this position). The Gitksan and Witsuwit'en case, headed by the initial signatories (Delgamuukw, the first signatory for the Gitksan, and Gisdaywa, first signatory for the Witsuwit'en), was to be pursued *not* by a collective of Department of Indian Affairs (DIA)–defined bands or by collective nations operating as a corporate sole, but by the local kinship-based, corporate agents. Individual chiefs would represent their matrilineal House groups; in addition, some of these chiefly women and men would represent other, closely related, Houses. The Tribal Council – later renamed the Office of Hereditary Chiefs – explained that this form of kinship land representation, and "old time" inter-clan[2] dispute settlement (particularly along inter-ethnic boundaries through clan solidarity and inter-ethnic marriage alliances), was central to indigenous practices of peace-keeping. This was a system that continued east and south among the Witsuwit'en and their neighbours, and west and north among the Gitksan and their neighbours (including their Nisga'a cousins and affines), and provided a common denominator, cutting across linguistic and government administrative boundaries. They stressed that the matrilineal system was a common structural edifice upon which First Nations nation building could advance within the nation-state of Canada, and upon which social life could, as in precolonial times, be legitimately structured.

My research contract involved producing a report on the local economy from approximately the early nineteenth century to the late twentieth century and on the social relations embodied therein. I was to help "flesh out" certain aspects of these multiheaded, decentralized, but complex societies and the changes they had experienced over the past two centuries, presenting the peoples' experiences and traditions in a conventional anthropological format. I was to be one of several "translators" of the plaintiffs' traditions and current ways of life for the court and the wider society.

In this work I have sought to reveal the "knowing subject" as something more than an unsituated and disembodied anthropological consciousness. I, as the knowing subject, seek to acknowledge my anthropological embeddedness in the historical moment, without disappearing the voices of those First Nations peoples who were not only my clients and the objects of my study but also the source of data I was expected to defend both before peers (who, along with members of the plaintiff community, sat in the audience during many of the almost 400 days in court) and before the chief justice of the Supreme Court of British Columbia. I was constrained by a series of overlapping competences of knowledge: the corpus of knowledge of my own profession and personal history, that of the researched, that of the legal profession, and that of the popular commonsense knowledge held by both participants and observers. As researcher, I strove to work with professional dispassion, within the limits of the "facts" and the relevant documentation, and within the discipline of my professional training; yet I was not especially assiduous in seeking to appear to be more dispassionate by desituating myself from the objects of study and the problematic of being party to one side in a court case. I did not subscribe to the obscurantist legal fiction that I was working as a transcendent subject who observes the phenomenal world from a non-phenomenal Platonic realm of forms, removed from the historical and partisan events pertaining to Aboriginal rights in Canada during the late 1980s and 1990s.

Having said this, I want to offer a personal caveat. Normally, anthropologists "go into the field" to gather data and then retreat to their academic commitments in the universities, where they write up their ethnographic monographs and engage in comparative work with the help of libraries and the Internet. In this particular instance, I was invited to live in proximity to the client community while gathering data, writing it up directly into my report, and revising it through ongoing observation and questioning in the local community (which is much easier to do when writing on site rather than at a university). In this way I could document ongoing social relations and changes in that community, and supplement information gathered earlier. The situation provided a considerable degree of access to the people's lives, particularly since I worked for the community – without what local suspicion frequently fears to be the anthropologist's "real agenda." However, it also left my work open to racist charges from the defendants' counsel, who insisted that I had "gone Native" simply because I practised a standard anthropological approach to data collection – namely, participant observation. (As an example of this approach, see Figures 11 and 12, photos taken during the Witsuwit'en and Gitksan highway blockade at Moricetown during the summer of 1990. This action was mounted in solidarity with the Oka uprising staged by the Mohawk outside Montreal and occurred well after I had given my opinion evidence in court.) Activities similar to this, but occurring prior to my presentation of evidence, were used as proof of partisanship and subjectivity by counsel for the *Delgamuukw* defendants, who argued that such participation proved me to be a subjective advocate of the current cause of my clients.

Well, I did not "go Native" (which is an ethnocentrically loaded and colonialist term), and I hope I did not go non-Native. I simply strove to fulfill my role as a visitor and a guest throughout my years in the area. The greatest part of my conscious local enculturation was discovering my "otherness" as a mainstream Canadian, living in the plaintiffs' territories as a tolerated guest possessing some utility in relation to the community's long-term aspirations. I learned that I did not belong, that these territories in the very region of Canada where I was conceived and born exuded rich but exclusionary cultural traditions. I learned that these territories had not been "vast and empty" or "pristine wilderness," as the chief justice was fond of saying, at least not since an interglacial period of many millennia past. I learned that local control and ownership of the region, in distinct territorial and fishing site units, seemed to have been in existence for much longer than Europeans could fathom. The immigrant mentality is so strong in the main Anglo-Saxon culture of Canada from which I hail that it tends to view First Nations peoples in terms familiar to an Anglo-Saxon self-image. In a word, First Nations peoples are often considered "primal immigrants" who happened to get here first and take up the pioneer project before the rest of us. Many Canadians still do not view First Nations peoples as the national inhabitants of their own ancient lands, the way they view Europeans in Europe, or Asians in Asia, or the way they view Canadian nationality in relation to Mexican or American nationality. They claim that everybody in Canada is a subject of the Crown and an immigrant. Full stop.

I did not "go Native" but I am, to an extent, partisan. I am partisan because I am an anthropologist living in a postcolonial world. Had I not been both fascinated by and concerned about indigenous peoples around the globe, their past and their future, I would not have entered the discipline of anthropology. On the whole, the profession of anthropology is overwhelmingly on the side of the indigenous populations studied. We all too seldom take up C. Wright Mills's challenge to "study up" and document the modus operandi of the elites. In *Delgamuukw* the government defendants were unable to get any leading reputable anthropologists to appear on the witness stand to testify against the claims of the First Nations plaintiffs. And those whom they did obtain limited themselves to archival work and to consulting the defence on how to cross-examine the plaintiffs' witnesses.

Most anthropologists are ethically partisan. We study living human subjects. We do not possess the dispassion of the forensic expert but we do recognize the existence of unsavoury, paradoxical, and/or frustrating evidence. In land rights cases these facts have to be faced with dispassion and objectivity. Our research need be no less objective, no less scrupulously assessed for biases, no less empirically based, than that submitted by researchers working for governmental defendants in such cases. At the same time, the work carried out by researchers for both sides – as part of the litigation process – has affected the lives of the plaintiff communities. Moreover, the partisanship of our opponents is constantly overlooked by judges in such cases because, I submit, the points of view offered by the defendants usually seem self-evident, based as they are on the sanctity of documents and a class and cultural perspective familiar to those who preside in the courts of law. Furthermore, anthropologists who work in conjunction with indigenous land rights issues usually work in an atmosphere of frustration. For the most part, the knowledge we create has little influence or lasting effect upon the level of enlightenment that nation-states bring to their policies on Aboriginal peoples' rights to land and self-governance.

Following the repatriation of the Canadian Constitution by Pierre Elliott Trudeau's government in 1982, Parliament allowed for the funding for several "test cases" that were intended to help define the specific nature of Aboriginal rights, which, in section 35.1 of Canada's Constitution, have provisionally been left without full definition. The Gitksan and Witsuwit'en First Nations land rights issue was one of these judicial test cases. The major players were (1) the judicial system of lawyers, courts, and judges; (2) the First Nations plaintiffs and their communities; and (3) those contracted to provide expert evidence (biologists, geologists, paleo-botanists, ecologists, meteorologists, archaeologists, anthropologists, linguists, historians, geographers, cartographers, administrators, and fishery officers) for either the plaintiffs or the defendants.

Because my research for this project was necessarily influenced by the actualities of a political and jural process in Canadian society, I have tried to make the text of what follows understandable to the general reader while, at the same time, allowing my teachers – some of the many knowledgeable members of the Gitksan and Witsuwit'en communities – to instruct the reader directly with their own ethnographic explanations. From a current anthropological standpoint, one could object that the text contains a degree of implied functionality that our discipline had more or less transcended by the end of the twentieth century. This was inevitable in that the project was geared to the court process. It was not the result of a doctoral thesis or the application of any specific fashionable body of theory to a body of ethnography. My mandate was to provide facts, information, and context for the plaintiffs' demand for the legal recognition of their full-fledged proprietorship, a tradition of self-governance, and their comprehensive knowledge and extensive use of the land in the course of what, broadly speaking, are and were their economic pursuits. Accordingly, *Our Box Was Full* tries to balance detail on land use, nutrition, ecology, and seasonal round with discussions on decision taking, exchange and trade, indigenous laws concerning immovable property, and, of course, the hallmark of Northwest Coast ethnography, the giving of gifts that reaffirms the rules and laws not only of ownership but also of everyday social intercourse.

Chapter 1 describes the juridical arena in which the research was presented for social interaction and verification before an audience of jurists, professional specialists, and the indigenous, or "lay," population – and which led to the rejection of this evidence by the trial judge who, at the end of the day, was unshaken in his belief that the life of the plaintiffs, before the just and magnanimous administration of *Pax Britannica*, was a Hobbesian world of all against all. Chapter 1 also examines the complexity of trying to present the trajectories of these peoples' ways of life over the past two centuries. It tries to do so in a way that reflects both the hierarchy of indigenous sociality, reciprocal gift-giving, and controlled competition without minimizing the foraging ethos. This ethos has a code of "gift-wrapped" reciprocity and respect, recognizing the ephemeral nature of good fortune while, at the same time, manifesting mistrust towards the enduring exercise of power beyond the immediate kin group (particularly in periods when there are no major crises affecting several families or villages).

Subsequent chapters are a response to a broad question I posed to myself at the outset of the research; namely, what are the necessary factors involved in the relationship between these two peoples and their land that impel them to demand recognition of their title to such a hefty section of what is today British Columbia instead of resting content with their contemporary life, either in a number of reserve villages along Highway 16 or as labour migrants in urban centres?

Chapter 2 is an ethnographic account of a *yukw*, or major feast, as an example of the ethics of social intercourse within and between members of these societies through the production and expenditure of material wealth. The totem-pole-raising *yukw*, or potlatch feast, outlined here is the result of my collaboration with a number of elderly female feast organizers who were eager to let the world know how and why they feast. Such events involve a set of distinct actions and transactions which, *when done properly*, constitute one of the culminating feasts in the regional feasting cycle – a feast that seldom occurs more than once in a generation. This feast is at once ceremonial, political, and social. While not strictly part of the economy in our modern sense of capital generation and distribution, it does legitimate the economy. It is the socially and jurally approved familial institution that sanctions the system of land tenure, the kinship politics, and the distribution of values, all under the cloak (or, more correctly, the chiefly robe) of gifting and reciprocity. The actions and behaviour of people discussed in all the other chapters reflect the ethic of gifting and reciprocity, of encouraging but controlling both status competition and the freedom of action of local kinship groups.

Chapter 3 describes the peoples' traditional diet and ecology, and their foraging strategies through the seasons and into the contemporary mixed economy. Chapter 4 examines the kinship structure of the economy, and Chapter 5 discusses the question of foragers in relation to storage/accumulation and social hierarchy. Chapter 6 focuses on gifts, sharing, and exchange – against the conditions of the late-eighteenth- and early-nineteenth-century fur trade. Finally, Chapter 7 outlines more of the armature upon which the economy has been played out since before European arrival, namely, the indigenous system of landholding and the exercise of authority with regard to territories and fishing sites. This is a system that underlies the gift exchanges and formal public procedures carried out in the potlatch feasts and that gives discursive shape to Gitksan and Witsuwit'en production, distribution, and consumption.

The direct citations from the Witsuwit'en and Gitksan are taken from the transcripts of the *Delgamuukw* trial, not because I did not interact with the plaintiffs in everyday life but because such cross-examined testimony formally holds more weight in a court of law than do interview notes. These statements were frequently first elicited in interviews and observation sessions (Daly 1986-88), then used to help the lawyers select lay witnesses and elicit similar information in the courtroom.

This work was assisted by many residents in the Witsuwit'en and Gitksan communities, and certainly not only by chiefs. I am thankful for the warm reception, hospitality, and forbearance I received over the course of more than a decade. Neil J. Sterritt and Don Ryan inspired and encouraged the work, and plaintiffs' librarians (first Gene Joseph and later Kathy Holland) have been tirelessly accommodating. Here, at the Ethnographic Museum Library in Oslo, I am deeply indebted to librarian Nancy Frank and the graphics assistance of Marija and Dragan Gacinovic. I thank Richard Lee in Toronto, and in another hemisphere, in South Australia, via cyberspace, I am indebted to Kingsley Garbett for decades of intermittent but stimulating discussion on the finer points of social theory. I also gained an immense treasure of information and experiences from my Gitksan and Witsuwit'en teachers, many of whom, since the trial level of *Delgamuukw,* have left this mortal coil and are once again between incarnations, yet the force of their various personalities remains a part of my inner life. Jane Smith Mowatt has been upbeat and patient in responding to my e-mails as I revised the manuscript. I also appreciate Bruce Rigsby, Jim Kari, and Sharon Hargus for some basic pointers in terms of orthography. They cheerfully did their best to make contextual guesses as to what my unschooled transcriptions referred.

Lillian O'Connor, Chris Roth, Margaret Anderson, Beverley Clifton Percival, and Dan Savard of the BC Archives; Frédéric Paradis at the Canadian Museum of Civilization; and the staff at UBC Press have all helped me seek out the appropriate permissions for use of texts and photos.

Moreover, I am grateful for the pithy criticisms of the anonymous peer reviewers over the years. I hope my responses to these have helped improve the reasoning in what follows. I am also grateful for both the impatience and encouragement of she who goes through life beside me, and the unbounded kindnesses and hospitality of my many vibrant neighbours in Hazelton/Gitanmaax, Moricetown, Hagwilget, Kispiox, Glen Vowell, Gitsegukla, Gitwangax, Gitanyow, Smithers, and Terrace. I also appreciate the occasional comradeship of some of the expert witnesses who laboured for the plaintiffs in the *Delgamuukw* case.

It was a fascinating ethnographic experience to work with some highly unconventional members of the legal profession; particularly, I luxuriated in the elegance of Professor Michael Jackson's thinking and writing, and his gentle suggestions for more mellifluous phrasing. At the same time, I was constantly encouraged by the excitement and humanity of Peter Grant's relations to plaintiffs, experts, and the world in general, not to mention the general assistance and good cheer of Louise Mandell and Stuart Rush, and the nocturnal black humour of Murray Adams. I appreciate the boundless support of Jean Wilson and the technical staff at UBC Press, especially Holly Keller. This book has been published with the help of a grant from the Canadian Federation for the Humanities and Social Sciences, through the Aid to Scholarly Publications Programme, using funds provided by the Social Sciences and Humanities Research Council of Canada. Finally, I want to offer deep-felt thanks to Richard Overstall, the vigilant but unobtrusive director of research for the case, and now a lawyer himself, who always managed to steer the work in such a way that we somehow remained within the relatively tranquil eye of the storm, or, as he might put it, on the complex razor edge of patterned existence protruding from the prevailing sea of chaos.

Orthography

The Gitksan revised the orthography of their name in 1994 to "Gitxsan," and the Wet'suwet'en, at a similar period, changed to "Witsuwit'en." In 2002, "Gitksan" and "Gitksen" were returning to favour.

Witsuwit'en orthography follows that used by Sharon Hargus (revised Hildebrandt): ï (i) high, front, unrounded vowel; ë (E) lower-mid front, unrounded vowel; gg (G) voiceless unaspirated uvular stop; c (c) voiceless, aspirated palatal/pre-velar stop; g (j) voiceless unaspirated palatal/pre-velar stop. Orthography used in the *Delgamuukw* case for names of Witsuwit'en clans, Houses, and chiefs has been retained here.

The Gitksan orthography follows the Bruce Rigsby popular transcription (Hindle and Rigsby 1973), somewhat simplified (not generally marking differences between hard and soft l, m, n, w, and y). Short vowels approximate English equivalents and long vowels are double letters; g (gutteral back g); k (soft front k); k' (hard front k); k̲ (soft back k); k̲' (hard back k); kw' (hard kw); p' (hard p); t' (hard t); tl' (hard hl); ts' (hard ts); ' (glottal stop).

Cover Illustration

The mask on the cover is called *Ghost Bear Transforming* (photo: Clinton Hussey; facilitated by, and with permission from the creator of the mask, Tsimshian artist Terry Starr and the Eagle Spirit Gallery, Vancouver). Terry Starr explains the mask as follows:

> Our people call this the Ghost Bear. It is also known as the Kermode, after Frank Kermode, the former director of the Royal British Columbia Museum. If it didn't have a recessive gene it would be a black bear. It's not albino because it has brown eyes and brown nose. For thousands of years its home has been the rainforest of Princess Royal Island on the north coast of British Columbia. The island does not have a human population today but it used to be a home to our Tsimshian people. Isolated on the island for so long, the bear's recessive gene did well for itself. One out of every ten bears is white. It even spread to the adjacent mainland. Our people have stories about how this bear came into being. Long ago, the world was covered in ice and snow. One day, Raven, the creator of the world, came down from heaven and turned the world green, as it is today. But as a reminder of the time when everything was white, Raven went among the bears and turned every tenth one the colour of snow. Raven decreed that the white bear, which the Tsimshian call Moksgm'ol, would live forever in peace.

Terry's mask reveres the past and reaffirms its continuity with the future. It speaks directly to the soul. It speaks to the way that the land gets under the skin of its people and the way the people are woven into the very roots of the land.

Our Box Was Full

1
Introduction

The hinterlands of the Western Cordillera of British Columbia have long been home to the Tsimshianic-Penutian-speaking Gitksan and their Athapaskan-speaking Witsuwit'en neighbours. The mountainous, riverine homeland of these peoples, partly along the Skeena and Nass watersheds that flow into the Pacific near Prince Rupert, and partly along the Fraser River watershed that enters the far-off Gulf of Georgia at Vancouver, has provided them with both access to, and defence from, the rapid changes occurring on the adjacent coast. These changes were wrought by land-based and maritime fur trading in the late eighteenth century, colonial settlement and administration in the nineteenth century, and, more recently, industrial extraction of raw materials and energy such as gold, salmon, timber, hydroelectricity, and coal (Daly 1999). Their territories were subject to the fur trade, and, briefly, to gold prospecting. From the 1880s, significant numbers of these peoples migrated to participate in the new commercial fishery on the coast during the short summer season, but not until the second half of the twentieth century were their territories exploited massively for hydroelectricity and forest and mineral products. The Witsuwit'en and the Gitksan, along with their coastal neighbours, have cultures that are firmly attached to the cycles of the salmon, but, like their more easterly Interior Plateau neighbours, they were, and continue to be, attached to seasonal land-based resources in the valleys and mountains of their territories.

Although distant from the coastal tempo of trading and raiding, these peoples have long traditions of marriage, trade, and other interactions with their maritime neighbours. Long before the arrival of Europeans, they developed elaborate reciprocal relationships expressed in ceremonial and sumptuary fashion, and by means of gift exchange and trade between different families, nations, and biogeoclimatic regions. Like their coastal neighbours, they were familiar with raiding and trading, with a rich artistic and ceremonial life, potlatch feasting, and totem pole raising (see Figures 1 and 2). Over the past century they have worked as wage labourers. In addition, they have been formed into reserve-based wards of government, with the usual problems of unemployment, welfare ennui, structural nepotism, substance abuse, and family discord; but, like the Tswana people studied by the Comaroffs in South Africa, to name but one of many similar situations in the contemporary world: "they also engage in productive and exchange relations that perpetuate significant features of the precolonial social system, one in which human relations were not pervasively mediated by commodities, and dominant symbols unified man, spirit and nature in a mutually effective, continuous order of being" (Comaroff 1985, 2). During gold prospecting days in the 1870s, and during the subsequent paddle-wheel riverboat navigation along the Skeena River until the early 1900s (see Figures 3 and 4), Gitksan leaders lodged protests (joining delegations to Ottawa and London) against illegal incursions into their territories. During the McKenna-McBride Royal Commission (McKenna-McBride 1915), they vigorously opposed the establishment of the "reserve system." They organized to take up "the land question" with government and participated in the Native Brotherhood, which had similar aims (Drucker 1958). In the 1920s, 1930s, and most openly at Gitsegukla in 1945 (Barbeau and Beynon 1915-57: BF 425-428; Anderson and Halpin 2000), they defied the "Potlatch Law" that had made their ceremonial activities illegal. In the 1950s, they were able to begin to change their approach to the "land question." The Nisga'a began their litigation process in the 1960s, and the Gitksan and Witsuwit'en did the same in the years that followed. They began the process of taking the Province of British Columbia and, ultimately, the Government of Canada to court in a bid to seek recognition of their landownership and the right to institute their own form of self-governance. Before the late 1950s this avenue had not been open to First Nations peoples in Canada.

Hunting and Gathering in the Courtroom
What kind of truth is adjudicated in a multi-ethnic courtroom situation such as that involved in a land rights case? Is Canada's much discussed multiculturalism reflected in the processes through which such cases are conducted?

Before the opening of *Delgamuukw,* my clients' political leaders did not hold very sanguinary views about multicultural respect or the scope and rules that would be employed for determining truth in the court. However, they pointed out that their constituents had vast experience with litigation from the "other side" and that the very act of being plaintiffs and not defendants, for once, was indeed a step forward in the struggle for social recognition. They viewed the court case as a step on the long road to gaining respect and status in the wider society, to pursuing a public political settlement of their grievances, and to achieving recognition of what they considered their rights. They rejected a strategy that would limit the nature of their case to what the cautious and ethnocentric courts might find "reasonable." They wanted to mount a case that was not limited to the identity paradigm of the Department of Indian Affairs and Northern Development with its "band council" system of elective departmental governance, indirect rule, and in-built agenda for terminating Aboriginal rights through either revised or new treaty agreements and a municipal model of governance. Rather, they envisioned a case based upon postcolonial governance according to long-standing principles of kinship and affinity – a form of reciprocal social life marked by the richness, complexity, and historical depth of their two traditions and cultures. They entertained the possibility of establishing sets of overlapping rights and jurisdictions with federal and provincial governments. They hoped to push back the boundaries of what constituted admissible evidence. They hoped to call on Canada and British Columbia to redress some of the injustices of colonial and postcolonial practices by recognizing alternative Aboriginal ways of being human and the values to be found in Aboriginal stewardship and management practices on the land.

Bodies of law, like moral or religious codes, can be used in many ways to prove many things, and in the period leading up to *Delgamuukw,* the First Nations plaintiffs realized that the extent to which their point of view could attain broader understanding through the courts depended considerably upon the enlightenment of the forthcoming adjudication. The day-to-day leaders of the Office of Hereditary Chiefs were aware that they and their witnesses would be walking into a conventional court, with its juridical disciplines and hierarchies. They knew that there would be great resistance to their attempts to broaden the existing positivistic and administrative vision vis-à-vis indigenous forms of social control and self-governance. Nonetheless this is what they tried to do. They said they did not expect to win their demands simply through the courts but felt that the courts should be used to broaden administrative minds, show alternatives, and plow the ground for future political settlements of such burning issues as land and governance.

The Courtroom as a Vertical Force Field

From an analytic perspective, the courtroom deliberations constituted an arena of interactions, or overlapping fields of interest, played out upon a sloping plane of power and powerlessness. Having experienced this courtroom situation from the inside, I have gained an existential appreciation of Pierre Bourdieu's field, habitus, and symbolic capital[1] (Bourdieu 1990a, 1993; Bourdieu and Wacquant 1992). The courtroom in which an Aboriginal rights case is tried is a social situation marked by a definite field of power – even spatially:[2] With the judge both at the top of the social promontory and at the elevated front of the room, and directly below his dais, the contending teams of jurists, together with the current witness, court stenographer, and clerk. To one side are seats reserved for the press, but during *Delgamuukw* they were almost always empty. Further down the slope, at the back of the room, almost out of earshot, are the seats for the public – in this instance, occupied by members of the plaintiff nations and sometimes by curious academics.

Bourdieu (1992 [1977], 126) points out that, in the configuration of relations that comprise a social force field, the socially closer the agents and groups within the physical space, the more common properties and common habitus they share; the more distant they are, the less they share. When one sits in the witness box at the front of the room, near the judge and the tables bursting with lawyers and documents, one is immediately encapsulated in a world of litigation and the administrative structures of the nation-state – an astral journey away from everyday life. Here the inner and implicit strategy, or the second-nature habitus, of the actors is highly conditioned by the juridical field itself. Repartee, tone of voice, body language all contribute to the role playing and impression management of specialists and professionals. This, of course, has been well documented in Goffman's (1959, 1961) interactional organization studies.

In their daily life, most witnesses possess a "sense of the game," or a habitus, that functions very imperfectly in the adversarial field of the courtroom. Witnesses are foreigners when they take their place in the box at the front of this room, and, in terms of social hierarchy, they usually come from the seats at the back of the hall. Be they anthropologists or First Nations witnesses, their contributions to the evidence are not accepted or rejected as lived experiential statements of "fact" that one side or the other is trying to present to the judge, or that two disputants might throw out to each other in an argument; rather, they are treated as raw material from which both sides will extract "evidence" for their generalizing arguments supporting the positions of their respective clients. As such, the evidence of witnesses is never heard at face value, that is, in the contextual terms expected by the witness. It is constantly subject to the professional habitus of the legal actors and their canon of rules and procedures for conducting the competition between the field's different interests. Once in the witness box, the witness, whether from the ranks of the First Nations or the anthropologists, historians, or biologists, ceases to be socially situated in her or his everyday life and becomes part of the firepower that each team of advocates tries to use to cripple its opponents and advance its own interests. Moreover, the witness who "breaks frame" and tries to assert her/his identity as a respected interlocutor, or to defend her/his interests in the proceedings, is severely devalued as a bona fide resource not only by the judge but also by counsel for both disputants. In fact, such "outbursts" contravene the rules.

They lack dispassion and objectivity. They are part of the messiness of contextualized everyday life (see Figure 5).

History professor Arthur Ray (2003, 273), who presented ethnohistorical opinion evidence for the plaintiffs in *Delgamuukw,* has written that historical experts in Aboriginal rights cases must be guided not only by the highest ethical and professional standards but also bear in mind that their primary responsibility is to the court rather than to their clients. This might be a plausible aim for historians working within the academy, removed from the everyday life of the clients and working on evidentiary materials that are contained in written, archival sources – in a word, a project with which the courts are familiar and comfortable. But this view is predicated upon an acceptance of the current power imbalance in society and the current positivistic administrative way of thinking based on fixed text-based categories for containing data rather than on context-based categories developed from various evidentiary sources, including the oral. Rather than moving with the times, the courts frequently seem to demand that the times fit into outdated and implicitly male, middle-class, Eurocentric ways of determining truth. Professor Ray seems to be implying that the only way to let the purity of one's objectivity shine is to be answerable to the court (despite its administrative biases). This, I would argue, tends to reinforce existing ethnocentrisms among the power-holders in society. Surely we, with our various bodies of situated knowledge, have to be answerable to more than one constituency and strive at all times, and everywhere in society, to advance the justice of our positions. It seems this has to be our pedagogical agenda so long as judges, as educated members of society, continue to allow nineteenth-century colonial views to cloud their twenty-first-century judgment. In *Delgamuukw* the court not only adopted a colonial and racist attitude towards the plaintiff cultures and histories, but it did so with the impunity of power.

To whom, then, should we anthropologists who are involved in Aboriginal rights cases, be responsible for our research and its educative function? I would hope that we can be responsible to ourselves as moral actors situated in society, as well as to our profession and to the basic ethics of recognizing our social engagement. Professionals have a right and a duty to contribute to the ongoing debate (in a society divided by class, gender, and ethnicity) about justice and injustice as these issues pertain to that corner of society about which we have specialized knowledge.

A corollary of Bourdieu's equation concerning cultural proximity and power is the substantive fact that the actors in the courtroom arena coexist uneasily. They have different worldviews and ways of constituting the truth. They are ultimately coerced to conform to the procedures and views of the judiciary. The officials of the judiciary, in general, neither accept nor acknowledge what is the aqua vitae of both everyday life and the anthropological universe; namely, an awareness of the importance of grasping the contextual complexity as it arises out of alternative cultural and historical trajectories of social action. The litigants and their arbitrator, the judge, play by a set of rules central to the organization of the nation-state – rules often little understood by other actors in the courtroom field of action. The indigenous witnesses and observers in this instance have their own rules of conduct for "occasions of state," and the anthropologist, to name but one of the professionals called in to give opinions on aspects of the case, has yet other rules of procedure for seeking legitimacy in public settings.

All these systems of regulation are employed to arrive at the truth, yet we normally observe only the most hegemonic rules of procedure at work: those of the nation-state, its administrative jurisdictions, and its judiciary. However, among the witnesses there are other, often tacit, rules of procedure in play, but since these are subordinated to the adversarial method of the court, their effectiveness as ways to arrive at the truth is usually obscured or obliterated. The epistemologies of lay and expert witnesses in an Aboriginal rights case fall into this category. Their evidence is not accorded the status of knowledge. It is considered no more than a small part of the fabric from which the opposing legal arguments are constructed and adjudicated.

Stifled Competence

Let us take for a moment a hypothetical elderly woman seated in the witness box, a female chief from one of the several Houses of one of the four Gitksan or five Witsuwit'en clans. She has grown up on the land under dispute and moved into the reserve village only so that her children could attend school. She herself may have received some "white man schooling," or she may speak only a bit of English. In town she looks poor and inarticulate, but she is a woman of reputation in her community. She is the matriarch of several generations; she holds one or more feast names of great power; she knows the history and the narratives of her matrilineal family's origins on the land, as well as those of her husband's family, and the histories of the Houses in their respective villages. She knows the names of her House's territories and perhaps of several others; she has organized many large feasts; she has prayed to the "Lord Above" to give her strength for what she has to do this day. She has communicated with her ancestors and the psychic force of all the living beings in her territory or territories. She has sought out intimations of their support for what she is putting herself through for her family, for those who "have gone before," for her village and her nation, and for those not yet born. The seat in the witness box is very hard and narrow and upright. It is meant for the criminals one watches on TV and is not a happy place for a chief to be. The judge is announced and she has to stand for his entrance, despite her own status, venerability, and arthritis. He sits above her and does not acknowledge her presence. The lawyers look directly into her eyes – something that, were they not so ignorant, they would know is insolent and discourteous behaviour towards chiefs and those born to be chiefs.

Still, she decides to countenance with dignity all this insulting ignorance. Her family members are in the audience to provide physical and psychic support. But her enemies are here too, the cousins who are bone lazy and venal and are waiting for her to misrepresent their land and their interests so that they can pounce on her – the witness who is suffering in court on their behalf. And they are zealous to pounce as well on any financial gains that might come from this court case. And the political representatives of the two main factions in her home community are here too. One of these factions wants to use her culture as an axe to clear a space for her people in the Canada of the future. They know the language and the old customs but are perhaps too glib, too well educated in the white man's way, although the spirits of the dead speak to them. And they who stand for the other faction are very cautious and basically do not want to rock the raft that "dem DIA" have built. To make changes, one has to let go of that raft and start "rockin'" a lot of canoes. She does not really trust any of the leaders.

She has been to the hairdresser and is wearing her gold jewellery embossed with her clan crests. Birth and age have propelled her into the ranks of royalty and she is planning to speak directly to the judge (who stands for the Queen of England) about the injustice suffered by her family and also about the justice of her people's claim. In the feast hall people of reputation speak to the history of any ongoing dispute, as they know it. Others listen and add on to what is said in order to contextualize and alter its connotations or put their own interests in a more favourable light. The matter is taken as far as possible by both sides. Then the gathering breaks up and the sides continue to push for their interests in other spheres of life. Perhaps other feasts will be needed to settle the matter, or perhaps the ancestors consider that tempers should cool off and that their descendants are moving too quickly or with the wrong motives. Things change, and the positions that reflect these changes tend to win out until somebody builds on to them in a new way. Next time the chiefs meet, the discussion will continue, diplomatically. To use hot words can lead to killings and disruptions. In the old days there was no standing army. Babies could die and people starve from the chaos that reigned when the peace was broken. It would get so bad that people could not even fish and hunt and trade. And so, a stern law bid the chiefs meet once more, in solemn dignity and respect. They exchanged presents and listened to their brother and sister chiefs, and when called upon, they spoke. Words were precious and they did not waste them.

But here on this witness bench she is not accorded the smallest scrap of respect. Any old lawyer can interrupt her words whenever she or he likes. The judge does the same. They then ignore her and argue fiercely about her words or the "justice" of admitting them into the evidence, and all this without consulting she who speaks the words. She soon realizes that in this room she is not the tall cedar tree she certainly is at home. In their eyes, she is only a pile of ol' weather-beaten planks, brought here only to fight over. In the golden days of her ancestors, this behaviour would have been grounds for war. But she cannot say this because "dem Judge" and "dem lawyer," they feel, in their bones, that her people's past was primitive and as low as you can get. They say you guys had no wheels, no pickup trucks, and, hey, no takeaway pizzas. They say you were cannibals and worshipped dem idol. And instead of religion, her community is said to be under the tyranny of crazy sorcerers, evil superstitions, wild masks, and pornographic dances.

She knows precisely what has to be said in this public forum. She holds her tongue in face of all the indignities and hopes that this case will at least put First Nations interests on the national agenda. She hopes that this will cause the white world to pay attention. Her people have a culture, a tradition, and a life, and the right to come out of the back alleys in the towns and down off the pile of rocks they call an Indian reserve, a right to stand up and demand respect. But she can feel the contempt of her cousin rivals in the back of the courtroom prickling the back of her neck; and she knows she must concentrate now so as not to compromise the precision of her answers. If she were to talk without clarity, or in falsehoods, the witnesses from the other clans would know and there would be hell to pay for generations to come, and Those-Who-Came-Before, they would turn their backs on her and her family and remove their power and protection. She must banish these thoughts, tell the truth, and find a way to get her message to the Queen.

Traitors or Subalterns to the Relations of Ruling?

The anthropologist who takes the witness stand is also from another world, with other competences and other habits of thinking. Yet, when interrupted by the adversarial skirmishes of the lawyers, she or he, as a consequence of the same educational ethos, is able to identify to some degree with the nation-state juridical process. The anthropological witness begins to detect the motivations, the contours of the arguments, the various game plans, and the rationale behind the thinking of the advocates. She or he is from a branch of the same system of higher education as the judge and lawyers, but the game rules exclude her/his active participation in the judicial dialectic of litigation. The rules of the game demand empirical objectivity, and the task at hand is to present an antiseptic view of the plaintiffs' life ways and traditions, filtered through the disciplines of social science and history. The plaintiffs' lawyers, with whom I worked, requested my help to "draw a picture or a map" for the court, showing aspects of the plaintiffs' society and economy through time. In other words, my task was one of providing contextual information to the court in an area of knowledge somewhat distant from the normal realms of law. My role was to be pedagogical. Fine, but one soon finds that the court is not a classroom.

One's usual forum of discourse, the learned journal and the seminar and classroom, are not available; rather, in order to be at all credible in the eyes of the court, one must act as though one were defending one's point of view in front of one's peers. But to attempt to do this puts one in an untenable position. One has to appear more knowledgeable and more dispassionate than the seemingly dispassionate, archive-oriented experts contracted by the defendants. Yet at the same time, one is expected not to jeopardize one's clients' search for redress for the injustices of invasion, colonization, and state-imposed in loco parentis relations. Like the evidence of the hypo- thetical female chief, the ethnographic evidence of the hypothetical an- thropologist is little more than a pile of old planks to be used for sectional interests, to build and house the respective contending juridical arguments. At best, anthropological opinion is material "that goes to weight," that pro- vides a perhaps exotic, but nonetheless rational, context. It is seldom ac- cepted as substantive truth. Evidence from the social sciences tends to be treated as tangential and not as something that illuminates the dark cor- ners of cultural ignorance. Nor is this knowledge debated in a manner that will test its truth and efficacy – the slow sifting process of discourse and the reciprocal process of testing, rejecting, and accepting that leads to the accu- mulation of academic or scientific knowledge.

Well, the court had its way with us, and was less than impressed with the lay and anthropological evidence presented by the plaintiffs. Although the social scientists involved in this case may have had the same training in what Dorothy Smith (1987, 1990a, 1990b) calls "the relations of ruling," as their juridical interlocutors, their contextual evidence did not enjoy the legitimacy and status of the more conventional documentary evidence pre- sented by witnesses for the "other side" – the defendants. The opinion evi- dence of the social scientists, with its specificity, its interconnections with political and social discourse in the society in general, and the lived com- plexity of ongoing weavings of ancient and modern realities was not the stuff a judge with an administrative habitus was willing to learn. Nor was he willing to become familiar with it.

Justice from the "Hovering Sovereign"
Much has been written about the underlying worldview of the chief justice and his Reasons for Judgment in this case, and his dismissal of Gitksan and

Witsuwit'en heritage as "nasty, brutish and short" (Asch 1997; Miller 1992; Cassidy 1992; Culhane [who introduced the term "hovering sovereign" to identify the myth by which the British Crown judicially sanctions its colonial land acquisition] 1998; Mills 1994). It is not my intention to cover this ground again, yet it bears pointing out that there remains in the Canadian courts a strong and rather narrow streak of "admin speak," or what is more commonly called narrow positive empiricism in which there is one set of document-based criteria employed for establishing "the truth," and where more reflexive, culturally embedded, and nuanced points of view are either rejected or, as in Chief Justice McEachern's ruling on the validity of oral narratives as evidence, accepted as evidence but evidence whose weight is subjected to stringent mainstream assessment.[3] Some consider the judge to have been too "conservative" in his ruling, but the Appellate and Supreme Courts, while overturning many of his legal findings, did not challenge his findings of fact. The higher courts were content to accept his juridical – and unexamined, unconsciously ethnocentric, commonsense – assessment of the substantive evidence on life and history in the disputed territories.

As far back as Immanuel Kant, philosophers were asking what it is, with reasonable certainty, that human beings could know, and these philosophers have concluded that such knowledge must be limited to the condition and experiences of the minds that are doing the knowing. In the present era, as we divest ourselves of empire-think, we are gaining new appreciation of the fact that understanding is prone to fallibility and that, as social scientists, we have to take ever-greater pains to improve our data and to verify and contextualize our conclusions. Nice, straightforward referentiality and cut-and-dried falsification – the stuff of narrow positivists and some sections of the natural sciences – is hard to come by in the real social world. Conditions and contexts change, and with them, meanings and connotations of words and the nature of the empirical evidence. In order to find everyday shortcuts, society and its administrative bodies try to limit the denotations by using dictionaries and rules of usage, as well as moral and legal codes. But despite these attempts, society's condition of flux, change, complexity, and development continues, and so too should the system for determining truth and reality within society's courts of law.

This is not to say that enlightened voices do not exist in the courts. There are even judges who join anthropologists in condemning McEachern-like pronouncements.[4] When the Nisga'a *Calder* case came before the Supreme Court of Canada in the 1970s, Justice Emmett Hall, in his minority judgment, took the then current British Columbia chief justice, H.W. Davey, to task for not acknowledging the changes in society and in the accretion of knowledge with regard to First Nations life and history: "The assessment and interpretation of their historical documents and enactments tendered in evidence must be approached in the light of present-day research and knowledge disregarding ancient concepts formulated when the understanding of the customs and culture of our original people was rudimentary and incomplete, and when they were thought to be wholly without cohesion, laws or culture, in effect, a subhuman species" (Hall 1973). Mr. Justice Hall elaborated this point by showing that, as enlightened as the early nineteenth-century rulings of Chief Justice Marshall of the United States had been, his understanding had been limited by the level of knowledge available in his day:

> This concept of the original inhabitants of America led Chief Justice Marshall in his otherwise enlightened judgment in *Johnson and Graham's Lessee v. M'Intosh* (1823), 8 Wheaton 543, 21 U.S. 240, which is the outstanding judicial pronouncement on the subject of Indian rights to say (p. 590), "But the tribes of Indians inhabiting this country were fierce savages, whose occupation was war." We now know that that assessment was ill-founded. The Indians did in fact at times engage in some tribal wars but war was not their vocation and it can be said that their preoccupation with war pales into insignificance when compared to the religious and dynastic wars of "civilized" Europe of the 16th and 17th centuries. (Ibid.)

In *Delgamuukw*, the trial judge did not see fit to assess the progress of knowledge about indigenous North America and move with the times. He opted for the form of straightforward subjectivity with which he was most familiar: he assumed that the plaintiffs' ancestry was peopled with those who shifted from savagery to the civilizing process of colonial administration, and he supported this preconception with selective textual documentation and selective statistical findings. The only findings he found convincing were those that accorded with his own ethnocentric views. He remained immune to complexities that fell beyond the immediate reach of mainstream legal considerations in the late twentieth century. I submit that this reflected his leading role in the ruling relations of society, wherein simplifying data from human populations, disempowering these populations by treating them as abstract types to fit into a priori categories, is an integral part of administrating the less empowered, and processing them through governmental agencies forged in the fires of colonialism. However, in subsequent decades, the courts have begun to realize the importance of trying harder to keep abreast of current knowledge regarding Aboriginal rights (see *Sparrow* [1990, 177] and *Pasco* [1989, 37-8]).

During the presentation of my evidence in court, the chief justice interrupted my account of ongoing spiritual beliefs and procedures associated with preparation for hunting big game animals. These were practices I had both witnessed and repeatedly been told about as part of the practice of respect towards, and reciprocity with, the ancestral forces of nature. He exclaimed, "Doctor, as a scientist, don't you need a control group before you can draw this kind of conclusion?" He then mentioned his uncle, who managed to shoot deer without any such beliefs and practices, and asked, "What am I to conclude?" I countered with the importance of recognizing the social organizing principles of a set of beliefs and practices, and, in terms of law and order, the ability of such a system to compel standards of practice. But this fell on deaf ears (Transcripts 1987-89, 12096). In other words, observable indigenous belief systems and their practice were not welcome in the courtroom as sociological, organizational facts – unless, of course, they had been greeted with appropriate skepticism by being tested against a logically constructed theoretical model, had been measured quantitatively, and had withstood the test of falsification that is one part of the European scientific method. There was no room for accepting the logic of alternative or analogous ways of seeing, or of analogous and socially standardized ways of practising one's proprietorship on the land. There was room only for the received "truth" that arose from the dispassion of science and mathematics, from the likes of Newton and Descartes – a dispassion that arose historically with industrialism in Europe but gradually laid claim to universality. But are the claims of objectivity from this epistemology universal? Ought they not – before being submitted to comparisons – be tested against the history and social structure of their genesis and the history and social conditions of wherever they are subsequently employed?

Through the judge's non-self-reflexive and pragmatic eyes, the plaintiffs were engaged in one of three things: telling the truth, dwelling in superstition, or telling tales to mislead the gullible anthropologist. In the eyes of the chief justice, my anthropological task was to eliminate the two least sustainable propositions by committing the *symbolically violent* act of attempting to disprove the pragmatic effects of the plaintiffs' beliefs and practices. Such an approach would, in the present case, have distorted the social reality and history of the plaintiffs into something understandable (if wanting in modernity) in the eyes of Europeans but very alien both to the logic of these cultures and to the process of cultural understanding in the wider society. This crude view of science from the bench assumes itself to be free of the encumbrances of culture, class, and gender. Thus liberated, it is free to judge as true or false any encumbrances it finds in other cultures and classes. I use Bourdieu's notion of "symbolic violence" to refer to imposing the rules used by one set of players in the intellectual game played in the court upon the rules used by the other set of players. These imposed rules govern the "truth" of the utterances of both the indigenous plaintiff peoples and the professional "expert witnesses." Today, these two sets of alternative rules are involved in the debate about building a more tolerant and democratic society, and they ought to be allowed to interface more effectively with the institutions and thinking of the nation-state.

Rejecting such blatant, symbolically violent approaches, or what has been termed judgmental relativism on the one hand and value-neutrality on the other (Harding 1991, 139-40), I would tend towards the standpoint epistemology proposed by certain feminists working in the sciences. Writers like Sandra Harding (1986, 1991) and Donna Haraway (1988) propose this epistemology for feminism, and it could well be profitably applied to the field of Aboriginal rights. As Harding (1991, 142) explains: "A feminist standpoint epistemology requires strengthened standards of objectivity. The standpoint epistemologies call for recognition of a historical, or sociological or cultural relativism – but not for a judgmental or epistemological relativism. They call for the acknowledgment that all human beliefs – including our best scientific beliefs – are socially situated, but they also require a critical evaluation to determine which social situations tend to generate the most objective knowledge claims. They require, as judgmental relativism does not, a scientific account of the relationships between historically located belief and maximally objective belief."

Haraway (1988), in commenting on Harding's position, argues that relativism and objectivity can become concrete only from the position of situated knowledges. This has also come to be known as "standpoint knowing," where the researcher works from a deep rootedness in one corner of society and does not conform to the conventional disembodied consciousness that has been the (male) model of science since before the Enlightenment. Being rooted and partial, the researcher, as proposed by Haraway, seeks to view the objects of study as having agency in their own right. The researcher seeks to engage in conversations both with the knowledge of those studied and with other, similarly rooted "situated knowledges," and not to resort to what she calls "the god trick" of posing as a disembodied, ecologically detached master seeker of truth: "A corollary of the insistence that ethics and politics covertly or overtly provide the bases for objectivity in the sciences is granting the status of agent/actor to the 'objects' of the world. Actors come in many and wonderful forms. Accounts of a 'real' world do not, then, depend on a logic of 'discovery' but on a power-charged social relation of 'conversation.' The world neither speaks itself nor disappears in favor of a master decoder. The codes of the world are not still, waiting only to be read ... the world encountered in knowledge projects is an active entity" (Haraway 1988, 593). According to this approach to objective truth and relativity, the field of law is called upon to reflect the changing, developing, and deepening nature of knowledge rather than to force knowledge to suffer the violence of being called upon to conform to a set of jural practices whose heyday was a time of social exploitation and colonial aggression that history is supposed to have transcended.

Bourdieu (1990, 183-4), too, points out that scientific objectification is bound to remain partial, and thus false, as long as it ignores and refuses to acknowledge the point of view from which it is enunciated – here, in the present instance, the totality of the courtroom "game" with its full force field of contending views played out according to one set of hegemonic rules. Bourdieu explains that true objectification requires a brutally objective assessment of all the "objective" positions at play in the scientific discourse used in any current arena of contention (such as he undertook with his own arena of contention in *Homo Academicus* [Bourdieu 1999]). By avoiding self-conscious construction, the hegemonic and administrative outlook leaves the crucial operations of scientific construction – the choice of the problem, the elaboration of concepts and analytic categories – to the social world as it is. It does not question the established order and fulfills a conservative function of ratifying the doxa, the received and unquestioned order of things (Bourdieu and Wacquant 1992, 246).

My standpoint of learning in the present case took place in the context of the partisanship of a court case. This has resulted in a type of ethnographic presentation of empirical facts that has had to steer a course between the narrow positivism acceptable to many judges as the basis of evidentiary proof and the more dichotomous, negotiable nature of local "social institutions." The litigious context has indeed had some effect on the subjects emphasized in this work. For current tastes there is probably an inordinate emphasis on "surviving the season with a sufficient surplus" and on interactive proprietorship, but that was the mandate for my work. Beyond this, however, I, perhaps unconsciously, engaged in a certain amount of self-censorship, given that my main readers would be members of the judicial community. For example, the work could have benefitted theoretically from a more expansive use of Gregory's analysis of gifts and commodities in postcolonial Melanesia. I treated this material lightly because my habitus informed me that the bench would hold economic marginalist assumptions that would regard Gregory's adoption of the political economy approach with either contempt or the wrath of God. The hegemonic economic thinking today follows the tradition of Jevons, Menger, Walras, and Samuelson on consumer choice and economizing. The political economy approach, following as it does the more radical ideas of Adam Smith, Ricardo, Marx, and Engels, would likely have fallen not on unsympathetic ears but on antagonistic ones. This of course is no issue around a seminar table. It can be argued and debated and lead to further research, dispute, and gradual consensus. In an arena of power like the courtroom, however, such questions become real material issues. This is an example of the qualitative pitfalls of consultancy research in an arena of winners and losers, where the researcher must try to remain dispassionate regarding the facts yet morally responsible to her/his employers (Daly 2003). I have used Gregory's analysis more extensively in reworking the material for publication.

In the same light *Our Box Was Full* over-emphasizes economic instrumentality and does not give enough indication of the complexity of indigenous practices and procedures. Due to the multifunctionality (from our cultural outlook) of social practices in First Nations societies, what we like to analyze into separate and discrete boxes (e.g., economy, kinship, religion, politics, or law) are often aspects of the same institutions and practices. Yet to discuss the spiritual sanctioning that backs up traditional laws and standards of behaviour, for example, would have caused already deaf ears to close completely. Again, in preparing this work for publication, I have tried to redress some of the imbalances caused by my own diplomatic stance towards the positivistic view of the bench.

The second issue that I want to raise is the incident that tore the largest hole in my evidence at trial, at least in the eyes of the judge. Counsel for the Government of Canada introduced as evidence, for my cross-examination, a social survey undertaken by Carleton University on behalf of the plaintiffs. I was aware of the existence of this survey and had asked to review it in the course of preparing my evidence but had been informed that, since it was poorly conceived and executed, it had been scrapped and destroyed. But indeed it was not destroyed. It was a prized weapon in the documentary arsenal of the defendants. My not having obtained this document proved to be a considerable issue for the judge:

> He [Daly] was not aware of a comprehensive survey of over 1,000 persons conducted by the Tribal Council in 1979 which achieved an 80% return. This survey disclosed, for example, that 32% of the sample attended no feasts, and only 29.6% and 8.7% engaged in hunting and trapping respectively ... Apart from admissibility as evidence of its contents (for I have no way of knowing if the survey is accurate or representative, although some of its results tend to confirm the view I obtained of present Indian life), its significance is more in the fact that it was kept from Dr. Daly. Many of his views of Indian life may have been markedly different if he had access to this substantial body of information in the possession of his clients. For these reasons I place little reliance on Dr. Daly's report or evidence. (McEachern 1991: 51)

I later had the opportunity to study this document, and it proved not to be substantial at all, as I was able to indicate in redirect. It did not contain the magical powers that the chief justice had attributed to it. I found that the results – even though the returns were far from the 80 percent the judge reported (80 percent of the questionnaires may have been returned, but the majority left most questions unanswered or only intermittently answered) – were not inconsistent with the determination of the plaintiffs' mixed economy and cultural continuity I had made in my report. The figures demonstrated a considerably higher degree of cultural retention than is found among many modern Aboriginal peoples in Canada. It appears that the judge accepted these questionable figures at face value because they seem to be numerically substantiated "concrete" facts. However, these figures are abstracted from the situations that generated them – the complexities of local, everyday life. Anthropologists are not averse to statistics, but we learn in undergraduate courses that "the figures" are only as good as the accuracy of their collection and the context and theory that situates and informs them. However, for this court, the figures sui generis told the whole story.

The figures of this highly incomplete survey revealed that 23.8 percent (not 32 percent as cited by the judge) of the plaintiff communities' members did not attend feasts. The judge saw this figure as nullifying the centrality of feasting and conveniently ignored or rejected out of hand a mountain of evidence on precontact feast conditions. These conditions continued well into the memories of elderly witnesses, if not directly, then at least in the feasting rules they learned from their grandparents. They learned that *only chiefs* and their *intended heirs* attended feasts and that open invitations to the whole community were initiated only in the twentieth century. But even those who today do not attend feasts are, upon death, usually subject to the traditional obsequies of a settlement feast, no matter what their social standing.

According to the judge's logic on this point, if this figure of 23.8 percent pertained to the Canadian electoral system, this system could not be considered a central institution in society because one-quarter of eligible voters do not participate in the electoral process – which is indeed frequently a fact at election time – without nullifying the electoral process. Furthermore, while 80 percent of those questioned in the survey may have returned their questionnaires, most of the returned forms were either not answered at all or only partially answered. Out of the 460 questioned about feasting, 390 gave no response. When asked for negative views of feasting, 432 of the 460 expressed no opinion. Similarly, the survey's reliance on the industrialized, 1950s-type nuclear structure of the family did not allow the figures to accurately reflect the more extensive family ties to feasting, landed territories, river fishing sites, and local social legitimacy.

Regarding continuing land-based subsistence activities in the survey, we find that only 33 percent of families (nuclear) possessed smokehouses (fish and game smoking are joint family ventures, with several households using one smokehouse). Fifty percent engaged in food fishing and 47.6 percent had been engaged in hunting the previous year. Again, as with the feasts, the question of hunting statistics requires contextualizing in order to be correctly appreciated. Normally each village has, and had, specialist hunters (those selected for apprenticeship as hunters were chosen from among the youth by elderly hunters who closely observed the coming generation). Indeed, traditionally there was a considerable extended family division of labour based on personal aptitude, be it for healing, weaving, carving, hunting, trapping, dancing, recalling oral history, trading, negotiating, or martial defence. In the court case, much was made of fur trapping as a central part of indigenous life. The survey figures showed that only 8.7 percent maintained traplines, but by the time of the survey, due to the international anti-fur lobby, the fur market had almost collapsed. While I worked in the Gitksan and Witsuwit'en territories, the Hudson's Bay Company closed down its Canadian fur branch after three centuries of trading. Its Hazelton warehouse is currently a cappuccino bar.

The scanty figures also showed that 51.6 percent of the respondents had received Aboriginal names, 66.7 percent had learned their Aboriginal language at home, 61.2 percent used this language at home, 30.6 percent taught the family oral history and knowledge of crests at home, while 47.7 percent knew their ancient narrative histories, songs, and dances. These figures from this questionable survey indicate support for my own findings as to the vitality and ongoing nature of Gitksan and Witsuwit'en ways of life, but, like the negative "facts," they count for little since the survey was so incomplete.

In relation to this undisclosed survey, and to my methods of work (document reviews, participant observation, interviews, incorporating observations and data from subsequent questioning of informants [and doing so directly into my growing report instead of compiling diary notes as one does when writing up the data far from the field, usually at a university]), I was characterized by the judge as duped and compromised and, as a researcher, less than searching, dispassionate, and objective.[5] In fact, I had the dubious honour of being cited in United Nations subcommittee documents on indigenous peoples' rights as the anthropologist whose testimony was rejected in a court of law because he admitted to subscribing to the American Anthropological Association's Statement of Ethics (which, at that time, contained a proviso that it was unethical to engage in activities detrimental to the well-being of those studied) (see Daly and Mills 1993).

Of course the qualities of icy objectivity, judicious dispassion, and equanimity are integral to both the bureaucracy and the academic and scientific professions. They are part of our society's ethnography, part of its system of myths and beliefs, and are integral to our higher education in virtually all fields. Both the bureaucrat and the social scientist operate in situated practice within an actual society and culture complete with a habitus that is coloured by the partisanship of the field of forces therein (although this is generally unacknowledged). As I see it, most of the social science professionals involved in *Delgamuukw* were to a considerable degree dispassionate and objective in the way they worked with the available data.[6] We all strive for dispassion and objectivity before the facts, but this is never done in a non-partisan way, whether the research and scholarship is pure, applied, or subject to litigation. We are all of us situated in a stratified society and, in order to transcend this actual partisanship, we rely upon the discipline of our professionalism. If we are honest and self-reflective about our own upbringing, education, and habitus, we all have to admit that, while we can present rigorous objective findings, these are always presented to a partisan world, as Bourdieu (1999) has shown so starkly.

The nature of the beast is quite different from forensic evidence, where opinions have far less to do with the contextualized world of social relations, although even here the "objective facts" are assembled and defended according to one's own professional stake in the forensic field. But I do not mean to imply that I ignored or distorted facts that did not accord with the clients' case. I strove to work professionally – paying attention to documentation and consistency of available information – for my clients (the plaintiffs), and I did so openly on the witness stand in front of not only the legal profession but also my professional peers. Social scientists working openly or behind the scenes for the defendants in this case were equally advocates for their clients, but, being less honest about it, and holding views less inimical to those of the judge, they avoided being chastised for the same. Indeed, some of their views, familiar in terms of commonsense skepticism towards other cultures, were incorporated, without attribution, directly into the Reasons for Judgment.[7] These opposing views were accepted by the court without question, partly, I submit, due to their conformity with the colonial mentality of "us and them," and partly to the daily habitus and doxa of the court, where decontextualized documentary evidence is privileged over the contextualized information of the empirically rooted anthropologist, archaeologist, or historian.

As Ray (2003, 263) has stressed, the counter-opinion given by the defendants relied upon pre-land-claim ethnographic work, partly because researchers for the defendants would not have been welcome in the communities of the plaintiffs. The work of those who did fieldwork among the Gitksan and Witsuwit'en was considered, rightly, to have a purposeful objective: to advance our understanding and put our findings at the disposal of the communities studied. This was something that, in the eyes of the court, made the plaintiffs' research "less objective." But much of the earlier research was problematic as well. When these apparently less purposeful studies were used to support courtroom arguments, especially as analogous examples from other First Nations ethnographies, their respective contextual purpose was ignored. These ethnographies usually had purposes very different from those pursued today in an era when the issue of Aboriginal rights is a major theme not only in litigation but also in relation to social theory. Our body of ethnographic knowledge changes and develops with the passage of time. Ray makes this point clearly by citing the experience of Alfred Kroeber testifying before the US Indian Claims Commission of the 1950s. Kroeber "noted that most of pre-claims anthropological research had been oriented to salvage or cultural-element distribution surveys. This work had emphasized material culture, mythology and religious beliefs; it had paid little attention to native economic systems, political organizations, or local tenure practices" (Ray 2003, 261).

I would add a point here. North American anthropological discourse of earlier decades tended to use ethnography to provide apt examples in on-going ideological debates. Such debates raged over issues such as race and intelligence, biological versus social determinism, the position of women, and the deterministic power of capitalism versus other forms of socio-economic life. There are many examples, but I want only to raise one here. I select this example because the defendants in *Delgamuukw* abstracted features from both sides of the ethnographic debate in question. They used these features, in a decontextualized manner, to support their arguments that, prior to European contact, there were no forms of indigenous exchange or land proprietorship in the territory that became Her Majesty Queen Victoria's Colony of British Columbia.

The debate in question dates back to before the Second World War. In reaction to the "communism of living" that Morgan (1965 [1881]) described among the Iroquois and other Native Americans, Frank Speck (1926), and others such as Robert Lowie (1936), Irving Hallowell (1943), and Loren Eiseley (Speck and Eiseley 1942), attacked the view that "free land-holding has generally been thought typical of primitive man." This, the Morgan view, gained its ideological colouring by being adopted by Friedrich Engels in *The Origin of the Family, Private Property and the State*. On the basis of Morgan's findings, Engels argued that, in the course of human history, there was a social and historical evolution of proprietary rights from the collective and the matriarchal to the individual and the patriarchal, and that only a communist revolution could reassert gender equality and collective social action and ownership. Speck used his ethnographic work in Canada's eastern subarctic region to argue for the indigenous existence of individually owned family hunting territories. Eleanor Leacock (1954) challenged Speck's argument on the basis of her ethnographic work among the Innu (Montagnais-Naskapi) and her ethnohistorical work in the archives. Her conclusion was "that prior to the influence of the European fur trade, the Labrador Indians had owned their lands collectively. Furthermore, fieldwork, plus a re-examination of reports by Speck and others made clear that even after the Montagnais-Naskapi became dependent upon fur-trading, it was not an individual's right to land as such that was recognized, but only the right to *trap* on certain lands. People could hunt, fish and gather food, birchbark and other necessary goods where they chose" (Leacock 1981, 31).

Leacock was challenging what she considered a privileged, male, middle-class approach that saw the world's cultures in the image of their own "eternal," and not historically specific and hegemonic, culture, ideology, and habitus. This debate extended through the McCarthy era in the USA, a period when women were being removed from the wartime economy. It was a time when anti-fascist common front sympathies for the socialist camp were being suppressed, particularly in the USA, in ways reminiscent – as Arthur Miller reminds us in his play *The Crucible* – of the witch trials in seventeenth-century Salem, Massachusetts.

Subsequent research, partly in relation to land rights politics and litigation, has revealed that in the region of the eastern subarctic, individual family heads, while not "owning" land in the Western sense of individual freehold, were nonetheless responsible for "managing" and "stewarding" the resources on a given tract of land and for supervising harvest levels (Feit 1969, 1973; Sieciechowicz 1986; Tanner 1979). Although they also controlled commercial traplines on these territories, these family heads appeared to have had responsibility as "keepers of the game" (Martin 1978); that is, they managed the sentient bio-mass that was not part of the cash economy. Bishop (1986) and Morantz (1986) have also argued that this stewardship extended back at least into the earliest documentary evidence of the seventeenth century.

Land rights movements developed in the 1970s and since. Leacock, too, was involved in such projects on behalf of First Nations plaintiffs. The new Aboriginal rights climate has given rise to a new emphasis on those aspects of indigenous land tenure that most closely resembled private, jural proprietorship in the wider Canadian society. Studies of land management and collective ownership have proliferated as part of the climate of the times. Today the research continues and a number of scholars, perhaps in "the spirit of the gift" that, like debate and criticism, is part of the advance of scholarship, call for synthesizing aspects from both sides of this earlier debate in order to better approximate ethnographic reality in light of current knowledge. (See, for example, Berkes 1986; Mailhot 1986, 1999; Scott 1986; Sieciechowicz 1986; and Tanner 1991.)

The land claim process itself has generated and propelled into existence new findings. It has helped expedite, refine, and clarify earlier research findings and concepts. Predictably (from a litigious perspective but ironically in terms of Leacock's own "standpoint of knowing") in *Delgamuukw*, the provincial government's defendants emphasized arguments from social science and history that privileged the fur trade land tenure demonstrated by Leacock. Simultaneously they ignored the existence of the incipient in situ capitalist-like relations found by Speck. Leacock was thus used in court to bolster an argument that no land tenure system existed prior to the influence of Europeans and their trade.

Ray (2003) outlines similar developments arising from the interface between anthropology and the courts, both across Canada and in Australia. He finds similar processes at work in Aboriginal Australian land rights cases from *Gove* to *Mabo* and the cases arising from the struggle over Hindmarsh Island in South Australia. In light of historical research, he concludes:

> Thus, the courts, necessarily one of the bastions of positivism, face an ever more difficult and frustrating struggle in their attempt to make such differentiations and deal with the fluid nature of cultural/historical evidence. Canadian Supreme Court Justice J.J. Binney highlighted the problem in 1998 in the course of rendering his decision in the controversial *Marshall* case. He wrote "The law sees a finality of interpretation of historical events where finality, according to the professional historian, is not possible. The reality, of course, is that the courts are handed disputes that require for their resolution the finding of certain historical facts. The litigating parties cannot await the possibility of a stable academic consensus." (Ray 2003, 272-3)

As an anthropologist who has been involved in such cases, I contend that our professions would be better served, and perhaps in the long run also our clients and the law, if the courts would grapple regularly with the current state of knowledge in various fields of expert opinion. In other words, it would be healthy for justice if the courts risked grappling with those state-of-the-art dialectical, open-ended, and situated expert knowledges that are offered up for consideration in the courtroom. I submit that this is a healthier approach to justice than trying to turn the profession of history or anthropology back fifty years (or more) and conforming to the outdated "necessary positivism" of the courts.

At the end of the day the judge chooses to ignore the charges of advocacy laid against whichever side makes the most coherent evidentiary sense. Given this situation, and the reputedly strange and complex nature of alternative cultures, oral history, and recent ethnography (that which has not yet achieved status as a historical document), these social phenomena are often given short shrift in courts of law. As one observer has noted:

> Anthropological opinion finds that jural arguments have a pronounced colouring of ethnocentric authority to them, aspects of which are seen at work in a striking manner when the Western court system is dealing with other cultural traditions and other legal paradigms. Anthropologists who have functioned as expert witnesses in court cases on aboriginal rights have been confronted with the legal profession's conceptual limitations and its self-ascriptive opinion that their concepts have a kind of universal and authoritative standing, to the effect that it has in some cases made

cultural translation a nearly insurmountable task. (Thuen 1992, 137 [my translation])

Multivocal Culture

As an actor in the land claim process, I was engaged in a set of social practices that spanned the worlds of anthropology, history, natural science, law, current politics, and everyday domestic life. I was also a neighbour to the plaintiffs and to the non-Aboriginal residents in the region. The ethnography was not only an individual production: it was socially constructed, socially constrained, and socially contested. Indeed, I came to see the process of consensus and discourse in the social sciences as analogous to that of a Witsuwit'en or Gitksan feast. In the feast, the point of view presented by the specific host family is hooked into, and tested against, the experience, interests, and point of view of the guest families and the wider society. In this process, for all its partisanship, the truth is gradually validated and/or repudiated. Social validation, whether in the sciences or on the potholed roads of "Indian reserves," involves a long and often slow process of assessing conflicting knowledges marked by ideological positions and criss-crossed by the stamp of class, ethnicity, gender, age, profession, and the many trajectories of social discourse. Are the discursive social practices for establishing "scientific facts" in general so very different?

With respect to the substantive issue of land, the discourse between indigenous peoples, the state, and the intermediaries has a long history. Indeed, this discourse goes back to the debate in Valladolid in 1550 between the priest from Chiapas, Bartolomé de Las Casas, and the philosopher of the latifundists, Juan Gines de Sepúlveda (Berger 1991, chap. 2). Although the Indigenes did not have their own voice in 1550, a little over a century later, in Iroquoian territories, they had many silver tongues. Thanks to the records of Benjamin Franklin we have many of the speeches of indigenous leaders in the 1700s who entered the discourse in defence of their rights to North America, which they called the "Turtle's Back." While government printer for the Thirteen Colonies, Benjamin Franklin published transcripts of "Indian treaty" processes in the pre-revolutionary British colonies and thereby preserved the words of some very eloquent indigenous leaders. One of the articulate speakers of that era was Onitositah (Corn Tassel), who had the following to say during his people's (the Cherokee) peace treaty (1777) with the government of the recently declared United States of America:

> Let us examine the facts of your present irruption into our country, and we shall discover your pretensions on that ground. What did you do? You marched into our territories with a superior force ... Your laws extend not into our country, nor ever did. You talk of the law of nature and the law of nations, and they are both against you.

Indeed, much has been advanced on the want of what you term civilization among the Indians; and many proposals have been made to us to adopt your laws, your religion, your manners and your customs. But we confess that we do not yet see the propriety, or practicability, of such a reformation, and should be better pleased with beholding the good effects of these doctrines in your own practices than with hearing you talk about them ...

The great God of Nature has placed us in different situations. It is true that he has endowed you with many superior advantages; but he has not created us to be your slaves. *We are a separate people.* He has given each their lands, under distinct considerations and circumstances; he has stocked yours with cows, ours with buffaloe; yours with hog, ours with bear; yours with sheep, ours with deer. He has, indeed, given you an advantage in this: that your cattle are tame and domestic, while ours are wild and demand not only a larger space for range, but art to hunt and kill them. They are, nevertheless, as much our property as other animals are yours. (Williams 1921, 176-8)

Once again, more than 200 years after Onitositah's words, the plaintiff chiefs in *Delgamuukw* viewed the case as a tribunal for carrying forward the same discourse, the same struggle to defend their land and renew their demands for recognition of their identity and rights as "first-comers." In April 1988 Simoogit Gwisgen (the late Stanley Williams) of the Gitksan Gisk̲'aast Clan, addressed the land question and the issue of cultural persistence and legitimacy. He "added on" to what his Cherokee and Iroquois predecessors had said:

Each time our people use our law, they make it stronger, and it still goes on today. We never deserted our grandfather's seat, and we never deserted our land, our territories. It's still the same today. Today the government wants to take all this away from us, and they want to take the laws of our people, of our ancestors, and they want to break our laws today. I don't think they could do this, because it's been passed on from generation to generation, and we've had this law for thousands of years ...

When a grizzly bear gets into the provisions of another person, then he eats it up. And when the owner comes back, then the grizzly gets mad – instead – gets mad at the owner. And that's how the government is treating us today concerning our territories. (Stanley Williams, Commission Evidence, *Delgamuukw*)

The field in which this discourse has been unfolding through the generations contains enormous gaps between the hegemonic sanctioning of one point of view – that of the technologically superior land-takers – and the local knowledge and sanctioning system of those whose land is being taken.

The playing field is not level, and thus the interlocutions often sound like monologues. In North America the anthropologist with a foot in one camp, and a toehold in the other, has a long history (from Lewis Henry Morgan on) of trying to fill an intercalary role in this discourse. The chapters that follow are but one small part of this lengthy tradition; however, it is first crucial to situate them within both the general field of hunter-gatherer studies and the literature on gift-exchange societies – categories that embrace both the Witsuwit'en and the Gitksan.

Foraging a Future

Recent debates concerning the temporal limitations of hunter-gatherer ethnographies and their questionable purity, and the limits of their use as rough analogues for social formations approximating human social origins, have, from one side, tended to be argued in terms of stationary snapshots of reified social entities. By virtue of the fact that classical forager bands have had interactions with agriculturalists and traders for considerable lengths of time, this position argues that the authenticity of earlier ethnographies and the contours of the hunter-gatherer social entities therein are, at best, historically specific and, at worst, subjective creations. Either way, they have been considered of little utility for comparative or evolutionary studies (Wilmsen 1983; Schrire 1984; Headland and Read 1989; Wilmsen and Denbow 1990).[8]

Some scholars regard forager bands, by virtue of their contact with more complex social formations, as having lost their cultural virginity, and they view them as "soiled goods" barred from polite society and unsuitable for donning the feathers of authenticity. Often such groups are considered to have no identity apart from that of faceless clients of the more complex social entities with which they interact. For instance, Jolly (1996) argues, in an either/or manner, that the dynamism of San ritual practices and rock art derives from surrounding agriculturalists rather than having either San origins or shared origins with interactive neighbouring peoples. There does not, however, seem to be conclusive evidence for pure origins among either the San or the cattle-keepers. This line of reasoning affirms the necessity of a close reading of historical context, yet its own epistemology is frequently a non-relational, non-processual historiography that replaces a classic forager snapshot ethnography with a colonially inspired snapshot, this time of peoples who are decultured subalterns to more sociologically complex peoples.

The emphasis on "all-or-nothing" synchronic social identities has led some researchers to consider the whole field of hunter-gatherer studies to be on the brink of extinction. This position rests upon the radically transformed way of life and outlook of descendants of earlier informants who were foragers (arguments outlined by Lee 1992 and, in more alarmist fashion, by Burch 1994). Perhaps the tempo of social change among hunter-gatherers is such that social scientists, enmeshed in globalizing social processes, see only the discontinuities between post-hunter-gatherers and their foraging past. Perhaps they do not see the distinctive and flexible nature of their interaction with the wider social forces or the ability of the old culture to requicken self-identity in current practices that are often responses to international social and economic shifts. Furthermore, many may forget to recognize the need that postcolonial nation-states have to keep alive the myth of noble savages as a measuring stick of stately advance and development (Francis 1992). The present velocity of change blurs the vision of what is, was, and will be the hunter-gatherer identity (Lee and Daly 1999, 1-19).

But beyond this there is a problem with theoretical concepts that substantiate features of dynamic social relations by using static nouns like "forager" and "hunter-gatherer." Marilyn Strathern (Ingold 1996, 60-6) makes a similar objection to the term "society" when it is treated as a group-like thing that is said to stand opposed to "the individual" and not simply as a designation for social relationships. "Foraging" or "hunting and gathering" run into trouble when they stand for groups instead of for a type of human activity, organization, and social relations. When they stand for a group, the classical "direct appropriation," "communism in living," and demand-sharing paradigm comes to the anthropological mind, and of course most hunting-gathering people measured against this paradigm come up wanting. However, the features that the paradigm presents are important and are often reflected in the less pure reality of ethnographies of people who engage in foraging. I suggest below that "foraging" be utilized for those activities, relations, and forms of organizing that approximate those of the classic paradigm wherever they occur, whether in fishing and hunting formations, "indirect appropriation" foraging societies, or even within the periphery of nation-states.

The theoretical crisis that mirrors current geopolitical and economic changes parallels the situation in physics in the early twentieth century, with the appearance of subatomic physics and Heisenberg's uncertainty principle, which was so inimitably described by Bertrand Russell (1985 [1955], 411): "Nobody before quantum theory doubted that at any given moment a particle is at some definite place and moving with some definite velocity; the more accurately you determine the velocity, the less accurate will be its position. And the particle itself has become something quite vague, not a nice little billiard ball as it used to be. When you think you have caught it, it produces a convincing alibi as a wave and not a particle."

If we keep the metaphors raised here for a moment, it might be argued that snapshot "particle" views of small-scale anthropological groups reflect general trends in recent geopolitics, wherein previous general historical "us-and-them" synchronicities are viewed as slices of time. One example is the timespan of mercantile capitalism in the societies generally studied by anthropologists. In many such societies "peace" was imposed on the locals by the metropole countries (whose forces, conversely, tended to wage wars on rival colonial powers). In such conditions, anthropological ethnographies have portrayed relationships as discrete, bounded entities, small in scale and often peripheral to the centres of empire.

By contrast, today's worldwide commodities market blurs both the boundaries and the image of hunter-gatherers, who every day seem to be living "more like us." We all live in a smaller world where globalization makes space and time omnipresent, creating every *place* as here and every *time* as now, and turning what formerly appeared to be discrete particles into waves. A corollary of this situation is the disregard for boundaries, social distinctions, and those tiresome "othernesses" that hinder the expansion of the market and its local conquests. The situation has gone so far that the postmodernist Jean Baudrillard (1997) laments that the Other is disappeared almost totally into a multiculturally appropriated cosmopolitan generic self. The most apt icon of this self, he says, is the pop star Madonna, who/which is a collage of style without the boundaries and distinctions that are necessary to identify what is authentically rooted from what is not. This postmodern trend is often bleakly construed as all-powerful and as steam-rolling over small social formations and the natural environment.

While the steamrolling is undeniable, we should clearly understand that such processes proceed unevenly, at different tempos, and varying degrees of resistance. Researchers should examine actual conditions carefully before privileging the workings of the international capital market and consigning to the past the "traditional" cultural identity of small peoples. Many small kin-based societies continue to live socially distinctive lives, with powerful senses of the past and future; as such, they challenge and provide alternatives to the processes of globalized commodity exchange and capital penetration (Solway and Lee 1990; Lee 1992). As Feit has pointed out, some anthropologists not only tend to privilege the power of these megaprocesses, but they also tend to disempower the practices and initiatives of hunter-gatherers when they speak of forager ways of life in the past tense[9] and describe their future in the most pessimistic terms: "Anthropological constructions of hunter-gatherers are implicitly and in substantial terms disempowering, for the anthropological models deny the planning and everyday processes of change that are essential to both effective intentional action and to the human role in historical process. In short, we construct hunters who have a past and a momentary present, but who lack a real future, one with possibilities they might set about constructing as social actors" (Feit 1994, 438).

In my estimation the hunter-gatherer concept need not become more exclusive and historically limited; rather, as I hinted above, the term should be broadened to denote a condition or enterprise existing within a variety of social formations. This is particularly apt among other small-scale kinship aggregations. What comes to mind are those groups whose traditions include having engaged in regular – or under certain extended circumstances, a modicum of – foraging activities and foraging social organization, even though these societies may combine these activities with other forms of economic activity. In some cases these peoples engage in swidden agriculture while hunting and gathering, be they in the Americas, South and Southeast Asia, or Africa. In other cases they combine pastoralism with hunting, as in Northern Eurasia and Africa. Others also combine foraging with agriculture *and* pastoralism as in South Asia, and today, many former foragers also combine hunting, gathering, and/or fishing with wage labour and stints of urban migration, as is the case with the Gitksan and Witsuwit'en. Foraging should not be viewed as something carved in granite. The Mikea of Madagascar, for instance, have been hunting and gathering for over a century, after fleeing to the forests, away from a more horticultural existence marked by colonial war and internecine strife (Kelly, Rabedimy, and Poyer 1999, 215).

Broadening the scope of foraging in this way gives researchers a fuller palette with which to paint the wide range of foraging processes and organizational forms. These can be studied in greater complexity, whether in relation to ecology and economy or in relation to culture and social relations. They deserve more nuanced understanding of the shift in forms of sociation, from predominantly foraging bands to broader organizational forms controlling stable natural produce or increasingly devoting energy to raising plant or animal domesticates. This breadth of scope is also useful for understanding the nature of present-day foraging and helps release us from the problems of the billiard ball particulate view of small social formations.

A complementary approach to what I suggest here is being developed in relation to forager-farmers in Amazonia, where research has been inspired by the debate as to whether or not foraging has been viable in the Amazon without agriculture and whether or not foragers there are "the real thing." This research shows that Amazonian foragers create biotic niches by combining various forms of human actions and consciousness to alter the patterns of natural fruition in the surrounding environment. This enables people to live from the land by enhancing the utility of nature without actually converting to full agriculture and dominating the landscape (Balée 1989, 1992; Posey 1983; Rival 2002; Sponsel 1989; Yen 1989). In a word, this is a way of looking at the human imprint on an environment that supports hunting, fishing, gathering, and some gardening. Most if not all hunter-gatherers studied by anthropologists carry out some environmental alterations by their very presence on the land and by their "managerial" activities in relation to the biogeoclimatic conditions, as Don Ryan (Masgaak) shows in his Afterword to this book (see also Bailey 1980; Ellen 1988; Fowler 1996;

Gamble 1986; Haeussler 1986; Gottesfeld 1994; Thomas 1990). Such areas of inquiry help expand knowledge about the continuum between foraged/extracted produce and domestication.

This general outlook – that is, regarding foraging and domesticating activities as two of the possibilities in which small-scale social formations might engage – relies on a relational and cumulative concept of historical development. (By "simpler" and "more complex" I mean something like Woodburn's [1980, 1982] distinction between a greater emphasis on direct appropriation from nature versus a greater emphasis on seasonally shared appropriations and a distributive emphasis on sharing.) In other words, the more complex does not always eliminate the simpler but, rather, may incorporate it, modify it, and, in turn, be modified by it (like Hegel's classic discussion in *The Phenomenology of the Spirit* about the complex two-way relationship between master and slave). Indeed, degrees of encapsulation or, at a minimum, some form of periodic interaction have marked the last several millennia of relations between hunter-gatherers and their more socially complex sedentary neighbours. On the Indian subcontinent it appears that agriculturalists and foragers have shared territories and interacted for the past 4,000 years (Morrison 1999; Misra 1973; Possehl and Rissman 1992). In northeastern North America, along the edge of the Canadian Shield, which is the limit of horticultural possibility in Canada, horticultural Iroquoians – themselves partial foragers – interacted with Algonquian hunters over the past millennium (Trigger 1962; 1963; 1972, 80-1; 1976, 344). Examples occur in many other regions. Along the northern portion of the Northwest Coast and the adjacent Cordillera, oral narratives (Barbeau and Beynon n.d.) and archaeology (Fladmark, Ames, and Sutherland 1990, 239) suggest two millennia of periodic regional interaction between those who were primarily land-based hunters and those who were primarily marine hunters and fishers. These peoples conducted their interactions by gifting, feuding, trading, bartering, and intermarrying.

This long-term and extensive interaction between small-scale producers possessing different social complexity probably reinforced the distinct cultural identities of the various types of participants and gave variety to the goods used in everyday life. This endemic interaction with Others is a central theme of Eric Wolf (1982, 18), who castigates the anthropological preoccupation with the search for pristine small societies, which, in reality, have never been pristine, but rather have always been formed through social interaction – locally, regionally, and even internationally. If this were not the case, then one could assume that, at least in regions of the world where foragers have enjoyed many centuries of trade and commerce with a wider world (as in the Indian subcontinent), such small groups would long ago have lost their distinctive social and cultural identities. Long ago they should have become alienated from their close kinship with the forests/

jungles and all the forms of life and power identified therein. It is not axiomatic that the simpler entity becomes culturally obliterated by virtue of its relations with, or knowledge of, a broader, more inclusive and complex social formation.

In the 1960s Turnbull (1965, 1968), and more recently Ichikawa (1978, 1996, 1999), examined the Mbuti of the Ituri Forest. These people were associated both internally and externally with foreigners and neighbours. Such works have gifted hunter-gatherer studies with vibrant examples of the enduring and flexible nature of forager-type social relations, which existed side by side with participation in other, wider social relations. Much of pre- and protocontact Iroquoian culture (based on horticulture, fishing, and hunting) demonstrated that foraging and horticultural activities existed, as it were, under the same longhouse roof and were exemplified by reciprocal relations between the women (who produced, prepared, and stored the crops) and the men (who fished, hunted, bartered, traded, and raided) (Stites 1905; Daly 1985). This is a relational approach to the definition and description of hunting and gathering rather than an essentialist categorizing approach wherein the presence of one set of subsistence activities precludes the existence of the other.

The same approach can be extended to the study of capital penetration into hitherto indigenous forest-based social relations. If we assume, and can gradually document, that foragers have long been defined in the context of their relations with non-foragers and non-foraging activities in general, then we should be more cautious in privileging those with more complex social organization (with whom foragers interact), even when this involves the expansion of capitalist markets into the forests of the world. We should not look at the market as a simple subversion of tappers and trappers (Murphy and Steward 1968); rather, we might try to determine the ease with which foraging societies adapt to new opportunities and limitations. To what extent are old customs and institutions abandoned in favour of new procedures? And to what extent are they maintained and reformulated?

Complex Hunter-Gatherers
Researchers in the field of hunter-gatherer studies have generally consigned the peoples of North America's northern Pacific coast (and those of the adjoining cordilleran hinterland [e.g., the Tsetseut, Tahltan, Interior Tlingit, Gitksan, Witsuwit'en, and Chilcotin]) to the role of problematic anomaly, the so-called complex (Price and Brown 1985; Burch and Ellanna 1994), affluent (Lee 1976; Koyama and Thomas 1981), competitive (Hayden 1994), and delayed-return (Woodburn 1980) foragers. In the literature, the major contribution of such peoples often seems to be foils for the "classic" ambulatory small-group hunter-gatherers in Australia (e.g., Spencer and Gillen 1927) or the African foragers of the Ituri Forest (Turnbull 1961, 1965; Ichikawa

1978, 1996, 1999), the Kalahari (Marshall 1976; Lee and DeVore 1976; Lee 1979, 1990; Biesele and Weinberg 1990), and the savannah near Ngorongoro (Woodburn 1970, 1979, 1982). When viewed from afar, peoples like the Witsuwit'en and Gitksan are assumed to negate notions of hunter-gatherer egalitarianism, "communism in living," and to replace the centrality of social fluidity and sharing with rigid hierarchy, slave-taking, agonistic gifting, and other acts of double-edged reciprocity. As stressed above, "simple-complex" polarized distinctions enter our discourse as synchronically conceived "snapshot" patterns of socioeconomic activity and association rather than as entities in motion, process, and interaction within a field of relations associated with both similar and different other entities and temporalities.

The peoples of the Northwest Coast are frequently considered to be complex hunter-gatherer-fishers by virtue of their storage of salmon and other species, their semi-sedentary existence, social differentiation, and forms of association. However, what is not as obvious is the fact that in the higher latitudes of the northern hemisphere, apart from perhaps the Arctic coast, most species sought by local human populations are limited to short, seasonal availability, with much more biodiversity available in the late spring, summer, and autumn seasons than during the winter. As a consequence, most of the peoples of this region have probably always been delayed-return foragers – due not to the enormity of resources available or to their "complexity" but, rather, to the need to tide themselves over until the next species can be procured for seasonal human use. Salmon and berries, dried and smoked, did of course fill the gaps when there were no other species available, and the hundreds of storage pits in the old village sites along the Skeena River of British Columbia attest to the delayed-return nature of distribution and consumption in the region.

However, a stranger in the region two centuries ago would probably have noted that the degree of centralization and hierarchy seemed to increase as he or she moved from the cordillera down the rivers and out to the estuaries and islands on the coast. Yet the inland Gitksan and, to some extent, the Witsuwit'en had a protocontact (post-1492) past characterized as somewhat competitive, reciprocal, hierarchical, and status-seeking, and they had a seasonal sedentarism with an active village life for much of the year. (The Witsuwit'en gathered in their main village only during the summer fishing season and telescoped much of their feasting into this season.) However, even the contemporary fieldworker observes that features of foraging remain part of the social life of these peoples. This is seen in their respectful but friendly attitude towards the natural surroundings ("our supermarket," "our real home"); it is witnessed in the belief in the sentient nature of material surroundings ("the spirit of the land," "the breath of the ancestors"). It is also witnessed in distrust and dislike of enduring leadership that extends its authority beyond the scope of the descent group. Moreover, it is evidenced in the presence of internal sharing and giving of foodstuffs, the encouragement of individuality, the development of special powers, and the independence in the young. It is seen in the considerable fluidity of political alliances, including repeated attempts to resolve disputes by seeking consensus, and a tendency to vote with one's feet when tough decisions are to be made.

The Gifts of Nature and the Nature of Gifts

Northwest Coast peoples are well known in anthropological history – from the journals of Captains Cook, Vancouver, Malaspina, Galiano, Caamaño, Alcalá, and Valdés (Gunther 1972; Suttles 1990b) as well as from the ethnographic writings of, among others, George Dawson, Aurel Krause, G.T. Emmons, Johan Jacobsen, Harlan Smith, Edward Sapir, Franz Boas, Marius Barbeau, and William Beynon (Suttles and Jonaitis 1990). The peoples of this region are known to be well-gifted by the bounties of nature. They are known for the complexity of their foraging-based social order, their plastic arts, their ceremonialism, and for their public form of gifting. They have given the anthropological world the phenomenon of the "potlatch" – a ceremony at which the apparently wanton giving of gifts shocked and stunned the first wave of Europeans and inspired the second wave to outlaw this practice in 1885; this so-called Potlatch Law was not rescinded until the 1950s (Laviolette 1961).

Gifting and feasting, practised by the Gitksan, the Witsuwit'en, and classical Northwest Coast neighbours like the Nisga'a, Coast Tsimshian, Haida, Tlingit, and the Wakashan and Salishan peoples further south, are central features of the region's cultures. They attest to the way that the horizontally organized social relations of foraging intersect with vertical tendencies towards hierarchy. For much of their history – barring the heyday of the sea otter trade between the 1780s and 1820s and subsequent decades of resource frontier market relations before the establishment of "Indian reserves" – feasting demonstrated a loose familial structure of power and authority. This authority was diffused through reciprocal gifting between the clans and their respective Houses, between villages, and even sometimes between neighbouring peoples.

The agonistic giving by prominent figures in this region during and after the maritime fur trade was recorded by Franz Boas and, following the publication of Marcel Mauss's eloquent essay, "The Gift," has engendered a century of debate concerning the comparative nature of gifting and lending, giving and investing. It is unfortunate, however, that the "potlatch" aberration has come to stand for "potlatch feasting" since what the people call feasting (then and now) appears generally to be, and to have been, more subtle in both conception and practice, and less overtly steeped in political economy.

Building on insights recorded by Mauss, Bourdieu (1992 [1977], 4-8) argues that the nature of social interaction in gift-giving kinship societies (in terms of temporal uncertainty in relationships) differs radically from contractual interactions found in state societies. In the former, the tempo of interactions is neither predetermined nor fixed, and each act of prestation involves ongoing risk and uncertainty of outcome, thereby requiring continuing social input into the relationship between givers and receivers. This point has also been made by Gregory (1982, 12), who writes: "non-commodity (gift) exchange is an exchange of inalienable things between transactors who are in a state of reciprocal dependence. This proposition is only implicit in Marx's analysis but it is, as will be seen below, a precise definition of gift exchange." With contractual relations – the dominant form of interaction in state societies – the result is fixed and settled at the outset of a relationship, in a contractual manner, such as in a bill of sale, a lease, or the terms of a loan.

Gift exchange presupposes what Bourdieu calls *méconnaissance*, or wilful "misrecognition" of the reality of the objective mechanism of exchange (and self-interest). In other words, it presupposes a subtle (if rhetorical) "family-like" intimate relationship between giver and receiver, even though gifts objectively signify not only care, affection, and gratitude but also obligation and debt. Bourdieu argues that too often we neglect the temporal aspect of the gifting process. Reciprocating too soon, or too late, can both have disastrous consequences. Giving a counter-gift on the spot concludes the relationship and puts it on a par with a contractual exchange such as occurs while selling or buying. Lapsed gifts, on the other hand, entail the receiver acknowledging the social superiority of the giver. Moreover, actors in a gifting relationship work on the assumption of "the sincere fiction of a disinterested exchange," a collectively maintained and approved self-deception, without which symbolic exchange, the medium of culture, could not function. The actors' habitus shows them to be at once aware of the value of their exchanges and refusing to recognize this awareness. In Northwest Coast feasting, the public disinterest of a recipient masks his or her gratitude and pleasure at having received, in kindness, something of the other. At the same time, it masks the gift recipient's frustration at being further indebted to the giver.

The lapse of time between gift and counter-gift enables the counter-gift to be seen as an inaugural act of generosity (as well as an expression of gratitude), which is given without calculation. If gifting were locally perceived as a transaction, then it could not exist as gifting. The time interval between gift and counter-gift allows for the coexistence of both calculation and generosity, and leaves the outcome of each initiative as part of an unfolding, cumulative, open-ended relationship. Of similar concern is the spatial element in reciprocal relations. Sahlins (1972, 199) finds a comparative trend towards negative reciprocity and profit-taking increasing with the decrease in the vitality of kinship relations from the local moiety or village to tribal and international sociological spatial categories. Ingold (1986) has refined this idea, showing how negative reciprocity (as demand sharing) can occur at the centre and how positive reciprocity (as barter) can occur at the periphery of consanguinity. One can, however, debate whether demand sharing is negative reciprocity since those who demand a share are equally subject to demand by others and one's continual refusal or inability to share (to always take or keep) makes one increasingly peripheral to the sharing group (Bodenhorn 2000; Macdonald 2000). Similarly, barter at the kinship periphery can often be viewed as relatively out of balance and negative. In general, there is usually a broad trend towards more local gratitude-oriented gifting close to home, and more overt or explicit profit-seeking at the periphery of kinship societies:

> The general law of exchanges means that the closer the individuals or groups are in the genealogy, the easier it is to make agreements, the more frequent they are, and the more completely they are entrusted to good faith. Conversely, as the relationship becomes more impersonal, i.e., as one moves out from the relationship between brothers to that between virtual strangers (people from two different villages), or even complete strangers, so a transaction is less likely to occur at all, but it can become, and it does increasingly become purely "economic" in character, i.e., closer to its economic reality, and the interested calculation, which is never absent, even from the most generous exchange (in which both parties account – i.e., count themselves satisfied) can be more and more openly revealed. (Bourdieu 1992, 173)

Bourdieu argues that objective economically oriented analyses, steeped in the assumptions of the social contract, generally ignore this socially constructed *méconnaissance* that is important in many face-to-face interactions, and particularly in societies lacking nation-wide institutions of social control: "In reducing the economy to its objective reality, economism annihilates the specificity located precisely in the socially maintained discrepancy between the misrecognized, or, one might say, socially repressed, objective truth of economic activity, and the social representation of production and exchange" (Bourdieu 1992, 172). From this perspective, northern Northwest Coast feasting embodies a finely tuned customary misrecognition that takes the forms of ceremony, etiquette, altruism, and respect, behind which economic and political calculations are set in motion. Only under extraordinary conditions do the latter break out into full view, in the form of the "potlatch," or what Mauss (1990, 7) called "total prestations of an agonistic type." In the agonistic potlatches of the fur trade, and to some extent today in the mid-coast region, the precious items, the coppers, were/are given aggressively and openly or sacrificed to squelch the status of a rival (see the recent Chief Mungo Martin example below). They were often sacrificed rather than being given to the rival, with the result that the rival was challenged to reciprocate at the same or greater magnitude. Failure meant losing one's public face.

Among contemporary Gitksan and Witsuwit'en peoples, such agonistic frankness is never admitted. The land tenure and the economy of these peoples cannot properly be comprehended without an appreciation of their own understanding of reciprocal relations involved in paying off their family gift obligations, their receipt of counter-gifts, and, in turn, countering these counter-gifts. I place these activities in this order of "misrecognition" since very few matrilineal kin groups in the ethnographic region ever feel free of the deep-seated obligation to reciprocate from their "hearts" and their "treasure boxes." They do not consider that they are initiating gifting; rather, they see themselves as responding to existing social indebtedness, to earlier rounds of kindness received. They constantly feel pressed to give in response to kindness born of friendship, customary kinship services rendered, and material gifts received by their House years earlier (or even gifts unrequited by earlier generations of House members). These are people whose social dispositions have arisen from generations of luring game and fish into their possession and, when successful, giving thanks for the gift of material well-being to the life forces around them. They set up alliances through marriage with other groups whose compliance and interests may not always coincide with their own, and they face the uncertainties of salmon runs, wild produce, weather patterns, gambling risks, and political enmities. Such uncertainties are countered in relational ways, through forms of reciprocity that assume transactions (between people and the life force in each other and in all things) can be undertaken in ways that, while open-ended, engender understandable reactions and standards of behaviour.

The prevalent form of positive reciprocity employed takes the form of gifting and counter-gifting. Actors gift other groups in order to cause social imbalances to swing more in their own favour (which then creates further imbalances elsewhere in the community, requiring subsequent gifting responses). These communities have a heritage marked by a reliance upon one another's goodwill, and, lacking central leadership, bureaucracy, and a police force, they probably could not have tolerated the blatant pursuit of naked economic interest by individual persons or groups. Their *méconnaissance* subsequently took the form of the gift with its built-in temporality. A gift given probes a relationship into life or extends an existing one. What that relationship will become, only time will tell.[10] This relational attitude also extends to human relations with what Western cultures see as a discrete entity that goes by the name of "nature." Among the Witsuwit'en and Gitksan the land is a gift to a matrilineal group, given by the energetic spiritual forces of that place. The human-sustaining resources of the place are likewise "owned" by the matrilineal group as the result of an ancient chain of gifting between those anthropomorphic forces that populate nature, and their counterparts, the descendants of the family's first ancestors. The "natural" revelations made, or "gifted," to the family's first ancestors are gifts assumed in theory and learned in practice by each generation, and, in the form of family narratives, songs, and crests, they are passed on, or gifted, to subsequent generations. Lands acquired through peace settlements have similarly been legitimized as payments for suffering negative reciprocity and have similarly been incorporated into the sacred family narratives *(kungakh,* or *adaawk'*). The possession of the gifts of nature provides the basis for sufficient prosperity to enable the family, through its talents and its labours, to maintain its name through feasting – the most social and public form of giving.

Most analyses, from Boas (1897; Codere 1966) to Godelier (1999), begin with a tabula rasa situation wherein a free individual decides rationally to accumulate prestige by initiating a round of giving. This appears to have been possible only to a few, and only during the resource frontier days of the nineteenth century (Cole and Darling 1990). However, according to Boas, the Wakashan-speakers of the mid-coast appear to have had a less ascriptive system of kinship statuses and more social possibilities for political entrepreneurship, or "big man" competitive giving, than existed on the north coast. Competitive potlatching and winter dance societies spread north and south from the middle coast as well as into the adjacent Pacific Cordillera (Drucker 1963, 1965). For example, among the Nlaka'pamux Salish of the Fraser Canyon and Douglas Plateau, as Mary Charlie explained to Marian Smith in 1945, people sometimes potlatched "if they were after a big name"; but, as she went on to explain, a mortuary feast was different. It was to honour the dead (M.W. Smith 1945, bk. 4:1, 268 p. 40ff.).

My experience (see also Drucker and Heizer 1967; Roth 2002) indicates that every generation is born into existing obligations that have to be parlayed into a better social situation. Perhaps we should call it social repression, but virtually nobody is in a position to begin, as if they were initiating a new round of giving. Everyone today explains his/her feast-giving in terms of the misrecognition of reciprocating (or "paying out") for kindnesses (especially the kindness of the community in rallying around at the death of a beloved House member, coming to the feast to cheer up the family and to witness the repairing of the status discontinuities created by the death of a name-holder). I do not intend to imply that such misrepresentation is conscious or that a genuine wave of gratitude does not underlie the conscious sense of indebtedness and need to pay back.

Mauss (1990), Godelier (1999), and Bourdieu (1977, 1990b) suggest that societies marked by the prevalence of gift exchange were, in terms of structural complexity, located somewhere between the realm of "total prestation"/ sharing (that of the classical hunting band perhaps) and the contractual relations of civil nation-state society. Godelier (1999, 160) has suggested that reciprocal gifting has proven important in societies where these relations are limited and relatively internal to kin grouping, and where kinship groups entail the transfer of goods and services in order to seal or renew alliances and webs of indebtedness. These alliances are expressed in idioms of friendship, kinship, and social morality.

What the Gitksan and Witsuwit'en themselves refer to as "feasting," with its complexity of giving and receiving, paying and paying back, discharging and creating indebtedness, allows for the achievement of status within a framework of ascribed rights and responsibilities associated with a hierarchy of family names. It is a means for de jure status to be made more de facto. The term "potlatching" is better reserved for agonistic giving in abnormal competitive periods of history. Godelier (1999, 153ff) points out that the potlatch is a highly useful institution in a social formation that does not have a hierarchy of overarching power and polity-wide leadership. In such conditions gifting can serve to channel competition and to create local temporary leaders within the ever-unfolding kinship system. Gifting, of course, is a major feature of social life among the Gitksan and Witsuwit'en. These societies also exhibit an analogous institution that results in limiting the accretion of power: that is, the common practice of patrilocal residence combined with matrilineal inheritance. This breaks up potential blocs of male kin who otherwise would acquire enduring power and authority held by men and their sons. In their role as nephews, sons inherit names and land rights from their mother's brothers and not from the fathers who have raised and trained them to hunt and fish on "foreign," or paternal, family land.

Annette Weiner (1976, 1985, 1992) has re-examined the giving processes in the Trobriand Islands, along with the body of production and distribution relations. Here, ceremonial givings are an integral part of society, and they include massive labour expenditures by women in the internal, or *sagali*, exchanges central to local social reproduction through mortuary ceremonies. Weiner points out the close bond between brothers and sisters, which is central to reciprocal giving between kin groups. She stresses that it is not strictly groups of men who give women, as Lévi-Strauss, Godelier, and Gregory have all asserted but, rather, groups of kin that give women's labour and uxorial rights to one another while, especially in matrilineal systems, *retaining* rights of geniture. The negotiated gifting of the rights to a woman's labour (in the form of giving a bride), and formerly, at least among the Witsuwit'en and Gitksan, groom service to the bride's family, is conducted not by men who exchange women but by matrons and their brothers. The siblings leading one such group negotiate with the siblings leading another such group. The sibling bond is certainly strong on the Northwest Coast, even though brothers and sisters are separated by virilocal residence.

Marriage, due to the incest rule, can also be viewed as a form of inter-group and inter-nation gifting (Lévi-Strauss 1969). As Weiner points out, the brother-sister relationship in reciprocal gifting stresses the paradoxical nature of giving. What is it about the gift, she asks, that binds giver and receiver in a manner that is lacking in a commodity transaction? She found that the most powerful gifts in *kula* exchanges are items that simultaneously contain both something that is given and something that is retained by the giver. Because brothers and sisters have to marry out to other clans, villages, and nations, their corporeal transfer is a form of gifting between kin groups, whose members retain rights in, and affections for, their members given in marriage. When a woman is given in marriage her husband's group raises her children, but they inherit from her and her brothers. Among the Gitksan and Witsuwit'en, both spouses are bound to help the other's siblings in their feasts. In other words, the validation of landownership, and rights to esoteric family history, crests, and songs, may be revealed or temporarily gifted to other families (in their narration and performance) but do not really leave the family of origin. These gifts and revelations are facilitated by the giving of large quantities of foodstuffs as well as subsidiary gifts. As Gregory (1982, 52) has pointed out in regard to Papua New Guinea: "The aim of an inter-clan gift transactor is not simply to maximize the number of gifts of a given rank he gives away, but to give away a gift of the highest rank. However, as these usually circulate amongst a small group of big-men, a young ambitious man must begin by transacting gifts of low rank and work his way up the ladder of rank."

In terms of the Melanesian cultures studied by Weiner, the gifts of greatest potency are considered to possess an inalienable essence that renders them distinctively owned by those who made them. They are known as *kitoum* items, and, although they enter into complex geographically and temporally extensive exchanges, they continue to contain the *kitoum* of their makers. While a *kitoum* as a gift may circulate widely through a gifting network or community, there is an invisible thread tying it to its original giver. The intertwining threads of altruism and self-interest implicit in gift-giving and receiving make significant contributions to the building of community. These threads also extend the political renown of the givers in a social context where the pursuit of "big man" status was conducted most visibly through *kula* gifting. Fundamental to *kula* gifting, but less visible, is the gifting of foodstuffs and craft items in other ceremonialized exchanges during the lifecycle (such as mortuary exchanges). Those who would rise in *kula* exchanges must also acquit themselves well in the giving of gifts at weddings and funerals.

On the Northwest Coast there was no *kula* equivalent. The mortuary feast (Barnett 1938, 1968; Drucker 1963, 1965; Drucker and Heizer 1967; Kan 1989) was, and is, the main vehicle for public, ceremonial gifting. Here too, as across the Pacific in the *sagali* giftings that were integral to grieving the dead of the Trobriand Islands, the more valuable gifts (given by brothers) are supported by public payments to the guests in the form of items of lesser value (produced by sisters). Weiner found the mats, intricately woven by the skilled hands of the women, to be the main items of lesser value that were given in large numbers. Similarly, in Gitksan and Witsuwit'en feasts it was also furnishings made by women that filled this role – fur robes, Chilkat robes, woven rabbit fur blankets, cured hides, fine mats and bark bags, and tightly woven raingear (and later, Hudson's Bay blankets). These items and the more luxurious special gifts made by men, such as inlaid feast dishes, elaborately carved kerfed boxes (the four sides of which are made from one board notched and steamed to form three corners, while the fourth is stitched up with spruce root fibre), carved horn spoons, copper-tipped daggers, slaves, and copper shields called *hayatsxw,* were equally socially constructed extensions of the giver and/or the giving group, marked mainly by emblems from the crest system.

Agonistic giving is documented on the adjacent coast, but the Gitksan and Witsuwit'en elders consider such practices to have been uncivilized, undignified, and infringements of the rules of feast-giving. Probably during the fur trade, regional gold rushes, and early commercial fishing and forest-cutting, some feasts and many of the winter dance ceremonies (see Figure 6) were occasions for vigorous but politically subtle agonistic gifting, or "potlatching," although the chief actors were hereditary chiefs and not self-made "big men."[11] In these mortuary feasts, and those feasts commemorating whole generations of departed kin (see Chapter 2), gifts are to "replace" the deceased, to firm up alliances weakened by deaths. When one dies in the Trobriand system, one's heirs return one's body and subclan property to the subclan in return for gifts. *Kula* exchanges are above and beyond the general give and take of *sagali* gifting but were built materially upon its local social foundation. In a similar fashion the competitive potlatching of the mercantile and colonial nineteenth century was based upon, and constrained by, the kinship status system of legitimacy (see Chapter 6).

In potlatch and *kula* regions, the most highly valued gift objects are often of little apparent utilitarian function. However, these valued objects serve as aesthetically crafted vehicles and symbols of social transactions and, hence, of power. Godelier (1999, 161) lists the qualities of such objects. His first point is that such objects are substitutes for persons. (The oral tradition of the Tsimshianic peoples is filled not only with gifting but also with people exchanged in marriage, whether by good- or ill-will, to strengthen the relationship between groups often socially and geographically distant from one another.) Godelier's second point is that these objects intrinsically possess psychic powers derived from deities, spirits, or ancestors and believed to be endowed with powers of life and death. Third, as comparable to one another, these highly valued objects provide their owners with a standard of self-measurement in relation to others. All these features resonate in Gitksan and Witsuwit'en gifting.

Among these peoples the most sacred group-defining incidents, as passed down in ancient songs and narratives, have to do with miraculous events that occurred in the past and at specific sites on their territories. These events are made visible in representational and plastic arts as crest figures. The combination and juxtapositioning of crest figures identify those descended from these narratives, the owning group, and the matrilineal clan associated with them. (See, for example, Figures 7 and 8, visual images of crests from Wilps Tenimget/Axti Hiix, as described and explained by Tenimget in his *Delgamuukw* evidence.) These figures and events overlap to an extent with the narratives and crests of certain other Houses and clans, such that a web of oral historical association is woven over the feasting area. Not all crest stories overlap with all others, but there is an outward-extending network of association. Crests have traditionally been carved and painted on talking sticks, house fronts, totem poles, interior house posts, and the illustrious coppers as well as upon virtually all hand-crafted items of domestic and gifting use. The items given in a feast – beginning with the foodstuffs (produced by the House members and coming from its land and fishing sites) and progressing to luxury goods – used to be accompanied by a description of their place of origin in terms of raw materials, labour input, history of the family at that place, and anecdotes about events in which certain feast guests participated at that place. As in the Trobriand Islands, owning is confirmed by giving. What is and was given in feasts is and was the item itself and the goodwill of the giver (a bit of the giver and the giver's family). What is retained is and was the ownership of the miraculous events that occurred on the giver's land and are represented by the specific visual representation of the matrilineal family's crest figures. (Vis-à-vis other clans and villages, that which is retained is legitimate proprietorship, recognized in the narratives of local "jurisprudence." However, vis-à-vis the land itself, this is conceived as a sacred gift exchange between spiritual forces and the ancestors.)

As I have indicated, at the time of contact, common feast gifts were fur robes and rawhide. (This was so obvious to outside observers that there was competition between feast requirements for beaver pelts and the demands of the Hudson's Bay Company and the North West Company traders for furs.) Other feast items were carved and woven works of art, and small items of copper. Slaves and coppers were uncommon luxury goods occasionally used in feast-giving. The fur robes were soon replaced by elk hides obtained from the south by the fur traders, stroud (woollen trade blanket material), and copper shields fashioned from commercially obtained rolled copper. Pax Britannica put an end to the capture and exchange of slaves. Copper, while available on the Alaskan Copper River and in the northeastern Gitksan territories, was very scarce. The trade copper was made into shield-like entities with a T-shaped skeleton surmounted by a convex "head" adorned with figurative designs. On the coast, these coppers became "the ultimate symbol of wealth" (MacDonald 1984, 133). Garfield (1939, 264) reported that Tsimshian chiefs' coppers would be broken up after the deaths of their owners, and the pieces, standing for the bones of the deceased, would be distributed to chiefly peers. Halpin and Seguin (1990, 278) state that the designs scored into the copper were not crests and that, since they changed hands, coppers could not stand for kin groups. My Gitksan teachers say that the main figure on a copper was indeed associated with the owner's crests: "You put your crest on the copper, whatever crest that is for your totem pole is what you put on your copper. Copper is of great value among us" (from a recorded interview made with elder Sophia Mowatt, Wilps Djokaslee, Lax Se'el Frog/Raven Clan, by Jane Smith Mowatt, who generously shared it with me). This indicates that, at least on the upper Skeena, while coppers could change hands (especially parts of the copper), they also contained inalienable qualities of their first owner, who invested them with crests. While the copper increased in value with each new owner, the crest figure that rooted it in a community of origin may also have increased its mystique. Miller (1997, 156) argues that, during the chaotic changes brought about by population devastation and social upheaval with the coming of Europeans, the ownership of coppers for potlatch use "provided a durable constant in the transmission of Tsimshian traditions."

Perhaps coppers did exist before the fur trade era, but none have been found extant in the postcolonial world (Jopling 1989). But copper, due to its scarcity and its ability to shine in the sun (the creator's illumination) when burnished, had long been an item of wealth. It is a material that, along with *haliotis* (mother-of-pearl), which was traded from as far away as California, has been used for jewellery and for adorning carved boxes, masks, rattles, talking sticks, and, occasionally, for blades on well-crafted daggers. Copper was considered to be a hard but living substance with a soul. It signalled prosperity, wealth, power, and well-being. Gitksan *adaawk*'s identify copper with high status, such as the Lax Gibuu Wolf narrative of bear mother. In this narrative, a high-born young woman was abducted by the bears for failing to show them proper respect. In order to maintain her honour and self-respect during captivity, she was counselled by Mouse Woman to hide her defecations and to replace them secretly with bits of her copper jewellery (*adaawk'* recounted by Art Mathews, Tenimget, in his *Delgamuukw* testimony, Transcript, 73).

Copper is also a central theme in the Hlgu lat' *adaawk*' of Wilps Djokaslee (which I have been given permission to cite by Simoogit Djokaslee, Ted Mowatt). The flatulent Hlgu lat' was ostracized for his noisy and annoying farting. He and his granny moved out of the village and lived beyond the boards where the villagers squatted to defecate by the river. There, in that undesirable location, they built a little house and made their own food. One day a copper canoe was revealed to the boy at the riverside. The copper-clad paddlers left the copper canoe on the riverbank and disappeared inland. They did not return. Hlgu lat' approached and found the canoe was solid copper. Inside was a copper box filled with furs and copper items: paddles, chiefs' regalia, rattles, and berry pickers. He took these items and cached them before running to his granny. Together they took all the wealth and hid the canoe. Hlgu lat' took copper and made a shield, on which he scored his frog and eagle crests. He made jewellery and a copper scratcher. He used the latter to pay a slave from the main house to take copper bracelets to the chief's niece, who, intrigued by the gift, came to visit him. They later married, and at their wedding, the bride's brothers paddled up the river to the main house in the copper canoe. The boy used his copper shield "to bring up all the coppers," or to engage in social giving and counter-giving until he became a man of substance. He became *simoogit* (chief), and chose as his name, Hlgu lat', which today would be translated as "Farts-a-lot." In addition to denoting flatulence, it referred to living downwind of the planks that were the village latrine. He took this unsavoury name and burnished it with feast-giving until it shone like copper. Copper had cured both his flatulence and his social ostracism, allowed him to enter the arena of feasting, and invested him with a wealth of social relations. These *adaawk*'s in particular show the two poles of value used by the Tsimshianic cultures to make moral and material judgments: copper and excrement.

Thus, symbolically at least, copper appears to have been the gold standard for social status and moral purity, even if its scarcity made it impractical as a currency before the fur trade (see also Chapter 6). Coppers increased in value as they passed through giving and counter-giving. Helen Codere (1990, 369), discussing Wakashan-speakers' coppers from the period of about 1780 to 1930 on the middle coast, writes: "A copper's value was that of the property distributed at the potlatch in which it had last changed hands, and it could be bought only at double that amount, a fact that so inflated the cost of coppers by the 1920s that even when options were taken on them and down payments made, transfers were rarely completed." Here, coppers were broken in rivalry potlatches, "burned" in fires, or "drowned" by being cast into the sea. To protect his honour and avoid acknowledging his inferiority, the main rival felt pressured to treat a copper of equal value in the same way. His actions were guided automatically by the same habitus of reciprocity found not only in relation to gifting and gambling but also in kinship and affinity. In an interesting modern note, Codere gives the history of the late Chief Mungo Martin's *Killer Whale Copper*, Max'inuxwdzi (see Figure 10). Mungo Martin, a well-known artist and chief, purchased this copper shield in 1942 for $2,010 from Peter Scow. The missing top section was cut away by guest chiefs invited to do so at the *hamatsa* dance initiation of Mungo Martin's son. The bottom piece was cut away when a rival questioned the status of Mungo Martin's son as a *hamatsa* dancer. During the fur trade era this would have been publicly presented to the rival, who would then be silenced if he were unable to reciprocate with a gift of double the value he had received. But in this case, the cut out piece was publicly withheld from the rival. Chief Mungo Martin silenced his rival by stating that he would not be giving the piece to his critic or opponent, as the latter would never have the wherewithal to reciprocate; instead, Martin threw the cut off piece of copper into the sea when his brother died. (Codere does not say whether or not this was considered an agonistic honour contest with a rival or a family sacrifice to mark a weighty death.) The copper was later displayed as the "coffin" for Mungo Martin's son. Having no other heir, he then donated the reduced-in-size but increased-in-value copper to the British Columbia Provincial Museum (370).

This fascinating information raises questions for those of us not from this culture. What is it that compels a response from, or at least entails a social effect upon, the rival when a luxury item like a copper is either destroyed or publicly precluded from being presented as a gift to a rival? What is it that impels a response from others when a donor selects a recipient in order to refuse publicly to give his luxury item to this selected rival? Why does he publicly consider the potential recipient, who is also an actual rival, to be insufficiently worthy or insufficiently wealthy to receive it properly and to reciprocate later with a gift of double the value of the one received? What impels the donor to deploy his wealth item in an act of destruction? Mauss, in *The Gift*, suggested that destruction was a form of sacrifice to gods, spirits, and ancestors. For me, a more satisfying explanation is given by Pierre Bourdieu (1990b, chap. 6) in the course of his discourse on the temporal aspect of gift exchange, where he argues that gift reciprocation has an inbuilt tempo and timespan. Here, using his Kabylia fieldwork experience in Algeria, Bourdieu examines contests of honour as competitive activities of *méconnaissance* that are similar to gift-giving in kinship societies.

Whereas in classical egalitarian foraging societies people spend much of their time thwarting and limiting sectional and personal accumulation and stressing sharing and equality, among Northwest Coast foragers a similar amount of time is spent accumulating within kin groups (that are nominally equal to one another) in order to pay off indebtedness in ongoing relations of reciprocity. The pressure to gift in return, to keep up with the Joneses, comes from public opinion, from social, moral, and ethical values:

in a word, from the socially constructed precepts of honour. Honour competitiveness can serve to divert what otherwise might become anti-social and violent competitions over material interests in society into less violently disruptive channels. Honour thus functions as do schools, churches, and the police in state societies – as an effective form of social control. Honour contests are in the same league as are other forms of non-contractual exchange including gifts, compliments, insults, marriage partners, and gambling: "The exchange of honour, like every exchange (of gifts, words, etc.) is defined as such – in opposition to the unilateral violence of aggression – that is, as implying the possibility of a continuation, a reply, a riposte, a return gift, inasmuch as it contains recognition of the partner (to whom in the particular case, it accords equality of honour)" (Bourdieu 1990b, 100).

Challenges to one's honour are only really properly constituted when they receive a riposte and are aimed at those deemed worthy of playing the game. Only those who are social equals can engage in contests of honour. Honour exchanges are duels, where everything the participant possesses can be risked. Or are they? The donor/challenger, once divested of wealth – or even his life (as in a duel) – still retains his (and it is generally a male game) high standing on the testosterone scale, his renown, and his family's pedigree and proprietorship rights. These things of immense symbolic value are not only retained following such disbursements (or physical destructions) of wealth but are also extended and multiplied. The social process involved is the antithesis of thrift, diligence, and capital accumulation by "the rational man" and, as such, was a red flag to the colonial authorities of Church and State. The waving of this red flag in such contests of honour led to the outlawing of feasts and other gift-based ceremonies across the land. With such honourable symbolic capital and renown, one may be temporarily poor in goods; however, in the long run, the one who has vanquished his rival by destroying his own wealth is wealthy in terms of those potent social relations that make for further material wealth and exchange.

He who would engage in such a competition with someone of inferior rank would demean himself, and he who would challenge an inferior risks a snub (such as Chief Mungo Martin executed vis-à-vis his rival when he publicly "non-gave" one of the segments removed from "the body" of his "killer whale" copper). Such acts rely upon a widespread code of honour if they are to be an effective element in advancing the flow of social interaction. Likewise, he who stooped to take up a senseless challenge would lose face.

I would add that these dispositions (contests of giving and challenges to honour) reflect the type of production activity common in many foraging societies. Here, given the limited technology, people engage in a relatively light predation of nature's resources. They do not dominate nature or bend it to their will; rather, they negotiate with it in a conceptually reciprocal fashion. What we call nature, or the home of raw materials, they consider part of the conscious relational and social world – a world not to be dominated (which, in any case, was not technologically possible) but to be dealt with by gifting, negotiation, gambling, even trickery. Goals remain secret because there is soul-to-soul communication between even the hunter and his game. As Guédon (1984, 141) has noted, the Tsimshianic hunter cannot openly express his intention to kill a bear, because the bear, hearing this, will consider the man to be boasting and will retaliate by killing him. To avoid such a fate, the hunter says he is "going to visit Grandfather" or "the old man of the woods." According to Guédon: "As a rule, one does not voice anything important in clear terms, for anything which is thought, and, more especially, anything which is spoken aloud, can be reclaimed in some way by other people, human or not. Nothing is hidden. The communication extends from soul to soul across the species boundaries, for instance from human to groundhogs, or mountain goats, or bears. It extends from the living to the dead ... thoughts occurring suddenly, seemingly from nowhere may have been sent by some dead relative."

These complex foragers gamble on getting the game, the berries, and fish in the right place at the right time, and they make return prestations both to society and nature to ensure that these ventures into risk-taking continue to pay off. The fluctuations of seasonal yield in different parts of the territories make harvesting an indeterminate art requiring flexible, open-ended, and reciprocal responses, which spill over into social relations. During the height of the coastal fur trade, when statuses were being reconfigured (particularly near the trading forts), contests of honour were the underlying basis for agonistic gifting. These struggles to save and destroy "face" were, after all, conducted between those who had to go on living beside one another and interacting in everyday life. They resulted in challenges that, in our own crass culture, would be called cycles of debt and obligation that can provide impetus to social production. In agonistic feast-giving, honour challenges between high-status equals tended to keep open the channels of interaction and to throw down the gauntlet to others in the economy to reciprocate, to assuage honour, or to save face. Not to do this was to lose political influence.

Copper and other precious gifts were supported by an ambient hospitality directed by the women, with great quantities of foodstuffs found on specific territories, the scarce items bartered or gifted up from the coast (e.g., oolichan and herring eggs on kelp), but especially meat, berries, and "grease." Food gifts were accompanied by crafted items made by the women (e.g., woven capes, bags, inlaid items, and sometimes a Chilkat robe with its complex tapestry weave of mountain goat wool and bark).[12] Other artistic works made by male carvers were also given. The hospitality involved music and dance, and everything was conducted with etiquette, metaphor, and respect for the honoured guests, whether the hosts' intentions were convivial or agonistic.

Even though I have described the cultural potency of copper as an ultimate gift, I do not consider the high-status gift as being the central aspect of giving in either feasts or potlatches. What counts in gifting is not what is given but, rather, the nature of the giving. Godelier (1999, 67) points out that it is not accidental that the theoretical difficulties with gifting "cluster around the interpretation of the nature of the precious objects" circulating in gift exchanges. He goes on to suggest, along with Annette Weiner (1992), that what really counts is "an immaterial reality present in the objects," composed of ideas and symbols endowing the item with "social power, something that, while given, is never completely alienated from the giver." Among the Witsuwit'en and Gitksan it can be argued that this something is the socially recognized spiritual power in the land owned by the clan or House as revealed, or gifted, to ancestors. The spiritual force of the crests, then, signals the donor family's unique identity and legitimate proprietorship of land and history.

Bourdieu (1977, 194), meanwhile, has taken this further. He writes that what distinguishes the gift from mere "fair exchange" is the labour and attention devoted to the *form*, the manner of giving, which must, in a public way, deny the objective interests of the exchange and symbolically transform it into socially acceptable customs and conventions. Through conventional and often ceremonial forms of giving there is a convenient masking of expressions of direct personal interest. Bourdieu calls such conventional masking of sectarian material interests the deployment of *symbolic capital* as a socially acceptable way to exert power without having to resort to physical coercion. He explains that "symbolic violence" takes the form of credit, confidence, obligation, loyalty, hospitality, gifts, gratitude, piety – all the virtues of a code of honour. The use of symbolic capital in conformity with such a code constitutes a highly effective form of domination and social order.

In the cultures of the Northwest Coast great efforts are made to follow the formal regional aesthetics of designing and making gifts and their presentation (see Figure 9). This attention to design and creation also applied to the other items, which, while involved in public giving, were not themselves given (such as totem poles and house posts). As the late Haida artist Bill Reid never tired of pointing out, the highest morality is craftsmanship. One can give nothing more precious of oneself than something well-designed and well-crafted (Bill Reid, personal communication).[13] Rare and precious materials, painstakingly worked and perfected according to socially constructed principles of formline design (Holm 1965), always adorned the actors and their goods in the cycles of feasts that radiated out across the region like ripples produced by raindrops on the surface of a pond.

To repeat, house fronts, house posts, talking sticks, chiefly robes, and totem poles are not feast goods, but they are both present in feasts and symbolically at the core of the group's being and proprietorship. Invested with life through the family crests they embody, their presence reinforces the legitimacy of the givers and their current actions of "giving back" (with a little extra). This act also "polishes the ancient name" by expressing goodwill and respect for others, and thereby leaving the House in good order for those who will come after. The crests themselves are considered gifts of power from the life forces in the land to the human beings living on that land. Enlivened by a life force, these gifts originally came from what the European cultures call "the world of nature." They were revealed, or given, to the ancestors of today's House members, and their power is revitalized again and again by their involvement in reciprocal gifting between kin groups. People say they give back in feasts in order to requite the gift of land, history, and legitimacy they inherited at birth.

The public form of giving gifts demonstrates that the giver is giving something of her- or himself. When the self is a kinship group in a "potlatch society" its identity is rooted in a position within a set of positions and dispositions that are in play across a whole region. These positions are geographically distributed and spiritually sanctioned. One (in the sense of the kin group representative) gives of one's ontology in public in order to retain or augment one's social identity within the existing configurations and dispositions of villages, clans, Houses, hunting territories, and fishing sites (and possibly to improve one's standing therein). One does so not as a lone entrepreneur (except in rare circumstances, as we shall see in Chapter 6 regarding the fur trade) but collectively, from within the corporate nature of the kinship system. In the long run, if a House does not requite these gifts, say, following mortuary ceremonies where the father's side has given the bereaved family a present of paying the funeral expenses, this can lead to the hosts eventually being pressed to forfeit land to their affines, their deceased chief's "father's side."

For these reasons much of what follows is presented in the spirit of the gift. The following chapter, an account of a totem-pole-raising feast, provides both a context and a paradigm for the gifting practices and symbols that inform so much of the economy and social life of these two peoples. It is an "ideal type" account, synthesized from several teaching sessions I was given by elderly feast specialists and made actual with many examples from my teachers' own life experiences, as well as my own attendance at pole-raising feasts.

In the courtroom, where this chapter began, both the plaintiff witnesses and their so-called expert witnesses engaged in the risky business of gift-giving. They made contributions to a community in search of truth, offering public education about an ancient way of life. Hyde (1999) makes a persuasive argument for the importance of gift-giving with regard to building a sense of community in the fields both of art and scientific inquiry. The gifts Hyde has in mind are scholarly contributions to free scientific or artistic discourse (something he acknowledges is rapidly being reduced with large corporations now financing and patenting research). Scholars agree to give (relatively free of vested interests in jobs and funding) their findings to journals, conferences, and university publishers, and to counsel neophytes simply with the aim of improving their status and making a contribution to the development of their field. (Hyde finds that in such endeavours – and, we might add, like any honour-based engagement – status and income stand in inverse proportion to one another.) I submit that the plaintiffs and their experts deployed their respective gifts in the *Delgamuukw* case. They sought to gift the public with particular knowledge and information, and to give what is at the core of all gifts, namely, ideas and relationships. Such procedures are political and moral in nature, and their recompense is certainly of a very delayed nature.

The gifting of one another with ideas, counter-ideas, and something of the personality of their donor is essential to the well-being of any community. In this sense, academic and scientific communities are no different from kinship-based communities. Gifting provides structural strength to the community. However, it has little currency in those fields of human endeavour where gift relations have been superseded by contracts, as in the courts of law.

The contents of *Our Box Was Full* were given to the court and returned unopened, but in order to avoid the breaking of the ring, this book has been prepared and given as a contribution to what, it is hoped, might become a future community of understanding.

FIGURE 1   Totem poles at Gitwangax. When this photo was taken in 1923 these
poles were already an established tourist attraction promoted by the Canadian
National Railways.

© Canadian Museum of Civilization, No. 59712. Photo: C.M. Barbeau.

FIGURE 2 Gitanyow (Kitwancool) in 1910. This village, the Gitksan settlement
closest to the rich Nass River estuary of their Nisga'a neighbours and relatives, remained outside the *Delgamuukw* litigation, pursuing Aboriginal rights in its own
way. However, Gitanyow people were closely involved with the *Delgamuukw* case,
even appearing in court as witnesses for the plaintiffs. The wealth and sophistication of this village is reflected in the complexity of its *xwts'aan* (memorial poles).
BC Archives, No. A-06900.

FIGURE 3 The paddlewheeler steamboat *Hazelton* nearing its namesake, Hazelton, the inland terminus of navigation during the early 1900s.
BC Archives, No. A-02004.

FIGURE 4 Awaiting the arrival of the paddlewheeler at Hazelton/Gitanmaax around 1900. Note the food cache on stilts (to protect the contents against vermin) down the hill below the clan houses. The steamboat landing was located beside the warehouse of the Hudson's Bay Company trading post. Much of this shore was eroded by the flood of 1936, and on the remainder there was a small house in which the author lived during the period of fieldwork.
BC Archives, No. E-08391.

FIGURE 5 Cartoon by Don Monet occasioned by a courtroom incident during the trial stage of *Delgamuukw* when Chief Antgulilibix, Mary Johnson, was asked to sing her wilp *limx'oo'y*, or song of mourning, a crucial feature of legitimacy of territorial proprietorship. This "breaking of frame" with courtroom decorum (albeit by the most solemn values of another culture) alarmed Chief Justice McEachern, who stopped her, saying that in matters cultural he had a tin ear. Antgulilibix did not lose her aplomb, and, in so far as the judge was the representative of the Queen of England, she consistently addressed him as "Your Highness" as she vainly sought to penetrate his senses. But alas, they were hermetically sealed, as he had warned, in a thick layer of tin.

Courtesy of the artist, Don Monet.

FIGURE 6   Secret society gathering at Hagwilget, summer 1923. Witsuwit'en chiefs
queuing to enter the hall known as Owl House. Elders of the 1990s recalled when,
as small children, they peeked in the window of this house to snatch glimpses of
the secret ceremonies and potlatch gift-giving inside. Among coastal peoples, and
the Gitksan, these ceremonies were held in the winter months, but the Witsuwit'en
fitted them into the brief summer season when they assembled at the river canyons
to fish. This was the type of ceremony that was despised by William Duncan, Robert
Tomlinson, and other missionaries; yet, despite negative moral pressure and being
outlawed under the provisions of the Potlatch Law, these ceremonies persisted.
From left to right: Burns Lake Tommy (Gitumskanist), Round Lake Tommy
(Wedexkw'ets), Felix George (Goohlaht), August Pete (Kweese), Jimmy Michel
(Samaxsam), and Bill Nye (Mediik).
© *Canadian Museum of Civilization, No. 62310. Photo: C.M. Barbeau.*

FIGURE 7   Totem poles at Gitwangax, with a pole of Wilps Tenimget/Axti Hiix in the foreground that has the distinctive lion crest, or *hawaaw,* on the top.
© *Canadian Museum of Civilization, No. 59698. Photo: C.M. Barbeau.*

FIGURE 8 *Hawaaw*, a crest of Wilps Tenimget/Axti Hiix, Pdeek̲ Lax̲ Gibuu, Gitwangax.
This crest, or *ayuks*, is also on the top of one of the *wilp*'s poles. The narrative of
its origin, and its cultural, jural, and social significance, were explained in the
Delgamuukw trial by Simoogit Tenimget, Arthur Mathews Jr. This *wilp* (House) had
decided to reveal a certain degree of its intellectual property to the court in order
to demonstrate to the judge the complexity, the philosophy, and the legitimizing
function of the system of *ayuks* (crests) and *adaawk*'s (narratives) of origin.
BC Archives, Accession No. I-028221.

FIGURE 9 (FACING PAGE, BOTTOM)   An example of gift-giving and litigation. This drum by Haida artist Bill Reid was photographed at the artist's summer home in the Gulf Islands of British Columbia. Bill Reid donated drums like this one to the plaintiffs in *Delgamuukw* so that they could auction them to raise funds for the court case. *Courtesy Bill Reid Foundation. Photo: L. Mjelde.*

FIGURE 10   Kwa̲kwa̲k'awakw *Killer Whale Copper (Max'inuxwdzi)* belonging to the late Chief Mungo Martin, which is described here in Chapter 1 and in Codere (1990, 370). Coppers like this were items of extreme value among Gitksan and Witsuwit'en chiefs as well. The "destruction" of coppers has long intrigued social theorists.
Courtesy Chief Peter Scow and the Royal BC Museum, No. CPN 9251.

FIGURE 11 "You are on Wet'suwet'en Land." Information blockade on Highway 16 on Witsuwit'en territory, July 1990. This blockade was in solidarity with the action in defence of Mohawk land at Oka, outside Montreal, and in support of the on-going land rights case headed by Chief Gisdaywa for the Witsuwit'en and Chief Delgamuukw for the Gitksan.
Photo: R. Daly.

FIGURE 12 Anthropologist at work. Participant observation during the information blockade in the Witsuwit'en village of Kya Wiget (Moricetown), July 1990.
Photo of Richard Daly: L. Mjelde.

2

The Reciprocities of a Pole-Raising Feast

This chapter contains an "ideal type"[1] ethnography of feasting[2] and seeks to reveal the unique vitality of social interaction among the Gitksan and Witsuwit'en. The ceremonial gifting of the feast can be regarded as a paradigm for social practice as far as this pertains to relations between local matrilineal kinship groups. Any one feast is a momentary slice of time that shows the relations of gifting between the mother's side and the father's side of every extended matrilineal family. The feast consists of a set of irreversible actions and counter-actions that perpetuate and interweave relations between kinship groups. These relations have similar contours throughout Gitksan and Witsuwit'en society, but the most paradigmatic for local society are those conducted between the holders of chiefly names, who represent their respective House groups.

Public accounting is carried out between these matrilineal Houses named for the group's dwelling, located in one of several villages along the mainstem Skeena-Bulkley river system. These social units formerly housed all members not married out elsewhere as well as in-marrying affines. Feasting events are publicly and jurally witnessed activities. In terms of convenient "social misrecognition," they provide the givers with a way to acquit themselves of their indebtedness and, simultaneously, shift indebtedness (expressed in the form of gratitude) over to other Houses of other clans. These recipients will, in turn, one day reciprocate in order to discharge their own social debts, usually in the context of death obsequies for family members (Daly 2002).

Feasting is ontogenic. Its gifting relations enact the succession of generations with their corresponding rights and duties, actor by actor. Feasting marks individual House members' sequential phases of life and the social connections that accompany these changes. Social relationships are adjusted as people age and die. Some societies invest most of their gifting in birth or marriage, while in the Northwest Coast culture area it is customary to focus upon bereavement (Kan 1989). People say the most meaningful, valuable, and beautiful things in life come into being through sadness and melancholy, associated with longing for those who "have gone before." Reciprocal gift-giving between the bereaved maternal group and a formally solicitous father's side embody basic relations of kinship and affinity. Gift-giving associated with feasts may be viewed as a socially reckoned template for everyday relations of credit and debt, and, ultimately, a demonstration of the appropriate management of family lands and fishing sites. Feasts validate the reincarnation of personalities, names, crests, histories, laws, and traditions of the hosting group, as well as the readjustment of relationships with linked kin groups.

At a feast, the hosting House, with its clan support, fulfills its obligations to the limits of its current collective ability, striving to live up to the locally recognized status and legitimacy of its matrilineal pedigree. It seeks to "pay its dues" and, thereby, reconfirm its ownership of crests, narratives, spiritual powers, and land. It seeks to do so in a way that is consistent with the prosperity and well-being exhibited by "those who have gone before," and to do so through respectful obsequies to these deceased predecessors. The most prevalent arena for competition is usually not between descent groups but, rather, within them, focusing on the question of succession to high names and the associated rights and duties – a competition usually conducted out of the public eye. Fierce internal competition attests to the continuing vitality of the feasts and the social relations and cultures in which they are embedded.

Feasting entails a formal etiquette and diplomacy that highlight the decentralized nature of decision taking and a strong distaste for long-standing political hierarchies. Loss of face by one chief at a feast could lead to feuds, charges of psychic ill intentions, or open violence. Etiquette, a corporate kinship procedure for offering presents, and listening to the legitimizing narratives of others are thus the order of the day.

Each House, or each set of linked Houses within a specific clan, can affect the course of public affairs only by means of its own members' demeanor, comportment, and collective strategies of persuasion. Public behaviour is not only witnessed and remembered, but it also comprises the historical record passed down through the memories of succeeding generations. As one chief said, "I cannot go over to my neighbour's territory and tell him what to do. I can only stand on my side of the boundary, look into his eyes, and tell him my history" (the late James Morrison, Txawok, personal communication). In the absence of centralized administrative institutions, this reliance upon historical narrative elaboration, moral suasion, diplomacy, and an overarching body of laws and beliefs lubricated by gift-giving is central to the social effectiveness of the feast system.

There is a considerable academic literature on the potlatch feast of the North Pacific coast.[3] Drucker (1965, 55-6) views feasting in light of existing ethnographies, personal observation, and practitioners' exegesis:

> The overt purpose of both feast and potlatch was the announcement of an event of social significance: marriage of an important person; birth of a potential heir to one of the group's titles, crests and high statuses; inherit- ance and formal assumption of one of these titles or crests, and its corre- sponding position; or rescue and ransom and restoration to free status of a war captive ... The guests were witnesses to the fact that the privilege was rightfully owned and rightfully transmitted to its new bearer. This sanction was the essence of the potlatch and the prime purpose of the wealth. The effect of the procedure may be compared to that of notarizing a document or of registering a deed ... It was usual to announce to guests, for example, that they were invited to eat sockeye from such and such a stream, which had been discovered, given to, or captured in war by an ancestor and trans- mitted to the incumbent head of the group. The public announcement and tacit recognition of the fact by the guest group, so to speak, legalized the claim.

Marcel Mauss (1990 [1923-24], 7-9, 19-21) had a similar understanding, although he also stressed that the potlatch feast was a shamanic event. He wrote that feasts are shamanic because the participant chiefs are human incarnations of the spirits associated with the names they hold, whose songs they sing, whose dances they perform, and whose spirits they merge with to mediate the mental and emotional well-being of their people. For Mauss, the core of the gift-giving at a feast was an exchange and mingling of spiri- tual power "in the wake" of which came the disbursement of valued items. In many locations this aspect has been downplayed due to censure by the churches and administrators. The spiritual dimension is also stressed by Halpin (1973), Seguin (1984, 1985), and Kan (1989). Kan argues that the feast is common to mortuary obsequies in many cultures and ought to be approached in terms of participants' emotional responses to the deceased, the ancestors, and the family heritage that continues to preoccupy each generation. Lévi-Strauss (1987) criticized Mauss as having accepted "emic" explanations of potlatch and *kula* gifts. Beneath such embedded explana- tions, Lévi-Strauss reasoned, lie "unconscious mental structures" that are manifested in constant exchange and reciprocity through the medium of symbols. The symbolic nature of the origin of human society is integral to the giving and counter-giving of gifts (Lévi-Strauss 1987, 30).

Goldman (1975) and Walens (1981) do not venture so far philosophi- cally, but they explore the symbolic context of nineteenth-century Kwakwaka'awakw potlatch feasts. Piddocke (1965), Suttles (1960, 1962, 1968), and Vayda (1961) consider feasting in light of ecological functionalism, although they overplay the centrality of feasts as venues for distribution and exchange. Much of Northwest Coast exchange was facilitated by, but did not actually occur within, feasts.

John Adams (1973), the only writer apart from William Beynon (Anderson and Halpin 2000) to publish a monograph on Gitksan feasting, also stresses the redistributive function of the potlatch feast. He does so in a qualified way, pointing out that most students of the potlatch look on the institution from a strictly economic perspective and stress the redistribution of food. He argues that the potlatch host distributes mostly non-food items, especially items of wealth, which signal prestige and social status. What Adams misses on this point is that formerly much food *was* produced and exchanged, not only to couch the wealth objects presented as payments to the guest chiefs but also to signal ownership of the land and resource sites from which the food came. Food-giving also reinforced local social relations through a "family-like" medium of commensuality, the sharing of food (Drucker 1965), and by demonstrating the productive health and well-being of the host group.

At the present moment, the direct production of foods from the territories is less than it was a century ago, although the present cash economy is largely derived from broader economic activities on the same regional lands. To a considerable degree, the fruits of wage labour buy substitutes for territorial produce. The limited wealth enjoyed is still extracted from the land (via the fishing and forestry industries), but it is not, for the moment, land that is directly controlled by Gitksan and Witsuwit'en matrilineal kin.[4] The cash fruits of this productive activity are fed into the present-day feast, which is the venue where ownership over these lands continues to be asserted and validated. The non-traditional foods are sometimes treated as standing in for the foods of the host's territories (Arthur Mathews Jr., *Delgamuukw* Transcript, 4607; Daly 2002).

When planning and preparing for a major feast, a chief will strive to establish needed credit and use whatever type of values s/he has at his/her disposal. These values may be traditional or home-produced foodstuffs, hides, or cash, and all such values will be parlayed into obtaining the wealth items that, along with supplementary foodstuffs, are needed as feast gifts. Cash, in various denominations, is used to acknowledge statuses of guests (chief, wing chief, adult, child). Formerly only chiefs and their intended successors attended feasts, and all would receive roughly the same number of basic furs, mats, hides, and foodstuffs in gratitude for their attendance. Hide and fur items were frequently divided up and given out to guests, a practice that continued in the era of trade blankets (Bridge 1998, 130). Today, cash has entered the system as a handy yardstick for age and status marking. Additional gifts are also given to certain guests. These are specific to the host

family and its network of persistent interfamily relations. Feast preparations promote a high degree of economic activity (as local shopkeepers and
traders have attested over the past century), even though feasting itself is
not, as Adams correctly points out, normally a significant venue of food
redistribution.

Adams argues that the concept of society-wide redistribution through the
chiefs stands in contradiction to the strong ethos of group self-sufficiency
in the Northwest Coast area. He says that this ignores the great importance
the peoples place upon all kinship groups being able to reciprocate with
like groups. Adams proposes that the functional significance of feasting lies
in the fact that the laws of reciprocity, serve to force the society to reallocate
personnel, through adoption, between House groups in order to keep the
component social units (the Houses) roughly balanced in population. In
order to maintain this system of reciprocity, each House must be able to
host a feast when called upon to do so. Houses weak in numbers, and hence
wealth, threaten the system's ability to maintain credit and to repay debts
efficiently. Hence, according to Adams, by arranging adoptions into, and
loans for, weak Houses, larger, stronger Houses readjust the goods and labour
between such kin units in opposing clans so as to perpetuate the social
system. Also, Adams (1973, 106) argues, large Houses tend to be centres of
conflict and competition, thus: "Those excluded from participation in one
House, because of a shortage of statuses, could move to another House which
had statuses unfilled."

Adams concludes that the Gitksan are impelled to make frequent personnel adjustments in order to deal with population fluctuation. This, he
proposes, is something that "will almost certainly require the periodic redistribution of people to those statuses if they are to be maintained. If those
statuses are linked with resource-holding corporations, then such redistribution of people helps to maintain a balance in the man/resource ratio"
(108).

Attractive though this hypothesis is, I did not find evidence of massive
adoptions in the genealogical materials prepared for this case. No doubt
some adoption has been a historically specific factor in the period between
approximately 1860 and 1950, which saw serious depopulation in the region,[5] although not of significant volume to warrant Adams's hypothesis.
Current population demography is more than healthy, and the adoption
phenomenon is relatively rare. While Houses are indeed units of reciprocity, they are not carved in granite. The reciprocating groups are malleable
and tend to expand and contract along lines of common heritage within
the clan. Often when a certain House faces natural depopulation (such as a
dearth of daughters), its survivors and their collective property will be subsumed, for a few generations, within another closely related House of the
same *wil'naat'ahl* (those Gitksan clan members sharing the same migration

narrative), until the population is sufficient to again enliven the original House names and statuses. Large Houses can divide in two, although not usually without enmity. Among the Witsuwit'en it appears that this drawing in and temporary consolidation has occurred even at the clan level, with Laksamshu and Tsayu feasting together. This also holds among the Gitksan (Gitksen in the western dialect) at Gitwangax, the Wolves and Eagles, who have common narratives of origin and who, with population fluctuation, have feasted together as one hosting unit in recent decades. Gitksan persons have told me that they, as children of women adopted into other clans or distant sections of their clan, find it nearly impossible to be accepted within their mothers' adopted House. There is social pressure for them to return to "where they belong" within their own *wil'naat'ahl*. Similar pressures are exerted on women who raise clan children not their own to return such children to their correct House of origin.

Adams also implies more free agency among feast-goers than actually exists. People cannot freely choose which relationships they express when they are in the feast hall. These relationships are preordained by blood, by public display through the feast seating order, and by collective decision taking within the House regarding which name and status will be held. This social position determines their relations both within their own House and to the host of the present feast. Every member of the society must work from within the context of these constraints.

On the individual level, a feast participant is free to enhance his or her interests, but the cultural resources (or "capital") are circumscribed by social structure, by the line of descent, by one's role as host or guest, and by current local interfamily concerns. Even a chief's scope for personal decision making is limited to deciding how he or she will fulfill various leadership roles imposed upon her/him by family circumstances and by the heritage of *wil'naat'ahl* history, crests, and narratives (Olive Ryan, Transcript, 4987-9).

Adams fails to take into account the flexibility built into the Gitksan system by means of the *wil'naat'ahl* institution, whereby a depleted House often acquits itself in the feast hall with the massive assistance of other clan folk. Clanspeople who help are those who share narratives about entering these territories together long, long ago.[6] Houses with few personnel are likely to be subsumed within another related House within the *wil'naat'ahl* for a period of time, their chief name being held, in safekeeping, by the leader of that related House.[7]

Adams's analysis is demographic, with an ecological orientation, which means he focuses upon only one of many possible interconnected aspects of the feasting phenomenon, without integrating them into local exegesis. Families among the Gitksan and Witsuwit'en, and their neighbours, feast one another and explain the process in a holistic fashion: feasting encapsulates "business," or the social relations that make up the shared experience of everyday life, although today these relations are generally expressed in secular terms.[8]

Certainly there has been some adoption in response both to the late-nineteenth-century population plunge and to changes emanating from European settlement in the area shortly thereafter. A major population shift occurred with the move of Guldo'o and Kisgagas people southwards to Kispiox and Gitanmaax, where they have, over the past century, integrated their respective Houses and clans from the northern villages into the interclan relations of these villages. In the feast, however, they continue to be recognized as descendants of their villages of origin.[9] This shift has complicated feast statuses somewhat, inspired some adoptions, and complicated the ranking of seating procedures.

With the decreased Guldo'o population, for example, the *wil'naat'ahl* of Wolf Clan Houses like Kyologet and Gwamoon are now one House, Wilps Kyologet (Daly 1986-87 [Mary McKenzie]). Similarly, Tenimget gave evidence of the near decimation of his House in the last century as a result of epidemics. He recounted how Simoogit Axti Hiix became the head chief because Tenimget and his brother chief, Wii'hloots, formerly House chiefs in their own right, had died without immediate matrilineal descendants. He explained how later, in the twentieth century, his paternal grandfather, Charles Smith, had had himself adopted into the Axti Hiix/Tenimget House to strengthen it at a time when it had few members and possibilities to carry forward its history and traditions. Charles Smith knew this history and these local traditions due to the long-term close ties between his House and that of Axti Hiix/Tenimget (Transcript, 4557-60).

But today many Houses have renewed their populations and are beginning to re-establish their own Houses.[10] The level of "in-adoption" in the process of amalgamation (fusion) of small House groups and the "out-adoption" and division of large Houses (fission) is today, in my opinion, not a major function of the social relations of Gitksan feasting.

Rather than primarily reallocating personnel between Houses, Gitksan (and Witsuwit'en) feasts function as paradigms for a cultural tradition that asserts ownership and management of historical emblems of legitimacy of place – land, fishing sites, crests, narratives, songs, and regalia (much as described in Drucker [1965, 55-6] or Barnett [1968]). Each such unit of joint heritage has a habitus that, through *wil'naat'ahl*, links it to that of several other such units. This, too, is manifested in feasts honouring the deceased, both recent and ancient. It is said that each such feast requickens human and spiritual relations with House territories and their ancestral (animal and human) life forms.

As well as animating ongoing community relations, the complex of exchanges within a feast (which are outlined below), constitute a semiotics of the society's ethos, symbols, and traditions by means of reciprocal giving and counter-giving. Sergei Kan (1989, 209), discussing nineteenth-century Tlingit feasts, points out the emotional comfort of food and gifts: "Food and gifts were perfect objects for expressing gratitude and affection since this was their role in daily life." Furthermore: "the exchange of potlatch food and gifts was a rich and complex system of communication, in which material objects carried metamessages about eschatology, power, and rank, as well as success in subsistence activities, trade, warfare, and key cultural values and structural principles. Using the artifacts circulating in the pot-latch system, the participants negotiated their social and power relations as well as expressed their feelings and attitudes towards each other."

Social relations registered by exchanges during feasts allow people to mesh with one another through the overlapping experiences of kinship and marriage, economic cooperation, credit and debt relations, political alliances, moral obligation, and formal social legitimacy. In a feast, the host House and its *wil'naat'ahl* "sort out their business" in relation to the other Houses and clans of the village (or the Houses and clans of several villages whose feastings overlap with one another). They make prestations that change the balance of power and esteem in local society, which will change yet again with the next major mortuary feast. In this way, their important decisions are witnessed and ratified by the whole community and the ever-changing equation of local credit and debt moves on.

In the feast hall, each matrilineal host group submits itself to the intense scrutiny of its peers. It minimizes its weaknesses and makes much of its strengths, yet its members' *primary* motivation does not lie in quantitative competition with other Houses. There is sufficient competition and sufficient satisfaction simply in being able to fulfill the House group's obligations whenever a member dies. This non-admission of competition, and its substitution by a sense of duty to ancestors and the community, can also be viewed in Bourdieu's terms of misrecognition of substantive interests, but it remains the cultural or "emic" basis upon which feasting rests. At each feast the House, its chief, wing chiefs, and elders are challenged to live up to the ancient name, to strive to fulfill their social obligations in a manner that is at least consistent with the prosperity and well-being exhibited by previous generations of House members. Living up to the name entails spending as lavishly as possible, yet without giving offence to other chiefs, all of whom are theoretically of the same rank.

In his famous discussion of Boas's account of competitive potlatching at Fort Rupert on Vancouver Island, among the Kwakwak'awakw (Kwakiutl), Mauss points out paradoxically that the supreme obligation to give is accompanied by the desire to break the chain of reciprocity to one's own advantage: "The ideal would be to give a potlatch that is not returned" (Mauss 1990 [1923-24], 122). But, except under unusually discordant circumstances, such wishes are not realized (or are realized only for short durations), especially since humans are not islands unto themselves, reproducing hermaphroditically. People are reproduced through social interactions with others, interactions often mediated through things that frequently stand for human relationships. Given this condition, a reasonable degree of "extra giving" is acceptable – even desirable – and beneficial to the hosts, but excessive extra giving can lead to the giver being ostracized rather than cherished and esteemed.

During a Gitksan or Witsuwit'en feast, the hosts are tense and vigilant. They cannot afford to be at ease because their actions are under the scrutiny of the greater community until all "their business" has been completed. Social errors committed by hosts in the course of a feast can blemish their collective image and lead to enmity between Houses, clans, or villages. Such errors may be assuaged with immediate reparations; that is, by rapidly presenting further gifts to wipe clean any blemishes caused to the reputation of other Houses. Alternatively, transgressors can hold a shame feast, a *glok*,[11] to wash away the memory and the hurt of their immoral acts.

A hosting House group can never feel at ease in the feast because the full weight of social expectation and responsibility rests firmly on its shoulders. The chiefly family at the core of the hosting House is also under the careful observation of its extended matrilineal kin: the *wil'naat'ahl* and even the whole *pdeek* (clan).[12] The combination of these internal and external social and political pressures provides the dynamic tension that gives force and vitality to the feasting process.

In the past, each household residential unit was coterminous with a core of "brothers" (uncles and nephews in a matriline) living together under one roof, with their wives and young children and those of their mothers and maternal aunts not currently married out. There are often people with whom individual members feel most relaxed and at ease living outside their House group in structural positions free of the tensions of joint socioeconomic responsibility and common inheritance. This often occurs between individuals of adjacent generations who are linked through fathers or spouses. They nurture one another at either end of the lifecycle. At the time of a feast, the sisters in the host House, if living in their husbands' places of residence, come home and take up the leading role in organizing the event and its preparatory planning.

The most common close matrilineal ties are between those individuals in structural positions of father and child. This close non-descent relationship is sometimes graphically explained by Gitksan as *ge'nax*, "to chew for someone who has no teeth." This term was used until recently for the life-long relationship between a young woman and the woman (often the sister of the girl's father) who helped her through her first menstruation "coming of

age." This entailed a full year of seclusion, when she was expected to prepare mentally and materially to organize her first feast. This term is also
used today for other close relationships, for those who are so close that they
are called *xshla'wasxw* – the foundation, or "the one who is as close to us as
our underwear." Such women helped the young to unlock their own gifts
and talents, and out of gratitude would be cared for in advanced old age by
their former acolytes. This relationship is highly significant for women learning their role as feast organizers.

Not to pay attention to the affairs of the House or to honour one's obligations to the feasting complex can lead to a lonely existence. To turn one's
back on the family heritage, against which older people caution the young,
and to ignore the old laws, is to embark on the road to ruin. Young people
are admonished to pay attention to their social responsibilities if they want
to live "to see their own grey hair."[13] If one does not honour one's feast
obligations, then one is considered to live like a slave, or like all who have
become immigrants to Canada, who are seen as strays, without pedigree,
"people of uncertain origin." Such people show up at feasts. They receive
gifts, but they never generate wealth. They live without honour, on the
kindnesses of others.

I asked one Gitksan chief, the late Pearl Trombley, G̱wamoon, the significance of the term *sitx'asxw,* which is used frequently during the speeches at
a feast. Another common term, meaning "to pay back," is *luu yeldin.* She
said: "Your name is mud if you don't *sitx'asxw,* if you don't settle your accounts. *Sitx'asxw* is paying back. If you don't *sitx'asxw* nobody looks at you
the second time round."

The Pole-Raising Feast: *Ba̱xmaga hed'msingan* or *Ba̱xmaga xwts'aan*[14]

Most of this chapter describes and analyzes a particular Gitksan feast. It is a
generic feast informed by the people's descriptions and from the writer's
participation in pole-raising events and subsequent questioning about the
observed proceedings. The feast outlined is that of the pole-raising, the culmination of a feast cycle carried out by a generation of chiefs and leaders of
a House. In its essential features the Gitksan pole-raising does not differ
from the comparable institution among the Witsuwit'en.

This description has been based upon exegesis provided by people who
are active in feast-giving today and who have given information about the
more elaborate feasts that occurred in the first half of this century. During
that period, feasts were prohibited under the Potlatch Law.[15] That was a
time when even the ethnologist of the National Museum of Canada, Marius
Barbeau (1929, 1950), declared that pole-raising on the upper Skeena was a
phenomenon of the past. I attempted to clarify which features of the
pole-raising are practised today and which, while they are not forgotten by
the feast specialists, are not.[16]

Raising a crest pole is a testament to the present prosperity of a House and its political fortunes in the community. In the past, as today, a whole generation of the primary host's *wil'naat'ahl* would throw all their resources into the pole-raising. Years of outstanding House business would be settled and witnessed by the greater community. The pole is the public face of the House and clan. It normally faces the main avenue of communication, whether this is the river or the highway (see Figures 13 and 14).

The pole stands for perhaps two or three generations, a monument not only to the predecessor being commemorated but also to the industriousness of the generation that raised the pole. The same ethic prevails. Today, as in the past, the raising of a pole and the associated feasting comprise the crowning event in the cycle of feasts a chief can be expected to host during his/her lifetime. Most chiefs never have the resources to complete this cycle, with the result that those who do generally command considerable respect. This feast incorporates into a complex settlement of accounts the main activities and transactions found in less elaborate feasts. It does so spiritually, materially, and socially on behalf of a whole generation of chiefs of the host group. Now, as in the past, a pole-raising is a sign of the good fortune and good health of the House, its *wil'naat'ahl*, and its clan. The fact that its hosts can mount such an event only with the assistance of their paternal kin *(wilksilaks/wilksibaksxw)* and affines *(ant'im'nak̲)*, and through massive sacrifice of their members' material well-being, attests to its rarity as well as to its compelling power.

The raising of a House crest pole is at once a memorial to a generation of House leaders and a periodic renewal of the dynamic relationship between the people and their land. Putting the elaborately carved pole into the ground renews the bond between the group and the land by focusing the will and desire, the labour and wealth, of a whole generation of House chiefs when they *adaawax̲* (verb intrans.), when they see their *adaawk̲'* (noun) "written" on their crest pole. This is what the chiefs mean when they say that the power of the generations, the *dax̲gat/daxget*, is suffused into the pole whenever it is raised. In the mind of the host chief, this power of the generations flows from the land, which is covered with the dust of the ancestors, and on into the living descendants. The living, by their meritorious actions, convey *daxget/dax̲gat* into the pole. The pole, once connected to the earth, allows this power to flow back into the territories, stronger for the reciprocal transactions it has experienced. The collective will and energy of the House is seen as the force that renews and concentrates this power, revitalizes the land's humanity, and enhances its productivity for yet another generation.[17]

The phenomenon of reincarnation is integral to this cyclical endeavour to renew the land and its owners down through the generations. Deceased holders of high names are said to reincarnate, their spirits usually returning to the babies of their own line of succession, to help out their descendants and maintain the House's human prosperity (Mills 1988a, 1988b; Mills and Slobodin 1994). According to Kan (1989), the feeding of guests in a nineteenth-century Tlingit potlatch simultaneously fed the ancestors with renewed social recognition.

The pole commemorates not only a former high chief of the House but also his or her counsellor chiefs, all the chiefly members of one generation (or possibly more if a pole has not been raised for many years). A crest pole is a commemoration of the recently deceased generation and usually survives for two or three generations if it is well cared for.

With the passage of time, the pole will lean and eventually topple. It will fall back to the earth and rot away, following the cycle of life, death, and rebirth. A new generation of House leaders will then, when they have judged the time to be ripe, take the decision to raise another pole and, with it, the names of their predecessors.[18]

Today, art museums and galleries, preoccupied with the recording and preserving of cultural artifacts, seek to collect, shelter, and conserve the splendour manifested in the old crest poles. Museums obtain grants to finance the carving of replica poles. The carving of poles and house posts has now become a branch of the international Aboriginal art market. (Poles are carved for art centres, the atria of skyscrapers, or to grace financial institutions. There is even a small generic pole, carved at the Kitanmax School of Art by Hlo'ox̲s of the House of Kyologet, installed at the top of the stairs leading into the Spadina Subway Station in Toronto.)

Art lovers may be appalled at the sight of a totem pole rotting relentlessly back into the floor of the rain forest (Reid 1971) or by the accounts that fallen House poles, as reported by Marius Barbeau (1950), were used, with the approval of the missionaries of the day, to keep the flood waters of the Nass River from people's potato patches.

The art-appreciating public, in lamenting "les temps perdus," forgets that its perceptions are informed by its own literate, written-down tradition of materially tangible artifacts. This public does not see past the rotting artifact to a culture alive and confident of its roots and its pedigree. That culture traditionally allowed its organic artifacts to rot down and rejoin the cycle of death and rebirth because its members are/were able to recombine the principles of design and the specific cultural components so as to give voice to the tradition yet again for the new generations. The Northwest Coast culture has retained the ability to combine images and narratives that express an ancient heritage, yet continues to render it immediate today.[19]

There is a fine crest pole of the Lax̲ X̲skiik (Eagle) Clan lying on the ground beside the totem poles at Gitwangax̲. It was entangled in tall grass and a profusion of wild flowers when I first viewed it in the summer of 1986, and it continues to lie in the same position. I knew it had been carved some years earlier, as a replica of an older pole, after museums had urged that its predecessor be removed and preserved from the ravages of the elements.[20]

Why, I asked myself, has this beautiful pole been lying on the ground for so long? As time passed during my fieldwork, I came to believe that I understood at least part of the answer to my question: in terms of Gitksan culture, the actual carving of this new pole seems to have occurred at the urgings of Polly Sargent, the Skeena Totem Pole Restoration Society, and the Royal British Columbia Museum rather than at the instigation of the Lax̲ X̲skiik owners in a series of preparatory pole-raising feast meetings. The preservation project was not an immediate part of the Eagle Clan's efforts to venerate a generation of chiefs and to settle long-standing House business.

According to Gitksan law, the pole cannot be erected unless the appropriate ceremonial activities and feasting are performed. This can be carried off only when the fortunes of the House and clan are strong and the capital necessary for the installation is available. If the family owning the pole were to raise the pole with government backing, or with only government backing, then their standing in the community would be damaged. Their only course of action is to grow strong enough (in members, skills, and resources) to raise the pole and the power of the ancestors through their own efforts.

Deciding to Hold a *Yukw*

The *li'ligidim pdeek̲* is the meeting of the clan (or at least to the scope of the *wil'naat'ahl* members). This *li'ligit* (feast) is an internal gathering to decide the most auspicious time to hold a *yukw*, at which a chief and his/her counsellors will honour their recent predecessors with a new carved pole. (*Yukw* is a general term for the most important feasts, where serious political, economic, social, and spiritual business is conducted. *Li'ligit* is the term for those feasts that are not of the same degree of seriousness as is a *yukw*. In the Witsuwit'en language the term is *dinï ne'aas*, "people coming together" (Mills 1994, 43).

Usually the decision to raise a pole is taken only after some time has passed following the funeral feasts of a generation of chiefs, their siblings, and cousins. This is because "their spirits all go ahead together." The *li'ligidim pdeek̲* may convene several times, as the raising of a pole is a major decision involving an enormous outlay of time and effort, a full-scale mobilization of the widest network of support and credit-seeking. The father's side (*wilksilaks/wilksibaksxw*) of the deceased high chief is consulted as this planning develops because it, too, will have major responsibilities in relation to the preparations. The *wilksilaks/wilksibaksxw* of the present chief will also be consulted.

From Cedar Tree to Crest Pole

The House now delegates a scouting party to locate the best possible tree or trees. In the past, each village had stands of red cedar relatively close to the settlement or at least where gravity and/or the river current could be used to transport the log(s). Such groves, in proximity to villages, were on House territories but were treated as resources open to any chief of the village who required two or three trees for carving poles. Today, as a result of the rapid tempo of large-scale non-selective logging, there are no cedar stands near the villages. Logs are now obtained from the Terrace region to the west (Earl Muldon [Delgamuukw] and Walter Harris [Ge'el], carvers, personal communication). Kyologet, Mary McKenzie, explained to me that the cedar trees from the Terrace area grow much more quickly than do those in the less temperate north around her village of origin, Guldo'o. Consequently, Guldo'o area cedars were much more close-grained and durable as crest poles.

The scouting party, composed of people from the chief's *wilksilaks*, together with the present *simoogit*'s designated successor nephew/niece (who, of course, is a member of the pole-raising House), would formerly select the cedars, which were felled and either skidded over poles or moved by river to the edge of the village. They would be left in the river near the village to soak and expand: *gyooksinhl gan* (the soaking of the log). The soaking would be done if the carving were not intended to begin immediately. In her evidence, Gwaans, Olive Ryan, explained that, in the past, there was a ceremony called *Ts'aa gantxw* to mark the cutting down of the tree and another ceremony, *X̱maas*, to mark the removal of the bark (Transcript, 1073).

Today, the same categories of kin (from the father's *wil'naat'ahl* or clan) go out to obtain the poles or to select or buy them and to arrange for transport if they are purchased from a distant area. The carver *(gahla)* was usually selected from among the matrilineal relatives of the chief's father (from the *simoogit*'s father's *wil'naat'ahl*). If there is no skilled carver available in this group, then the chief's *wilksileks/wilksilaks* may contract the services of an outside carver. The same situation prevails today when there are a limited number of professional carvers carving for the whole community. Walter Harris, Ge'el, ceremonial head of the Kispiox feast system and a *simoogit* of the Gisx̱'aast Fireweed/Killer Whale Clan, informed me that, when his House was ready to put up a new pole, he (being a professional carver), designed it, and his *wilksilaks* did the actual carving. Earl Muldon, however, being of the Lax̱ Se'el House of Delgamuukw, was in the right relationship to carve the pole of his father's House, the Gisx̱'aast House of Gitludahl, and of the correct "father side" clan/*pdeek̠* to carve the new Gisx̱'aast pole for Wilps Ha'naamuxw (see Figures 15-18).[21]

The fees for the carving, as for the many other services rendered in the process, will be acknowledged in the feast and recompensed by the House (the *wilp*) and those closely related to it. The crests are replicated every time a replacement pole (a new generation's pole) is carved. A House crest of the chief's father's side can be placed at the bottom of the pole (among the eastern villages this sometimes occurs, and among the western villages it generally occurs). A further crest may be borrowed from another House or *wil'naat'ahl*.[22]

If a crest has been borrowed from another House, then the next pole-raising generation of House leaders is required to return the borrowed crest to the House to which it belongs. If the succeeding generation, instead of returning such a borrowed crest, uses it again on a new pole without properly seeking permission, the chiefs run the risk of having this crest chopped away from their pole by members of the House to which the crest belongs.[23] If this occurs, then the pole-raising group has no redress because it did not properly seek permission to renew the use of this crest. Each family's crests are insignia reflecting their narratives of origin on the land.

In the past the carving process involved not only the master carver but also his assistants, all of whom had to be paid and given board and lodging during the time they were working on the pole. The carving may extend for months at a time, over a period of one or two years. The carving crew, in the past, was fed by different villagers at different times. The carvers' tools were maintained by men in the local community. At present, carvers have become skilled craftspeople and artist entrepreneurs in the role-specific Canadian society. Some are paid according to the rates of income enjoyed by established international artists. Their services have to be contracted, even by members of their own communities, at something like the going rate. Today, a portion of the cost of carving is borne, in some cases, with the assistance of government grants.

This has proven a contentious issue. Some people feel it is yet another Canadian intervention in the First Nations ways of doing things. Whereas in the past the carver worked for his father's side, shared whatever they had, and was acknowledged with gifts and a portion of the contributions at the subsequent feast, today his work has become much more costly to the pole-raising group. Consequently, some families now opt for the assistance of a grant to defray some of the expense. Yet, when they do so, others say that they are cutting corners and only pretending to possess the power necessary to raise a crest pole. A pole-raising is meant to crown a lifetime of important feasting, standing for the internal prosperity, hard work, and self-reliance of the House group. Ganeda *simoogit* from Gitanyow, G̲amlax̲-yeltxw, the late Solomon Marsden, spoke to this effect at the Gux̲sen pole-raising feast in Gitsegukla in 1986.

The *wilksilaks* of the pole-raisers also arranged the digging of the hole, with its angled approach, into which the pole would be slid as it was laboriously, and with infinite good humour, hauled upright by means of ropes and crossbar supports. Today the carving team constructs a concrete footing and iron support brackets. Poles are still raised with crossbar supports, ropes, and the muscle power of not only the *wilksilaks/wilksibaksxw* but also of the whole assembly. The carver used to be paid in standard feast gifts: tanned hides referred to as *hliyun* (see Figure 24) and fur robes known as *gwiislip'ast* (*gwiis:* groundhog, *lip'ast:* sewn). Today various items of merchandise as well as cash make up the *hliyun* and *gwiislip'ast.*

Formerly, these services were accounted for and remembered in people's minds. They would be repaid in the feast. Today the pole-raising feast accounting is done on the basis of detailed records kept of time expended and materials used. Feast transactions are recorded with state of the art technology, including computers and video cameras – a fact that shows the vitality of the institution and the enjoyment of new technological means to serve existing traditions and social relations. The feast is not an old, fragile family heirloom, and the Gitksan and Witsuwit'en are not nostalgic, ultra-conservative people. They do, however, maintain dynamic relations with their ancestors who, through dreams and meditation, often reveal certain intimations regarding how to act successfully both today and in the future.

The necessary goods and services for sustaining and financing the carving and associated preparations take the form of two types of gifts, or loans, that are metonymic of preparing the corpse. The first, the *suxw'daa/sixw'daa,* or "mattress," is raised and offered automatically by the chief's *wilksileks.* (These loans come to the House automatically, in the form of gifts from the persons in the appropriate kinship relationships. They are acknowledged in the feast and returned from the pocket/treasure box of the chief and not from the sum of goods and cash contributed publicly in the feast.) The second, the *sugwilat/sigwilat,* or "blanket," is raised by the spouses of House members. Again, this is an unsolicited gift/loan to the host: it is from the host's spouse's House group. (In Chapter 7 we will see that the word *sigwilamsxw* is used by Tenimget to describe the process of putting the blanket around a new spouse's shoulders and announcing to the guests where she or he could fish, hunt, and gather on the host family's House territories. The sugwilat is a payment by the spouse group "in gratitude" for these privileges; the host must repay this "gratitude" in the course of his/her feast.)[24] Similar loans are made for a funeral feast by the same categories of kin and affines.

A year before the actual pole-raising, which is generally planned for the autumn or winter months, the preparations intensify. The women begin the long and complicated process of obtaining and preparing special foods. In the past these included sweet hemlock sap cakes (to which Don Ryan, Masgaak, refers in the Afterword), dried wild rhubarb, salmon roe, salmon strips and soups, berry cakes, and coast foods such as oolichan grease (to mix with berries and to combine with dry-smoked salmon), oolichan, dulce seaweed, herring roe, halibut, clams, and winkles. Some of these foods are still prepared or purchased from the coast. When the actual preparation takes place just before the feast, each item must be a culinary perfection in order to satisfy the honour of the hosts and the enjoyment of the guests, who will be comparing the quality with that of their own feast standards.

Ant'im'nak' people (spouses of members of the host group) are expected to assist in these preparations. In the past, the work the spouses invested in the preparations reflected well on their own respective Houses and was, in a sense, repayment for the right to use fishing sites and territory belonging to the host *wilp*. The women who had married into the *wilp* plaited large cedar-bark mats over which the pole of their husbands would be slid as it entered the village and was moved to the site.[25] (The *gan*, or pole, is not allowed to touch the ground until it is actually on site and has been invested with the *daxget* of the *wilp*.) The male spouses would traditionally make the cedar-bark and nettle-fibre ropes. They would soak the rope in special solutions to increase their elasticity and strength; their reliability would be tested before the actual pole-raising. These men also constructed the cross-braces *(ha'mingahla,* or *xgajaak)*, made from two long sturdy poles lashed one to the other near the top (with rope) and used to support the heavy pole as it is gradually pulled erect (see Figures 16, 17, and 22). Today the *ant'im'nak* are very much involved in the preparations, in mobilizing funds, in preparing food, and in assisting with the pole-raising itself.

The *K'otsgan*

Both in the past and at present the pole becomes a crest pole, or *xwts'aan –* often called simply *gedimgan* (man/figure *[gedim]* on a pole *[gan]*) once it is carved. (The pole in the sketch [Figure 22] was photographed about twenty-five years later [Figure 23] and still stands today in the village of Hazelton.) When the new pole has been roughed out it is customary to formally transfer the life force, the living power and authority (the *daxgat/daxget* – which is an integral part of the ancient history of the crests of the House and is replicated on the old pole, the regalia, and in the songs) into the new, green pole. Ha'naamuxw (Transcript, 5026) explained the continuity involved in this transfer of heritage from pole to pole and generation to generation:

> Certainly it's a way of maintaining the heritage from – from our grandfathers, and in making sure that the pole is put up again. We have taken it down to restore it, and also to put a new one, with an added crest [the crest of her Ganeda[26] Clan father] to indicate that it's my pole as opposed to the previous owner. It's a way of reaffirming and confirming the daxget of Ha'naamuxw. It's a way of establishing that the property of Ha'naamuxw has not been abandoned, nor will it be in the future. It's a way of telling the

other chiefs that the House is as strong as it was before, and that it will continue to exist, because we do have a fair number of people in our House who will continue with the activities within the House of Ha'naamuxw – who will ensure that it will continue in the future. It's also a way of releasing the spirits of those who have passed on ... of giving thanks for having had them in ... in your House. It's a way of giving recognition to the contributions that they have made to your House. It's a way of acknowledging to our Creator too, the privilege of having had them share their lives with you. It's a way of saying that we have completed the business of caring for them. It's a way of saying that they have added a dimension to our lives. And when I say our lives, I'm taking about the members of my House, and to you as an individual. And it's a way of saying that we respect them, and we are saying that they are important to us. That's it. (See Figures 15 and 20.)

Ha'naamuxw's words are applicable not only to the *k'otsgan,* or pole-cutting ceremony, but also to the whole process of raising a new pole to revitalize the House and venerate those who have gone before.

The *k'otsgan* ceremony of Wilps Ha'naamuxw, held in April 1987, was recorded on a video film and was shown to the court on 11 June 1987 in Smithers (Transcript, 1142). I witnessed both the *k'otsgan* and the court viewing of the video. The *k'otsgan* is a service provided by the *wilksilaks,* the father's side (in this case, the *wilksiwitxw* [sing.] was Simoogit Lelt of the Ganeda [Frog/Raven] Clan). This chief puts the power into the new pole and recalls, in word and song, the power and authority of the House and *wil'naat'ahl* through history. He is paid for his assistance by the pole-raising House, and all those who have attended and witnessed this event are similarly paid and hosted to a small feast at the conclusion of the ceremony.

Tets

When the carving is complete and the feast food preparations are ready, the host *simoogit* sends out the *tets,* the inviting party, to give his invitations to the chiefs of each House. Some aspects of the *tets* practice are not always observed today, although it is my impression that the invitation process for a major feast, a *yukw,* is growing more elaborate than it has been in the recent past. The Burns Lake Carrier people and the Witsuwit'en send a *tets* delegation to one another in which the spokesman spreads eagle down to bless those who are being invited. More chiefs are going back to the use of *tets* delegations with regalia, and even eagle down, which compels those invited to attend. For some people the *tets* usually consists of a printed invitation; for others, an invitation or a telephone call is unthinkably *k'amksiwaa* (i.e., the white way of doing things).

The *tets* party embarks upon its work following a short ceremony called the *halaydim tets,* wherein the messenger party will be protected and strengthened by the chief and his spirit power and House authority for their journey to the other villages. Usually the chief does not go with the *tets.*

At all times the *simoogit* is expected to show public reticence and modesty. On those occasions when he is not able to delegate another House member to speak for him, he must be coaxed to speak himself. The words of a chief carry considerable significance so long as they are used sparingly and appropriately. Chiefs will speak on important occasions: during the settlement of disputes; to welcome new brides and grooms to the House and to blanket them and award them fishing sites and land to use; to acknowledge the proper succession of chiefs in other Houses; to address their own feasts with their *limx'oo'y* (song of mourning for the ancestors), their *adaawk̲'*(s) and the names that define their territory; and in matters pertaining to foreign chiefs.

The representative of the chief in the *tets* is generally his/her nephew. The speaker is the chief's *galdim'algax̲,* "the container of the word" *(galdim':* container; *algax̲:* word or speech). The *galdim'algax̲* may be accompanied by one or more senior advisors, usually his/her mother, the chief's sister or the chief's brother, and several other *wilp* members. Today, the *tets* can be as brief as an apologetic telephone call or as elaborate as a robed *tets* party sent out with the chief's blessing, a drum, a rattle, songs, eagle down, and *amhalayt* headdress (a forehead mask representing the wearer's spiritual power, framed by tail feathers of the woodpecker, a crown of sea lion whiskers enclosing eagle down, and a train of ermine tails down the back of the body [see Figure 20]).

The *tets* party proceeds to the neighbouring villages. Here it follows a strict order of procedure, adhering to a ranking protocol that demands that the senior *simoogit* for each clan in the village be invited first, then their respective counsellor chiefs, then the other *simgiget* of that clan (together with their respective counsellors), and finally the heirs, or *hlguwilksihlxw* (the *guslisim get* [nephews]and *guslisim hanak̲'* [nieces]), of the high chiefs; that is, those from among whom a successor will one day be chosen. In Gitanmaax today the *tets* go first to Gyedimgaldo'o of the La̲x Se'el and Spookw of the La̲x Gibuu. In Kispiox it is G̲e'el of the Gisk̲'aast, Delgamuukw of the La̲x Se'el, and X̲hliiyimlax̲ha of the La̲x Gibuu. In Gitwangax̲ the order is Lelt and Wii Hlengwax of the Ganeda/La̲x Se'el, Tenimget/Axti Hiix of the La̲x Gibuu, and Sakxwm Higook̲x of the La̲x X̲skiik (Eagle Clan). The chief to whom the *tets* go first in each village is determined by which clan in that particular feast will have the task of providing the principal witness and acknowledger – called *'nidinsxwit* – to all that is publicly conducted by the hosts in the feast. (This moiety focus of binary feast divisions is more easily detected in the western villages with two founding clans, where each chief has a "village opposite" that witnesses his *'nidilx.*) In the past the *galdim'algax* struck his carved talking stick on the floor before the high chief. Someone in the *tets* would shake a rattle and begin to sing the ancient *limx'oo'y* that referred to events that occurred in the early history of the House and *wil'naat'ahl*. The singing venerates and mourns the passing generations and one's own previous incarnations. In singing for the departed generations of ancestors of the *wilp*, the chief expresses his combined joy and sorrow. (The really fine things in life, people say, are worthy of tears.) The singing is a component part of some *tets* today as well.

The *galdim'algax* explains to the chief the significance of the forthcoming *baxmaga/hed'msingan* and the importance of having this chief attend, witness, and lend his or her wisdom to the matters of business to be transacted. The chief may answer right away or may prefer to consult with her/his counsellors before deciding. In the past, the chief would signal acceptance by wafting eagle down *(mixk'aax)* on the *tets* party and would give the *galdim'algax* an acceptance gift to convey to the chief who would be hosting the *yukw*. This gift is also called a *mixk'aax*. Formerly, this was preserved food that the *tets* would take home for the host chief. Today it is cash. (The *mixk'aax*k is returned by the hosts during the feast.)

After this visit the *tets* go on to the next chief, where again the *galdim'algax* stresses the importance of the *simgiget* attending and assisting the procedure by witnessing the transactions and ensuring that what is decided is correctly done. These invitations took weeks in earlier times. Invited chiefs usually indicated their acceptance of the invitation by asking the *tets* to attend a small feast. There may well have been one such feast given by each clan in each village. Today the *tets* does its task at a much more rapid tempo and often in an abbreviated form. Sometimes a decision will be taken to do it with greater elaboration.

At this small feast formerly held for the visiting *tets* party, the *tets* would be greeted by the *naxnox* power of their host chief. (Figure 21 shows Simoogit Guxsen, "The Gambler," revealing the shamanic, or *halayt*, knowledge belonging to his *wilp*.) This is a form of shamanic strength obtained through meditative training and is specific to the name of each House chief. It is a power from a being that, nonetheless, belongs to the House. (Among the Witsuwit'en it is more individuated, more personal and esoteric, yet its presence, like the Gitksan *naxnox*, must be hinted at in the ceremony to authenticate the identity of the chief.) This *tets* procedure is described in some detail by William Beynon in relation to the pole-raising feasts that were held in Gitsegukla in 1945 (Barbeau and Beynon 1915-57, B-F-425-28; Anderson and Halpin 2000).

The *tets* members would counter this power with some of the *naxnox* force that had been imparted to them by their own chief before they had left home. The *tets'* host would now dance, wafting *mixk'aax* from the crown of vertical sea lion whiskers topping his *amhalayt* headdress. The *mixk'aax* would hang suspended, on minute air currents, over the heads of the *tets*, signalling the ultimate law of peace and goodwill between Houses and between different peoples. In turn, each high chief hosted the *tets* to a small feast and gave special foodstuffs from their territories, which the *tets* members placed in their boxes to carry back for their people to sample in the home village.

Today, during the visit of the *tets*, both the host and the visitors retain the dignity and formality established in the past. It is not correct for the host to invite the *tets* to sit down and relax: the members of the *tets* make the invitation while standing and generally avoid eye contact. They sing and express their wishes, and the chief who is being visited responds by means of a *mixk'aax* gift, which will later be returned with interest.

After visiting each village, and inviting the chiefs in the proper order of precedence, the *tets* returns home and continues its visits there. Here it follows the same protocol, visiting the senior chief of each clan. Today this is accomplished rapidly with the assistance of motor vehicles. In the past, the *tets* would often be away for weeks or months. When it returned home, the *tets* went to its chief and local *wil'naat'ahl* to share out the food and gifts received. It would explain the diplomatic nuances of the different receptions it experienced in each village so as to prepare the chiefs of the House and clan for any possible problems or disagreements that may be expected at the feast.

The final days are devoted to ensuring that the mechanics of pole-raising are complete, that the food is prepared, that the songs and dances are practised, and that the protocol for receiving the guests is reviewed. (Figure 19 shows the preparation of food gifts for a Witsuwit'en feast at Hagwilget in 1923.) The *wilp* members' *ant'im'nak* (spouses of the host group) would be busy at this time preparing skits, comic dances, and satirical songs to perform during the feast. These preparations still carry on, though the general tempo is faster and the elaboration of detail is less extensive.

Bagunsxw

The invited guests arrive on the appointed day (the day before the actual raising of the pole) to welcome the new crest pole, the *xwts'aan* – now carved and ready – into the village. The chief's *wilksilaks* bring gifts of foodstuffs and money, and place these on the pole, which at this time lies horizontally on cross logs. This father's side contribution is called the *aye'e*, the grandfather gift. The *aye'e* is the equivalent of the *k'otsgesxw* (literally, "cut" or "knifed hair," or "the haircut payment"), which occurs in any burial feast. (Formerly the hair of the bereaved was cut off by the *wilksiwitxw* of the mourning chief.) Today the *k'otsgesxw* is a payment made in funeral feasts for burial services rendered. In feasts other than for funerals the k'otsgesxw is replaced by the *aye'e*. The *aye'e* too will be recompensed in the feast.

In the past, guests were welcomed into the host village the day before the pole-raising for the *bagunsxw*, or reception feast, which received the guests who arrived from other villages and honoured the arrival of the *xwts'aan/hed'msingan*, the carved pole. All chiefs of one clan from one village arrived together. They would be hosted by the pole-raising host's own local clan members. For example, arriving Wolf chiefs and Fireweed/Killer Whale chiefs would be greeted by the Frog/Raven Clan if a Frog/Raven House were raising the pole. The Frogs in this case would have prepared some food for their guests, and they would dance it to the guests, holding it high in the air and usually announcing the territory from which it had come.

Let us assume that we are back in a *bagunsxw* a century ago. In this instance the Frogs prepared salmon or game. This would be displayed on strings or on the points of spears. Next the Wolf guests (and often the Eagle guests would join them) would sing and distribute their food gifts to the other visiting chiefs, the Fireweed/Killer Whales. If this food were not large pieces of fish or game but, rather, berries or sap cakes or coast foods, then it would be displayed in elaborately carved and painted bentwood boxes. The Fireweed, in their turn, would sing and present all the food – their own and that of the Wolves and Eagles, together with that donated by the hosting Frog clan, to the pole-raising host chief. Most of this food would later be used for specific gifts and payments during the main feast the following day. This process is repeated with the chiefs of each village, and the whole assembly carefully notes what has been donated, from where, and by whom. In the past, the *bagunsxw* of a particularly large feast might require two or three days to complete before the proceedings could move on to the actual pole-raising.

All the guests would witness and remember from which territory each item originated. They would also witness the social interclan and inter-village transactions relating to these items of food. These items gained more and more semiotic weight, more connotations, as the feasting events unfolded. (This is something that cannot be visualized the same way in today's feast transactions, where most of the items exchanged take the form of money.) Later, in the main feast, the guests saw these items become involved in further social transactions and payments. Thus, particular goods denoting the land and family of each participating chief were visible items that wove back and forth across the feast hall through succeeding social relations, like the cross weft of a Chilkat blanket (such as that worn by Ha'naamuxw, Figure 20).

The same reciprocal transactions are conducted today, but the highly fluid medium of exchange does not display the social relations as graphically as did these *bagunsxw* procedures. The metaphor of the interweaving of relations through marriage and kinship, through the mother, the father, the mother's father, the father's father, and so on, remains a vital and eloquent part of present-day Gitksan and Witsuwit'en culture, as was evidenced by Tenimget when he explained that his social relations were many and that they were woven into a fabric (Transcript, 4777-8):

> Like I indicated and tried to show here that we have interests, quite high interest in our own territories – Xsi gwin ixstaat and Tsihl gwelli but our interest reaches far out to other territories through *wilksiwitxw* [*wilksileks* pl.], both your mother and your father's side, and like relatives from other villages. This is what we call the helping of each other, a phrase that we have in our language – *nahlimoot* – is to help each other. And what is so unique about that is – we have a phrase that my grandparents ... said that – the phrase about our Gitksan and Witsuwit'en relations, interconnections of marriage, we are like a *sgano,* a woven fabric, solid. That is the way we look at ourselves, as a woven fabric, together.

Baxmaga: Raising the Xwts'aan (Figures 16, 17, 22)

In the past, as well as today, the morning after the *bagunsxw* ceremonies the carved pole is met at the edge of the village by the whole community and welcomed. The pole may be decorated with cedar-bark garlands and woven mats or with streamers and balloons. In Kispiox, poles were carved down on the flat beside the Kispiox River (today's soccer field), above its confluence with the Skeena, and carried and slid into the village from there. The late Mary Johnson recalled Kispiox poles in her childhood being slid over the ice and snow on woven mats, and the feasting sometimes happened outdoors around a fire. Today the pole is trucked in from the artist's carving shed.

The pole and the guests are greeted with food. Sometimes the host *wilp*'s *naxnox* spirit powers are revealed at this point, to the accompaniment of a special song. This is the *nii laxlaginsw,* the invocation of the powerful spirit of the host chief. On other occasions the *nii laxlaginsw* occurs in the main feast. At winter pole-raisings the snow in front of the *xwts'aan* is strewn with spruce and cedar boughs. Then, as the pole approaches the site, its path is strewn with the cedar-bark mats prepared for this reception. The *xwts'aan* is treated with the respect that one would afford to the bones of the departed. In the past the pole was not allowed to drag on the earth: it had to be lifted or slid on mats.

Today, mechanized equipment is used to move the pole and suspend it such that it does not touch the ground before reaching its designated spot. In the past, the assembled guests and the villagers danced their respective

welcomes to the souls of the dead chief and counsellor chiefs of the generation being venerated, while the *xwts'aan* passed them on its entry to the
village.

The passage of the pole is considered to be the passage of the remains of a
generation of chiefly souls. In a manner similar to a funeral procedure, young
people escorting the *xwts'aan* would urge the souls to go gently, just as they
urge the soul of the departed in its *xbiist* (cedar coffin box, as in Figure 8) to
go to its burial (during the nineteenth century) or cremation (pre–nineteenth
century) in a state of grace and harmony. "Welcome," they say, "and take
care. Here is your pathway."[27]

Until the last few decades, boxes of berries – often the whole season's crop
– together with boxes of oolichan grease and other highly prized foodstuffs,
would be fed into the *xwts'aan's* base to ease its passage. Today the blood
red of the berries and the richness of the grease are substituted with pails of
red fruit juice. In this way the spirits of the dead are ritually fed and welcomed to the *mindax gan*, "the place where the pole goes up." Children may
be placed on the pole as it is moved to the *mindax gan*, signifying the continuity of the House through the generations. Placing children on the *xwts'aan*
is called *ha nun nit'aa*, which I observed during the 1991 Ha'naamuxw
baxmaga.

Both in the past and today a number of technical services, all of which
are rewarded in the course of the feast, are performed during the actual
baxmaga (sloping, raising): the decorator ensures the *xwts'aan* is in the most
festive condition possible when it is being moved into the village. A pole
handler, the *t'alganit,* directs the raising. (These days the *t'alganit* is often
the carver.) There are diggers, captains for each rope, and handlers of the
cross-braces. These services, like every single ceremonial service performed,
will be remembered and recompensed in the feast later in the day.

If the pole seems to be inordinately heavy as it is being hoisted aloft, it is
said to be a sign of reluctance on the part of the spirits to leave the living,
and the mourners must urge and coax the spirits to go softly. The *xwts'aan*
envelops the souls of a whole generation or more of leaders and chiefs of
the *wilp*. Their collective will, their force and energy and strength of personality, is fed with the food wealth, the berries and grease, which the House,
by its size and influence, has been able to mobilize. The living generation of
House leaders is expending the accumulated production of the House so as
to renew its legitimacy and authority by clearing its accumulated debts.

When the pole has been raised halfway, to the shouts of the guests to the
spirits of the deceased – "Take care, chiefs! Take care!" (Hawlii'in, simgiget!
Hawlii'in!) – all the guest chiefs are expected to take their places on the
ropes and assist in the final installation (Figure 16). One chief explained to
me that she had once been urged to take her place on the rope at a
pole-raising, at least symbolically, when she was eight months pregnant.

The host chief, or her/his delegate, sings the *wilp limx'oo'y* and mourns all the many generations who have gone before, who have returned again, and now are leaving once more. The *simoogit* and her/his nephews and nieces stand beside the erect *xwts'aan,* behind the chief's crest blanket, which is held like an unfurled banner facing the guests, and with them stand the chief's *wilksilaks/wilksibaksxw.* As the pole goes up, so do the names of all the high chiefs and counsellor chiefs who have died since the last *xwts'aan* was raised. The *wilp* members stand together and bear witness to their deceased: "Dim ambaxye'es" (We raise up), the chief announces; then he calls out the name of one of the deceased. This is repeated for each of the commemorated deceased *simgigat* and elders.

The time of the feast is now announced. The nephew who acted as *galdim'algax* goes up to each guest chief with his talking stick to *nebax* (run into) him/her, to remind each guest to attend the feast, and to reiterate that her/his presence is particularly important for the success of the feast. The ropes are pulled down from the pole and cut into useable lengths. Each guest *simoogit* is presented with two lengths of the rope. The rope cutter, too, will be rewarded for this service.

Yukw

The feast usually begins a few hours after the actual pole-raising, in the local community centre or hall. In the intervening period the guests are urged to wait and are fed with snacks and warm drinks either at the hall or in private homes. Lesser feastings are called *li'ligit.*

Wanimsxw: Welcome

If they have not been so greeted at the pole, the guests are introduced to the host's *naxnox* as they arrive at the feast hall. In response, each *simoogit* directs his or her own *naxnox* power at the hosting chief. This exchange of psychic power is called the *'niilaxlaganst.* Sometimes today this exchange occurs at the entrance to the hall, and sometimes the host takes his *naxnox* around to the tables where the *simgiget* have been seated. In the past this was a lengthy performance with masked dancers, semi-psychic competition, and joking. Many of these performances today are very humorous and are even executed on occasion with sexual overtones; sometimes they are conducted by a host group in costume. In the past they were very dramatic and awesome, as Tenimget graphically demonstrated when he told of the *naxnox* performance in which his grandfather's head was hacked from his body with a kitchen knife and then replaced and healed (Transcript, 4611-14). Herb George (Sats'aan, of the Witsuwit'en Gilserhyu Clan) says he will never forget the terror he experienced in a feast as a child at the moment a *naxnox* bear walked up on its hind legs, snarled, and "mauled" his father. (Some of the feast items, such as masks, carved feast dishes, goat horn spoons, box drums, and crest-carved "talking sticks" are recorded in National Museums of Canada [1972]).

The seating is organized by the *wanimswit/wenimswit* (welcoming party), who announce the guest, *tsi lim extxw,* and conduct each to the appropriate seat, tapping the floor by the seat with a cane. This must be done with extreme care so as not to insult any chief and thereby embarrass the host's *wilp.* One's *ant'aa* is one's seat in the feast hall and one's position in the whole social structure. One inherits *ant'aa* "like an *ayuks* [crest]."

In the past, if a chief happened to arrive late at a feast due to unforeseen circumstances, then s/he would not enter if the food had already been served, because the seating would have been completed, with each guest being located as accurately as possible in the correct configuration. A latecomer would only disturb the proceedings by forcing the rearrangement of the seating. Late arrivals are tolerated today but only over protest from elders and to the utter consternation of those charged with seating the guests.

Even though the order of seating is worked out with the greatest possible care, it is a matter of great difficulty as there are always conflicting opinions about the exact seating order of some chiefs. For example, a relatively young person may have been chosen to hold the name of the high chief, but in order to carry out his responsibilities properly, his senior advisors, even if they do not have the appropriate high names, must be seated beside him so that they are available for close consultation. Also, the move of northern Houses to Kispiox and Gitanmaax, together with the decimation of the populations of many Houses, disrupted the warp and weft of what is said to have been a stable ranking system.

While all high chiefs formally hold the same rank, their counsellor chiefs' ranking is based partly on the names they hold and partly on their ability. The person seating the guests must know all the chiefly names in each House as well as who is occupying them at any one time. The seater must know who the senior advisors are for each House and which Houses combine the names of more than one original House while remaining consistent with their common *wil'naat'ahl* heritages. The hosts must also recall who is absent and acknowledge these absentees in the appropriate parts of the proceedings.

Four welcomers and escorts are expected to stand at the door and greet the arrival of each chief and his party. One or two members of the welcoming party are *ts'imwil atitxwit* (those who call people in), who call out the names of each chief entering the feast hall. Each chief is greeted by the host and the host's *naxnox* before being announced again and led to his seat. The members of the welcoming delegation who are the seaters are called *ant'aadit.* They welcome the chief, call out his or her name, and urge her/ him to take care of her- or himself. They are expected to chant "Hawlii'in, simoogit! Hawlii'in, simoogit!" as they escort the chief to the correct seat.

One of the *ant'aadit* strikes the talking stick beside the chair to which the chief has been escorted, while the other helps him/her get settled. Thus a chief is installed. Her nephews and nieces bring the chief's dishes and extra containers for taking away food and gifts. This chief's attendants are then seated as well.

Food *Hawaal*

The feast is opened when one of the *ts'imwil atitxwit* (announcers) calls upon one of the chiefs to bless the gathering. The same chief will be called again to close the feast. Formerly, a song was sung and the special gift foods brought by each chief were displayed on strings and spears in the hall. The song explained for whom these food gifts were intended and from whence they came. Today, while the guests are being served by young members of the host clan, the food donors are announced, along with what they have contributed.

Foods from the land add an important lustre to the feast today but are not considered essential. In some Gitksan feasts there is moose meat and beaver; in most Witsuwit'en feasts barbecued beaver is served and sometimes moose meat as well. When this food is "called up," the customary order is followed: first, the food of members of the hosting House is announced, then the food of chiefs from the same clan as the host, then the *wilksilaks* food, and finally that of the *ant'im'nak̲'*, or *ant'imhanak̲'*.

Well into the 1930s, a high chief who was a spouse to the hosting House would fulfill *ant'im'nak̲'/ant'imhanak̲'* obligations by preparing a game animal or by slaughtering a steer. When the announcer, the *ts'imwil atitxwit*, called up this food, members of the *ant'im'nak̲'* stood up and sang, displaying the hooves and tail of the animal, either holding them high on spears or wearing them as a crown. Today, as the formal announcements of all food donations are made, their monetary value is noted down in the feast account book and added to the appropriate contribution figures.

Li'ligit: Dinner

Today the main dish of beef or game is served as a thick soup, together with deep-fried bannock, buns, muffins, crackers, oranges, bottled berries, tea, coffee, and juice. Sometimes this is accompanied by game, salmon, and salads. As the guests are eating, the hosts distribute the *so'o*, the food to take home and share with those who did not attend. (The usual *so'o* items today are fresh fruits, loaves of bread, buns, sacks of sugar, boxes of crackers, and dried soups.) The order of giving is from the head of a clan table to the foot, from the leading chief of the table to the chief on his/her right then on his left, then to the next on his right, and so on, alternating left and right. The servers, who are from the same clan as the hosts, must follow the etiquette of precedence of high names over ordinary names, elders over younger people. And they must exercise great care in serving carefully, politely, and with dignity so as not to embarrass the hosts or cause inadvertent insults. They must exercise great care in serving the *simgigat,* spilling nothing, jostling no one, never reaching across the table to fill a glass or cup, never emptying "the dregs" of a soup pot or coffee jug into the dish or cup of a chief but always serving from an adequately full vessel. Similarly, the chief must never eat his/her soup to the bottom of the dish as this signals to the host that the recipient is not being properly fed and hosted.

The hosts call one of their children to come forward in full regalia to sing a special House song, the *xsinaahlxw,* or "breath song," which laments the passing of a generation of great chiefs who, by the way they lived their lives, have honoured the ancient names and crests of the House. The host *simoogit,* or his/her delegated representative, speaks about the pole that has just been raised, acknowledging the carver and the *wilksilaks* relationship between the carver and the pole-raising *wilp.* The speaker explains the crests and recounts the *adaawk'.* A *wilksiwitxw* announcer stands with the chief and explains the force of the chief's particular spirit power, the essential *ts'imhalayt* psychic force of the chiefly name, House traditions and history, crests, fishing sites, land and its boundaries.

The host clan does not eat with the guests. They serve and sit along the back wall near the kitchen. As Gregory (1982, 52) has stressed, commensuality, or sharing food, implies a close family or conjugal relationship, while giving food implies social distance.

Bats'aa

Gifts that acknowledge the stature of the high chiefs and express the ranking order of each House and each clan in the respective villages are then distributed. They are given in thanks for the kind presence of men and women of authority who, consenting to be guests, are assisting the hosts to settle their business appropriately. This gift-giving by the hosts is called the *bats'aa* (to lift up, hold high). Today it consists of both food – boxes of bread and of crackers, crates of oranges and apples, sacks of flour and sugar – earlier it included boxes of oolichan grease and items presented in carved gift containers: sap cakes, berry cakes, rendered groundhog fat, kidney fat from mountain goats, as well as non-food items like *gwiislip'ast* (groundhog robes) and *hliyun* (tanned hide) and special gifts that were prepared for individual chiefs.

Before contact these gifts could range from a pair of snowshoes or a carved inlaid feast dish, to obsidian spear points or a special rare medicine. After contact other useful items were included: rifles, knives, Hudson's Bay blankets, kerosene stoves and lanterns, battery radios, pack-boards, axes – all the subsistence items useful for everyday life on the land. Today, a large part of the *bats'aa* is paid in cash and goods: blankets, quilts, kitchenware, cloth, electrical appliances, electronic goods, rifles, and clothing.

Part of the *bats'aa* is payment for services rendered. The digging of a grave in a funeral feast is paid for in cash and is further rewarded with something in the order of a Coleman stove, a sleeping bag, or a duvet. These additional gifts (sometimes called by outsiders "the interest payments") are the *'niimaga*. Those who provided services in the pole-raising receive special *'niimaga* gifts.

Legi am daal and *Hawaal*

After the guests have eaten, various categories of people are called upon to make their contributions, which the hosts will use to pay their debts. The host's *limx'oo'y* is normally sung at this point. Usually before this occurs, the *guxsmagan mixk'aax* is paid. The hosts will give each of the guest chiefs an envelope that contains money that repays "with something extra" each guest's *mixk'aax*. (The *guxsmagan mixk'aax* is the repayment of the cash gift given earlier to the *tets* group, signalling the chief's intention to attend the feast.)

All whose mothers are members of the host House are called upon to make significant contributions to the feast, in proportion to their age and the status of the names they hold. The *wam simgigat*, those with chief names, are called first. The first contributor is the host chief himself, the successor to the name of the high chief of that generation that is being venerated by the pole-raising. This contribution is the *legi am daal*. Those hosts who are close in rank to the chief also contribute *legi am daal*. The subsequent contributions of all other members of the *wil'naat'ahl* and the non-House members of the clan in general are called *hawaal*.

The *wilksiwitxw*, usually father's brother or sister, will call up the *wamsimgiget* to the front of the assembly, using their baby names *(wam ts'uusxw)*, telling them to come up and take care of their grandmother's burial for, in a sense, the pole-raising is a final funeral for a whole generation of the matriline.

Beyond the pole-raising feast there is one further gathering that is the ultimate culmination of the feasting cycle – the feast that is held to ensure that the spirits raised with the pole are properly venerated. This is the *Gwalgwa 'amgan Feast*, the final major *yukw* of a chief's life. Few chiefs are ever prosperous enough to hold this feast, where the high chief takes back his/her baby name, the *wam ts'uusxw*, and in effect retires from active management of *wilp* affairs (though until death the chief will remain a leading authority on family history and cultural-jural procedure).

The *gwalgwa 'amgan*, "the drying off of the pole," if it is held at all, occurs one to two years after a mature chief's *baxmaga*, or pole-raising feast. The *gwalgwa 'amgan* puts the final touches on the *wilp*'s cycle of feasts for a generation of chiefs of that House. It is a joyful occasion in which the *simoogit* who hosts it cheerfully prepares to depart from this life by leaving the House affairs in a clean and prosperous condition: "He leaves behind his hands that they may conduct his own burial."

The chief, upon being called up by his/her baby name, approaches the announcer and makes his/her payment, the *legi am daal,* which is placed in the pot, the *tsek.* The same procedure occurs with the counsellor/branch/wing chiefs, who pay a lesser amount than the chief, *wiisimoogit.* Beynon made the following notes about this step in the 1945 pole-raising of Ha'naamuxw in Gitsegukla after Ha'naamuxw himself had made his *legi am daal* payment:

> Then he stood up, "With this I am going to look into my brother's face," meaning of course that he was now going to take the place of his uncle [actually, his predecessor was his mother, Fanny Johnson (Figure 20)]. Before the name Ha'naamuxw is assumed, the successor always refers to the predecessor as his uncle. When his name has been assumed, the predecessor becomes the brother. And so in this case, as he had already in the past had assumed the name Ha'naamuxw he refers to the deceased uncle as brother, and he is now able to gaze upon his full responsibilities. (Barbeau and Beynon 1915-57, B-F-428: 4-5; Anderson and Halpin 2000, 167-8)

Then other members of the House make contributions according to the ranking of the names they hold. When these relatives are finished, more distant members of the *wil'naat'ahl* queue up to do their *hawaal. Hawaal* is paid first by one senior matron and her children, then by her younger sisters and their respective children, and by "cousin sisters," until all House members have made their contributions. The announcer calls out the name of the contributor, the value contributed, and the category of payment that it constitutes.

Aye'e

The second category of contribution to the *tsek* is the *aye'e,* literally, the "grandfather" payment. The *aye'e* is made by those who are related to the host *wilp* through their fathers. The fact that the grandfather term is applied to these payments may indicate the long-standing intergenerational ties between the host's and the father's respective matrilineal groups. Consistent intermarriage between two Houses results in the father's group, over time, giving rise to grandchildren who can inherit from the grandfathers. This is more striking when we remember that the majority of Gitksan villages were either composed of only two clans or else the village was divided on the occasion of ceremonial events into two sides called *nidilx,* the two

voices of the village. The diligent reader will recall that the *aye'e* was introduced above in the *bagunsxw* section. It rightfully is paid, or gifted, directly
onto the pole to help bring it to life the day before the actual raising. If this
is not done it is made in the course of the feast, following the *legi am daal*
and *hawaal*.

Ant'im'nak̲/Ant'imhanak̲'

The third category of donation payment is the *ant'im'nak̲* of spouses to the
wilp members. This is traditionally a humorous and spirited set of donations. Those who are *ant'imhanak̲'* or *ant'im'nak̲* dance, sing, and joke. Frequently *ant'imhanak̲'* members secure their contributions about their bodies
in ways that challenge the dignity of the hosts, who are required to detach,
with aplomb, the money from the bodies of contributors of the opposite
sex, announce the sum and the name, and put it in the *tsek*.

Young men and young women known to be enamoured of a *wilp* member
will frequently be called up to join the *ant'im'nak̲* – to their embarrassment
and to the general merriment of the gathering. *Legi am daal, aye'e,* and
ant'imhanak̲' payments are all contributed to the *tsek*. In the days before the
existence of currency the gifts were all distinctive and readily identifiable at
all times, a fact that suggests the assembly could actually see the sequence
of giving and receiving that their respective gifts followed in the course of
the feast. Now, in monetary times, it is considered appropriate for the sums
donated from each of these categories of relationship to be accounted sepa-
rately before being added to the *tsek*. This indicates their separate identity
and value; it should be announced as it is being donated and reiterated in
summing up the evening's transactions at the end of the feast.

Interval

Two people are invited to count the *tsek*. They are the *t'aaphl hayatsxw*
(*t'aaphl:* to hammer; *hayatsxw:* copper), or the "coppersmiths," from those
who were called upon to break up the host chief's copper shields for distribution to the guest chiefs. Today the *t'aaphl hayatsxw* record every transaction, every single donor, and tally up the *tsek* with pen and paper, a pocket
calculator, or notebook computer.

The goods or cash distributed to the guest chiefs from the *tsek* are *x̲gwiikw*
(groundhog pelts). Formerly marmot pelts or robes were a standard Gitksan
gift payment to chiefs who bore witness to the host's business. Only rarely
did a host have coppers to break for the guests, but they always had groundhog pelts and sections of caribou hide or moosehide.

During the intervals in the feast, and especially the lengthy period when
the *tsek* is being tallied and prepared for distribution, various incidental
debts are paid. In the course of the *bax̲maga* many guest chiefs employed
the services of other guests when they revealed their wild, untamed *nax̲nox̲*

spirits in response to the *naxnox* of the host. For these small assistances it is customary for each individual *simoogit* to reciprocate with a gift. Such "payments," called *sa'etxwhl naxnox*, are made in the intervals between sequences of major business. So too are payments by the hosts for help with their own *naxnox*: to the person who danced and performed the *naxnox* spirit, and to those who were its guardians, ensuring it did not harm the guests. *Sa'etxwhl naxnox* are personal debts that do not come out of the *tsek*. The hosts may also pay for the services of a singer if they did not sing their family songs themselves. In the past, hosts would occasionally hire singers to perform aspects of the House group's history and crests, and to entertain the guests during lulls in "the business."

Another type of transaction that occurs before formal proceedings commence, or during intervals, is the payment of certain personal debts that individuals have run up in the recent past with members of the hosting House. People say, "You pay these back in the feast because you feel guilty not to do so at a time when the host's every resource is taxed to the limit by the payments that must be made in the feast." I have observed people announce they are making a gift and cash payment to individuals in the host group who showed kindnesses to the giver, such as driving her to visit sick relatives in hospital or providing firewood at crucial times.

Individually, guests go to the head of the hall to announce what they are paying and what is being added to it. They then present these payment/gifts to the hosts. As well, individual members of the host *wilp*, and some people closely related to the House but not actual members, give gifts that fall into the category of personal debt payments for loans, gratitude for kindnesses shown, or past services rendered to these various individual "father's side" relatives. These are announced, and the recipient is called to the head of the hall and paid directly. These are usually merchandise gifts termed *xk'ayhl*. *Xk'ayhl* is the giving of a gift in return for unsolicited past goods and services "from the heart." The same term is used for the payment made by a chief, at a name-giving, to those among the *wilksilaks* who acknowledge the individual successions to names (see below). Everyone making contributions in the form of personal debt payments is expected to give a list to the feast accountants of the cash and/or goods contributed.

Succession to Names

Intervals are also utilized to announce new successions to names within the host *wilp*. There are a number of levels of names: a baby name *(wam ts'uusxw)*, a child's name *(wam tk'ihlxw)*, a young woman's puberty name *(wam giniitxw)*, an adult name (man, *wam gat*; woman, *wam hanak')*, and a chief name *(wam simoogit)*. There are also *k'ubawilksihlxw* (*hlguwilksihlxw* sing.) names for those who one day will inherit chiefly names. A person in a chiefly line of succession may "wear" four or more names in the course of a lifetime, or she/he may pass smaller names on to others.

All leaders of Houses must keep abreast of the changes of incumbents to *wilp* names all over the community and in other villages so that in future feasts their ranking configuration can be correctly maintained despite the constant changes brought about by the lifecycle. When a person moves up to a name of a higher status, the old name is, on the same occasion, "floated" (*gyooksint*) to a new incumbent. However, people generally retain their baby names and will sometimes resume them in advanced old age.

The name-taker, *uxwshedint* (sing.), *uxwslidint* (pl.), "the one brought forward," stands up at the head of the hall with a senior member of the *wilp,* who announces to the guests that names will be put on this person or persons. S/he will explain who the *uxwshedint* is, what his/her qualities are, who their relatives are, and what the new name is that the person will wear. S/he then explains the name's origin or relates anecdotes about previous holders of the name and concludes by saying that this person is the legitimate heir to the name because of his or her position in the kinship configuration (i.e., because the person is *hlguwilksihlxw* of the lineage).

The *uxwshedint's wilksilaks* members are then named. These persons then speak their *ayesxw,* a sentence that acknowledges the new name and shows its link to one's self, that is, to the name-taker's *wilksiwitxw.* This acknowledger from the father's side will probably tell about past colourful personalities who wore this name. It is also considered appropriate to make a pun or a riddle that links the name with the speaker's clan or crest. For example, if the *wilksiwitxw* is of the Lax̱ Gibuu Clan and the new name of the *uxwshedint* is Latecomer, then the *ayesxw* may include a phrase such as "the little wolf comes in late."

A gift, a *x̱k'ayhl,* is then given by the naming hosts to the person from the father's side who has thus validated the name. The senior House member then explains the seating location of the new name-holder in relation to the other names in the *wilp.* This is witnessed and remembered by the guest chiefs. If the new name-holder possesses another adult name, this will usually now be "floated" to a new incumbent.

"The Amount in the *Tsek* Is ..."

When the *tsek* has been counted, the debts incurred in the pole-raising are paid first: the mattress (*sixwdaa/suxwdaa*), the paternal relatives of the chief, the blanket (*sugwilat/sigwilat*), the male chief's descendants – those to whom the host chief is "father's side" – these gifts given immediately after the death (or, as regarded by the recipients, "loans") are repaid from the pocket of the chief rather than from the *tsek.* Expense payments are deducted from the *tsek;* occasionally, these may include outstanding business carrying over from earlier feasts (especially with grave and cemetery expenses and out-standing debts that the deceased left unsettled).

All services and materials involved in the pole-raising are paid for. These are summarized below. Next, the sum that remains in the *tsek* is paid out to the guests for having witnessed the proceedings. This, technically, is part of the *bats'aa* payment, the first portion of which was paid out in foodstuffs during the banquet.

The announcer says, "It will go around to where it runs out" (lip ligi an dim wil luu goodit). Kyologet, who for years was actively involved in organizing feasts, maintains that this part of the proceedings always makes her nervous not only because the money must not run out but because proportions according to ranks of chief, counsellors, *k'ubawilksihlxw,* ordinary people, and children must be accurate. It is, after all, not only the hosts but also the guests who are making the calculations, and the latter know almost exactly what sum ought to be placed in front of them. Accounting errors have direct political and social repercussions. They can damage the authority that the *wilp* is demonstrating through the public and judicious discharge of its debts, its decisions concerning its territories, its appointments to high names, and its general conduct in the feast, as well as its standing in the ebb and flow of credit and debt relations in the village.

Absentee chiefs are paid *am xosint,* absentee payments, out of common courtesy even though they have not witnessed the proceedings. The *wilp's simgiget,* who are allocating funds, stop at the absentee's seat and one of them thrusts his or her arm in the air, shouts the name, and leaves the payment with relatives of the absent *simoogit.* When a chiefly name is vacant following the death of the previous incumbent, and no decision has been taken by the House to retire that name, then the hosts will continue to leave a place for the name. As well, they will continue "to feed the chief's bowl" for some period of time even if a chief is absent due to a dissolute lifestyle. But eventually the name will cease to be honoured in feasts. When this occurs, shame falls not on the hosts who neglect to provide a place for the absentee but, rather, upon the House that has allowed its chief to ignore House business and proper behaviour.

If a chief engages in improper behaviour he is required to hold a *k'ilgal gimks* (*k'ilgal:* surface; *gimks:* wipe off), a cleansing feast, at which he presents each guest with a basin, towel, and soap. He then apologizes publicly for having acted in a manner demeaning to the dignity of his chiefly name. He must explain that his undignified and immoral activity has, of itself, stripped him of his authority and regalia. In the cleansing feast he asks to be reblanketed and reinvested with his regalia.[28]

In addition to allocating the correct sums, the hosts must proceed according to their understanding of the formal ranking and the de facto structure of authority; for instance, if a high chief is young, his senior advisors must be accorded standing almost at his level, as they are his essential mentors. The *tsek* usually begins with chiefs from the home village. The place in the hall where it begins will determine the order in which the guest chiefs will speak to confirm the proceedings that they have witnessed. It begins with the senior chief of the host's *wilksilaks,* or the senior chief of his *nidilx,* "the opposite side" of the village.

When the *tsek* is empty it is held aloft, upside down, while the hosts announce that their transactions are finished. They have given out all their *ha'amwil* (all that they brought to the feast to give away). The hosts now hold up the *simoogit*'s crest robe, and the chief's speaker, usually from his/her *wilksiwitxw* (father's side), speaks to the guests about the *wilp*'s origins and the history of the crests of the House (Figure 18). The chief may recount a version of the House *adaawk̲',* or one of them if he or she possesses several, as well as announcing other decisions of the House and summing up what has been accomplished during the *yukw* in the previous hours.

Tenimget gave evidence that at the Gux̲sen pole-raising of October 1986 the host family announced, among other decisions, that Tenimget's mother, Kathleen Matthews, in *wilksiwitxw* relationship to the host, would be given the right to use some of the host's fishing sites during the remainder of her lifetime. In the same announcement, Tenimget himself was given the right to assist his mother at these sites by virtue of having *ye'e* (grandfather) ties to the host through his mother. His rights are called grandfather rights, *amniye'etxw,* while his mother's rights are *amnigwootxw,* rights through the father (Transcript, 4747). When all such announcements and business are completed, the host will say that he/she has revealed the treasures inherited with the name and has "broken the copper" (Figure 10), with the result that now the wilp's business has been completed. The host then thanks the chiefs by name for having attended before declaring, "Now it is for those with wisdom to speak." Beynon reported the closing words of Ha'naamuxw in 1945: "Now this is the tradition that we have which was related to me by my grandmothers and uncles, and it is in their memory that I have erected this pole, which you all have helped me in. I have showed you what is mine that I have inherited. So what you have done to me, Great Chiefs, I cannot thank you too much for your help to me, and I hope that when you return to your homes, you will find everything pleasant."

'Nidinsxw: Acknowledgments by Witnesses

Kyologet gave evidence that chiefs are invited to feasts, especially an important *yukw,* to witness the business and see what the host group chooses to reveal from the heritage treasure box of the House:

> As soon as you enter into a feasting house you have to watch and you
> have to listen, and if one chief doesn't agree with what is going on in that

feasting house, he will let you know. So each of the head chiefs that are guests ... they have to listen to what is said by the host ... and what has been done, they have to witness that, and if anything went wrong they, the guests, have to say right there that this is not right. (Kyologet, Transcript, 307)

The authority of the host is confirmed by his/her peers as long as, in their estimation, the host acted according to the law, the procedures of etiquette, and in keeping with the history of the House and *wil'naat'ahl*. When the guests feel that matters have not been properly handled, then the chief who is in the appropriate structural position to initiate the acknowledgments will point out the errors. Ha'naamuxw testified that in one feast she recalls Haalus's House business was not fully acknowledged by the *'nidinsxwit*, (Transcript, 5010-11) who, on that occasion, was Gisḵ'aast Clan chief Simoogit Gwisgen (a territory had been incorrectly described). In a subsequent feast this error was corrected and then proper acknowledgment was accorded.

When all the chiefly guests have been paid, and the host or his representative has addressed the guests the way Simoogit Jeffrey Johnson did in the 1945 Ha'naamuxw *baxmaga* feast, the host's *wilksiwitxw* chief, or his *nidilx* (the senior chief of the opposite clan of the host's home village), will begin the speeches that deal with the legitimacy and correctness of the business that has been conducted by the hosts. In the 1945 Ha'naamuxw Gisḵ'aast Clan feast, this was the Ganeda or Frog Clan chief, Mool'xan, who said at the Ha'naamuxw pole-raising on 14 January 1945: "My son, my son, Chief Ha'naamuxw, all that you have now told and shown to the chiefs here is true, and what you have shown and told is the truth" (Anderson and Halpin 2000, 174). Mool'xan commended the host on his explanation of the crests and his knowledge of the elaborate history of the House, and said of Ha'naamuxw's territories: "You have great territories, both here, and farther up into the hills. Your berry grounds are the most abundant of all, and now these are being lost to the white man. I remember seeing many of the naxnoxs that are from your uncle's House at former feasts of your uncle's, and some of these you have shown to the chiefs who have gathered here. I for one acknowledge that what you have told us and what you have shown us is true" (Anderson and Halpin 2000, 174-5).

Next, the other high chiefs of the Houses of that clan in the village have their chance to speak before the turn comes of the third clan (if there is a third clan in the home village). Then the speakers from other villages begin. The village order for a Kispiox feast is Kispiox, Gitanmaax, Kisgagas, Guldo'o, Gitsegukla, Gitwangax, Gitanyow/Kitwancool. For a Gitsegukla feast the order is Gitsegukla, Gitwangax, Gitanyow/Kitwancool, Gitanmaax, Kispiox, Kisgagas, and Guldo'o.

It is now time to *dim segapditsxw* (add on to what has been said and done). The guest chiefs speak in order; they explain which chiefs they are speaking for and they thank the hosts by name, reiterating the parts of the hosts' business that they think are particularly important and have been conducted according to the law. They elaborate with stories and examples from their own experience to illustrate the importance of the law, the established boundaries of the land and the crests and *adaawk*'s, which accord with their own knowledge. When all the representatives have spoken, the feast is closed by the same person who opened it.

As discussed above, the prosperous House that has succeeded in hosting the important lifecycle feasts of all its members – birth, puberty, first hunt, marriage, death (funeral, gravestone, grave fence, and pole-raising) – can seal the process to ensure that all the deceased were *dem hap menye'es*, or "ancestors raised with the pole." Now the *simoogit* can legitimately retire from active leadership of *wilp* affairs. The final feast in the cycle, the *gwalgwa 'amgan*, is "like putting the final seal on a document. It really brings the xwts'aan to life" (Daly 1986-88 [Trombley]).

Summary of *Baxmaga* Feast Transactions

The main transactions of the pole-raising feast: the House and its allies contribute fresh food, *bats'aa* foodstuffs, and lay out large sums for *'nimaga* gifts. They also contribute *legi am daal* and *hawaal* from the chief and other children of the women of the *wilp*; *aye'e* contributions come from those whose fathers are *wilp* members or those whose brothers are fathers to *wilp* members (in a funeral feast this is the "haircut" contribution: *k'otsgesxw*, and *ant'imhanak'/ant'im'nak* contributions from the spouses of the House/ *wilp*). At an earlier point the hosts have also been lent the "mattress" *(suxwdaa)* from the father's side and the "blanket" *(sugwilat)* from the spouses of the *wilp* members. Certain personal debts are repaid to House members as well. The guest chiefs each contributed their *mixk'aax* token of acceptance of the invitation at the time the *tets* delegation visited their respective villages.

The hosts must make the following payments: (1) cash sums and goods "from their own pockets" used to discharge loans (the *suxwdaa*, the *sugwilat*, and any outstanding debts from previous funeral feasts); (2) the *guxsmagan mixk'aax*, the repayment with interest of the guests' *mixk'aax*; (3) sums to discharge feast-related debt for services rendered *(hlgo'um)* and, in particular, *luuye'edim*, "paying the casket" or, in this case, "paying the pole" ([a] to the *wilksilaks* for help to select, cut, haul, preserve, and carve the pole or to have it carved by someone else; [b] to the carver, the *gahla*, and his assistants; [c] to those who gave board and lodging to the carving team and maintained their tools); (4) other feast-related services rendered *(xw'u'um)* (in the funeral feast this payment covers all other burial and ceremony expenses not covered by the *luuye'edim*; the *xw'u'ums* in the pole-raising feast covers payments to the one who festoons the pole, to the movers, to the handlers at the site [the *t'alganit*], to the diggers, to the cementers, to the cross-brace handlers, to the makers of rope and cedar-bark mats, to the lead men on the pull ropes, to the singer of the *limx'oo'y* at the raising, to the rope cutter, and for all the supplies and tools used. This also includes payments for services at the actual feast provided by those who are not members of the host clan to the welcomers [*wanimsxwit*], the escorts [*ant'aadit*], the announcers [*ts'imwil atitxwit*], payments to those who count the *tsek* [the *t'aaphl hayatsxwit*], and to other helpers and assistants); (5) from his or her pocket the host chief pays the *naxnox* performers and *naxnox* escorts who assisted the host's performance; (6) individual guests make similar payments "from the pocket" for assistance with their respective *naxnox* performances *(sa'etxwhl naxnox)*.

Most of these payments – all those except *suxwdaa*, *sugwilat*, and those made by *simgiget* for *naxnox* performance assistance, come out of the *tsek* total. When these payments have been deducted and distributed, the main *bats'aa* payment, the *xgwiikw*, made to the guests for witnessing the proceedings, begins. *Xk'ayhl* gift payments are also made during the name-giving to each *wilksiwitxw* who has acknowledged the name. Payments are made for food donated by the guests at the *bagunsxw* as well as to defray guests' travel costs, for attending as witnesses, and for *dim segapditsxw* ("adding to" the proceedings and, in the speeches of acknowledgment, for elaborating upon what has transpired in the feast).

A person with empty pockets can very well go to a feast hosted by his or her own *wil'naat'ahl*, yet when it is time to contribute to the *legi am daal* or *hawaal*, the empty pocket has become full through the matrilineal credit network that blends gifting, sharing, and reciprocity.

These, then, are the major contributions, loans, and repayments in a *baxmaga/hed'msingan*. The hosts have gone into their heritage and history, their crests and songs and territories; they have drawn their legitimacy from their treasure boxes, the *anxhlo'omsxw*, the place they store their wealth. Here they have used the power and energy of their whole matriline and its links to other Houses through marriage, their whole wealth and estate (their *ha'amwil*), which has been needed to fulfill their social responsibilities. If everything has gone according to the law, then the guests will go home saying of the hosts: "*Kwasinhl ligiwil* [They have paid back]. *Sitxhasxw*, they have truly broken the wealth that they have gathered from their land and distributed it according to the law!" "*Dim helda kw'adiksxw* [It will come back many times over]."

The Feast System

According to the *adaawk*'s, the reciprocity of feasting has been practised for millennia.[29] Archaeological data suggest that feasting may have arisen with the transformation of regional hunting bands into semi-sedentary communities of diverse, salmon-fishing foragers (Matson and Coupland 1995, 229). Feast memories link the present with narrative memories of an ancient past.

Feast-givers aim to settle debts and disputes, strengthen trust, renew credit, and challenge, by their example, others to follow suit. Both the Witsuwit'en and Gitksan say that a "great giving" is a sacrifice that will clean social relations the way rain will clear the air, a point echoed by Seguin (1985). The feast is able to fulfill many overlapping functions because it manages and sorts out a broad range of social relations through the reciprocal exchange of histories, emotions, goods, and services.

Socially evaluated prestations are exchanged, paid, borrowed, and repaid in the feast. While the flow of these goods is small in terms of the total flow of goods and services in everyday material life, their ceremonial giving expresses and reinforces traditional reciprocity. Feasting in itself has probably never been a highly effective vehicle for goods distribution, but, through its ceremonial mask of gifting and gratitude, it both underlines and facilitates social and economic activity, and economic-related social interaction both within the local society and with more distant peoples. Gisdaywa (Daly 1986-88) said all Witsuwit'en chiefs are and were rich in one way or another, but by attending feasts one learns what other Houses are *not* rich in. There has long been interdependence and exchange between Houses such that all can attain a general level of well-being, given an equal labour input, using one another's lands, goods, and special skills. The gifts between chiefs in the feast hall signal these differences and interdependencies.

As we have seen above, the pole-raising feast involves years of preparation on the part of hosts and long hours of intense concentration upon the transactions presented for public scrutiny. Feasts mark the changing generations, the shifts in privilege and responsibility. As hosts look forward into the future, they feel that generations of ancestors who held their chiefly names centuries ago are looking with them and at them. The hosts feel the steering hands and voices of the generations of House leaders, those who are venerated in the pole-raising, and this ethos contributes to the forward thrust of feasting into the coming generations. These intimations from the past accompany each family into the future.

This multifaceted institution has long perplexed outside analysts. Perceptions of the social relations that take place during a feast are highly coloured by the observer's own cultural upbringing and implicit values. The viewer who is steeped in market relationships tends to equate feast-giving with "a wasteful and time-consuming way of putting the others in the host's debt" (as is reflected in academic literature and the Potlatch Law banning indigenous sumptuary ceremonies into the middle of the twentieth century). On the other hand, for members of a society steeped in centuries of social relations centred around the appropriation and exchange of goods that come into their prime with the roll of the seasons, feasting demonstrates the flow of responsibility, respect, and gratitude between human groups and between these groups and their natural surroundings. Hosts provide hospitable conditions in which to discharge their obligations and debts to their peers, season after season and generation after generation. The host group that has expended everything in a major feast has "cleared the air," has vindicated the ancestral standing of the House, *wil'naat'ahl,* and clan, and has, for the moment, made good its name.

By singing their songs of mourning in the feast hall, hosts reveal the epiphanies and the anguish experienced by their ancient namesakes. "Those who came before" are so close to the chief at such times that they feel like parts of his/her own body (Transcript, 4643).

Feast payments tend to be greater than the values of the debts that are being paid off. Participants explain that this is not equivalent to "paying interest." They say that the extra they give is only sending a bit of oneself to those who have shown kindness. The Other is thus woven into the never-finished fabric of obligation and counter-obligation, as expressed in the idiom of the gift.

The Gitksan and Witsuwit'en deny the charge that they "pay no taxes." They point to their sacrifices to society, to "the millions and millions" paid in the feast hall "for the right to enjoy the lands of our ancestors." Today it is said that feasting does not balance out. Perhaps it never did; however, elders point out that "before the whites took the land," families had more wealth to draw upon for feast payments. "Back then," they say, "our box was full."

Gregory (1982) has shown how the twentieth-century meeting between the Western culture of commodity exchange and the gift economy of Papua New Guinea did not result in a unidirectional change from gifting to buying and selling. He says that the essence of the region's economy today is ambiguity: "A thing is now a gift, now a commodity, depending upon the social context of the transaction ... The colonisation of PNG has not produced a one-way transformation from 'traditional goods' to 'modern goods,' but complicated a situation where things assume different social forms at different times and in different places" (115-16). This parallels present-day Gitksan and Witsuwit'en feast-giving. Many of the items given are purchased with money, the ultimate commodity. This money has been obtained in wage labour, transfer payments, and the sale of goods and materials from the land. Money itself plays the role of a good given as gift in the feast. Its quantitative standard of value has been adopted to signal the levels in the hierarchy of statuses, from chiefs' names to wing chiefs' names, adult names, guests without names, children, and babies. It can also stand for other symbolic items traditional to feasting, such as the *mix̱k'aax,* the white eagle down (symbol of peace and of relations between a host chief and guest chief), which the guest gives to the host's messengers to signal his or her acknowledgment of attendance in the coming feast, and which the hosts return with something extra during the actual feast. It has not led, however, to the supplanting of the enduring and open-ended relationships of gifting and feasting, with the cut-and-dried relationships associated with buying and selling. And the main reason, here as in Papua New Guinea, is that land has not been alienated as a commodity, and thus the basis for clan organization has been sustained, even though government refuses to recognize Aboriginal title except at the moment it is surrendered to the Crown. The Gitksan and Witsuwit'en are not landless proletarians. They have clan and House lands, where their ancestors reside, and the preferred form of exchange is through gifting.

Alfred Joseph, Gisdaywa, the first Witsuwit'en signatory to the Statement of Claim in *Delgamuukw*, said there is still an attitude that seasonal wage labour is a windfall or a sideline to real economic activity on the land. He cited the years of summer travel to the coast to work in canneries. The money made was "easy come, easy go," and the migrant workers often had to be fed in the subsequent winter by those who stayed home. Those who came home with cash to invest in feasting were viewed as three-day wonders, who might expend everything they had, but then, not having their feet in the land, and not gathering goods year round, would have to be fed by others. The villages were mostly empty in summer, until well after the Second World War, and the people who kept things going – accumulating year-round, "the stay-at-homes" – were the chiefs and those born to be chiefs. As Gisdaywa explained: "The stay-at-home people put out much more than those who go to the coast, for example. The high names always held back, steadily gathering things all year round. These were the people who could be relied upon. There were one-shot people who came home with money from logging contracts, gill-netting or trapping. They tried to come up in the feasts, but they got no leading names. It is always the elders who stayed home who had the names and put up the feasts, at the same level. Steady feasts. These one-shot people didn't like that. They were shamed."

The Houses and clans demonstrate in their day-to-day lives the reciprocity at the core of their being and the ethic of paying back and giving. They feast together and break their respective wealth, as the law demands, so that again and again, now and in the future, *dim helda kw'adiksxw:* it will come back many times over, or, in the words of the Witsuwit'en, "Our family can hold up its head and be decent, *c'izu*, and never lazy." And, unlike their non–First Nations visitors – be they unadopted anthropologists, men and women of the cloth, or others from the immigrant cultures – they are clearly and publicly seen to be free from the shame of always being fed by others.

A New Sharing

The heads of Houses and families closely guard and protect their feast knowledge. While the general contours are known across the region, the finer distinctions, elaborations, and connotations of feast procedure have been protected within the family and cautiously imparted to descendants. The esoteric nature of feasting and its detailed significance, its procedures and sentiment, invest this knowledge with the same spiritual and social power accorded to the narratives of origin, the crests, and songs that hosts revealed (fleetingly) to guests.

Now, following a long century of direct administration by Canada, these peoples are "opening their boxes" to reveal tantalizing whiffs of this old knowledge to the uninvited non-indigenous guests who have become their neighbours – some of whom, over time, even become "family." These fleeting revelations of esoteric knowledge are signals of gifts being offered, of sharing, and tentative overtures to reciprocity directed to those from the newcomer society who are willing to respond with humanity and respect. This chapter is an instance of just such a fleeting revelation of esoteric knowledge to the wider world. How we of the newcomer society respond to these proffered gifts of knowledge will determine the quality of the social fabric we weave into the increasingly global future.

In Chapter 3 we leave the feast hall behind and explore what Nurit Bird-David (1990) has called "the giving environment." Here, I outline the ecological and dietary basis for human life on what the trial judge in *Delgamuukw* called "a vast and empty land," through the seasonal round of economic activities that puts the Witsuwit'en and Gitksan into a perpetual round of indebtedness to "the spirits of the land."

FIGURE 13　Gitwangax totem poles on the riverfront at the old village site in 1915.
© *Canadian Museum of Civilization, No. 34596. Photo: H.I. Smith.*

FIGURE 14   Timbered houses from the colonial era and totem poles at Anspayaks (Kispiox) during the early twentieth century.
Royal BC Museum, No. PN 6828.

FIGURE 15   Simoogit Ha'naamuxw, Joan Ryan, with her newly adopted House member, Niis bins, local artist and cartoonist Don Monet, on the occasion of the pole-raising *(hed'msingan)* of Wilps Ha'naamuxw, Gitsegukla, October 1991.
Photo courtesy of Gwaans, Beverley Clifton Percival.

FIGURE 16 *Sigid'm hanaak,* or female chiefs, contributing their *daxget* and muscle power to the raising of one of Ha'naamuxw's two poles erected in Gitsegukla in October 1991.

Photo courtesy of Gwaans, Beverley Clifton Percival.

FIGURE 17 The *baxmaga:* raising the *xwts'aan.* This Ha'naamuxw pole was first raised when the incumbent to Ha'naamuxw was Fanny Johnson, the grandmother of the current Ha'naamuxw, Joan Ryan. It was raised again in 1945 by the next incumbent to the name, Jeffrey Johnson. The 1945 raising was occasioned by the great Skeena River flood of 1936 that washed away the Gitsegukla totem poles from the old riverbank village. The reraising of these poles required the Gitsegukla chiefs to defy the Potlatch Law, which outlawed such jural, social, and spiritual ceremonial events. This event was recorded by ethnographer and participant William Beynon. In this photo the same *xwts'aan* is being raised for the third time, in October 1991. Beside it is the pole of the current Ha'naamuxw, Joan Ryan (not in picture). Her pole is slightly different in that the bottom crest is that of her father's Ganeda (Frog Raven) Pdeek.

Photo courtesy of Gwaans, Beverley Clifton Percival.

FIGURE 18 During the pole-raising feast, a *wilksiwitxw* (father's side) announcer explains the host's crests and *adaawk̲'* narratives, the force of the chief's particular spirit power and essential *ts'im halayt* psychic force, *wilp* traditions and history, fishing sites, and lands and their boundaries. In this photo the House displays its *ayuks* – Person of the Rainbow returning from heaven down through the stars to the everyday world on Ha'naamuxw territory. This button robe is worn so that the figure's head points down towards the earth.

Photo courtesy of Gwaans, Beverley Clifton Percival.

FIGURE 19 Preparing for the funeral feast of Chief Woosimlax̲ha at Hagwilget, 1923.

© *Canadian Museum of Civilization, No. 59572. Photo: C.M. Barbeau.*

FIGURE 20 Ha'naamuxw, Fanny Johnson, Andimaul, 1924. Maternal grandmother to Olive Ryan (Gwaans), paternal grandmother to Gertie Watson (Gaxsgabaxs), great grandmother to Joan Ryan (Ha'naamuxw) and, among others, Don Ryan (Masgaak). The character of Sunbeams in C. Marius Barbeau's novel *The Downfall of Temlaham* is based loosely upon the life of this woman. Active with the Salvation Army, she moved out of the home village of Gitsegukla for a time and was among the leaders of the Salvation Army village of Andimaul, across the Skeena River and downstream from the parent village.
© *Canadian Museum of Civilization,*
No. 62619. Photo: C.M. Barbeau.

FIGURE 21 Gu<u>x</u>sen ("The Gambler") Charles Mark of the Gis<u>k</u>'aast (Fireweed/ Killer Whale) Clan, in his *halayt* costume, as used in healing procedures. Gitsegukla, 1923.
© *Canadian Museum of Civilization,*
No. 59803. Photo: C.M. Barbeau.

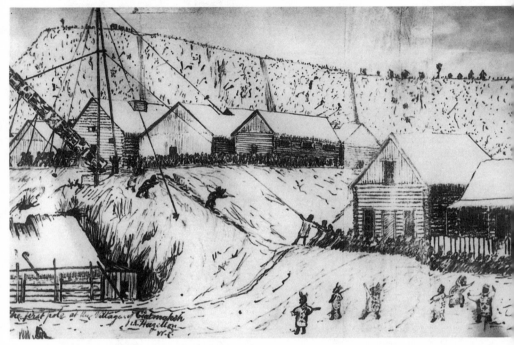

FIGURE 22 "Raising the first pole at Giatmaksh." This sketch was made in January 1881 by Helen Kate Woods, younger sister of Alice Tomlinson, wife of the missionary Robert Tomlinson, who lived near Kispiox. Helen and her brother had travelled north from Victoria to the Nass River estuary, up the mostly frozen Nass, and over Cranberry Junction to visit the family in Kispiox Valley. This was one of several sketches made by Helen and used as illustrations for the *Hazelton Queek,* a shortlived local paper inspired by Bishop Ridley and his wife. It records the raising of the pole of Simoogit Gyedimgaldo'o of the Lax̱ Se'el Clan. This was the first pole to be raised at the new village site, in front of the new, colonial-era, timbered longhouses of the clans. Gitanmaax elders in the 1980s said that the village had earlier been located "down near where [the museum village of] 'Ksan is today." Thus one should not consider this the first pole at Gitanmaax but, rather, the first at its modern site.

BC Archives, No. B-00047.

FIGURE 23   Gyedimgaldo'o's *xwts'aan* in front of the Lax̱ Se'el house/*wilp* in the
new square-timbered village of Gitanmaax. Photo probably taken about thirty
years after Helen Woods's sketch of its raising.
BC Archives, No. A-06886.

105

FIGURE 24   Maggie Jackson of Wilps Miluulak scraping a moosehide at Kisgagas, 1920.

© Canadian Museum of Civilization, No. 49475. Photo: C.M. Barbeau.

3
A Giving Environment: Nutrition and Seasonal Round

This chapter examines seasonal rounds in the territories and discusses Gitksan and Witsuwit'en diet at the time of contact. The subject matter here is certainly not at the cutting edge of anthropology today, but at the time of preparation for *Delgamuukw*, evidential requirements included a description of the management of successful ecological relations on the land. As late as the 1980s the Canadian courts would not entertain any claims to land unless a detailed usufruct could be established. This chapter, then, is intentionally historically dated in order to give the reader a flavour of how the court's understanding of Aboriginal issues tends to lag far behind ongoing research interests in the field of Aboriginal studies.[1]

Nutrition and Ecological Zones

The Witsuwit'en, who, along with their Babine and Takla neighbours, speak a northern Athapaskan language, were formerly known as northern and western Carrier (Morice 1895; Jenness 1943; M. Krause 1973; Tobey 1981). The ethnonym "Witsuwit'en" locates the people geographically (Widsu: Wedzenkwe – around the Bulkley/Morice River; *h^wit'en:* people of this place). Some of their hunting territories drain not into the Skeena watershed but, rather, into the Nechako-Fraser River system. The Witsuwit'en's western neighbours are the coastal Wakashan-speaking Haisla (from whom they are geographically separated by the precipitous Coast Range) and the Tsimshianic- speaking Gitksan (*git:* people; *'Ksan:* Skeena River), whose territories lie along the Skeena and upper Nass River watersheds. Witsuwit'en territories fall within approximately 53°N. and 55°N. and 128°W. and 124°W. Gitksan territories extend north roughly to 57° N. between 130°W. and 126°W. longitude, and south, to 55°N., roughly between 128°30'W. and 127°W. longitude.

Within this region, the fishing, hunting, gathering, and trading inhabitants have developed unique societies and ways of life deeply rooted in the natural surroundings that they both adapt to their needs and to which they adapt. Located in the cordilleran interior adjacent to the Pacific coast, these peoples have made effective use of the economic possibilities afforded by the existing biogeoclimatic zones.

The past two centuries have seen the Witsuwit'en and Gitksan subjected to lethal epidemics of measles, smallpox, and influenza; an increased tempo of trade and war followed by forced sedentarization; acculturation into the Canadian nation-state; and increasing dispossession from traditional lands. Yet this period has been marked by land-based economic strategies consistent with those employed in precontact times. Intimations of precontact conditions are cautiously assembled from present-day archaeological knowledge and the consistency of the oral history of the region. Archaeological evidence (Albright 1987; Ames 1979; Coupland 1985, 1988; Inglis and MacDonald 1979; MacDonald and Inglis 1976; Matson and Coupland 1995; Turnbull 1966) suggests that the precontact populations on the upper Skeena and Bulkley system, the recent predecessors (of the past two millennia) of the people who have come to be known as the Coast Tsimshian, Gitksan, Nisga'a, the Naadut'en, and the Witsuwit'en, followed a similar annual foraging cycle, using tools of wood, stone, bone, antler, and shell. Activities included the appropriation of salmon, fur-bearing animals, game, and botanical products as well as the import, by gift and barter, of obsidian, shell, copper, and other industrial products (Carlson 1983; Albright 1987, 5-3).

The distribution of obsidian from a few known sources, often over great distances, attests to interregional social relations (Carlson 1983). The existence of rows of multi-unit domestic dwellings in Kitselas Canyon dates back at least three thousand years (Coupland 1988) and suggests a social structure similar to that of early contact Tsimshian society (MacDonald 1986). It appears, then, that one may ascribe considerable antiquity to the main contours of the kinship organization in the area, by means of which land and labour were combined when first recorded at European contact.

This assumption is reinforced by the oral history of the Gitksan and their Tsimshian and Nisga'a neighbours in so far as the *adaawk's* narrate the harvesting, preparation, and exchange of many products "in the ancient times" that remained integral to the production activities of the region during the postcontact nineteenth century. The *adaawk's* abound with references to the produce of fishing, hunting, gathering, and exchange. I have selected, as an example, the *adaawk's* of one of the four Gitksan clans, the Lax Se'el, or Ganeda (Frog/Raven Clan).

These *adaawk's* refer to clan history over the region without respect to the linguistic boundaries of the present-day communities. I have tried to limit my selection to those events that occurred roughly in the area of the Gitksan: the Skeena, the upper Nass, the headwaters country between the two rivers (Gitangasxw), Kisgagas, Bear Lake, Kispiox, and Hagwilget. These references are found in *Raven Clan Outlaws on the North Pacific Coast*.[2] These Frog/Raven *adaawk*'s refer to oolichan fishing and social interaction concerning oolichan grease. We learn that oolichan grease was exchanged, was cached on the Nass, and, along with caribou and moosehide moccasins, was used to pay warriors for joining a raiding party. We learn a multitude of uses for red and yellow cedar on the Nass and Skeena. We find that mountain goats were hunted along the Skeena and in the Stewart area, that mountain goat horn was used for weapon points. We learn that, along with a special hard, blue "clam shell" obtained on the coast, goat hides and robes were feast gifts and that goat hunts were conducted at Gitanyow/Kitwancool (the upper Nass and Kisgagas areas). Marten pelts were made into robes on the upper Nass and were trade items in Kispiox (along with marmot [groundhog], caribou, and moose).

We find out that clubs and hammers were made of stone, that eagle feathers and abalone shell were valued items, that spruce gum was collected and used in weapon-making, that shells were used for knife blades and arrow points. In the Kitsumkalem-Kitselas area the Frog Clan hunted mountain sheep, groundhog, caribou, and grouse; hemlock bark was used for string and rope; fireweed fibre was spun into string; beaver was hunted for the making of robes at Meziadin Lake and along the Skeena and upper Nass. We learn that the fishing of humpback, sockeye, spring salmon, and steelhead was carried out in Kispiox (Anspayaks) and Temlax̱amid (T'imlax̱'aamit), and that fishing was done by pronged spear and by employing fishing weirs with basket traps attached (see Figure 25).

Berry-picking occurred in the autumn after the salmon season (and while the men were taking groundhog and mountain goat) around Kisgagas and Bear Lake as well as around Gitanyow. Berry-picking is mentioned in many other regions as well. Feast gifts at Gitwangax and the upper Nass included grizzly bear and mountain goat hides. Cedar houses, log defences, and bridges are described in the Gitwangax and Kisgagas areas. In the Stewart area and on the upper Nass it is said that marmot territories were extremely important because the pelts were a highly valued trade item. *So'o,* a favourite sweet springtime food, was prepared from the inner bark of the hemlock (Book Builders of 'Ksan 1980) as well as the inner bark of pine and birch. There is mention of devil's club medicine; caribou hunting; a chief's headdress decorated with dentalia, abalone, and copper shields; cranberries; huckleberries; beaver; black bear; grizzlies; mink; and crabapples. Finally, containers were made from birchbark, and drums were often bentwood boxes.

The economic pursuits of the Gitksan and Witsuwit'en prior to the contact and protocontact periods appear to have been contiguous with the economic life of the two peoples in the contact period (Matson and Coupland 1995, 274; MacDonald 1983; Croes 1989a, 1989b).[3]

Subsistence Strategies and Nutrition

So as to provide some understanding of the material basis for the traditional and ongoing social relations these peoples engaged in during their daily lives, it is useful to begin with a discussion of nutrition. Nutritional requirements for good health include a modicum of proteins, carbohydrates, fats, vitamins, and minerals to provide *essential nutrients*. These make up the carbon compounds and minerals that biological organisms must obtain preformed from the environment so as to form and maintain tissues and the life-sustaining metabolic processes. The energy potential of these compounds is measured in *calories* (Lee 1984, 54; Wirsing 1985; Stefansson 1946). The ways of obtaining a necessary nutritional intake and balance over time depend upon the type of technology and know-how of the population, the food resources available to that technology, and the attendant cultural values and traditions.

There are various ways by which peoples in different economies and ecologies achieve their nutritional needs. Studies have been undertaken that compare the dietary philosophy of the industrialized nations (that stress a balanced intake of proteins, fats, carbohydrates, and small amounts of needed minerals) with the dietary philosophy of other economies. Subsistence among many peasant societies, for example, is based largely on grains and vegetable matter. Such diets, while nutritionally sound, are quite different from the industrial diet. Peasant diets are based upon "protein complementarity" in which a number of combined foodstuffs, mainly grains, nuts, and vegetable matter, function together to provide the body's metabolism with its necessary complex of protein/amino acids (Lappé 1982, 161, 172ff.).

Researchers such as the anthropologist and Arctic explorer Stefansson (1945, 1946) and his associates have examined Inuit-type, single-species, all-meat diets and, after having lived on them for a full annual cycle, have found them to be as healthful and sustaining as an industrial diet. Some diets are almost exclusively composed of flesh, others of grains. Both types are capable of sustaining populations. The peasant-type, grain/vegetable diet satisfies the body's caloric needs by combining different types of protein foods with carbohydrates. Hunting diets, on the other hand, are based largely on the consumption of flesh and are relatively high in protein (Lappé 1982; and Dr. Harriet Kuhnlein, personal communication), yet they tend to require supplementary sources of calories, especially in times of prolonged physical activity and climatic extremes. In northern regions such as the Gitksan and Witsuwit'en territories, where until the last century the technology and climate precluded the cultivation and consumption of carbohydrate sources of calories (with the exception of wild berries and springtime cambium from south-facing young trees), this supplement was provided by oils and fats extracted from fish and game.

Meat-eating hunting peoples who live in cold habitats have the greatest ease in obtaining their requisite fats; at the same time, lacking substantial alternative sources of caloric intake to maintain energy and body heat in the winter months, they are among the world's greatest consumers of fats. These fats and oils generally occur side by side with the substantial protein of the flesh of the game animals hunted. Perhaps the greatest concentration of these two needed substances is to be found in sea mammals, particularly the seal, dolphin, whale, and sea lion of the polar and subarctic seas. These are the species upon which relatively non-diversified hunting economies, such as coastal Inuit (Chance 1966) and the Yamana (Lothrop 1928), generally concentrate their harvesting energies. This also pertained in the postglacial Namu culture, which existed on the middle of the British Columbia coast (Carlson 1979), and the equally ancient postglacial, non-diversified economies of the Baltic region of northwest Europe (Zvelebil 1986; Tringham 1971).

In hunting and fishing economies there have been two general strategies for obtaining an annual nutritional balance. First, among peoples such as the coastal and inland Inuit, the diet has been limited to the few species in stable supply in the region's ecosystem (Birket-Smith 1929; Chance 1966; Draper 1977; Speth and Spielman 1983; Stefansson 1945, 1946; Worl and Smythe 1986). Many of the coastal Inuit still rely considerably upon seals and whales, and, to some extent, caribou, to supply a large part of their material needs for most of the year. Similarly, within the last few decades the inland Inuit have continued to rely upon the seasonal barren land caribou to satisfy many of their material needs (Burch 1986; Csonka 1995).

The coastal Inuit and postglacial populations on the middle and northern portions of the British Columbia coast have solved this nutritional equation by focusing upon fish and sea mammals. Other hunter-gatherers, such as the Gitksan and Witsuwit'en, have solved the same problem through the pursuit and storage of a number of diverse sources of high energy foods that successfully combine the protein of the dietary staple (stored, dried salmon) and the carbohydrate of berries, sap bark, and root produce with various sources of fat. The cornerstone of this diet was fat and protein obtained from the combination of fish and game. In the indigenous Gitksan and Witsuwit'en economy this form of annual dietary combination was achieved in the course of fishing, hunting, plant harvesting, sharing, and barter. The produce could be combined in a sustaining manner over the course of the annual economic cycle by means of highly efficient drying and storage skills. Moreover, the well-developed network of exchange and trade in fat- and protein-rich foodstuffs was traced across the land in the form of sinuous trails linking the settlements of peoples over the general region.

A central ingredient in both the Gitksan and Witsuwit'en diet until the 1940s, and for many families to the present time, is dry-smoked salmon.

This protein-rich foodstuff also contains an amount of fat and is supplemented with additional fatty foods such as the oil (locally called "grease") rendered from freshly caught oolichan as well as from salmon, groundhog, beaver, and big game. Fat rendered from salmon heads was prepared in summer, hung in bladder pouches in the rodent-resistant family meat caches, and saved for winter use (Book Builders 1980). In the cold of winter, fat is a highly important source of energy (Figure 26).

The salmon themselves contain varying amounts of oil, although they utilize much of it in the course of fighting their way upstream to their spawning beds (Morrell 1987, 22). Spring and sockeye have the highest oil content. Most animal species hunted in the late summer and fall have been pursued at that time of year expressly because they have generally finished rearing their offspring and have fattened over the summer months. Fat game was taken for its hides and furs as well as its oil riches. The marmot/groundhog of the Alpine Tundra Biogeoclimatic Zone is especially noted for its luxuriant autumn fat. Gitksan hunters describe both its stripes of lean and fat flesh, and its taste as "bacon-like" (Daly 1986-88 [David Blackwater]). The mountain goat too is a fat game animal, its head, neck, and backbone yield fat that can be rendered to oil. The fat encasing the kidneys is rich and sweet. Formerly, according to the late Mary Johnson (Antgulilibix), David Blackwater (Simoogit Niist), and the Ganeda *adaawk*'s of Simoogit Haimas, goat fat was a suitable gift for an important guest in the feast hall. Haimas, in hosting his first major feast, showed his guests that he was not the poverty-stricken eater of shellfish (which was considered, in the vicinity of his coastal village, as fat-poor starvation food that coastal peoples resorted to in late winter), as had been rumoured by his rivals. He invited his guests to join him in his "shellfish diet." He then almost drowned his guests in the plethora of mountain goat fat that he had prepared in advance. Deer, moose, sheep, and caribou also yielded considerable quantities of fat. "Friendly" rivalries between chiefs are remembered by today's elderly. At these events hosts challenged guests to out-consume them in grease, and they would sit, tied by etiquette, through the many hours of the feast seance without being able to exit in order to relieve themselves.

Sometimes fat-rich grizzly and black bears were also taken during the autumn hunt, though some informants have stated that bear dens were known as permanent resource features of the House territories. Bears from such dens might be taken in late winter and early spring if other food sources were scarce. Bears wake from hibernation with the bulk of their autumn fat intact (Art Mathews Jr., Transcripts; Daly 1986-88). This fat is the bear's sole energy source for the first six weeks following hibernation, when the spring breakup has not yet provided the new plant growth and the new cycle of voles, insects, and grubs that constitute hors d'oeuvres to the summer's foraging.

The importance of high-energy foods to the diet and to the peoples' general prosperity was signalled culturally in the feast by the lavish expenditure of these rich foods towards the attainment of social status rather than nutrition. The people explain how they have witnessed their grandparents using such labour-intensive produce as rendered fat and berries in such ceremonial practices as pouring them into the track of a new crest pole as its base is slid into the hole. The *adaawk*'s recount the use of oil or grease on the fires to enhance the dramatic revelation and dramatic performance of the host chief's psychic power in feasts and winter ceremonies. The first Frog/Raven *adaawk'* (*Raven Clan Outlaws*, No. 1: 12) tells of a red glow within the host house: "It was secretly produced by rotten wood pulverized into dust and scattered over the floor. Some of it, mixed with candlefish [oolichan] grease, cast by ladlefuls into the fire was burning with a sizzling noise." In this unearthly light the spirit power of the host was revealed before the guests and gave rise to a name and crest of that chief: "Inside the Red House of Marvels."

Ganeda (Frog) chief, Gamlaxyeltxw, the late Solomon Marsden, spoke of an occasion when a man visited Gitanyow/Kitwancool from the Nass River to ask for a young woman's hand in marriage. Coming from the "home of the oolichan" he had brought a quantity of grease with him, which he poured on the fire at the welcome feast when he expressed his desire to marry the woman. The prospective bride ultimately declined the hand of her suitor. After assessing the amount of oolichan grease he actually poured on the fire, she concluded he was a niggardly man, who took no risks and who lacked generosity and largesse (personal communication).

In early spring many of the Gitksan and some of the Witsuwit'en journeyed to the coast to obtain the oolichan grease and storage oolichan,[4] which are smoke-dried. According to Kuhnlein et al. (1982, 159-60) the oolichan is not only a fat-rich food but a vitamin-rich substance that has both nutritional and medicinal uses: "the saturated fats of *ooligan* oil are similar to lard and higher than that present in corn oil and corn oil margarine. The total unsaturated fat, that is the combined monounsaturated and polyunsaturated fats, of *ooligan* grease is similar to that of corn oil. There is no doubt about the superiority of *ooligan* grease in providing vitamin A, E, K in comparison to the other three fats."

Ninety-nine percent of the content of oolichan is composed of fats, of which approximately 33 percent are saturated, 56 percent are monounsaturated and 1 percent polyunsaturated (Kuhnlein et al. 1982). The oolichan swims shoreward at the end of the winter season, when other sources of fat are scarce. It has long been regarded as a dietary saviour for the people of the region. In the Tsimshianic languages the arrival of the oolichan, from which the oil, or *t'ilix*, was made, was traditionally announced with the cry: "Hlaa aat'ixshl halimootxw!" (*hlaa aat'ixshl*: it is just arriving;

hali: for the purpose of; *mootxw:* healing people), or: "Our Saviour has just arrived!" This bounty was indeed conceived as a gift from nature to the people at a time of year when there were few other fresh food sources. Consequently, it was a prized gift in feasts and between neighbours. This was one of many gifts the people were permanently indebted for, and they could counter only by regarding the natural world with respect and gratitude.

Oolichan grease has traditionally been in high demand by both coastal and interior peoples (Poudrier 1891; Hart 1973; Drucker 1963, 1965; MacDonald 1980). It became the conduit for barter networks along the coast and inland as far as the Rockies. The "grease trails" (which are discussed later) carried oolichan and other sea products inland, and inland products coastward.

The Gitksan and Witsuwit'en obtained and continue to obtain special coast foods by exchanging for them their stores of dried salmon strips and dried berries. While enough salmon is taken annually to satisfy most family needs, the quality and quantity of berries fluctuates. Rather than consume all of these much loved and sometimes scarce items themselves, the Gitksan and Witsuwit'en preferred to use at least part of their annual supply (and today, part of their cash) to obtain the grease that cures all humanity. They sought out oolichan, together with the piquant and salty coast foods that add variety and a different set of vitamins and minerals to the diet. No doubt the desire for variety played some role in the decision to engage in this exchange.

In precontact times the neighbouring coastal peoples were also fishers and hunters (Fladmark 1986; MacDonald and Inglis 1976) who obtained their needed caloric intake largely from flesh and fat. Here, the calories were primarily obtained from fish and sea mammals such as seal, sea lion, dolphin, and porpoise, and secondarily from deer, berries, roots, and bulbs. These foodstuffs were obtained largely from the coastal waters and along the adjacent shores. In the mountainous interior however, among the Interior Tlingit, the Tahltan, Tsetseut, Gitksan, Naadut'en, and Witsuwit'en, the flesh and the fat needed through the course of the year were not found simply in the river and along the adjacent coast. These items were obtained by trade with the coast and from a number of different eco-niches spread over considerable distances and at different elevations. The carbohydrate component of the diet was also located in different niches. Given the partial sedentary settlement pattern and relatively high valley bottom population density, regular access to these disparate, and often distant, niches was essential to the dietary well-being of the Gitksan and Witsuwit'en. The diets were further enriched and varied by means of the trade and gift exchange of foodstuffs between peoples living in generally different climatic zones and regions (see, for example, Morrell [1987] on the exchange of salmon products between the Babine and Witsuwit'en peoples).

Whereas the Gitksan and Witsuwit'en have been able to support themselves well with salmon from the main-stem Skeena and its tributaries, this
was not a complete diet in and of itself. *To obtain the additional requirements
necessary to sustain their population with sufficient caloric intake and balance of
nutritional components, these peoples could not rely simply on dried salmon; they
also needed access both to trade and to diverse hunting territories that could be
regularly harvested and husbanded for the future.* This probably became more
important as the population grew and was, at least among some of the
Gitksan, concentrated in large villages for at least several months each winter. Schalk (1981) has argued that the northern Northwest Coast region developed its complexity not as a result of abundance of resources but, rather,
from the clustering of the essential resources (particularly the marine and
anadromous produce [like salmon]), from the necessity to manage and
manipulate access to these sites, and from consumer relationships that derive from clumped resources subject to periodic fluctuations. He notes that
the northern temperate rain forests are less resource-rich than are those
further south, yet social complexity tends to be greater in the northerly
regions due to the heavy reliance on, and organization of access to, fish and
sea mammals.

Environmental Conditions and Resource Distribution
(Three Major Biogeoclimatic Zones)

Haeussler (1986, 2-8) and Gitksan-Wet'suwet'en[5] Chiefs (1988, legend for
Map 2) indicate that the two peoples are virtually unique in that their territories lie astride the intersection of three major North American ecological
and climatic regions. Haeussler has termed these regions the *Coast*, the *Interior,* and the *North*. The Coast Zone is a narrow band of temperate coniferous forest bordering the Pacific Ocean from Alaska to northern California,
parallel with the Coast Mountains/Cascade Range and penetrating some
river valleys. The climate is mild and wet, with heavy snowfall at higher
elevations. Lower elevation vegetation is that of the temperate rain forest –
hemlock, cedar, coastal Douglas fir, amabilis fir, red alder, and maple. The
zone abounds with seabirds, sea mammals, black and grizzly bear, and coastal
black-tail deer. It contains saltwater and estuarine fishing grounds noted for
salmon, halibut, oolichan, trout, cod, herring, and various shellfish.

The Interior Zone includes the Rocky Mountains and other ranges on the
Interior Plateau extending down through central British Columbia to Colo-
rado and New Mexico. The climate is continental, with warm summers, cold
winters, and variable precipitation; much of this area is in the rain shadow
of the Coast Zone. The vegetation is mixed conifer and deciduous forests,
with shrub/grasslands in dry valleys and alpine tundra at high elevations.
The Interior is noted for lodgepole pine, interior Douglas fir, aspen, interior
spruce, and subalpine fir. Major faunal species are mule and white-tailed

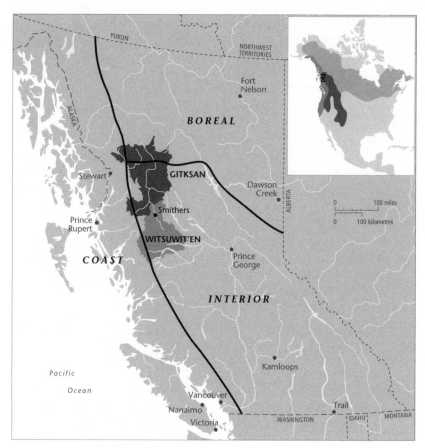

MAP 2 Gitksan and Witsuwit'en territories in relation to three major continental biogeoclimatic zones
Source: Haeussler (1986).

deer, bighorn sheep, and elk. Fishing consists of inland salmon and resident lake species.

The North (Boreal) Zone, the boreal forest, which extends in a broad band across Canada and Eurasia, has a subarctic climate with cold winters, a short growing season, and low precipitation. On the western side of the continent the typography of this zone is marked by a complex of northern mountains and plateaus, interspersed with extensive open tundra and muskeg. The vegetation is boreal conifer forest: white and black spruce, subalpine balsam fir, aspen, willow, and birch. The major mammal species are caribou, thinhorn sheep, moose, and wolf. Fishes consist of Arctic species and resident lake populations.

The location of Gitksan and Witsuwit'en territories in relation to these zones is laid out in Map 2 (after Haeussler 1986). While it appears that the

Gitksan and Witsuwit'en territories lie mostly in the Interior Zone, the broad river valleys of the Nass and Skeena form openings in the coastal mountain barrier. These openings allow moist Pacific air to penetrate much further inland and lose its moisture more gradually than is possible in any other part of the Interior Zone in British Columbia. Consequently, the Gitksan and Witsuwit'en territories occupy a broad transition zone in which ecological characteristics are intermediate between Coast and Interior in the south, and between the Coast and Northern Boreal in the north. The following ecological/territorial descriptions are summarized from Haeussler (1986), Map 2, G-W Map Atlas (Gitksan and Wet'suwet'en Chiefs 1988), and from the work of Hatler (1987) and Morrell (1987).

Biogeoclimatic Regions within the Territories

The transition from Interior Zone influence to Northern Zone influence at the northeastern portion of the territory is also gradual due to the open structure of the mountain ranges, such that the location populations have had ready seasonal access to resources of all three zones. For example, the red cedar upon which the peoples of the Northwest Coast culture area have traditionally been dependent extends up the Skeena and Bulkley Rivers. All the major Gitksan and Witsuwit'en villages availed themselves of this tree. The bark, needles, roots, and straight-grained wood of the cedar were used in house-building, as well as in plaiting, weaving, medicines, storage containers, canoes, crest poles, weapons, tools, baskets, mats, rainwear, and as a component of Chilkat robes. And cedar was present in a hundred other forms of construction and craft-work.

Similarly, the caribou and moose of the Northern Boreal Zone find their way into the valleys of the Gitksan and Witsuwit'en territories through the climatic blending of zones. Black and grizzly bears exist throughout the area, and the alpine tundra species such as marmot, ptarmigan, and mountain goat, live at higher altitudes throughout the area.

Northern Gitksan areas of the upper Nass and upper Skeena reveal features of both Coastal and Northern forests. Southern Gitksan areas lie in the centre of the Coast-Interior transition. The mid–Skeena Valley, Kispiox Valley, and the lower Bulkley and Segukla Valleys enjoy a vegetation that mixes elements of both Coastal and Interior Zones. Witsuwit'en territory below Moricetown[6] is Interior, or Sub-boreal in nature, but its climate is milder and moister than is the case further east.

All summer villages of the two peoples lie within, or at the edge of, the Hazelton Variant of what climatologists call the Interior Cedar-Hemlock Zone, Northern Transitional Subzone (ICHg3). The availability of red cedar made these locations attractive for building, but the Witsuwit'en also constructed large houses from spruce poles when living in their Interior Zone territories during the winter months. Johnny David (Commission Evidence,

69-70) has explained how firewood was cut from logs in the days before iron tools. The people would split the felled spruce, gradually and methodically, by applying wooden wedges along the grain. Although the straight-grained cedar was of great assistance to the house builders and woodworkers in general, its availability was not a crucial limiting factor in the economy. The fact that the Gitksan and Witsuwit'en settlements were located at phenomenally successful and reliable fishing sites, which in turn could be used seasonally in conjunction with the people's hunting territories, had much more bearing on the location of the villages.

Each of the major biogeoclimatic zones in Gitksan and Witsuwit'en territory contains a wide variation of types and quantities of subsistence resources. These resources are affected by elevation, the moist air of the river valleys, the cooling effect of the boreal forest, and the drying effect of the Interior Plateau. Dominant valley vegetation gives way to mid-elevation and high elevation biotic areas (Haeussler 1986, 12-13). Bisected by so many mountain ranges the territories are subject to many microclimatic variations. Zone C, where most of the population lives, and where all the villages are located, contains a moderate-to-good abundance of all major species, including hemlock, cedar, and the all-important salmon runs. The other zones have their special types of abundance and scarcity. It is of benefit to the families of these regions to have territories in other regions or at least kinship connections to other regions and other configurations of abundance. The Witsuwit'en Zone D, prior to settlement by outsiders, was noted for its marmot, caribou, and mountain goat (autumn species), while Zone E was famous for lake fish and beaver (early spring) and deer (autumn).

The major areas into which one can initially subdivide the biotic zones of the G-W territories (as shown in Map 3) are Zone A (the north), Zone B (the northwest), Zone C (the central zone consistent with the biogeoclimatic zone of ICHg3 at the valley bottom elevations), Zone D (the southwestern Witsuwit'en areas), and Zone E (the southeastern Witsuwit'en areas).

Zone A: Northern Gitksan Territory

This area, running roughly from Kisgagas to Guldo'o, northwest to Bowser Lake, and across the top of Gitksan territory to the northeast corner and down to the Babine River Valley, includes the headwaters of both the Nass and the Skeena. This is the region where the territories of such Houses as 'Niik'aap, Wii Gaak, and Meluula$\underline{k}$, and part of the territories of such Houses as Kyologet and $\underline{X}$hliimla$\underline{x}$ha, are located. The climate is relatively cold and winters are long. The landscape in this region is marked by extensive alpine and subalpine vegetation. The high altitude meadows and tundra, and the semi-alpine scrub forest, provide excellent habitat for huckleberries and

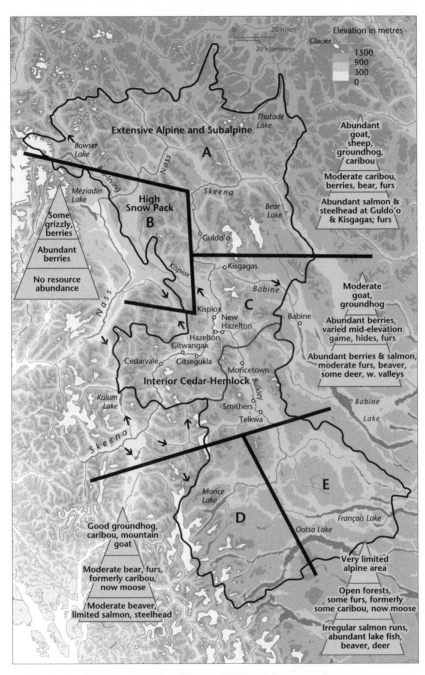

MAP 3 Biogeoclimatic zones of Gitksan and Witsuwit'en territories
Source: Gitksan and Wet'suwet'en Chiefs (1988).

blueberries, bear, groundhog, caribou, mountain goat, and mountain sheep. Lower elevations, both in the east and to the far northwest, are noted for good fur harvests. The upland resources in Zone A are for the most part at their prime in the autumn months. In the forests the main harvest in the past century has been fur-bearer species. In the valleys the main harvest consists of the summer sockeye salmon and berries, and the autumn coho. Some steelhead are taken at other seasons. Looking at the north part of this zone, the valley elevations are, on the western side, a variant of the Interior Cedar-Hemlock vegetation, while the central and eastern portions are dominated by boreal black and white spruce.

Zone B: Northwest Gitksan Territory

The region west of Guldo'o, north of the Cranberry and Kispiox Rivers, and west to Meziadin Lake and the Bell-Irving River, is where part of the territories of such Houses as Delgamuukw, Kyologet, Wii Goob'l, X̱skiigimlax̱ha, and Antgulilibix are located, as well as many *wilp* territories of Gitanyow. This zone is an area of high precipitation, with a deep snow pack, lush coniferous forests, considerable underbrush, and mountains with steep elevations and relatively small amounts of accessible open subalpine country or alpine tundra. Spring salmon and sockeye are taken by Gitksan fishers at Meziadin, and mainly sockeye on the Bell-Irving system up to Bowser Lake, but the region is known more for the steady and abundant runs of fall coho. The mid-elevation berry-picking used to be of great abundance before the government banned spring burning. In the autumn, above the treeline, people continue to take quantities of blueberries and grizzly bear.

Above 1,000 metres elevation in both Zone A and Zone B, the subalpine level is spruce/willow/birch in vegetation and gives way to alpine tundra conditions at the 1,500-metre level. The lowest elevations are clothed in variants of Interior Cedar-Hemlock, blending with spruce, while the middle elevations are marked by Engelmann spruce and subalpine fir vegetation.

Zone C: Central Area – Valley Bottom ICHg3 (Hazelton Variant)

The area between Kitselas on the west, Kisgagas on the north, and Moricetown on the south encompasses all the present-day Gitksan and Witsuwit'en villages. This is the area where the territories of such Houses as Lelt, Tenimget, Ha'naamuxw, Gwisgen, Sakxum Higookx, Nikateen, Luutkudjiiwus, Gitludahl, Spookw, Delgamuukw, and Wedexget are located as well as part of the territories of such Houses as Wedexkw'ets, X̱hliimlax̱ha, and Antgulilibix. All of the major main-stem salmon fishing sites are located in this zone, where the rivers are either sufficiently constricted to concentrate the fish or at least to allow for the placement of weirs/traps. The following factors have ensured that Zone C has historically been a major centre of salmon production for northwest British Columbia and parts of southeast Alaska. The major factors are the relative ease of harvesting large numbers of salmon, an efficient drying and smoking technology, dry summer weather, and a good ratio of fat to lean flesh. This means that, while drying occurs quickly, there is enough fat to flavour the dried strips (especially when toasted over a fire) and to provide considerable energy to the consumer (supplemented with fish oil rendered during the salmon runs and stored for winter). The river fishery in this zone begins early in the year with steelhead and chinook salmon, develops into sockeye salmon fishing, and continues in the fall with coho and steelhead. The mid-Skeena and tributaries also contain supplies of lamprey eel, which, while not eaten by the Gitksan, are smoke-dried by the Witsuwit'en.

Virtually all of the Interior Red Cedar and much of the Western Hemlock are located in Zone C. The valleys have an abundance of tubers, bulbs, roots, bark, and greens available from late spring to early fall as well as the plentiful hazelnut (from which the town of Hazelton took its name). The western valleys support deer, and there is a moderate yield of beaver, hare, marten, and other fur-bearing animals in the valley forests as well as ducks and geese in the autumn. Today the Skeena and its tributary valleys, from Kitselas to Kisgagas, support a healthy moose population.

Of course these species did not stand still. They moved with the climatic and seasonal possibilities open to them, through the various biotic zones, as, for example, the marten (Richard Benson, Commission, 109): "In the spring you see, the marten moves up a little higher on the mountain. They don't stay down. In the fall, that's when we were right down along the river. But in the spring ... real early in April, that's when we move further up, because the marten get after the blue grouse."

Zone C has a growing season that extends the period when it is usually possible to harvest plant foods in the Interior Plateau Zone; it enjoys a dry summer climate, great diversity of useful plant species, and a relatively low snowpack, with the result that winter travel has generally not been impeded.

Both the valleys and the middle elevations yielded a variety of game and fur animals. Each chief had access to some alpine tundra land for autumn hunting and gathering. While we were driving up the Kispiox Valley one morning in April 1986, David Blackwater, Niist, pointed out the peaks and alpine meadowland on either side of the valley. He gave the names of each mountain and of the owners. He explained that it was very important for each House chief to have access to alpine country because the alpine autumn harvest has long been an essential part of the annual economic round. It is in this high country that the people have obtained the rich, fatty groundhog with its soft, luxuriant fur, as well as caribou and mountain goat, and some species of berries, many herbal medicines, and a number of plant foods (such as dwarf hemlock). These same elevations, from river valley to treeline, support an abundance of berries.

Zone C is indeed blessed with several different elevational biotic subzones with a rich variety of resources. It should be remembered, however, that while the zone's salmon and steelhead resources are sufficient to sustain a high population, it would probably not have been capable of supporting the estimated population's winter energy needs. The population of approximately 2,000 Witsuwit'en and 6,000 Gitksan obtained this energy from large and small game and fur-bearing species. These species helped balance out the diet, provided some fresh food, supplemented the dried and smoked foodstuffs collected in the summer season, and provided items for trade.

The Men of Medeek *adaawk'* (Robinson 1962) explains the enmity that resulted in ancient times when the subsistence species were over-taxed by the additional predation from refugee hunters. The narrator, Chief Walter Wright of Kitselas, said that these hunters had dispersed downstream from Temlaxamid following an ancient (either natural or psychical) disaster. We should remember that populations did not grow willy-nilly. Informants suggest that conception was seasonally restricted according to the hunting rules imposed, generation after generation, by the head of the clan and House group.[7] Fertility may also have been impeded by the spaced births and subsequent lengthy periods of lactation in the mothers, as children were not generally weaned for two to three years (herbal medicines, too, were known as antidotes to unwanted pregnancies).

While I do not subscribe to the view that there can be any one single set of determinant variables to explain patterns of human behaviour, I feel it is useful to provide some ecological context to Gitksan and Witsuwit'en seasonal rounds, and to the management-type economizing of resources on the part of House leaders. In the middle of the last century the plant physiologist, Justus Liebig, proposed a hypothesis, now known as the Law of the Minimum, which states that, in any environment, species' population size will be limited by that material which is in shortest supply (Hardesty 1977, 196-7). In recent decades this law has been applied to some human populations. In reference to Aboriginal Australian populations, it has been argued that the material in short supply, which limits population, is not one or another species but, rather, the amount of seasonal and annual rainfall (Birdsell 1953).

How would the Law of the Minimum affect the Gitksan and Witsuwit'en? In general, in the days when the territories had not been appropriated by outsiders – and to some degree this carries on today – the chiefs direct(ed) the degree of harvesting on their lands on the basis of information obtained personally from those who used their various lands in various seasons. They assess(ed) the crops of berries, along with the numbers of each animal species and the patterns of their movement around the territories. They issue(d) instructions to ensure that a margin of unharvested foodstuffs be left: Art Mathews even explained the living, reserve food that hibernates in the bear dens of Tenimget/Axti Hiix territory. This reserve margin of various species provides a cushioning against sudden crises in the salmon runs, the caribou migrations, or the bear population. It also provides protection against the fluctuation of berry crops.

The crucial material likely to be in shortest supply during a part of the annual cycle of economic activity has most likely been fat, or grease, as the local people call it. Sharing in the coastal oolichan fishery or obtaining it by gift and barter were important during the hungry weeks of early spring.

When the oolichan, *Thaleichthys pacificus* (*thalei:* rich; *ichthys:* fish [Gr.]), form into massive schools to converge on their spawning river in the early spring, they become the object of the harvest activity not only of human beings but also of other species. These include dogfish, sturgeon, halibut, cod, porpoise, fin-back whales, orcas, sea lions, seagulls, and, at other seasons, salmon and seals, some of which were harvested in major estuaries such as that of the Nass (Hart 1973, 150). One of the largest annual runs of oolichan on the Pacific coast occurs on the lower Nass River. Many of the neighbouring peoples traditionally journeyed to join the Nisga'a in the harvest, including the Gitksan, Coast Tsimshian, Haida, and Tlingit. Some of the Gitksan and many of the Witsuwit'en obtained oolichan grease from the Haisla-speaking people from Kitimaat, Kemano, and Kitlobe. Regarding the journey over the trail to the Nass, the late Arthur Matthews[8] Sr., Ts'iiwa, explained (Daly 1986-88):

We'd go over the trail in early spring. Everybody did their own fishing. There was so much oolichan that it was more or less open to people from different places. People from here kept gear down there. They'd share forty-foot nets. The nets were set between two canoes and then pulled in. The fish were dipnetted out. If the river was still iced in, the net would be pushed underneath between two holes and tied. The oolichan were left to sit for four or five days in a vat or tub, then boiled with some water. The bones drop to the bottom and the oil was skimmed off. It was put in big grease boxes and the lids were sealed with crushed fish eggs to make them leak-proof. Some of the oolichan were dried on racks, others were salted. We had to pack it all the way back from the Nass – two or three loads in relay.

The availability of fatty flesh placed a limit on local population and ensured that a much wider territory was exploited in the course of each family's seasonal round. The proper management of this cycle of production was a chiefly task and was fundamental to participation in the wider political economy of the region, where, through feasting, barter, and trade, goods were exchanged between various ecological zones. Today the chiefs are still aware of the need to leave a margin of safety in the harvesting of species on their lands, although this has become increasingly difficult, as Pete Muldoe explained in his evidence, due to the rapid expansion of clear-cut logging (Transcripts, 6157-9). The peoples' ability to utilize their lands has been curtailed by utilization by outsiders, with the result that even the diet of the people has been altered towards that of the mainstream society. Among Native populations in British Columbia one finds there has been a change from a major reliance upon fatty wild meats and salmon to carbohydrates – especially sugars and starches (Kuhnlein 1984).

Zone D: Southwestern Witsuwit'en Territory

The biotic area bounded by Smithers on the north, the Bulkley River on the east, Ootsa Lake on the south, and the Coast Range on the west is the Sub-Boreal Spruce Zone (SBS) in the valley bottom elevations. It is noted for warm dry summers and winter temperatures somewhat more moderate than those in the plateau area located further east. In this zone one finds the territories of such Houses as Knedebeas and Gisdaywa as well as parts of the territories of Goohlaht, Hagwilneghl, and Kweese. Prior to European settlement this was an area of open forests and meadows (Hauessler 1986; Hatler 1987), with abundant black huckleberries *(digi)*, soapberries *(niwis)*, and saskatoons *(lhighikh)*. On the mountainous western perimeter there are considerable areas of accessible subalpine forest and alpine tundra, with mountain goat, groundhog, and caribou as well as grizzly and black bear. The valley bottoms yield sockeye – in the Morice in the summer – as well as lake trout, beaver, marten, and muskrat in late winter. The western portion of Zone D, in the Coast Range, has Coastal Western Hemlock vegetation that gives way to Sub-boreal Spruce as one moves east or gains elevation.

Zone E: Southeastern Witsuwit'en Territory

The area marked by Smithers and the Bulkley River at its northwest corner (the lower Babine Range), down to the southeast corner below Burns Lake, and westward below François and Ootsa Lakes is a Sub-Boreal Spruce biotic region contiguous with Zone D. This area sheds water partly into the Skeena drainage and partly into the Fraser drainage. The territory of Namox straddles Zone D and E but is mostly in Zone E, as are portions of the territories of such chiefs as Hagwilneghl, Gitumskanees, Kweese, and Goohlaht. At the southeast corner the Babine Mountains have given way to hills, open forest, and areas of grassland. The general lowland elevation in the southeast is higher than in the west. This is due to the topographical formation of the Nechako Plateau. The southeast has cold dry winters and warm sunny summers devoid of coastal climatic influence. It is an area with deer and moose at the present time and, formerly, was home to caribou. The area supports beaver, ducks, geese, some fur-bearers (seasonally), and hare (year-round). The large lakes dominating this area are spawning sites (some 1,500 kilometres upstream from the estuary near Vancouver) of Fraser River salmon stocks, though the runs appear always to have been sporadic. Late winter ice-fishing on the eastern lakes provides abundant harvests of trout, freshwater ling cod, sucker, and other species. Many Witsuwit'en House groups traditionally used the lakes in this region in late winter. Whitefish are taken in the fall. The southern Witsuwit'en territory, both east and west, is today a major moose wintering area, where the animals forage on willow, poplar, and birch when snowpack impedes other grazing (Andrew George, Mike Morrell, and Dave Hatler, personal communication). Zone E has elevation vegetation consistent with Zone D, except that the valley bottoms are home to Interior Plateau vegetation with climax forests of subalpine fir and spruce, aspen, and lodgepole, and seral Jack pine.

Of the nine main mammal species regularly hunted by these peoples (Hatler 1987) – mule deer (*Odocoileus hemionus* [three subspecies]), hoary marmot, or groundhog *(Marmota caligata);* beaver *(Castor canadensis);* woodland caribou *(Rangifer tarandus);* mountain goat *(Oreamnos americanus);* moose *(Alces alces andersonii* and *Alces alces gigas);* snowshoe hare *(Lepus americanus);* black bear *(Ursus americanus);* and grizzly bear *(Ursus arctos)* – most have adapted to more than one biotic zone. The marmot and the mountain goat are found almost exclusively in the Alpine Tundra. Formerly, mountain goats were said to live at lower forest elevations as well.

Caribou and grizzly may be found in either lower- and mid-elevation forests or Alpine Tundra. The other species are forest dwellers. Beaver, moose, and deer prefer the seral forest with its edible saplings. Moose, for the most part, appear to have moved into the region, or at least to have moved back into the region after the abatement of the "Little Ice Age" (LeRoy Ladurie 1971) that gripped the northern hemisphere from the fifteenth century to the late nineteenth century of the present era.[9] The gradual warming trend of the past century has been accompanied by the arrival and growth of moose (see Figure 24) and a slight decline in the caribou population.

Hatler (1987) indicates that, prior to the construction of rail and highway lines, one important caribou herd ranged seasonally over the Nechako Plateau and the Hazelton and Babine Mountains. Other herds exist in the headwaters of the Stikine, Nass, and Skeena Rivers. The seemingly lowly snowshoe hare is an important item in the diet of the eastern Witsuwit'en and as "trail food" all over the territories.[10] It is an important source of food for lynx and other fur-bearers as well. All the above-mentioned species, with the exception of the moose (the history of which is unclear at the present stage of research), have either a long fossil record or appear in archaeological sites throughout the region (Hatler 1987).

For the most part, the fishes are located in the valley bottom lakes and rivers, though some higher elevation lakes are well supplied with a variety of species. Some berry species are found at virtually every elevation. The same applies to medicinal plants and edible greens, roots, and bulbs.

These biotic zones indicate the resource base of the economy and show the general distribution of essential species on House lands in Gitksan and Witsuwit'en territory. All participants in the subsistence economy at the time of contact required access to salmon and steelhead fishing locations, valley bottom and low elevation forests, mid-elevation forest and meadow-land, and high alpine tundra. The diverse seasonal round required that every-one have access, either through lines of descent or through one's father, to each of these biotic zones. The evidence of Alfred Joseph, Emma Michell, Johnny David, Florence Hall, Bazil Michell, and Alfred Mitchell has indi-cated the way this accessing of different resources at different seasons through links of marriage and descent works across the Witsuwit'en territories, with their various local ecological niches and specialties. The same interlinkage of territorial use pertains among the Gitksan, although, as Tenimget, Art Mathews Jr., explains, the territories of some Houses, such as that of Tenimget/Axti Hiix, have traditionally been so productive that they are called the local banquet table, or *an t'xookxw* (Transcripts, 4777). Moreover, use rights to the various subsistence species have long been granted to many people of different kinship and marriage links to the owners.

Hunting Diversity under Postglacial Conditions

The move from single-species subsistence to a reliance on a diversity of species appears to be a common shift found by archaeologists in various regions. This shift certainly occurred in both northern Europe and northwest British Columbia. Research indicates that postglacial foragers of northern Europe shifted from single-species to foraging diversity and storage after two periods of reliance upon a limited number of species. They moved from ungulate hunting, at least from the recession of the ice until about 9000 BP, to an equally narrow range of aquatic hunting – mainly seals from approxi-mately 9000 BP to 7000 BP. After this point in time the ancestors of today's northern Europeans adopted a multi-species type of hunting economy. They moved to a diversity of harvesting by about 5000 BP (Zvelebil 1986; Tringham 1971) and developed their domestication skills.

The material artifacts left behind by these postglacial diversified Europe-ans reveal a settled, fairly sedentary form of social organization with so-cially differentiated societal features not unlike those of the Gitksan and Witsuwit'en (both archaeologically and as reported in early ethnographic accounts). While technologically foragers, the north Europeans of yester-year – and the Gitksan, the Witsuwit'en, and their ancestors – appear to have enjoyed sophisticated cultures generally associated with "post-foraging" agricultural economies.

The developing archaeological record on the Skeena River region has be-gun to reveal data that tend to corroborate the oral history accounts of millennia-long occupations at such riverside locations as Xsi Gwinixstaat

(Wilson Creek), Laxwiiyip (headwaters of the Nass, Skeena, and Stikine), Gitangasxw (Blackwater), Temla<u>x</u>am (Skeena-Bulkley area), and Dizkle (Skeena-Bulkley) (Albright 1987). The present level of ongoing research permits a cautious anthropological reconstruction of a somewhat similar pattern of diverse resource exploitation by the predecessors of the present-day Gitksan and Witsuwit'en and their neighbours at almost the same time period and under postglacial northern latitudinal conditions similar to those that prevailed in Europe.

Charles Borden (1975, 98-9), who devoted much of his life to the development of archaeology in British Columbia, argues that this highly adaptable microlith culture spread down the coast, following the recession of the ice, from refugia in the Yukon region:

> Accustomed to subsist on the resources of a wide range of habitats, from tundra and steppe to river and lakes, these hardy northerners of Early Boreal Tradition evidently possessed as part of their cultural heritage many of the important technological innovations and other cultural advances and elaborations that had been made in Eurasia and Greater Beringia during the Upper Paleolithic and early Mesolithic ... Equally adept at fishing, fowling, and the hunting and trapping of land mammals, those northern groups, though newly arrived from the interior, were subsistence-technologically preadapted to the exploitation of many of the rich food resources along the northern seaboard.

Technologically, the cultural record over the postglacial northwest was obviously highly complex, revealing a successful hunting system. As Borden concludes: "The distribution in space and time of micro-blade industries, variants of which all Early Boreal groups shared, makes it possible to trace their early southward advance to once-glaciated but evidently still uninhabited parts of the Northwest Coast. The apparent rapidity of this expansion from the Icy Strait region around 9500 BP to Namu at about 9150 BP, and across a broad stretch of open, often storm-tossed water to the Queen Charlottes by at least 8000 BC, suggests these groups possessed seaworthy boats which they evidently were able to handle with considerable skill" (99).

The cultural sequence succeeding the micro-blade period, at Kitselas (4000-3500 BP) and Hagwilget (5000-4500 BP), is also noted for its considerable flexibility of tools. Unfortunately the acid soils of most sites have not preserved the faunal materials, including bone tools, in such a condition that they are easily identifiable. Nevertheless, this sequence, dubbed the "Skeena Complex" by Allaire (1979, 46), shows evidence at Kitselas of caribou, fisher, groundhog, skunk, beaver, hare, black-tail deer, black bear, and a number of large and small mammal bones as well as unidentifiable fish vertebrae.

Both in Europe and on the Northwest Coast postglacial hunting societies were able to overcome inherent instabilities in the environment by combining specialization with wide adaptability to obtain stable access to all the necessary dietary nutrients. In both regions, the diverse hunting economy was marked by flexible, multi-purpose tools side by side with those that were developed to be task-specific. This technology and its organization appear to have led to a stable, quite sedentary, social life, with a degree of social ranking otherwise found only among agriculturalists.

Seasonal Round

The calendar of harvesting activities among the Witsuwit'en and Gitksan follows the changing round of the seasons and the cycles of birth and growth on the land and waterways. Foraged products have been both locally consumed and utilized in interregional barter, trade, and gift exchange. Harmon (Lamb 1957), Brown (n.d.), and Brown (HBC 1822), and other traders of the 1810-30 period describe the diet of salmon, beaver, winter trout, sturgeon, berries, bear, and game with which the Witsuwit'en and their more easterly Carrier neighbours provisioned the traders in the different seasons. They speak of the use of game and beaver in the feasts, and how these feast foods reinforce the connection of the food to the land of the chiefs. Similarly, the coastal traders and missionaries of the early nineteenth century found cultures sustained by ongoing processes of hunting, fishing, and interregional exchange.[11]

Since that time, the annual economic cycle of harvesting from the land has persisted in between, and sometimes in spite of, modern economic pursuits. Wage labouring and small enterprises like working as transporters (backpacking, and later, pack trains of horses and mules), pole-cutting, cannery work, homesteading, and casual labour jobs all fitted into the seasonal round. They did not interfere with salmon and berry appropriation in the summer and fall; hunting in the high country before snowfall in lower-elevation forests in winter; and fishing, trapping, and beaver hunting in the early spring waterways. Today many people live mainly from the proceeds of selling their labour year-round or they receive transfer payments from government agencies, but they still rely upon the land for part of their economic needs and much of their sense of cultural identity.

The seasonal round still involves a flexible system of seeking and granting use permission from the House group's owner-manager chiefs and the reciprocal use of territories by neighbouring chiefs, who often have kinship or marriage links with one another. The seasonal round of hunting, fishing, and gathering is organized socially in relation to the principles of House ownership. The question of who is going to be living and working with whom in any coming season is worked out by reference to kinship relations and House membership.

The Seasonal Round Today

In the winter of 1986-87 I observed Gitksan people in Hazelton regularly giving and receiving fresh steelhead, lake trout, moose meat, and moose liver, and using coast foods like herring eggs, dulce seaweed, and oolichan grease for special dinners. As well, on many occasions I noted spring salmon or sockeye, moose or beaver, either in storage or in preparation for cooking or storage in and around their homes. I enjoyed smoked beaver tail and barbecued moose at a feast in the late winter of 1987 and have kindly been given dry-smoked salmon, half-smoked salmon, frozen salmon, canned salmon, frozen moose steaks, jars of moose broth, preserved venison, and jars of blueberries. When I inquired where these items had been obtained, the hosts of the feasts or the persons who gave me food named the specific territories of origin. Adam Gagnon showed me the rock (and named its House ownership) from which he gaffed the spring salmon in Moricetown Canyon on which I lived for two weeks. Kathleen Matthews told me that certain berry species that they use in the Tenimget/Axti Hiix feasts come from their own territories and that formerly, before the controlled burning of old berry patches was made illegal, all the berries for Tenimget/Axti Hiix feasts came from their own lands. The smoked moose meat at the Delgamuukw funeral feast[12] was provided from the territories on which the Muldoe family members had rights to hunt – the lands of Delgamuukw (maternal, Lax Se'el Clan rights) and Gitludahl (paternal, Gisk'aast Clan rights).

Despite involvement in the modern Canadian economy, the peoples continue to pursue the seasonal round for foodstuffs. They are no longer able to utilize it legally as a source of goods for trade. The Gitksan and Witsuwit'en have been removed from traditional lands and proletarianized. What they have to sell in the market is basically their own labour power. The labour market, particularly the forest industry, is highly unstable and provides very partial and temporary security. This situation reinforces local insistence on the necessity of retaining their hunting and fishing skills, their ties to and ownership of the land, as Niist, David Blackwater, maintains (below).

In the 1850s gold exploration brought a certain amount of cash to the Gitksan and Witsuwit'en as guides, trail builders, and packers. Hankin opened his fur trading post near the confluence of the Skeena and Bulkley Rivers in 1866. The Collins Overland Telegraph Company's survey and construction began in 1865, from Quesnel to Fort Fraser, Hagwilget, and Kispiox. It halted north of Kispiox in October 1866, when the dream-destroying news of the successful laying of a transatlantic telegraph cable reached Collins, thereby ending the plan for a communications link between North America and Europe via Siberia. Coastal fish cannery employment began in 1876 and grew rapidly, employing Gitksan and Witsuwit'en people as well as indigenous peoples from along the coast for an intense period of six or seven weeks each summer.

There then followed a period of prospecting. Gold was pursued at Omenica; speculators opened the Lorne Creek Mine below Gitwangax in the 1880s; some wage work was provided by government mapping and survey crews that went through the area in the 1870s and 1880s. Later, the telegraph line was completed to the Yukon, with maintenance and provisioning supplying a little seasonal work until 1936. Road and rail construction provided sporadic wage work. During the riverboat era at the end of the nineteenth century and almost to the First World War, the Gitksan earned some cash for cutting cordwood for fuel needed along the paddle-steamer route between tidewater and the Hazelton terminus.

These intrusions into the indigenous economy were both ephemeral and seasonal. They did not disrupt the seasonal rounds of hunting and fishing, though they may have led to an increasing concentration upon the nuclear family as a unit of production. They also introduced new technology: guns, iron tools, horses, manufactured clothing, garden produce, flour, sugar, tea, and cook stoves. Cordwood cutting and garden preparation were done in the spring while people got ready for the season of river fishing. Freighting and packing involved large numbers of men and pack dogs in spring and summer and the use of snowshoes and sleds in late winter. Road work, gardening, and, later, cannery work at the coast entailed intense labour for about six weeks in the summer.

None of these activities eclipsed or eliminated the seasonal round, though some, like cannery work, involved some adjustment of labour within the extended family to ensure that all the needed goods were procured to see the family through the winter. The necessary production activities at this period involved gardening, salmon-smoking, grease-rendering, game-drying, and cash acquisition for new winter staples. These activities were coordinated by the greater family composed of local House members and affines. At the end of the nineteenth century the major Gitksan and Witsuwit'en occupation was still listed by the Department of Indian Affairs as "hunting." It is the opinion of geographer and historian Robert Galois (1978, 18) that, through this period, the people continued to make effective use of their traditional resource base.

Entrepreneurial activities and wage labour did not in themselves effect dramatic changes in Gitksan and Witsuwit'en social relations; rather, it was the accompanying social institutions of the Canadian society that had greatest consequence. These included the establishment of "reserves," the sedentary effect of church and school, corporal punishment of children caught speaking their own language at school, and the general tutelage of the Department of Indian Affairs (DIA) administration, as well as increasing pressure on the land by settlers and corporations. These are the factors most salient to the peoples' reduced "traditional" exploitation of the hunting territories in the present century.

The modern seasonal round of the Witsuwit'en has been more severely curtailed because their forest lands have been extensively transformed by non-Native settlement, clearing, homesteading (including land scrip awarded to veterans of the Boer War), mining, and logging; and the Department of Fisheries and Oceans has reduced the fishing potential on the Bulkley River due to blasting, thereby doing away with the rocks that formed the back eddies and pools where salmon formerly congregated to rest on the way upstream.

However, in other Witsuwit'en areas, as Alfred Mitchell and Madeline and Henry Alfred testified, where the degree of settlement and change has not been as intense, the territories continue to be hunted, trapped, fished, and enjoyed for their power and beauty, their berries, bulbs, and medicines. Henry Alfred, Wedexget, for instance, explained to the court how he had to change his trapline route and cut a new trail so as to avoid large cut-block logging operations on his territory in the late 1970s (Transcripts, 2979). Despite these changes Henry Alfred goes on doing his best to trap and hunt his territory.

The seasonal round stubbornly persists despite the pressures exerted by fishing, hunting, and trapping regulations. And the skills necessary for its future are passed on by men to sons and nephews, and by women to their daughters. This production know-how, or "bush smarts," persists to a considerable extent because it has to do with the land and the challenge to each individual to make a success of the subsistence activities and memories inherited from forefathers and foremothers. The seasonal round of hunting and fishing remains an important feature of the informal domestic economy today, as the following example indicates.

David Blackwater, Simoogit Niist of the Guldo'o Wolf Clan, was raised on the hunting territories in the north and schooled there by his grandparents in the 1930s. This training was based on a deeply established tradition of technical, historical, and topographical knowledge of the territories and their species, as well as on a knowledge of the techniques necessary for survival. It also included elements of the European way of life and technology: rifles, knives, axes, steel traps, flour, tea, sugar. It involved transport into the hunting areas by horse and the subsequent sale of furs to supply the necessary provisions for the next season (or to pay for what had been advanced at the start of the previous season). This way of life developed during the nineteenth century, having emerged from the traditional seasonal round and the fur trade. It became a new tradition in the area among both Aboriginals and non-Aboriginals. (David's early years are discussed below.)

David's life changed quite suddenly after the deaths of his grandparents when he was fourteen. He then went to work for his father, for no pay, bucking logs with a crosscut saw, until he obtained a job during the 1940s in a small sawmill that paid him one dollar a day plus room and board. Two years later he took up cannery work at the coast between mid-June and August. David worked summers at Sunnyside Cannery until 1956 when, with a young family to support, he moved to Cassiar Cannery where the season was a bit longer. In the winters, back in Kispiox, he worked in sawmills and became a sawyer, and worked on pole-cutting subcontracts for a man who sold cedar poles to the BC Telephone Company. He has worked as a timber faller since 1960 for several different logging companies. Some of these ventures have been run by Gitksan, whether as private companies or as band-organized logging and sawmill operations. (The present-day large-scale concerns have eliminated most of these small forestry operations.)

To an outsider this work biography might appear to be divorced from the old seasonal round of activities in which David participated as a child. The economic reality for David's family was more complex, however, because it involved its continuing reliance upon a land-based, informal economy. Through the whole of the 1950s, as well as the 1960s, David and his family planted their gardens and entrusted the success of their vegetable patches to people to whom they were related and who were not going to the coast to fish or work in the canneries. They would give coast foods and purchased commodities to relatives in return for salmon caught and prepared along the upper Skeena. (Most cannery workers took berries and salmon strips and hides to the coast to exchange for coast foods.)

David's family also used to hunt, and they continue to hunt each winter for moose and each spring for beaver. As well, they have tried to put up as much salmon as possible, fishing on the Skeena before the cannery season and trading some of the resulting smoked strips for coast foods and oolichan grease from Kitimat or the Nass. David has gained permission from the chief of the House that owns an accessible territory nearby in the Kispiox Valley to enter that land from time to time so that he can teach his son to hunt and trap. Throughout the late 1940s and up to 1960, David regularly went to the family's own northern territories with his parents to help them out with the winter trapping, spending long periods in the hunting grounds and even quitting jobs in order to be able to do this.

The Witsuwit'en Seasonal Round (1820-1950)
There are sources of information on the Witsuwit'en seasonal round in the early-nineteenth-century contact period that can be used to supplement the data available in the form of recollections of the elderly. The seasonal round of the last century has been described by Morice (1888-89, 1892-93) in relation to the material culture of the contact period, and Jenness (1943, 530-2). The Hudson's Bay Company records also make reference to the Witsuwit'en beaver hunt in the 1820s, and the difficulty the trading post factors confronted when they tried to persuade the senior chiefs to sell their beaver rather than "stubbornly to conserve them" for feasts (HBC 1822,

107ff.). Trader Brown also reported (HBC 1822, B/11/e/2) his reconnaissance visit to the Bulkley, recording that the Babines and Witsuwit'en assembled regularly at villages on the river for the salmon fishing season and to hold their feasts before going out to their winter encampments on the land.

The oral history of the Witsuwit'en is couched in the activities of everyday life. Historically significant events appear to have occurred in the course of the annual economic cycle while the people were on their way to their camps from Moricetown, while they hunted caribou, beaver, and bears; while they consumed the ever-present hare, caught fish, took lake trout (and dried them and the roe), dug wild potatoes and ate them with the roe, and dried chinook salmon at Moricetown Canyon. This oral tradition also reveals a preoccupation with food shortages in winter and with the importance of guarding and sharing whatever dried food remained in times of want. In years of shortages, journeys were undertaken to obtain end-of-winter foods from the coast: seaweed and dried clams, oolichan and oolichan grease – either from the Nass or from the Haisla peoples at Kemano and Kitimat. One such journey to Gitlaxdamks on the Nass River to obtain oolichan from the Nisga'a in the nineteenth century was recorded by Jenness in 1924 (Jenness 1943, 479-80).

Summer and Autumn

In describing the Witsuwit'en seasonal harvests and movements, it is useful to apply the provisional paradigm sketched out by Martin Weinstein in relation to the Beaver people (Denne-za) and utilized by Hugh Brody (1986) for the Witsuwit'en. The contours of this cycle of seasonal activities and travels reflect conditions after missionization, when people tended to return to the village for the Christmas season. My interviews have confirmed the accuracy of this model. However, the pattern of residence depicted here was influenced by the new seasonal opportunities afforded by the late nineteenth-century economy and the gradual settlement of the people for longer periods of the year at Moricetown (Kya Wiget) and Hagwilget (Tse Kya). Prior to the establishment of reserves, these were mainly summer fishing settlements.

Fur species had been trapped and prepared mainly for local daily use as food and clothing material and for feast gifts until fur trading centres were established on the coast and in the interior following the burst of sea otter trading at the close of the eighteenth century. Some pelts and, of course, tanned hides had long been gifts and trade items between Gitksan and Witsuwit'en and their neighbours (e.g., Boas 1916, Introduction). In the 1820s the newly consolidated Hudson's Bay Company opened trading centres at Fort St. James, Fort Fraser on Fraser Lake, Fort Kilmaurs ("Old Fort") on Babine Lake, and Fort Connolly at Bear Lake. Shortly thereafter, the coastal posts at Fort Simpson and Metlakatla armed and outfitted certain Tsimshian trader chiefs who travelled the Skeena by canoe and regularly enticed and intimidated the Witsuwit'en and, to some extent, the Gitksan to trade their furs and hides and to barter regular foodstuffs. What they received in return were coastal specialties and trade goods.

In the nineteenth century the Witsuwit'en and their Fort Babine relatives would return to their fishing communities of Hagwilget (Tse Kya) and Moricetown (Kya Wiget) in mid-June and fish the respective canyons with dip-nets, basket traps, gaffs, and jigs. They fished and processed their catch through the spring salmon and sockeye runs until mid-August. The Witsuwit'en report that, prior to the coming of the Europeans, many of their ancestors went to the Moricetown fishery only every second or third year, obtaining needed salmon by exchanging dried game and hides, and functioning as territory caretakers through the summer.

This general pattern continued into the twentieth century. Alfred Joseph gave evidence that some of his uncles and grandparents lived all year round at Owen Lake on their Kaiyexweniits land (Transcripts, 2238). This indicates an economy with a certain informal division of labour in which part of the family could stay on the land and part go to the fishing sites. Alternatively, family members could take turns in various economic activities for a specific season (with the understanding that the fruits of these various activities would benefit the broader family and serve its overall economic and social needs).

The Witsuwit'en salmon fishery is centred today on Moricetown Canyon. About 1820, due to a rockslide on the lower Bulkley, the salmon did not pass through Moricetown as was customary. The Witsuwit'en responded to this disaster by temporarily going to live with relatives both in the Hazelton area and on Babine Lake. William Brown of the HBC Babine trading post spoke of the failure of the salmon on the Bulkley and the arrival of Witsuwit'en families at Babine. On 17 January 1823 he noted in his journal (HBC:B/11/a/1:66): "There being no salmon this year in Simpson's River [Bulkley River] the greatest part of the Natives of that place have come over to the Lake to live." This was apparently a temporary solution to the problem because Sats'aan of one of the two Witsuwit'en Frog Clans travelled to Hagwilget Canyon to meet with his clan brother, Gyedimgaldo'o of the Gitanmaax Lax̲ Se'el. They asked permission of the Gitanmaax Frog and Wolf chiefs for their people to fish in the canyon since the salmon were not getting through the slide to Kya Wiget, Moricetown. Barbeau's informant, Peter John, said "there was too much water and the people above the canyon at Hagwelgate [sic] starved." Peter John had learned this history from an old lady who had witnessed the meeting when she was a child (Barbeau and Beynon n.d., BF-89.22): "The chief of the Hagwelgate [Witsuwit'en] was Sedza'n [Sats'aan]. Sedza'n took a present to each of the chief [sic] – a reindeer skin. And these he presented before exchanging them for permission to come and move to the canyon as the fish was gone from where they were ..."

So upon that, Sedza'n returned to his people. He told them the fact that there was much fish on the other side of the canyon and that he had received Galomgaldo [Gyedimgaldo'o]'s permission to move near the canyon and fish on the other side. That is why they are there today. Before that the Gitksan used both sides of the canyon."

The informant goes on to say that Gyedimgaldo'o and other Frog Clan chiefs held fishing sites on the right bank of the river and that the Wolf Clan and Gisk̲'aast (Fireweed) held them on the left, or Hagwilget, side. The Witsuwit'en worked to open the river channel at the slide as well as fishing at Hagwilget. They fished consistently in that location until the blasting of the rock in the canyon in the mid-1950s. Probably many Witsuwit'en had fished at Hagwilget long before this slide. There have long been marriages between bordering Gitksan and Witsuwit'en House groups, and each clan assisted its counterpart across the line whenever a funeral feast was held (Barbeau and Beynon 1915-57, BF-89.16). The Witsuwit'en established the Hagwilget Canyon village at an old site of habitation, with permission from the Gitksan at Gitanmaax, after the Bulkley River rockslide around 1820 (Figure 28). The newer village of Hagwilget (Figure 27) was established at the top of the canyon.

The oil-rich spring salmon, or chinook, is the first salmon species of the season to be caught not only by the Witsuwit'en but also by the Gitksan. The chinook run is overlapped by the dominant species, the sockeye, which reaches the area in late June and early July. For the Bulkley-Morice part of the Skeena system, this sockeye run, together with the springs, is the main source of salmon taken annually from the rivers. On the Skeena River itself, and on its Babine tributary, a later migration of sockeye arrives in mid-July and passes through the system to its spawning grounds by early August. This "second run" is the main source of the salmon the Gitksan put up for winter storage. Enough sockeye were taken traditionally to feed the immediate residential group through the winter, to provide for the elderly and all those unable to catch and process sufficient quantities for themselves, to have sufficient on hand to meet sudden feast and gift obligations, and for barter with other peoples. When this quantity of fish had been taken (and during the processing when no fishing occurred), the weirs would be opened and traps pulled out to allow the salmon run to carry on its journey upstream, ultimately to the spawning beds.

The sockeye fishing usually stops/stopped when the sheer volume of pink salmon (humpback), a species that is not usually of good quality in the rivers, made/makes sockeye fishing onerous. In the autumn, after the berry season and the groundhog trapping, coho salmon were (and are, though in fewer numbers) taken as they return to their place of birth to spawn the next generation. The sea-going steelhead trout come up the Skeena system in the late summer and fall and stay in the river until their spring spawning season. They are smoked and dried, as well as eaten fresh during the winter months.

The late fall fish, especially coho and steelhead, were often allowed to freeze on the ground in the night frost, then stored whole in earth pits or root cellars until needed. Another anadromous species (those that ascend the rivers from the sea for purposes of breeding) used quite extensively as a smoked storage food by the Witsuwit'en is the lamprey eel. Eels were taken especially at Hagwilget and by the Gitksan further downstream by regular fishers such as those in the House of Tenimget at Wilson Creek (Transcripts, 4635-7). Today, the western Gitksan give eels to the Witsuwit'en in exchange for smoked meats, tanned hides, and beaded craft-work. Traditionally, the variety of species available, and the staggered nature of the runs, allowed those people who for one reason or another did not harvest sufficient fish at their own normal location to make arrangements to borrow sites elsewhere so as to participate in one of the other runs.

Even at the height of the long fishing season the weirs were often opened and the traps pulled up and the gaffs laid down; today, in addition, the nets are pulled so that the processing and smoking work can catch up. The bottleneck in the production process has been the labour-intensive work involved in carrying out the many steps that go into the preparation of the red-fleshed salmon, as well as the many specific tasks needed for the gourmet preparation of special portions of the fish.

Some berry-picking would begin at the end of July and continue into September (in the vicinity of the villages), though the bulk of the berry harvest occurred back in the Witsuwit'en territories themselves. Meanwhile on the Bulkley River (Wedzenkwe) the salmon harvest continued and, with it, quantities of lamprey eel and steelhead were taken. September was, and is, the time for coho and increased numbers of steelhead.

Hagwilget and Moricetown pulsated with activity through July and August, both in terms of production and processing of foodstuffs and concentrated feast-giving. Here is what the Witsuwit'en told Jenness (1943, 531) about the month of July: "This month, and the month following, were periods of abundance, when the diet of salmon could be varied with fresh berries, with wild rice *(diankatl)*, and with the roasted roots of the wild parsnip *(djanyankotl)* and of the *djinitlrets*, an unidentified plant whose root attains the size of a pumpkin ... many days and nights were given over to ceremonies and potlatches, attended not only by all the villagers, but by numerous guests from neighbouring sub-tribes."

It was customary at Kya Wiget, Moricetown, for each of the leading chiefs to organize a feast to honour the first salmon to be caught by the House of that chief. (Today, Moricetown generally has a first salmon "fun" feast for all the surrounding people, including passing tourists, where the salmon are venerated, the neighbours hosted, and the Fisheries officers roasted.)

The fishing season began with a feast each night, hosted by a different chief. Lilloos, Emma Michell, mother of Wigetimschol, Dan Michell, says that in the days before the Moricetown fish ladder was constructed her grandmother, Chief Wilat, and Mooseskin Johnny, who held the name of Kweese – also of the Tsayu clan – had smokehouses on opposite sides of the canyon. They would host first salmon feasts and call all the clans to attend. The spring salmon would be cooked the day after it was caught and cut up into small pieces to be shared by the guests. Mrs. Michell said that they still cut up the first spring salmon and give away pieces, but it is not done with much ceremony. She explained that in 1986 she received some of the first salmon, which was caught and prepared the traditional way lower down the river system and given to her family by Gitsegukla people (Daly 1986-88). The contemporary first salmon ceremony was described in court by Ha'naamuxw (Transcript, 5026-7).

The spring and summer season was the time for collecting plant foods, the source of all carbohydrate and most vitamins and minerals in the Aboriginal diet in these territories. The most important item was the variety of abundant berries, rosehips, and crabapples ripe for picking from late July to September at different elevations. At mid-elevation (about 1,000 metres) the black huckleberry *(Vaccinium membranaceum)* is dominant on the moist sides of the Skeena and Bulkley Valleys. This sweet, easily dried and preserved berry has always been a major item of trade to the coast, where its high sugar content is much prized. The prominent berries of the lower elevations are the sweet dwarf blueberry *(Vaccinium caespitosum)*; the soapberry *(Shepherdia canadensis)* – valued for its taste and its ability to form a stiff pink froth when whipped; the saskatoon *(Amelanchier alnifolia)*; kinnikinnick *(Arctostaphylos uva-ursi)*; and the high bush cranberry *(Vibernum edule)*.

Most berry species, as well as rosehips and crabapples, were prepared by pulping and heating them to a boil, then spreading the pulp on large leaves spread on racks over a cool smoky fire. The dried berry sheets were rolled and stored in ground pits until needed, as were rice-root bulbs, hazelnuts, fern-root, and hemlock sap cakes composed of pounded and mashed cambium of young, sun-exposed western hemlock. Sometimes this was mixed with fireweed syrup and formed into rectangular cakes dried and stored like berries. Large quantities of both berries and hemlock sap cakes were prepared annually (Book Builders of 'Ksan 1980).

The cambium layer of pine and balsam would be stripped from the tree's south side and eaten fresh, usually in the month of June. It is said to taste fresh and sweetish and to have the consistency of noodles (see Afterword by Don Ryan).

The tempo of interaction between the Witsuwit'en of Hagwilget and their eastern neighbours (other Carrier peoples and the Sekani) increased in the nineteenth century. New European goods from the coast, as well as traditional coastal foods like dulce (dried seaweed) and oolichan, were exchanged for the berries and the hides that traders needed for trade with other Aboriginal groups. Some wage labour was available in the Hazelton area as well. These new economic opportunities, together with the superb fishing conditions created at Hagwilget as a result of the landslide on the Bulkley in the 1820s, drew most of the Witsuwit'en population to Tse Kya (Hagwilget) for longer periods of residency than was normal in earlier times.

Autumn

The headwaters Witsuwit'en people, who travelled down to the Morice, Ootsa, and François Lakes in the days before the vast Alcan (Aluminum Company of Canada) hydroelectric inundations, would generally pack up their stores of dried fish at Moricetown and Hagwilget and head south before the end of August. For some of the families this was a journey of two or three weeks to their home areas. Travel was shortened by the introduction of horses, although the cutting of hay for the winter provisioning of these horses then became a necessity. Haying occupied the time saved by travelling with horses compared to packing on foot. Later, rail travel and the automobile shortened the journey yet again.

In the period from contact to the end of the Second World War, the technology of hunting and trapping changed, but the calendar of economic activities retained its overall features. After this period, increasing settlement and land clearing, as well as hydroelectric floodings, mines, and extensive logging, radically altered the seasonal round of many Witsuwit'en. However, until the past few decades, many families remained out on the land until the following June. After tending to the haying (in the era of the horse) and to berry-picking, the families would spend some weeks camped at high altitudes hunting groundhog and mountain goat, and picking alpine berries. (August was known as *Binin dzilh K'its tsitidilh*, "the mountain-going time.") When the families were established at their lakeside settlements the men would hunt caribou and mountain goat through October and November. November and December would also be the first months for trapping, especially for marten and ermine.

Those people who wintered to the southeast, in the Topley and Burns Lake area, would fish the spawning whitefish (the September-October moon is known as "Small round Whitefish" *[hlots uze']*); then they would hunt groundhog and pursue caribou and deer in the Babine Forest until snowfall. Those with territories closer to Moricetown – east of the Bulkley River, up towards the Suskwa, and west around Hudson Bay Mountain, McDonnell Lake, and the Gitsegukla Valley – would follow similar pursuits up to December. Some of these people used Kya Wiget as their autumn base camp, thereby diminishing the amount of packing of needed dried foods and equipment during the fall season.

When I asked Andrew George, Tsibasa, if the annual economic cycle of the Witsuwit'en revolved around the villages of Hagwilget and Moricetown, he replied that the Witsuwit'en regarded Moricetown and Hagwilget not as home villages but as summer fishing sites. He said that the "real" home sites were spread over the territories. People returned to these settlements immediately after the salmon run. He added that life was centred on the hunting grounds. The river villages were used mainly for fishing, fish processing, and feasts; people with territories in the vicinity, like Chief Henry Alfred today, also took small game and picked berries. Tsibasa described the exodus to the south in late August as people went home to spend the winter on the giving land.

Winter and Early Spring
Throughout the pre–Second World War era winter was the time of prime consumption of the stored protein, fat, and carbohydrates gathered the previous summer. This included the dried flesh, the oil substances, the berries and crabapples preserved in oil, the dried rolls of berries and sap cakes, the soapberries (which could be soaked in water, then whipped with oil and snow), the fern-root and rice-root, and the accumulated coast foods. The spiritual and symbolic significance, along with the sense of well-being, denoted by the possession of fat and berries has been observed in many Aboriginal cultures of North America (Hamell 1983). Among both the Gitksan and the Witsuwit'en, rendered grease and berries, items of high value whose production traditionally entails a high labour investment and a foreign demand, symbolized the blood and life force in ceremonial events.

Until well into the present century, the villages were empty in February and March, during the height of the trapping and winter hunting season. At the end of this period people on the more northerly territories would return to the villages to prepare the fishing sites and gear, to gather firewood, and to do some steelhead fishing. Some of these people may occasionally have travelled to the Nass with Gitksan parties at this time of year in order to engage in the oolichan fishery or to barter for grease at Gitksan "grease distribution centres" such as Gitanyow/Kitwancool, Gitsegukla, and Kispiox. Most Witsuwit'en, however, would be more likely to receive oolichan grease at winter's end through the network of gift-giving in the region, which took the form of a flow of foodstuffs between Houses, clans, and villages. The Morice, Nanika, and Tahtsa Lake Witsuwit'en obtained oolichan grease from the Haisla, traversing the steep trail (Poudrier 1891, maps) to the coast where the Haisla fished them in the Kitimat, Kemano, and Kitlope Arms of the fjord, the Gardner Canal. As well, some oolichan made their way into southern Witsuwit'en territory from Kimsquit on Dean Channel near Bella Coola. Late in the winter of 1990, I accompanied Witsuwit'en men on a successful mission to Kitimat Village to ask permission to come for oolichan and to assist with the fishing, which was expected to begin within the coming fortnight.

Late Spring
In late winter and early spring, the bulk of the stored fat and carbohydrates has generally been consumed. The remaining stores of dried fish and game strips may now be dipped in recently acquired oolichan grease, rendered beaver fat, bear grease, or specially aged fish eggs. Those who are wintering on the land near a lake are able to supplement their fat supply with spawning trout and, to a greater degree, with the oil-rich liver of the freshwater ling cod. Stefansson (1945, 235) refers to the importance of cod liver oil in winter: "A thing known to some Europeans is a common place in the North, that cod liver is the most delicious form of fat. The greatest of all delicacy is the liver of the fresh water cod, the ling."

From late April through the month of May, men who had come back to the village to prepare for the summer fishery would go out from the villages again to hunt beaver. Headwaters people, however, were already out on the land; they would continue their beaver hunting before moving to the larger, more easterly lakes for concentrated fishing. At this season they took a variety of lake species, used fresh and stored and prepared either by combining sun- and frost-drying in the open air or smoke-drying. Hare and some fowl would supplement the diet at this season. In southeastern Witsuwit'en country, lake fish provided the mainstay of the diet in the spring prior to the return of the salmon fishing on the Bulkley.

Following the spring breakup, people gradually made their way back downstream to Moricetown and Hagwilget for a summer of fishing and berry-picking, feasting and preparing marriages, paying debts and planning the next winter's hunt. I have been told that if people had to travel in the spring before the snow melted, they would try to do so by moving downriver with cottonwood canoes made on the spot so as to avoid deep wet snow and mud, and to save energy, time, and food supplies. Otherwise, spring travel was onerous; progress could be made only during the night and the early morning hours while the snow was cold and hard.

Typical Witsuwit'en Seasonal Rounds
The Witsuwit'en clans all had general patterns of seasonal movement for the harvesting of different species within and between their territories (see, for example, Commission Evidence: Emma Michell I: 16-23, 30, 62, 65; II: 6; IV: 134; V: 138; Johnny David III: 59-67; Bazil Michell I: 32-44, 54-71). According to Emma Michell, in her lifetime and that of her grandparents before her, the House of Kweese of the Tsayu Clan would leave Kya Wiget

and Tse Kya at the end of summer and move southwest up the Telkwa River to Mooseskin Johnny Lake on a tributary of the Telkwa. On their territory in this region, around the Burnie Lakes and Eagle Peak (in the high Coast Range separating the Witsuwit'en from their Haisla neighbours on the Gardner Canal), they hunted bear and mountain goat. In late fall, they moved to their lands at Goosley Lake, south of Houston. Here they passed the winter months fishing through the lake ice for trout, sucker, freshwater ling cod, and other species; at the same time they trapped and hunted.

In the spring they made their way east – usually joining relatives on the way – to Maxan Lake, Rose Lake, and finally Decker Lake, where their target was the rainbow trout assembling in preparation for spawning. They also took suckers at this time. The April-May moon is known as *gusgï uze'*, or Sucker Moon. This late winter lake fishing seems to have been entirely consistent with the practices of more eastern Athapaskan groups. Harmon (Lamb 1957, 140) notes of the Stuart Lake people: "June 16, 1811: our Indians who about the middle of April (as I am informed they are wont to do every year about this Season) left their Village to go and live upon fish that they take out of the small Lakes no great distance from this, now begin to come in as they say that the season has arrived that they cannot take fish at those places."

The fish were smoked and, along with the trout roe, were prepared as trail food for the leisurely downstream return to Moricetown, which the people would reach in time to prepare for the summer salmon runs at the canyon. June and July were known as *bining kyet:* "when the salmon come up" (Jenness 1943). (More probably: *binin c'itcis:* "Moulting Moon" when cottonwood and other fluff is blowing [May-June], Sharon Hargus, personal communication.)

The Gilserhyu Frog Clan members from the headwaters country, who are known as the Unistot'en (people of distant water), left Moricetown annually in August and moved down to the headwaters of the Morice and its tributaries for autumn hunting. They then worked eastward on different combinations of their own and their in-laws' land, to Ootsa and François Lakes, before once again returning to Moricetown for the brief salmon season.

The Wolf Clan House members, the Gitdumden, moved in a somewhat narrower circuit, closer to the Bulkley and the Morice, from Moricetown to Lake Kathlyn near the present Smithers airport, to Tyee Lake at Telkwa, up the Morice River system and to Bulkley Lake at the Bulkley headwaters.

The Laksilyu Small Frog Clan chiefs moved to their own specific winter lake sites: Wedexkw'ets to Round Lake; Gitdumskanees, who, through the nineteenth century, travelled from Hagwilget to his winter territory at Burns Lake and his Dikyanulat territory at Dennis Lake.

The Laksamshu Fireweed/Killer Whale Clan House members wintered on their respective territories, including such locations as the important winter village of Lhë Tait, "The Crossroads," north of Houston and south of

Grouse Mountain. They also wintered in the area between the Parrott Lakes and François Lake, along the south shore of François Lake and between Tahtsa and Troitsa Lakes.

It bears repeating that, due to the flexible system of sharing and reciprocating with seasonal use rights to hunting territories, members of each House, and each territory group within a House unit, had the option (given the practice of leaving fallow specific mountains and watersheds, especially for bear, groundhog, marten, and beaver) of spending the bulk of the winter with either a set of in-laws, with their father's kin (that of their senior male member's wife or of her respective father), or simply with their own chief or one of the counsellor chiefs of the House (the evidence of Alfred Mitchell provides many examples of the options open to hunters and trappers during any one winter). This seasonal pattern is consistent with those of neighbouring cordilleran Athapaskan peoples like the Tahltan (MacLachlan 1981; Adlam 1985), Inland Tlingit (McClelland 1981a), Tagish (McClelland 1981b), and Tutchone (McClelland 1981c), although the degree of reliance on salmon differed from region to region.

The Gitksan Seasonal Round (1820-1950)

Spring and Summer
The spring and summer in the western Gitksan areas have been devoted to river fishing as far back as people can remember.[13] Antgulilibix's testimony about the names of the months of the growing season (Transcripts, 804-6) indicates the general seasonal concerns that have become fixed in the Gitksan language: "*Lasa hu'mal* – March, when you can get around by canoe; *Lasa ya'a* – April, when you start to catch spring salmon; *Lasa yanja* – May, when the leaves come out; *Lasa maa'y* – June, when the berries are forming up; *Lasa 'wiihun* – July, when the fishes come up the 'Ksan; *Lasa lik'i'nsxw*, when the grizzly bears come around and they kill them; *Lasa gangwiikxw*, when they begin to hunt groundhogs."

The spring harvest season begins with steelhead trout fishing in the rivers. Martha Brown (Commission II, 31) said that her grandmother would take three hundred steelhead from her special fishing site on the Kispiox River. This was a deep pool where she trapped and netted the fish under the ice in early March. Steelhead fishing occurs in the early spring today to provide welcome fresh fish after the winter.

The Gitksan go to their fishing sites as soon as the weather gets warm, usually towards the end of April, to take spring salmon and steelhead, as well as to cut wood and to prepare for the summer fishing (note woodpiles in Figure 30). In the past, and as recently as the 1930s (before the practice was discouraged by Fisheries officials and before the warm weather brought the late spring flood to the river), part of these preparations involved setting the fish weir across the river under the direction of the chief (Richard Benson, Commission, 12-3). The young men would pound the stakes in the riverbed with specially formed sledgehammer stones, some of which are part of the archaeological record of the whole Northwest Coast region (Duff 1975, 183). Today these items are to be found in the art museums of the world, but for several thousand years they were used annually to drive the fish weir pilings into the riverbeds and into the mud of tidal estuaries on the coast.

Today in the Gitwangax area the Skeena is too broad and deep to be spanned by a fish weir, but before the nineteenth century (which saw the end of the climatic cooling trend called the "Little Ice Age," the presence of which was felt across the northern hemisphere between the Middle Ages and approximately 1850 AD [LeRoy Ladurie 1971, 222-3], the river had a much smaller flow. Elderly people remark today that the glaciers have receded drastically in their own lifetime. The early spring was also the time for firing those berry patches that the senior matron had assessed to be in need of clearing from the advancing forest. It was also the time for burning insect-infested stands of trees before the larvae hatched and spread (Daly 1986-88, Mathews interviews; and Don Ryan's Afterword).

People usually stayed at the fishing sites through the spring and summer, catching, dressing, and smoking each species as it came through (see Figures 29, 31, and 32). The second sockeye run is followed by the arrival of pink, or humpback, salmon. At this point, people stopped fishing and turned to berry-picking. This shift from fish to berries remains a feature of the present-day seasonal round. Sometimes Gitksan people continue to fish the pinks and leave them at certain locations near the river for the bears, who, in recent years, "don't get enough to eat." People report that the bears are skinny due to a decline in the customary quantity of spawned-out salmon carcasses to feed upon (the spent bodies of the fish used to line the river banks in the days prior to the commercial fishery at the coast).

Like their upstream neighbours, the Gitksan concentrated their summer economic activities in the river valleys, harvesting salmon, berries, and other plant items. The importance of the salmon runs to both nations is expressed by the location of the villages at strategic fishing sites along the Skeena at some of its tributaries. Able-bodied persons of all ages participated in the harvest of the salmon runs and the berry crop. These quality fishing sites all coincide with the Hazelton Variant of the Interior Cedar-Hemlock Biogeoclimatic Zone.

In the late nineteenth century the summer also became the season of gardening. (By this time, both peoples planted vegetables that they could store for the winter so as to add variety and useful carbohydrates to the winter diet, particularly potatoes, carrots, and turnips.) Both Gitksan and Witsuwit'en also engaged in freight packing in the nineteenth century, which entailed the maintenance of horses and occasionally a few head of cattle – all of which had to be supplied with hay.

A phenomenal amount of labour was expended in a matter of a few summer weeks. Martha Brown, X̱hliimlax̱ha, explained that she and her mother would annually process 3,000 sockeye for the family's winter needs, usually in a three-week period beginning in late July, then smoke between 1,000 and 2,000 humpbacks for dog food over the winter. Then, by way of holiday, they would pick and smoke-dry forty to sixty pack-loads of berries.

The sockeye and spring salmon preparation was, and still is, highly labour-intensive. I observed the following process at Gwin'oop fish camp at the confluence of the Kispiox and Skeena Rivers in July 1986. The first stage – *pt'ikw* – involves dressing the fish, which have been allowed to stiffen in the river, and hanging them in a smokehouse on a sapling pole (which has been thrust through the tails) for the day over a small smouldering fire. (In Kisgagas Canyon the sockeye could be hung to dry in the constant river wind [Figure 32] – Wii Gaak, N.S. Sterritt, personal communication.) Then the fish are wiped down and cut. Two fillet strips are taken and each remaining side of the fish is partly filleted again so that the flesh opens out flat in four attached panels cut away from the bones. Women from each House group have their characteristic identifying marks in the cutting technique, as Tenimget reports (Transcripts, 4652). (The thin fillets and panels dry rapidly, thus minimizing the chance of spoilage.)

The fish are then hung back in the smokehouse fairly close to the smoke. Later they are bundled and hung from the top racks of the smokehouse until fully dried. The fire must be kept cool and smouldering "just right" day and night to guard, on the one hand, against overheating (which ruins the fish) and, on the other hand, "under-smoking" (too little smoke enables the flies to attack the flesh and transform it into maggots). Each phase of the operation is carried out in lots of forty fish (by both Gitksan and Witsuwit'en). Gift and barter items composed of sockeye and steelhead are packed in bundles of forty. In the Gitksanimx language the word for a bundle of forty is *kil'dahl* (Martha Brown Commission III, 11; Art Mathews, Transcripts, 4658), although the dried bundle of forty salmon is also called *gahlgoosxw* (Book Builders 1980). Spring salmon, being much larger than sockeye and steelhead, are bundled in lots of twenty each. Members of a production team are allowed to take a break only between processing sets of forty fish.

While into the early decades of the twentieth century the men caught fish with spears, gaffs, dip-nets, weirs, and basket traps (and today with gaffs, dip-nets, and gill-nets), the women, the old people, and the young were pressed into service to carry, wash, and cut the fish for drying and storage. At the same time, special processes are involved in preparing the heads – drying or boiling them for oil – as well as the eyes, bellies, and eggs.

Most of these processes are followed at the river sites and smokehouses today, the only difference from times past being a change of technology. Today the majority of fish are caught with gill-nets; steel knives have replaced slate, shell, obsidian, and bone blades; and storage is by canning and freezing in addition to smoke-drying.

Martha Brown said that her family would complete the bulk of the fish smoking by the third week of August. Then the berry harvest began, both in the Kispiox Valley and on the mountain slopes. In less than in a month they would have prepared (picked, boiled in wooden boxes with heated stones, then spread on leaves to dry on racks over the fire) forty to sixty pack-loads of berry cakes for transport back to Kispiox. Both the dried salmon and the dried berries frequently had to be backpacked in relays from House fishing sites and main berry sites several kilometres home to the village for winter storage. Sometimes Martha went up the Kispiox Valley in the late summer for combined coho and steelhead fishing and the picking of crabapples *(t'imi'yt)* and swamp cranberries (Commission III, 14-5).

The salmon are considered to be both important food and a fraternal nation, possessing the same life-force marvels and mysteries as the rest of the faunal kingdom, including *Homo sapiens*. This is indicated in the crest origins: informants referred to the *adaawk*'s of certain Houses that recount the narrative of a young member of the House having been taken by the salmon to live with them. Here they gifted him with the secrets of their ways and then allowed him to return to his people and use his knowledge to ensure that their relationship with the salmon would always be respectful and mutually beneficial. Boas (1916, 192) recorded one of these narratives collected at Kitselas; he recorded a similar narrative from among the Oowekeeno people of Rivers Inlet (Boas 1932, 54-8). The enormous importance of salmon is to be seen in the density of named and owned fishing sites in the territories, as indicated in Maps 4A, B, and C.

The salmon are the anchor and focal point of the subsistence economy (Figure 38). They comprise the protein mainstay of the diet. When this protein was combined with their own fat content and that of other fish and game species, as well as with the seasonally available carbohydrates (mainly berries, sap, bark, and bulbs), the salmon provided a secure and balanced diet to the precontact First Nations of the region.

In *Book Builders of 'Ksan* (1980) the Gitksan list twenty-four names associated with delicacy cuts of the salmon, succulent parts of the anatomy, methods of preparation of everything from oversmoked fresh salmon to salmon roe, eyes, the rich and delicious belly strips called *ts'okxw,* and the triangular piece of the neck, *t'ul.* The heads of the springs were rendered by boiling in water and squeezing the oil from the waxy nose; then each container would be boiled again (in the old days, by means of red-hot rocks) and the squeezing would be repeated.

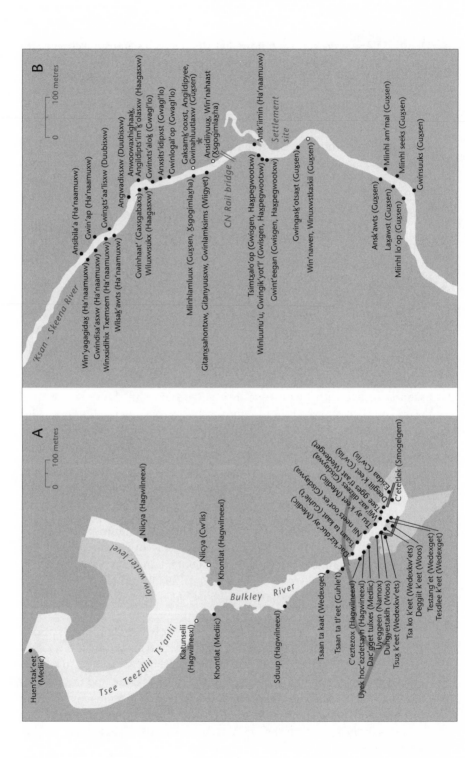

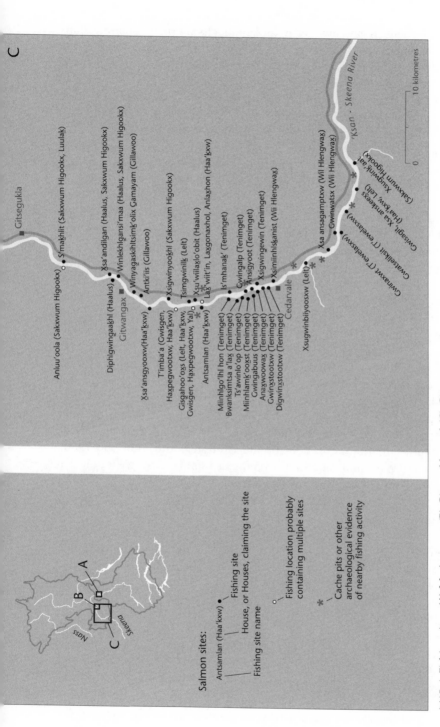

MAP 4 Fishing sites: (A) Moricetown, (B) Gitsegukla, and (C) Gitwangax

Source: Gitksan and Wet'suwet'en Chiefs (1988).

Much energy was/is, invested in the summer food fishery: catching, transporting, processing, preserving, and storing salmon and feeding the large workforce. These activities are still organized such that salmon remains an important part of the regular diet of both peoples. Today, as in the past, river gill-netting disperses Gitksan families to their owned sites along the rivers during the summer months. People enjoy getting away from the villages to their fishing sites. Mary McKenzie, Kathleen Matthews, and Audrey Woods all told me that going to the river in the summer is more than just fishing: it is part of their very identity as Gitksan people. They said that camping along the river offers a respite from the tensions of life that arise from being concentrated into "reserves."

In the late summer the women of the western villages would spend a few weeks in the mountains at their well-tended berry patches, picking blue huckleberries *(sim maa'y)* and blueberries *('miiyahl* and *miigan)* on the sites where their grandmothers picked before them. They might also make trips down some of the valleys for swamp cranberries and wild crabapples, saskatoons *(gam)*, and soapberries *(is)*. They would also pick the thorn-berry *(snax)* and rosehips, and dry them in cakes (as with most of the other species). The same procedure was carried out by the northern and eastern villages. In fact it was common, at least in the northern villages, for everyone available to participate. It was a festive occasion, a camping trip, and a change of scene after the hectic activity along the riverbank. Today people generally seek road-accessible berry patches.

Summer and early fall was also the time of the annual harvest of the most important and most common medicines (Olive Ryan, Transcript, 1253-9; Mary Johnson, Transcript, 808-10; and Gottesfeld and Anderson 1986). Johnny David (Commission III, 67-8) provided similar evidence for medicinal collections made in Witsuwit'en territory.

In general, medicinal plants attained their period of maximum efficacy only briefly or became more toxic in the summer growing season (e.g., devil's club, *wa'umst,* and the cow parsnip), while others grew less toxic as they matured (e.g., the powerful hellebore, *malgwasxw,* mentioned in relation to *sesatxw* purification in Chapter 7). Harvesting of these plants was scheduled precisely to coincide with other gathering activities in specific regions. Upon harvest, they would be dried and stored for future use. Other plants were picked as needed and used fresh (e.g., conifer pitch).

Hellebore root, or *malgwasxw (Veratrum viride),* would be gathered in the mid-elevation pine meadows and alpine regions when people travelled to their annual berry-picking at the higher altitudes in late August and September. Devil's club *(Oplopanax horridum)* was gathered from wet areas at lower elevations from late October until spring. The root of the yellow pond lily *(Nuphar polysepalum)* was also taken in the autumn months. In the spring and early summer, cakes would be made from the sweet inner bark of the western hemlock. Pine noodles, the cambium of inner bark, were also taken for eating fresh in early summer, as were soapberry teas and nettles for twisting into twine and rope.

Malgwasxw and *wa'umst* are used extensively for general tonics, for purification of the body, strengthening against heat, cold, tension, and stress. The *wa'umst* inner bark and root are used for rheumatism and arthritis, stomach ulcers, and gynaecological cancers. The fresh inner bark assists the rapid healing of wounds. *Malgwasxw* is of both physiological and spiritual efficacy. It contains toxic alkaloids (Gottesfeld and Anderson 1986, 9) and is normally not taken internally. *Malgwasxw* smoke is inhaled as an incense for calming a troubled mind; the grated root can be added to bathwater to treat skin ailments. The root is carried for general well-being, luck in bingo, and protection against malevolence.

Autumn

Martha Brown reported that, in the past, indigenous people "never sat around at home. We were always busy." After the berry season the people with territories around Kispiox made trips up the mountains for groundhog and goats. Martha's grandfather regularly hunted mountain goats. Martha herself went up to the alpine meadows with Joe Brown, her husband, for groundhog and caribou. Her grandfather made snares from cedar bark that he had softened over the fire and rolled and twisted together. In her grandfather's youth, one would snare the goats then get up close so as to dispatch them with bow and arrow. They also snared grizzly in the fall. They used cedar-bark nooses that caught up the front paws of the bear before shooting it, at close range, with bow and arrow.

The groundhog fat was stuffed into the stomach of the groundhog and hung to dry, sometimes over the smoke of the fire. This was called *ts'ee'wa'-gwiikw*. The mountain goat fat was rendered to oil; the meat would be cut into thin strips, smoked, and put away in cache houses with the salmon and steelhead strips. At this time as well, bear fat would be prepared for winter use (Richard Benson, Commission, 10-11). In his youth, Richard Benson would travel up the Cranberry River in the fall. For some weeks his family caught and dried coho and steelhead for winter food. Then they moved on north to gaff sockeye in the falls below the outflow of Meziadin Lake. There were late sockeye that wintered at Meziadin "as sleek and silver as the ones in the sea" (Daly 1986-88 [Benson interview]; Benson, Commission, 24 November 1987). Gitwangax and Gitanyow people would descend from the alpine country with marmot and mountain goat after the first hunting trip and return to the river for coho and steelhead at the end of September.

In the western Gitksan villages at the end of summer, each House chief ensured preparations were carried out for the groundhog trapping and the hunting of mountain goat and bear as well as the woodland caribou. He would be expected to ensure that only certain areas would be hunted each season, while others were left fallow. Today he is still expected to warn against over-harvesting and to make sure that, when hunting parties go out, they repair the trails and stone cairn trail markers above the treeline so that no one gets lost in the fog and blizzards of late fall (Art Matthews Sr., [Daly 1986-88]).

The late fall and beginning of winter marked the start of the feast season. Most people were and are home in the village at this time, having returned from the fishing sites, from their hunting and trapping, and from seasonal employment on the coast. In this region they generally carry out fall hunting in a series of short trips from the village instead of moving into the territory for months. With snowfall, trapping began on the territory and was intensified in January.

These pursuits are still followed, though less intensively. Trapping in western Gitksan areas, however, has been eliminated due to the extensive nature of the clear-cut logging since the 1970s and as a result of the international anti-fur lobby. In many locations the giving forest has been removed. I have seen a photograph of Johnny Wilson's (Skiigimlaxha) trapping cabin near Bowser Lake, taken in the summer of 1985, nestled in the woods. Now, according to Charlotte Sullivan, who at the time held the name Biniiks,[14] this cabin is "sitting in a clear cut without a tree in sight." (See also Figure 39, which shows Lax Gibuu [Wolf] chief Wii Muk'wilixw on his devastated territory.)

Northern and northeastern Gitksan wintered in their territories in the early decades of the twentieth century, after they had moved south from their home villages to settle at Gitanmaax and Kispiox to be near the schools. Each year, in the period from 1900 to 1950, a large group of people would leave Kispiox together around 20 August with pack horses. Once the people had reached their destinations in the distant territories to the north, some of the young men would take the pack horses back out to winter them at Kispiox. They would then hike in again to rejoin their families. David Blackwater spent the fall and winter of his childhood and early youth with his grandparents at Galanhl'giist, on the upper Skeena.

As soon as people arrived in these northern territories, they went up in the mountain for groundhog. Rather than risk losing and wasting a wounded marmot (they go into their burrows to die), David Blackwater told me, his grandfather would snare them, making the snares the right size to catch the two-year-olds but too large to snare the yearlings. They took one or two from each burrow and left the rest for the following years.[15] They would camp in alpine basins, boiling grease, drying the meat, and curing the pelts.

David explained, "We'd get mountain goat up there too, and blue grouse, porcupine and bear. We dried everything and rendered grease from ground-hog and bear fat by boiling it in water and skimming off the oil as it cooled." They alternated between three alpine regions in different years. In about three weeks, David's grandfather would say that they had enough meat. They would then return to the camp at the lake. The trip back down to the cabin usually took two days, as they painstakingly relayed the packs loaded with meat, grease, and skins all the way down the trail. The meat strips were stored away in the cache house six or seven metres above ground level.

Immediately they would go back, halfway up the mountainside, to start berry-picking and drying. As soon as the berries were dried and put away, they turned to gaffing coho in the creek and setting snares for black bears, which were also visiting the area for the coho run.[16]

Winter and Early Spring
David Blackwater explained that, in the northern territories, the coho were put away before the end of October, at which time preparations were made for trapping. They would clear the trails of windfalls and overgrowth and stack firewood for three regular campsites along the trapline. Grandmother had her own trapline, something she could handle on a daily basis from the lake. Trapping began in mid-November and ended in March: "We trapped just long enough to earn enough money for the next winter's supplies. We took marten, fisher, mink, squirrel and weasels. Lynx only brought 50 cents in those days. We took timber wolf and wolverine." They walked the trapline every few days to keep the trails open in the heavy snowpack.[17] From mid-March until the end of April, they pursued the beaver downstream from the lake. Also in March: "We'd do ice fishing for whitefish with a fine mesh net, and we'd get Dolly Varden and cutthroat. We'd drop a piece of chewed salmon strip in the hole of the ice. In a little while the fish would come and eat it. It's only 8 or 10 feet deep there. We'd gaff them and eat them fresh. We'd gaff steelhead in the spring too. You could sun dry fish at that time of year."

Winter was also the season of most of the Gitksan major feasting. At the time of first European contact, the winter was also the period devoted to the dance society ceremonies and socializing with visitors from other villages and regions (Tomlinson 1875). This appears to have been a common cultural feature of much of the Northwest Coast area in protocontact and the early contact period. Drucker (1963, 168-9), for instance, is of the opinion that the winter ceremonies of the Kwakwak'awakw, especially the *mitla* (*gami'hla* – Tsim.), which was probably acquired from the Coast Salish, "the ones returned from heaven" and the *nutlam* (*galuhlim* – Tsim. "dog eaters"), or wolf spirit performance, were in the process of expanding northward at contact. His reading of the evidence is that these ceremonies were established among the Tsimshian-speaking peoples by protocontact times and had begun to be adopted by the Haida and Tlingit only at contact. Sophia Mowatt of Gitanmaax recalled the *galuhlim* performances when she was a child (she was born in 1901), and the Reverend Tomlinson had the following to say about the ceremonial activity he observed at Kispiox in early winter, during the 1870s. His point of view is complete with Christian moral outrage, useful for generating funds from the readers of his report back among William Duncan's supporters in England: "All night long the drumming and rattling, the wild singing and howling were continued ... the person being initiated into the mysteries of the medicine work – after a certain amount of incantations, drumming, rattling and singing has been performed over him is supposed to become temporarily mad and unconscious of, and unaccountable for, his actions." Tomlinson then describes the seizing, killing, and skinning of a dog by the naked, maddened initiate, who then dashes from the house with the dog's remains, followed by "a whole troop of medicine men": "This is the signal for all in the village to hide themselves, as he may bite anyone he finds uncovered. He enters each house with yells, grunts, grimaces and gestures as diabolical as he can make them ... he began howling, hissing, spitting ... he entered the house again, holding the dog in his hands and tearing its flesh with his teeth" (Tomlinson 1875, 283-4).

Margaret Austin recalls as a child in the 1930s having sneaked up to the window of the Owl House in Hagwilget (Figure 6) to catch glimpses of "those secrets" (personal communication). These dances were frequently accompanied by lavish and competitive gift-giving that may indicate that such ceremonies were a medium for expressing changing social statuses at the time of the fur trade, as discussed in Chapter 6.

After a period of feasting and ceremonial activities, most Gitksan would hunt and trap in the late winter. Martha Brown recalls that, during her childhood early in the twentieth century, the late winter was also a time for lake and river ice-fishing. Char, Dolly Varden, whitefish, and other species would be taken, either by gaffing or with nets. For netting, the best method was night fishing with a fire built about fifteen metres from the holes between which the net was set. Martha says that this would continue until two or three in the morning. Someone would usually fall through the ice to add to the excitement. There would be up to 150 fish to dress, hang, and smoke the next day. Some people went out in spring for beaver and others went to the Nass for oolichan grease. Then, when the river was still high, steelhead and spring were caught, and the *t'in*, or weir fences, were made ready for summer.

Richard Benson recalled that, at the end of winter, after hunting and trapping around Meziadin, his family and other people from Gitanyow would travel to the Nass to Fishery Bay to participate in the oolichan fishery (Commission, 17-18). Richard reported that his family would exchange their labour, hides, and their dried salmon and berries for the grease. Sometimes the boxes of grease were loaded into canoes obtained on the coast and laboriously taken home by paddling on the open stretches of the river and, where it was frozen, by hauling grease and canoes over the ice. Sometimes the Nass people themselves travelled to Gitanyow with grease that they gave in exchange for berries. "We really fed ourselves from the land," Richard said. "Our people did not have to take welfare money in those days. Our box was full."

Regulation of Seasonal Activity

The detailed laws of trespass, exclusion, inheritance, and the delegation of use rights to House territories of the Gitksan and Witsuwit'en (Chapter 7) were essential to the successful maintenance of economic activities. These combined the seasonal but sedentary harvesting of anadromous species on the main-stem rivers with the complex harvesting of game and fur-bearing animals. Since they have been ingrained in people's "instinctive" cultural ways, or habitus, and since they go back into the oral narratives of these peoples, they have undoubtedly existed for a very long time. The animals pursued live in a variety of habitats; many species move through different eco-niches at different seasons or different phases of their lifecycle. These peoples have devised a regulatory kin-based system of use and ownership that is both enduring and flexible. Their system of proprietorship and extensive land use appears to have enabled them to maximize their beneficial relationships with those other species that are part of their lives and traditions – the species that make up their widest kinship network.

Salmon harvesting, as the evidence of Art Mathews (Transcript, Vol. 73) makes clear, is highly labour-intensive and, together with gathering berries and other plant foods, extends over half the year. Busy harvesting, processing, and storing the summer produce, the labour force has long been faced with the problem of how to obtain the supplementary fresh foodstuffs and sources of clothing and shelter needed to sustain a relatively large population over the winter season. This has required a well-planned and coordinated use of surrounding hunting grounds.

The territories claimed by the two peoples in their court action – about 54,000 square kilometres (22,000 square miles) – with an estimated population of 8,000 to 10,000, would approximate the human population density that non-industrialized hunting societies in other parts of the world have been able to sustain without domesticated crops. This figure is generally considered to be from two to five persons per square mile (Birdsell 1958, 1968, 1972; and R.B. Lee, personal communication). Moreover, as Rolf Knight (1968) has so elegantly pointed out, the density of cooperative social relations involved in food extraction, the degree of seasonal sedentarism, and the necessary extent of hunting territories all have much to do with the ecology of the actual species appropriated. In the Gitksan and Witsuwit'en regions the activities of spring/summer/autumn have centred on salmon, freshwater fishes, wild fowl, caribou, and berries – species that engage collectively with their environment in schools, flocks, and herds. Many of the winter species, by contrast, such as moose, bear, small game, and fur-bearers, grow and sustain themselves more or less in solitary numbers. Territories of human beings relying on these latter species in winter consequently tend to be extensive. Other solitary species, like mountain goats and deer, bridge the seasons but occur only in limited ecological zones. The coastal neighbours had available to them a year-round succession of species in the form of fish, sea mammals, some land mammals and plants – and the relative ease of trade by sea-going canoe. The Gitksan and Witsuwit'en, by contrast, appear to have engaged in extensive winter hunting and springtime oolichan barter or gifting with the adjacent coast. This would compensate somewhat for the unavailability of foodstuffs in the hungry springtime before the salmon returned from the Pacific and when the winter stores of fat were otherwise exhausted.

There were more than a hundred House groups among the Gitksan and Witsuwit'en in the early nineteenth century, before the devastation of European-introduced diseases. At the beginning of the nineteenth century, Ogden (1853) counted twenty-eight large dwellings at what is today Moricetown, with six or seven families in each. If we take a conservative estimate of six family units of seven members per house, we can cautiously calculate a Witsuwit'en population in the 1820s of roughly 1,200. If, at that point in time, there existed the same number of House groups as today, average House size would thus have been around a hundred. Witsuwit'en say that some people remained year round on the territories and did not travel to the river to fish. Such people would have been absent during Ogden's visit, and his calculated average House group size was thus somewhat conservative.

The Gitksan themselves suggest the figure of a hundred members for an average House group. Tenimget gave evidence to the effect that before the Gitksan were severely reduced in number by European disease, those living in a House group's dwelling would be about a hundred (Transcripts, 4775) and would become higher temporarily as people came from some distance to share certain resources or species controlled by a specific House.

With a maximal population of 8,000 to 10,000, derived from an average of a hundred House members and an approximate total of ninety Houses for the Gitksan and Witsuwit'en combined, there would have been considerable demands placed on those seasonal resources located in or close to the rivers. Extensive territories distant from the riverside gathering points (village sites) ensured fall and winter access to foodstuffs and special materials that could be both consumed locally and exchanged with more distant peoples. Despite the fact that, for at least part of each year, the bulk of the population lived clustered in a number of fishing centres in the Hazelton Variant (ICHg3) of the Interior Cedar-Hemlock Biogeoclimatic Zone, the resources located there would not likely have sustained this many people year-round. The population required a territory of much vaster proportions to maintain itself through all seasons and prepare itself for potential human lifecycle crises, natural disasters, and unforeseen emergencies. The existence of a cut-and-dried system of control, ownership, and management of territorial resources helped to cope with the considerable human pressure upon these lands and resources, given the prevailing technology (see also Ball 1985, 37; Schalk 1981; Cohen 1981).

4
A Kinship Economy

Underlying both the elaborate reciprocities carried out in the feast hall (Chapter 2) and the organization of seasonal rounds of harvesting on the lands and at the fishing sites (Chapter 3) is a matrilineal kinship form of social and economic organization. Eric Wolf (1982, 91) has explained how the economy of a small kinship society contrasts with that based upon the modern market economy:

> Put simply, through kinship, social labor is "locked up," or "embedded," in particular relations between people. This labor can be mobilized only through access to people, such access being defined symbolically. *What* is done unlocks social labor; *how* it is done involves symbolic definitions of kinsmen and affines. Kinship thus involves (a) symbolic constructs ("filiation/ marriage; consanguinity/affinity") that (b) continually place actors, born and recruited, (c) into social relations with one another. These social relations (d) permit people in variable ways to call on the share of social labor carried by each, in order to (e) effect the necessary transformations of nature.

What Might Be Called Production Units

In today's global world, the basic social entity that encompasses economic "production" activities is the commercial firm or corporation, the enterprise organized by owners or managers, who generally seek to combine quantities of labour and raw materials to produce goods or services for sale in the market. If we regard this as one end of a continuum, the other might be exemplified by the classic foraging band, found until recently in the deserts of Australia, in parts of southern and central Africa, south and Southeast Asia, the High Arctic, and elsewhere. Here, the production and consumption unit is very flexible, with loosely structured, highly open sociation, much sharing, individual autonomy, and egalitarianism.

The Gitksan and Witsuwit'en situation is at a point between these two poles, yet within a foraging modality of economic activity. Despite re-adjustments due to the colonial process (gold rushes, riverboats, suppression of indigenous laws, and gradual colonial administration of most aspects of life), the basic jural unit carrying out the annual round of economic activities has been a matrilineal kin group. The actual social unit, however, is always both more extensive, and more exclusionary, than House group membership might suggest. In terms of the "social imaginary" of these peoples, the core of the family economy is composed of those who, in precolonial times, lived together under the common roof of a split cedar "big house." These were members, spouses, and young children; aged parents; and other clanfolk. Hence the local term, "House group." One worked, shared produce and wealth, cooperated and competed on an intimate every-day basis with people in, and associated with, one's House. This de facto residential and work group overlapped with, but did not include, the whole membership of the matrilineal, proprietary House group. It also included many, mainly female, affines, while half of any House group – its married women members – lived under the roofs of others, usually of the father's or spouse's House group. The House was, and remains, a ritual, ceremonial, jural, and political entity, but family relations crossed, and continue to cross, the thresholds of many Houses. In other words, transactions between a set of individual actors often activate the crosscutting interests of several tenure-holding bodies of kin and extend spatially through a local watershed.[1]

The primary social relationships here are among House members and between intermarrying House groups. When necessary, the House expands to include other kin (the *wil'naat'ahl* among the Gitksan [those matrikin who by local reputation claim a common narrative of migration into the home area in ancient times] and the clan, or *pdeek*, among the Witsuwit'en). This contrasts with the market economy, where primary sociological relations bind individual citizens with the central state bodies administrating a national territory. Central governments around the world have long striven to replace the kin-based relationships of indigenous peoples with the proto-typical relationship between the individual and the nation-state. Among First Nations peoples in Canada, the latter form has, over time, supplemented rather than replaced the kinship form, although there is always pressure to conform to the standard norms of the nation-state. Observers without personal experience of kinship societies and economies tend to overlook the fact that there are many more direct political interventions of a filial, consanguineous, or affinal nature in kinship economies than one expects to find in international or nation-state market economies.

In a matrilineal kinship economy and society, where descent and inheritance of rights and obligations are reckoned through mothers, relationships between members of descent groups are immediate and face-to-face. This holds true for one's own matrilineal House members, one's father's matrilineal group, and the kin group of one's spouse, one's mother's father, and one's father's father. These relatives are bound together by blood and marriage, and by a formal body of rights, the core of which involves the reciprocal use and management of land and labour through the juridical units of proprietorship, the House group. The House also holds the songs, dances, crests, narratives, and psychic powers that legitimize this local proprietorship.

Each Gitksan and Witsuwit'en individual is born into a landholding group through her/his mother; she or he enjoys additional rights and privileges on the basis of links through spouse, father, and grandfathers. From a structural perspective, Gitksan and Witsuwit'en economic life is composed of property-holding House groups, while from an ego-centred point of view it is composed of a network of social relations that involves each member in both the bloodlines and activities of several House groups. House groups cannot be regarded as equivalent to market-oriented enterprises, even though they might engage in similar activities. Many of the interests of their members are different from one another since members have different fathers, grandfathers, and spouses, all from different House groups or from more distant societies. Common interests lie with succession to names and the feasting system which publicly sanctions this succession. A kinship-based modern economy requires groups of interested people, and their respective Houses, to work, if not cooperatively then at least reciprocally, through the idiom of the gift.

The premodern local family economic unit associated with a House chief is composed of persons linked through both blood and marriage. However, the members of the House, linked by blood, were and are distributed through marriage into a number of different domestic and production units and different villages. This gives rise to the mass of crosscutting local relationships that anthropologists so often encounter in their fieldwork. Houses are paradoxical and contradictory. They worked, and continue to work, to a degree, as political and economic units but in a manner that involves many other such units. No one House can operate on its own without affecting the personnel, interests, and activities of others. Houses are collective bodies whose strengths and weaknesses are relative to all other such units around them. A traditional, under-one-roof household was a living articulation of members of several House groups, just as are specific areas within "Indian reserves" today.[2] Often these residential units are composed of members of specific long-term, intermarrying "House groups" that hold contiguous territories.

Gitksan Houses fall within four clans: La<u>x</u> Se'el, or Ganeda (the Frog Clan, with Frog and Raven crests); the La<u>x</u> Gibuu (the Wolf Clan, with Wolf and

Bear crests); the Gisḵ'aast (the Fireweed Clan, with Fireweed/Killer Whale/ Owl/Grizzly crests); and the Lax̱ X̱skiik (Eagle Clan, with Eagle and Beaver crests).[3] Among the Witsuwit'en, Houses fall within five clans: the Gilserhyu Frog clan, the Laksilyu Small Frog Clan, the Gitdumden Wolf Clan, the Laksamshu Fireweed/Killer Whale Clan, and the Tsayu[4] Beaver Clan. Among the two peoples, and including the Gitksan village of Gitanyow,[5] there are probably eighty to ninety Houses today, each with chiefs, wing chiefs, high feast names, and everyday named positions in relation to the feasting system that marks progression through the lifecycle by commemorating "those who came before."

Some Houses are considered to be of the "original settler" category, descended from "the ancient times"; others are the fruits of fission and fusion through recent millennia. There are many chiefs, wing chiefs, and "those born to be chiefs." The constituency of each is small, family-based, and includes those matrilineal segments known to be closely related, though not always traced by actual genealogical links. These segments comprise a House; sometimes several Houses work closely together and share common ancestors, crests, songs, and narratives of origin.

A chief has no right to represent non-House members unless, due to unusual circumstances, she/he is asked to do so on a short-term, one-issue basis. This tradition makes the present-day band council type of local government instituted by the Government of Canada highly volatile. In the generations that led into the fur trade, certain Coast Tsimshian chiefs succeeded in extending their ability to represent their whole clan, village, and region. This appears to have been leading to permanent hierarchic chiefdoms in the century immediately prior to European contact,[6] something that seems to have arisen through an upsurge of coastal trade, physical coercion, slave-taking, and diplomacy. These conditions were quite specific to one era in the long, long span of Tsimshianic history, a time that overlapped but was not contiguous with the contact period, as discussed in Chapter 6 (see also Cole and Darling 1990; Fisher 1977; Robinson 1978; Wike 1957; Wolf 1982).

Today, wage incomes are earned by individuals and are usually disbursed among immediate family members. However, the wage earner, or the recipient of a pension cheque, knows he or she may be called upon at any time to contribute to a feast or assist on the not-infrequent occasions of family crisis. In terms of feast obligations, people with access to money (and those without money borrow from persons in the correct kin relationship) respond either as a member of a host group or because one's relatives were fathers to the host chief. Alternatively, one responds because the host happens to be a member of the group to which one's spouse belongs or on the basis of some other family connection relative to practices based on matrilineal descent. There is a division of labour at work within clan groupings, Houses, and families, whereby both the subsistence and market-oriented sectors of the mixed economy are mobilized reciprocally to serve the material needs of all, particularly in relation to life crises.

The kinship production group recruits its membership primarily from the House (in the Gitksan tongue, the *wilp*, and in the Witsuwit'en language, the *yikh*). However, there are always members of the production group who do not belong to whatever House is at the core of the group. House members rely to a considerable degree on the labour and skills of others who are linked to, but not members of, the House. Using other terms, the House group is a cultural and jural construct used to orient actual on-the-ground residential and work relations. The House finds its fullest incarnation within feast situations. Here a chief, a House, a *wil'naat'ahl*, or an entire clan can be evaluated by the quality of its distribution of values and its acquitting of social indebtedness. The conceptual House is fleshed out by the assembly of its members and their relations, and the fruits of their common land, by its commitment to its own sense of destiny, and by the public and ceremonial assertion of collective rights and prerogatives relating to history, land, and labour. Feast-giving brings the House and clan together, usually under the direction of elderly women and their brothers, to organize the ceremonial event.

It bears repeating that among the Gitksan and Witsuwit'en and their neighbours of the northwestern cordillera of British Columbia, Yukon, and Alaska – as among the Iroquois of the Eastern Woodlands – it has been matrilineal groups symbolically constituted as Houses (Daly 1985) that have been the units of ownership (as they are today), but they did not, and do not, constitute de facto residential or production groups.

Rules of exogamy state that Witsuwit'en and Gitksan must marry outside their own clan, with the result that those who reside together, and who even today pursue the seasonal round together, are both House members and non-members. The owning group, the House, cannot exist alone economically. This is due to the exigencies of kinship and exogamy: the biological and marriage ties to other units, as well as the fluctuations of resources on House lands. Today the observer sees points of social interaction in the society where "families" (i.e., relatives from more than one House) intersect with one another. These participants share their economic life even though they do not all live under one roof or gain most of their livelihood from hunting and gathering.

The Gitksan and Witsuwit'en maintain that one ought to spend one's adult life in proximity to, and interaction with, one's House people. Until one or two generations ago they practised matrilocal bride service (an initial period during which the bridegroom lived with, and worked for, his wife's family); thereafter, the couple would move to the groom's family, among his own House or that of his father. In this arrangement the children tended, and became socialized on, their father's land rather than that of their maternal uncle's (their own House land). Thus, many tended to take up economic activity on their fathers' territory and fishing sites, where they have use rights only.

This apparent contradiction is, in part, counterbalanced by marriage ties that link the mother's and the father's people over several generations, and permit temporary usufruct and residential rights within one another's area of authority. Thus, Houses are interlinked by many overlapping strands of blood and history, like raindrops imprinting themselves on the surface of a pond. Intergroup relations are manifested semiotically in the feast hall by payments made between the host and the various categories of his/her kin, as is outlined in Chapter 2. For participants, family relations are cycles of rebirth and reincarnation, uncoiling within broad tracks emanating from, and leading back to, the edges of time and the mind.

The actual residential group, in the era of the Big House, enjoyed flexible use rights to different territories in the course of the year. Each domestic unit of the House might at any one time be found using the territory of another House: either that of the chief's father, his *wilksiwitxw* (sing.) and *wilksilaks* or *wilksibaksxw* (pl.) group among the Gitksan, or his *bits'ac'elts'it* (father's clan) among the Witsuwit'en; or it could be the territory of the spouse. This has to be worked out between the chiefs and elders of the relevant territories. Among the Witsuwit'en, a domestic unit from one House frequently uses the territory of a second or third House (that of an adult's father or spouse). Members of these Houses may accompany one another on joint hunting trips, in a planned sequence, on each other's lands. Witsuwit'en of the same clan can use one another's lands freely, though all usufruct is traditionally subject to the overall planning and approval of the senior chiefs. The intergenerational movement of families between the territories of two Houses linked by successive generations of marriages is reflected in the pattern of use of the hunting territories.

This distinction between House groups and the families that articulate them can be seen today. So long as a kinship system serves as a template for social organization, it exerts its logic over social relations. Social interaction (including atypical behaviour) is explained, justified, organized, and censured in relation to this formal logic.

In his evidence to the court, the accomplished hunter and trapper, the late Alfred Mitchell, listed a number of House territories on which he has pursued game and fur-bearing animals over the past half century (Transcript, 5255). The territories that Alfred described include some of the high alpine regions where mountain goat and groundhog/marmot are found; the forests, swamp, and meadow frequented by moose, deer, bear, and fur-bearers; and the waterways that support beaver and trout in the spring. In the course of explaining where and how he has hunted, Alfred told the court why he has the right to use the different territories, from whom he gained permission to hunt, and his relations to those who invited him to join their hunting parties.

Alfred's father was Witsuwit'en and his mother was Gitksan. Thus he was born into the Gisḵ'aast House of Wiiseeks, of the northern Gitksan villages of Kisgagas and Kispiox. His mother died while he was a child, and his father took him to live in Moricetown on Witsuwit'en territory. His father was a member of the House of Namox, Tsayu Clan; his father's sister, Emma Michell, who held the chief name of Lilloos in the House of Namox, raised him. Her husband, Tommy Michell – also known as "Little Tommy" – was the Laksilyu Clan chief, Skokum Wasas of the House of Hagwilneexl. The second wife of Alfred's father was Mary Tom, a member of the Laẋ Gibuu/ Gitdumden House of Spookw – a Gitksan Wolf Clan House with territories bordering the Witsuwit'en and with numerous affinal and filial links to Witsuwit'en Houses. Mary Tom's father's side was Laksilyu; her patrilateral cousin, George Naziel, also shared this Laksilyu father's side (i.e., the fathers of George and Mary were brothers). George Naziel was Mediic of the Gitdumden House of Mediic and one of Mr. Mitchell's hunting colleagues. This link through Mary Tom was a factor in Alfred's ability to accompany his father on hunting trips to Laksilyu and Gitdumden territories.

Alfred Mitchell married into the Laksilyu House of Hagwilneexl. Hagwilneexl, Sylvester William, was Alfred's most frequent hunting partner. (Sylvester was also a matrilateral cousin of Alfred's successive wives, who were sisters.) Alfred's father-in-law, Dick Naziel, held the chief name of 'Ahk'ot in the Gitdumden House of Mediic. The brother of Dick Naziel was the above-mentioned George Naziel. There are many other kinship ties which, for the sake of brevity, we need not consider here, but which in fact further legitimize the actors' rights to use Wedexget's Laksilyu territory (discussed in the following example).

Within the territory of Wedexget there are areas of high elevation that have long yielded mountain goat and marmot/groundhog. Two of these areas are near the upper reaches of Corya Creek and John Brown Creek. *Tsë Ts'iwis To K'ët* (Place in the rock where water flows in, foaming up, *Ut'akhgit* territory) is noted for mountain goats (Transcript, 3271), and *Cas Winïc'ditiy* (Grizzly's trail over the ridge, part of Brian Boru Peak, *Ut'akhgit* territory) is noted for groundhog. Alfred Mitchell has been invited to hunt in these regions with other Witsuwit'en men. (It is customary for a group of men from all the clans to hunt mountain goat together. The technology, skills, and organization of the process are explained in Alfred's evidence [Transcript, 3176]).

Alfred was invited to these Laksilyu Clan areas by Sylvester William, Chief Hagwilneexl. According to Alfred, Hagwilneexl was the best hunter in the area. Alfred and Sylvester were accompanied by Dan Michell. Dan Michell was Alfred's patrilateral first cousin. It was with Dan Michell's father, Tommy, and his mother, Emma, that Alfred spent his childhood. Dan Michell is Wigetimschol, House of Namox, Tsayu Clan, and was raised by his Laksilyu father to hunt the Laksilyu territories of Hagwilneexl and Wedexget. The hunting party also included George Naziel, chief of the Gitdumden House of Mediic, who, in turn, was married to a woman of the Tsayu House of Namox – the House to which Alfred's father belonged. George Naziel, Mediic, had rights to use Wedexget territory because his fellow Mediic House chief, Kanoots, Peter Alfred, was married to Dzee, Madeline Alfred of the House of Wedexget.

On other occasions (Transcript, 3272) Alfred Mitchell hunted mountain goat and groundhog in the highest elevations of Wedexget territory with Dan Michell (whose relationship is explained above) and other, younger members of Dan Michell's Tsayu clan: Amos and Jimmy Naziel. On still further occasions (Transcript, 3273) Alfred hunted on Wedexget land with his father-in-law, Dick Naziel, House of Mediic and brother of George Naziel. Dick Naziel's wife, Mitchell's mother-in-law, belonged to the Laksilyu House of Hagwilneexl, together with her daughters, two of whom became Alfred's (successive) wives. Accompanying Dick Naziel and Alfred Mitchell on this occasion were Dick Naziel's young Mediic nephews, Gordon and Jimmy Joseph, and his Tsayu nephew, William Naziel.

These, then, are some of the inter-House and interclan links exhibited in the legitimate use of these sites for hunting mountain goat and groundhog in Wedexget territory. This territory and the nearby Laksilyu lands of Hagwilneexl and Wedexkw'ets were important to the structural kinship position of Alfred Mitchell's father, who, although in the House of Namox, had long-standing ties with his father's side, the Laksilyu. When Alfred hunted and trapped on Namox territory around Sam Goosley Lake, he was accompanied by members of the House of Namox and by their father's side: Laksilyu hunters like the brothers Pat and John Namox (Transcript, 3293 [N.B., the transcript erroneously reads "Joe" Namox]). Pete Muldoe, the present Gitludahl, from Kispiox, testified that he trapped on Namox territory when he was a young man (Transcript, 6092), and Alfred recalls accompanying Mr. Muldoe. Gitludahl was on Tsayu land (Namox territory) because he was living at his sister's residence; his sister was married to a member of the House of Namox. Hence, for a brief period of time, both Alfred Mitchell and Pete Muldoe – members of the same *wil'naat'ahl* in Kispiox, a Gitksan village – hunted and trapped legitimately on Namox land in Witsuwit'en territory by virtue of ties of marriage within their respective families.[7] This interweaving of people from various Houses into seasonal round activities brings the whole community into play when work is being performed, and it articulates the extended family relationships that make up daily life. A similar example is found in an old manuscript describing, among other things, the many mother's-, father's-, and spouse's-side relatives and in-laws who assisted in the building of a big house at Port Simpson ([Susman, Garfield, and Beynon?] n.d.).

Ties of kinship and marriage linked these hunters to the rights and duties of land use and ownership. These ties applied equally to all the personnel listed on the other sites where Alfred Mitchell hunted, such as the Caspit territory of the Gilserhyu Clan (Transcript, 3275 for mountain goat, 3284-5 for deer and moose); the Namox territory at Goosley Lake (3293); the northern Namox area above Goosley Lake (3293 and 3283-4); the Gyologet (House of Woos) Gitdumden territory (3276); and, for beaver hunting on Knedebeas territory, Gilserhyu Clan, at Gosnell Creek (3311), Pack Lake, and Poplar Lake (3317).

The kinship links to House ownership and permission to use the land can be worked out for all persons listed by Alfred Mitchell on the basis of the House genealogical charts (prepared for *Delgamuukw*) and local knowledge of family histories. Intergenerational ties between chiefly lineages of certain Houses, or at least certain definite clans, recur at fairly regular intervals. Such recurrences facilitate established patterns of hunting territory use and ownership. The ownership features are asserted in the feasts when the chiefly names are passed on, when debts are cleared, and when the beaver meat and game from the territories is served to the witnessing chiefs from the guest clans. These transactions, and many others, exemplify the interplay of different owning groups articulated by family relations. The example of Alfred Mitchell's hunting network shows vividly how Houses are woven, one into another, as into a Chilkat blanket, by blood and marriage.

Dora Wilson, Yaga'lahl, of Clan Lax Gibuu, addressed the interconnected nature of local relations that articulates the ownership groups. She was asked in court if her claim to territory was limited to the lands of her own House, Wilps Spookw. She replied (Transcript, 4485): "the way that question is put, it seems like we are only interested in one particular little spot. The way our system is, and the way we depend on one another and support one another, I think there is more interest than in just in our own personal territory. Like, for instance, I have mentioned already the different Houses that we helped in the feast, and the different Houses that helped us in the feast. So what happens to those territories is of concern to all of the chiefs, and concern of all of the Houses." Dora Wilson explained that, while she has an ownership claim only to Spookw's territory, she has some jurisdictional rights through family and clan to wider territories. She explained part of this jurisdictional claim in terms of the close ties between Houses in her Wolf Clan, both among the Witsuwit'en and the Gitksan (Transcript, 4485-6). Recent, post-*Delgamuukw* consultations over tree-cutting, between tree farm licence-holders, the Ministry of Forests, and Gitksan and Witsuwit'en chiefs have totally ignored these overlapping interests, with the result that – if there is any consultation at all – only the individual House chief is approached. This naturally leads to strife and disharmony in the community.

Family members still live in relative proximity to one another; family ties remain strong. The communities keep up relations even with members who move away, so long as these persons honour their obligations to their families and feasting in the home area. People still relate with one another interpersonally on the basis of kinship and marriage. In the course of a year, they use the land and they fish the rivers; they engage in wage labour and small business activities. Yet they utilize a portion of the fruits of this wage labour work and small enterprise activity in the maintenance of the indigenous system of House group collective ownership, especially through their contributions to gift-giving in the feasts.

The House does not own a person's fish boat, store, or sawmill but, rather, the House, at times of feast-holding, exerts a moral demand on its members to contribute a portion of their cash income to the proper conduct of House affairs. Those who remain in the home region produce country foods for those who have emigrated or who work solely in the non-subsistence sector of the economy. Those who die in distant places – even those who ostensibly have turned their backs on their own culture – are brought "home" for interment.[8] Their funerals are arranged and paid for by the appropriate relatives/affines, and their hereditary name or names are passed to new incumbents. Those without feast names are also commemorated in this way. The researcher experienced two such funerals during the winter of 1987. Both involved the untimely deaths of youths living in urban centres far away from the territories.

The conduct of marriages is one of the most important aspects of managing a kinship production unit because, as leading kinship scholar Meyer Fortes (1953, 30) has explained: "in a homogeneous society there is nothing which could so precisely and incontrovertibly fix one's place in society as parentage." Fortes's statement has two important implications. First, children are the source of the expanding fortunes of the corporative House as much as is territory. Consequently, influence over the labour and the offspring of the daughters of the House, no matter where they are living, ensures a definite continuity to the Gitksan and Witsuwit'en social systems. Parental or House or clan selection of marriage partners is no longer the norm, though considerable moral and social pressure is exerted on young people to observe the rule of exogamy (marrying outside one's clan) and to marry within the culture and the region. However, due to the nature of matrilineal succession, all children born to Gitksan or Witsuwit'en women inherit a position in the kinship system through their mothers, without regard to paternity. (The lack of patrilateral ties can, however, "thin the weave" of a child's local relationships.) Whether or not the daughters marry outside the local area, their children are ascribed House membership and (often) House names (Olive Ryan evidence, Transcript, 1358). Outsider spouses may also be adopted, usually into the same clan as that of the member spouse's father, so as to maintain the ongoing flow of reciprocal interrelations between those Houses in different clans.

That the children inherit through the mothers is attested to in the oral histories. Here one finds many accounts of women of chiefly lineage being kidnapped or married away at a great distance, such as occurs in the *adaawḵ'* of Neḵt's mother (*Raven Clan Outlaws*, Adaawḵ's 46-9), in which the Frog/Raven chief's niece is carried off during a raid and married to a Haida prince. She knows her children will have no standing and no respect in this nation since they derive their status from her bloodline. Consequently, she kills her husband, cuts out his tongue, and stuffs it in the mouth of her infant son, Neḵt, so as to make a silent escape with the baby. Today's situation is similar, even though women are not kidnapped and tongues are not amputated.

Often members of House groups are born in distant parts of the Pacific Northwest only to come back to settle in the home village, as Gwaans, Wilps Ha'naamuxw, recounted in her *Delgamuukw* evidence. In other families, however, the elders of House and clan play an active role in modern marriages and are consulted by the young people before the marriage is settled. The late Madeline Alfred (Transcript, 2764) explained that four of her daughters have married through such consultation and that, among the Witsuwit'en, grandchildren frequently consult on this matter with the grandparent generation.

There are Houses that, to the present day, intermarry regularly with certain other specific Houses. Striking examples arise in all the villages. In Kispiox, for instance, the Gisḵ'aast House of Gutgwinuxs regularly intermarries with the Laẖ Gibuu House of X̱hliimlaẖha and with the Gitanmaax village's Laẖ Se'el House of Nikateen. The Gisḵ'aast House of Tsibasaa/ Antgulilibix similarly intermarries regularly with the Laẖ Gibuu Houses of Niist and Wii Muk'wilixw. These recurrent marriages serve to consolidate the use and control of adjoining territories and watersheds.

As the fortunes of specific Houses wax and wane, their members seek to use marriage ties to their best long-term advantage. Persons born into long-standing interrelations perform reciprocal ceremonial services for one another in the feast and exchange gifts standing for day-to-day services rendered. Because the hunting and fishing lands are so highly prized, people continue to pour their production earnings into the community's reciprocal transactions at the feast in order to maintain traditional legitimacy to perceived land rights. They do this today, even though in most families the greater part of the earnings are not derived from the lands whose traditional ownership they defend.

Circulation of Goods and Services

In market economies the circulation of valued goods and services tends to be analyzed as the leading factor involved in the economy. In subsistence economies the circulation of goods is predicated upon the exchange of what is locally perceived as value equivalence, or a common sense reciprocity where goods are valued primarily for their consumption use, for the assistance they can provide the people in their basic production and ceremonial activities. Among the Gitksan and Witsuwit'en of the early nineteenth century, the bulk of items in circulation (although due to their perishable nature not available to much of the archaeological record)[9] consisted of goods that were socially necessary for the satisfaction of the basic material needs of the population. Today this same emphasis on supplying useful, needed "gifts" and "payments" in order to renew ongoing relationships is an important feature of the circulation of goods.

The exchange of goods and services within a political economy is part of the system of decision making. In a kinship society the implementation of decisions and the consolidation of authority and influence is frequently effected with the liberal giving of gifts, the provision of hospitality, and other forms of gratitude towards the other kin groups and their leaders. This has entailed the giving of certain luxury items (today considered objets d'art) that symbolize the heritage and value of the collective kin group, and which have been exchanged ceremonially between the hereditary leaders of these groups. Such prestations are based upon the prior production of useful consumables that allow the world to see that the House is a viable producer of basic subsistence and a good steward of the land. In the course of making these reciprocal expenditures, the family group consumes a portion of its production and accumulated wealth or assets, which raises the demand for further production. A successful giving reflects well on all the associated Houses linked by blood and affinity to the hosts.

At contact, the bulk of the values tended to circulate between House groups or (especially on the adjacent, protocontact coast) villages (Boas 1916; Garfield 1966; Halpin and Seguin 1990, 278). These consisted of ceremonial gifts, as well as goods and services related to subsistence and the sharing of fruits of the seasonal round. This circulation usually entailed some political negotiation between senior chiefs and the recognition of multigenerational reciprocal ties between intermarrying House groups.

Some of the Gitksan also have long-standing kinship ties to the Coast Tsimshian and Nisga'a peoples. These ties are cemented again and again by cycles of giving and receiving (goods and marriage partners), and by common family concerns and mutual participation in funeral feasts. The Witsuwit'en have similar ties to their neighbours, both to the Babine people to the east and the Kispiox, Gitanmaax, and Gitsegukla Gitksan. They also appear to have had long-standing, though not always harmonious, relations with the Haisla-speaking Kitimat on the Gardner Canal.

The "family" paradigm for social relations that ensure proper reciprocity is the feast, of which there are two types (see Chapter 2). The first type is the *li'ligit* (Git.), or general feast, in which food is given to the guests but gifts are not necessarily offered (or at least not major gifts), and where minor business may be conducted. The second type, the *yukw* (Git.), is where serious business is conducted, where a wider range of high chiefs are invited, and where the gift payments to the guests are substantial.

In kinship societies the possession and circulation of non-subsistence goods (the luxury goods mentioned above) are distinguished from but linked to the goods derived from the subsistence sphere. The prerequisite for the possession and exchange of luxury items usually entails rights over the production and disposition of subsistence goods (Malinowski 1922; Bohannan and Dalton 1962; Godelier 1966; Sahlins 1972). Malinowski (1922, 64) has reported that, among the Trobriand Islanders, one of the prerequisites for a chief to participate in the ceremonial *kula* exchange was the management of a bountiful subsistence economy and storage system. Weiner (1976, 1992) has added that this is accomplished by the close cooperation between brothers and sisters in the labours involved in preparing for ceremonial events and gift exchanges.

Among the protocontact Gitksan and Witsuwit'en and their coastal neighbours, the items that were revitalized and made more socially significant through exchange were copper shields (which were invested with names and personalities [as discussed in Chapter 1]), the occasional slave, crests, and sometimes even hunting territories (Boas 1916; Barbeau and Beynon n.d. [especially Eagle Clan *adaawk's*]; Barbeau 1950; Garfield 1966; Kan 1989; Oberg 1973; Sapir 1915a; Swanton 1905).

The manufacture and purchase of these goods depended upon the ability of the House to pay for them and upon the group's production and trade abilities. This procedure began with people working the land and the rivers, deploying their labour and entrapping, shooting, and collecting what the "Great Nature" provides (Book Builders of 'Ksan 1980).

Usually in the winter, after the completion of the most intense and active portion of the seasonal round, the fruits of House-controlled labour power would be most clearly revealed and "completed" during feasts and the winter ceremonies. Here important social and political decisions were formalized, elaborated, and sealed by the hosts, giving special luxury items to the head chiefs of other Houses and leading Houses of other villages. These items were, in themselves, an expression of the House group's dogged expenditure of effort to maintain the social and material standing bequeathed by its predecessors. Embedded within these goods (and their treatment as gifts) were the seeds of imbalance – the inalienable quality of the gift that drove, and continues to drive, the recipients to further production so as to be able to reciprocate at some point in the future. Social standing, then and now, is dependent upon public reciprocity. To be effective, such reciprocity is conducted with patience and equanimity down the generations. The evaluation of special feast gift items was contingent upon their being exchanged and consumed, or broken up and redistributed (as in the case of games of honour, especially in relation to the copper shields discussed in Chapter 1).

Today the luxury aspect of gift-giving is somewhat reduced. Chiefly gifts keep pace with present-day technology; they tend to be expensive yet useful. This has been the guiding principle of gift-giving/feast prestations along the upper Skeena and Bulkley. The principle has not changed since contact, although the goods given or counter-given certainly have. Animal pelt robes, aesthetic sculpted items, and coppers gradually gave way to manufactured goods, to Hudson's Bay blankets, then later to Coleman stoves and lanterns, tents, sleeping bags, bush clothes, and rifles, and again to suits of clothing, coats, duvets, food processors, television sets, and DVD players.

Whenever the storage pits and cache houses of the past were filled with the fruits of the territories, and supplemented with goods obtained by trade, the House could fulfill its feasting obligations and keep its names and reputation vibrant. Today, by combining food-getting on the land with wage labour and transfer payments, members of a House aim to achieve an approximation of past corporate kinship well-being and economic viability. They participate in barter and trade, as before, and also, as before, this market sector is harnessed to the gift economy. Those Houses not making great sacrifices so as to keep their standing high in the community become perpetual receivers of foodstuffs and of feast hall money. Their social standing in local affairs remains low and casts shadows on the various Houses to which they are linked by family ties. Moreover, if they are name-holders, the lack of response to gifts received also tarnishes their hereditary names.

In the past, those who managed to fill their storage pits and make the necessary sacrifices of personal well-being so as to fulfill the material requirements of their public feasting obligations gave social impetus to production and accumulation throughout the region. They have also tended to possess the highly valued items in the society – the masks, dance blankets, *amhalayt* (strong power) headdresses, raven rattles, copper shields, crests, ancient songs – all of which keep alive the ethos and identity of the chief and the House for yet another generation. In the eyes of the Gitksan and

Witsuwit'en, if the House fails to mount its feasts, the life force that surges through the regalia, the masks, the copper shields, and totem poles of the chief grows weak and feeble. These powers and the life force were formerly renewed through the kin group's proficiency in subsistence and barter, through unstinting giving to fulfill the needs of others. Today the situation is similar, except that economic proficiency now entails the widest involvement in the very limited opportunities available in the market sector of the mixed economy.

The late eighteenth and the nineteenth centuries saw an increase in barter and commodity exchange in relation to goods flowing between the Gitksan and Witsuwit'en and their neighbours. This was due to the expansion of the sphere of convertibility of indigenous goods – foodstuffs, tools, furs, and hides – into quantities of useful new European items: imported foods and manufactured goods such as knives, axes, pots, beads, and blankets. Yet this commodity trade was not a new innovation but, rather, an established tradition enjoying a quantitative increase and a more rapid tempo. Early eyewitnesses reported that feasting uses for furs outweighed considerations of accumulation through trade (Lamb 1957; Ogden 1853; and Brown in HBC 1822).[10] The salmon strips, tanned hides, groundhog robes, marten furs, dried berries, and sap cakes had long been used in a commodity fashion as items with values of equivalence in other goods.[11] What was innovative, however, in the nineteenth century was the tempo of exchange. Production for exchange probably increased, but it did not become the major force in the local economy at least until after the establishment of the industrial economy of raw material extraction and the formation of "Indian reserves" late in the nineteenth century. In the vicinity of major trading posts, the increase in competition and power-seeking distended the feast system to include extreme negative reciprocity with competitive, agonistic givings. Yet commodity trade on the coast adjacent to the Gitksan and Witsuwit'en did not destroy the basic economic emphasis upon kin-based subsistence, gift reciprocity, and the avid desire to obtain established luxury goods (Cole and Darling 1990; Fisher 1977; Suttles 1951; Wike 1951; Wolf 1982).

In the past, feasting obligations informed and inspired the planning and harvesting activities on the land; today these obligations drive some members of the community to work extra shifts in the sawmills.[12] The impetus for exchanging non-subsistence luxury goods is not to be found in an assumed propensity for maximizing material gain and prestige through forms of market exchange, as pointed out by Godelier (1966); rather, it is to be found in relation to the maintenance of ownership of the lands where the ancestors have made their living for many generations (see Chapter 7).

Economic studies frequently stress the primacy of distribution and exchange, particularly the market relations of economizing, and, finding these lacking or masked within other institutions in "anthropological" societies, they assume that these cultures have no exchange. Thus, even among Canada's public officials, precontact First Nations Canadians are considered to have been too crude and primitive to have engaged in systems of exchange. The Indian Act of Canada does not recognize the existence of goods circulation as integral to Aboriginal economies.

Economizing, in modern economic theory, is the economic decision taking in which it is assumed that profit-oriented participants will allocate scarce resources – labour, capital, and land – to alternate ends so as to best serve their respective entrepreneurial interests in conformity with the economic principle of market supply and demand. At one pole, this modern (and ethnocentric) economic outlook has led to feasting or potlatch analyses that emphasize market competition in the game of prestige accumulation. From this polar position, feasting is viewed as exemplary of a rich prestige economy wherein the public destruction of property is evidence of a system of credit and debt gone awry (Herskovits 1952, 415). At the other pole, we have the Indian Act, 1985, and the viewpoint adopted by Chief Justice McEachern that Aboriginal society had no production. From this perspective, Aboriginal peoples were considered to have simply eaten directly from nature and allegedly enjoyed no trade (i.e., people lived in discrete, isolated villages with minimal contact with each other or the land surrounding them). Economic and ethnographic realities are far from either of these extremes.

In the past, subsistence demands of the Gitksan and Witsuwit'en seasonal round placed limits on the possibilities for acquiring wealth through exchange. Still, this is not to say that exchange has not been an integral feature of the economy; but it is important to point out that regional exchange was closely related to seasonal economic productive activities on the land and at the fishing sites. (Landed property rights gave stability to, and protected, the important seasonal round from unplanned harvesting by others and from incursions by strangers, thereby protecting the rights to allocate kinship labour within fixed territories.) At the present time the profitable allocation of scarce resources to alternate ends by Gitksan and Witsuwit'en peoples is limited. It is limited more severely than in the past by immigrant, large-scale mining, logging, recreational, and other ventures on the lands and rivers the people describe as their food box, their treasury, and their home. When asked where they plan to hunt, young Gitksan and Witsuwit'en often say, "We are going to the Indian supermarket, to our land."[13]

The peoples' oral histories indicate that there have been definite periods of intense barter, raiding, and diplomacy across the region (Barbeau and Beynon n.d.; Duff n.d.; Halpin 1973; Marsden 1987). Probably the proto-contact period between the seventeenth and late nineteenth centuries constituted one such era when trade goods, always important to the subsistence economy, began to take on an existence of their own. This is the period when they increasingly became exchangeable goods – goods that gain their value mainly from their convertibility: in a word, *commodities*. Commodities are considered to have had their origins on the margins or fringes of kinship economies where it is often socially easier to maximize one's returns than is the case among one's kinfolk (Gregory 1982, 12). The control of commodity-cum-barter trade and trade routes at this point in Northwest Coast history led to wars and intense competition throughout the northeast Pacific area. In those cordilleran regions adjacent to the more volatile coast, even when coastal trading was not in a period of great competitiveness, the local economy was annually affected by external exchange. This has been particularly noticeable during the oolichan season and in the autumn and winter months when many of the large ceremonial gatherings occurred, both on the coast and inland.

Admittedly, periodic competition and conflict with neighbouring peoples (in times of intense trade) strengthened the Gitksan and Witsuwit'en system of clearly defined, House-owned hunting territories and fishing sites owned by matrilineal House groups. The ranking, stratification, and clearly defined property rights associated with trade activities existed at least in protocontact times (Bishop 1987). The oral culture and the archaeological record affirm that such stratification is of considerably greater antiquity than is accorded by Bishop.[14] If an archaeology of genealogical tables were possible to prove, I am confident we would also find a lengthy tradition of exchanges of personnel between families across the general Northwest Coast region and the adjacent cordillera. It is almost certain that there have been extensive ties of marriage and affinity, the conduits of gifting, barter, and trade between property-holding kin groups down through the generations.

But of course property ownership did not evolve simply from trade between different ecological zones. It also evolved from the need to regulate resource use, given a relatively densely clustered population (at least seasonally) in relation to the technology used to procure, prepare, and store the various runs of returning salmon, and the additional dietary and material needs of the population.

Other researchers (Ball 1985; Schalk 1981) subscribe to this view as well. Ball (1985, 37-8, fn.) outlines the debate that occurred in Canadian anthropology in the 1970s and 1980s concerning the nature of land tenure in precontact Canada. She adds her voice to those who see the Pacific Northwest as an area marked by well-defined ownership due to population density, regular salmon runs, and indigenous trade: "I contend that there is convincing evidence that the Indians of British Columbia developed land tenure systems within recognized territories during aboriginal times ... I can offer three possible reasons why: the first reason is that the comparatively dense Indian population on the Pacific watershed put pressure on the resources; the second is that the Pacific watershed Indians relied heavily on anadromous fish for sustenance and trade items – consequently they lived rather sedentary lives compared to many eastern tribes; and the third is that the Indians did not exploit the resources solely for local and tribal use but also for intertribal trade."

It is likely that the system of land tenure developed at the time of original settlement in the area by the ancestors of these peoples. The archaeological findings at Hagwilget, for instance, suggest a long period of regular, productive habitation along the section of the bank of the Skeena River that the oral histories call Temlaxamid, or Dizkle, their ancient home location. This appears to have been a long riverine settlement, extending many kilometres. The probable location was the vicinity of the junction of the Skeena and Bulkley Rivers. The Gitksan and their *adaawk*'s refer to the settlement extending from the present-day Hazelton area almost to Gitsegukla, and the Witsuwit'en and their *kungakhs* refer to a similar original large village on both sides of the Bulkley somewhat upstream from Hazelton.[15]

The Gitksan oral histories suggest that the first settlers in an area took the best territories they could find (i.e., those in conjunction with the best river fishing sites), while subsequent settlers established themselves in conjunction with or beside those who preceded them. Local awareness of population and resource balance is evidenced by events that are said to have followed the Gitksan dispersal from Temlaxamid, when the oral tradition suggests the land tenure system was already in place. Refugees from Temlaxamid were taken in and hosted by neighbouring settlements until the additional human predation on the main subsistence species led to enmity between the refugees and their hosts, as recounted in the Medeek Adaawk' (Robinson 1962). This *adaawk'* recounts that the refugees moved on to other regions, often further downstream, either settling unoccupied territory or breaking into small groupings and joining existing settlements.

Most conflicts between peoples in the region appear to have arisen over the monopoly of trade routes. They appear not to have arisen from scarcity of land and goods until enmities generated by the westward and eastward expansion of the European fur trade were felt in the region, probably in the early nineteenth century (Jenness 1937; Morice 1895/1971; and note is above). Intergroup feasting, barter, and trade were vital and integral features of the economy; however, their importance was limited by the necessary attention paid by the peoples to the production processes associated with the seasonal round.

Mixed Economy and Circulation of Values

Today the Gitksan and Witsuwit'en have a different mixed economy. Families combine subsistence hunting, fishing, and berry-picking with participation in the wider Canadian economy through limited wage employment, trapping, commercial fishing, farming, small business ventures, positions in the professions, and considerable reliance on government social service payments. This mixed economy is the legacy of European settlement in Canada. As the newcomers' social order consolidated, Aboriginal peoples suffered population decimation, and their economy and society experienced pressure and influence from the social system and expectations of the immigrant populations.

The Gitksan and Witsuwit'en have participated in the economy of the newcomers. Yet they have sought to do so without abandoning the hunting, fishing, and berry-picking lifestyle that is at the core of their respective cultures. They are trying to update the planned use of resources and assert their managerial rights in their traditional territories, which Canada and British Columbia consider Crown land. They are seeking to do this in accord with both modern economic processes and the principles of decentralized decision making – as exemplified by the reciprocal relations of the feast hall. The present-day economy, with its adherence to the land, its technological change, and its partial reliance on the Canadian market economy, is referred to here as a "mixed economy."

Long adept at exchanging goods with coastal and interior neighbours, the Gitksan and Witsuwit'en have been able to make the change to commodity production with considerable ease, supplying primary resources for sale whenever, in the past century or more, the market conditions have been favourable. They have produced furs, gold, railway ties, power poles, and wild mushrooms; they have provided guide-outfitter services, fish, meat, fuel, and transport for survey crews, trading companies, construction crews, and prospectors. They have operated sawmills and fishing vessels, small shops and handicraft operations. Today, with the large-scale nature of market-oriented production ventures, they are unable to compete financially – at least under prevailing conditions – with governments and large firms.

As the global market economy expands and contracts in its trajectory of development, Gitksan and Witsuwit'en participation is severely affected. In the early stages of resource production, there was room for indigenous peoples to participate by means of their own small-scale production enterprises and by selling their labour in wage employment. Due to the uncertainty and fluctuations of the modern economy, the Gitksan and Witsuwit'en continue to keep at least one foot on the land. The berries continue to be picked; the salmon runs are netted, gaffed, and smoked; the fall hunt and wild mushroom collection for the Japanese market continue; and the system of reciprocal kinship-related feasts is still the focal point of community life.

Since the *Delgamuukw* decision at the Supreme Court there is considerable emphasis on demonstrating sustainable management and use of the lands, even though territorial land title remains denied to the Gitksan and Witsuwit'en. Building on work developed in the 1980s, the Gitksan in particular are combining sophisticated mapping and inventory techniques, as mentioned in Don Ryan's Afterword, merging traditional ecological knowledge (TEK) and state-of-the-art data collecting methods. They are setting up watershed authorities and trusts to demonstrate their responsibility towards and use of the land, and to demonstrate alternative forms of forest and other resource extraction. See, for example, the plans laid out in the Gitxsan Strategic Analysis Team's (1999) *The Gitxsan Model: An Alternative to the Destruction of Forests, Salmon and Gitxsan Land*.

The annual domestic economy of a family in a modern mixed economy situation is often multi-stranded: the family's material survival is the result of combined activities in two spheres: (1) producing food and shelter and (2) producing market commodities. People in most economies evaluate some goods and human activities on the basis of their usefulness, and other goods and activities on the basis of their convertibility into money (or into social capital through gifting). In the dominant society and economy of Canada market relations predominate. In the Gitksan and Witsuwit'en mixed economy, however, the evaluation of goods and services on the basis of use and direct need on the part of one's extended family and relatives continues to be highly important. This continues to be the case today, despite the fact that participation in the cash economy is essential even to outfit oneself for hunting and fishing pursuits on the land.

Let us assume for a moment that the gift exchange implicit in feast-giving is part of the everyday "subsistence round" of social activities. What happens when the "commodity of commodities," money, enters this subsistence sphere? Are the relationships of feast-giving converted to contractual market relations? No. To the contrary: a commodity from the market sphere is taken up for use inside the gift-based feast system. There are parallels with First Nations demands, in the fur trade era, to have European goods that could fit into indigenous systems of gift exchange (Cole and Darling 1990; Wike 1951). Similarly, indigenous peoples have used money for feasting by adapting it *from* the market economy *to* the social needs of the gift economy. The cash used in feast transactions today is viewed not as "market style" payment but, rather, as a handy token for marking and recognizing levels of wealth and difference of status in the community – a medium that provides a "gold standard" for gift reciprocation and for services rendered. The cash is shown to feast guests in the same way as is the produce of the land – as part of the semiotics of accounting, proprietorship, and social and political legitimacy. Monies are explained metaphorically, as a stand-in for the wealth of the lands, such that a $40,000 or $50,000 feast (at the end of the twentieth century) attests to the strength and industry of the family.[16] To the extent that people engage in the sale of resources in their daily lives, they may indeed be concerned to turn a profit, but this sphere of economic endeavour is kept conceptually separate from the ceremonial.

People dip into the market sphere and its cash to obtain items necessary to continuing life on the land, including feast payments.

This taking up of cash for use in another sphere – the feast system – parallels the situation described by Godelier (1969; 1999, 138-40) in Papua New Guinea. He describes the use of Baruya salt money, which functions as a general currency in commodity exchange with neighbouring peoples but, when used internally in the local community, serves as an item of ceremonial consumption, lending sacred grace to the proceedings. Present-day cash in the Gitksan and Witsuwit'en feasts can be considered in a similar light. Money is an affair of the mind. It stands for relationships, standards, and convertibility of wealth and value. This parallels the functioning of gold, over a century ago, as the ultimate standard, the item that contained "something inalienable," something that, while at the core of market relations, was kept out of circulation so that everything else could circulate. In Marx's day, as a standard of value, gold was merely nominal money, and money, nominal gold. As a medium of circulation, it was symbolic money and symbolic gold, but in terms of its metallic entity, gold was money, or money was real gold, and as such it stood behind the bank notes that circulated in commodity exchange. Indeed, "here, in the very midst of a market economy, of universal currency, and generalized competition, we discover that something needs to be kept out of circulation, to be voluntarily withheld from the sphere and the movement of exchange in order for the mass of market and bank exchanges to be set in motion, for everything that can be bought or sold to begin circulating" (Godelier 1999, 28). In other words, money is not that far away from the inalienable nature of the pure gift and need not be the nemesis of the gift. In certain conditions, it can comfortably find a role to play in the gift sphere.

Such goods predominate in all subsistence economies. Even full market economies contain both goods for subsistence and goods for exchange. Indeed, there would be no impetus for exchange in any economy if the flow of goods had no ultimate practicality. And, one could add, no feasts could be conducted without the commensuality between guests and hosts. While market-sector commodities are valued as exchange items, they are hard pressed to maintain their value of convertibility without their connections to the useful, directly consumable items of every day.

The contemporary commitment of Gitksan and Witsuwit'en to their land, within the context of a mixed economy, is a reflection of their economic experience since contact. They have conducted small enterprises such as pole camps, sawmills, hand logging, and commercial fish boats – viable mid-twentieth-century concerns. More recent enterprises, which are larger in scale and are sometimes organized at the DIA administrative band level, like the present logging and sawmill venture at Moricetown, are conducted in the raw materials sector. These enterprises are geared to selling their products not to satisfy the expectations of investors for maximum returns for their support of the enterprise but, rather, to provide jobs, increase the tempo of local exchange, and enable indigenous peoples to gain some benefit from resources that otherwise would be totally lost to the outsiders who are awarded forest contracts. The Witsuwit'en of Moricetown, with their forest enterprise, have tried their best to stem the invasive "development" of their territories by developing these themselves so as to provide an income that would help satisfy their general subsistence needs. The results have been far from satisfactory, due, in part, to the massive scale of tree removal required by government licensing.[17]

The relationship between work, the utility of goods, and their public acknowledgment through gift-giving in feasts is a common theme in these communities. Alfred Joseph referred to this in the course of his testimony (Transcript, 1622) when he explained that one of the qualities that people look for in a prospective chief is industriousness. The candidate is expected to be not only responsible but also a good worker. A good worker is defined as a person who is alert and "ready to give assistance to someone in need and one that takes leadership and advice, and [is] always participating in feasts."

To be able to fulfill these obligations the candidate for chiefship must be a regular and productive worker, capable of providing the material assistance required of him or her. Today this includes the acceptance of wage labour work, which the Witsuwit'en elders view differently than do members of the main Euro-Canadian culture. The Euro-Canadian culture views wage work as a simple economic transaction wherein those who possess labour power, on one hand, and capital, on the other, exchange their goods in the market through the medium of money. And thus the relationship ends. Witsuwit'en elders see another, moral dimension to the job, namely, that of a gift relationship with its ability to reveal the participants' relation to work, productivity, and future long-term reciprocal possibilities.

Prior to European contact and throughout the nineteenth century, other forms of exchange did exist. A few definite items were linked with market-type convertibility; however, the values that these items stood for are specified and limited by feasting rules and procedures. A few of the items in these transactions, specifically copper shields (as discussed in Chapter 1), were highly symbolic, spiritually vibrant, and ceremonial. Their value increased with each pay-out or each giving. Similarly, they could be exchanged for only a few other items of wealth.[18] The degree of intense human interaction associated with these ceremonial items, which passed from chief to chief, increased the power and value of the items in the symbolic and political sense – that is, as long as these symbolic transactions were underwritten by the daily productive activity of the members of the community. Over the course of the twentieth century, cash used in public inter-House affairs has gradually acquired some of these same values and has likewise been constrained from exhibiting its commodity aspect in relation to feasting. As we shall see, especially in Chapter 6, there are limits to what money can buy in a reciprocal kinship form of organization.

FIGURE 25 (PRECEDING PAGE)   Sockeye basket trap in Hagwilget Canyon, 1923. Since the rockslide on the Bulkley River in 1820 the Gitanmaax people have shared this canyon with the Witsuwit'en. An early traveller, Helen Woods, wrote about such fish traps in April 1880: "This large cage is let down with the open side down stream. The salmon going up get into the cage & cannot get out, then the man goes out on the sticks and draws up the cage & takes out his salmon" (Bridge 1998, 141). Fishing is no longer bountiful here since the Canadian Department of Fisheries exploded a rock in the middle of the river in the 1950s; salmon were no longer able to rest in the same eddies on their way upstream through Hagwilget Canyon towards their spawning grounds.

© *Canadian Museum of Civilization, No. 59634. Photo: C.M. Barbeau.*

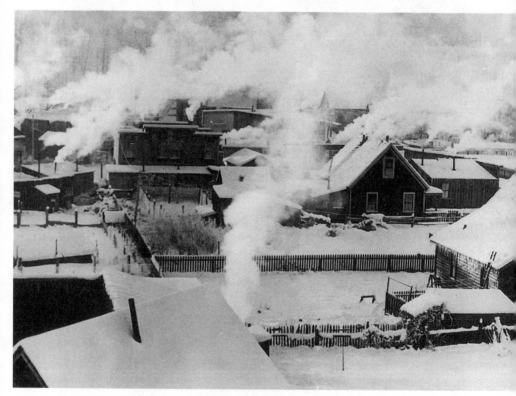

FIGURE 26   "Warming a cold snap." Winter in Hazelton during the early twentieth century, when temperatures dropped below –40°C. Located at the confluence of the Bulkley (Wedzenkwe) and Skeena ('Ksan) Rivers, near the villages of Gitanmaax and Hagwilget, Hazelton became an early trading and administrative centre in the area.

BC Archives, No. A-4008.

FIGURE 27 The new village site of Hagwilget, above the canyon, with Mount
Rocher de Boule, or Stikyoo'denhl, "Home of the Mountain Goats," in the
background.
BC Archives, No. I-021833.

FIGURE 28   Hagwilget, the original village down in Hagwilget Canyon. This village was established by the Witsuwit'en shortly after 1820, with permission from Gitksan *simgiget* of Gitanmaax Village, as a fishing station. This followed the devastation wrought by a major rockslide that blocked the Bulkley River and impeded the return of the salmon upstream to the main Witsuwit'en fishing area of Moricetown Canyon. The current Hagwilget Village is above the canyon.
Royal BC Museum, No. PN-3399.

FIGURE 29   Smokehouses in Kisgagas Canyon, summer 1920. Gitksan elders spoke of the volume of sockeye sometimes being so extreme here that, at the height of the Babine run, this stretch of the canyon contained more salmon than water.
© *Canadian Museum of Civilization, No. 49469. Photo: C.M. Barbeau.*

FIGURE 30 "Old potlatch houses at Kisgagas," 1920. The village seen here was composed of houses built of squared timbers in the style of the day. The fish-drying and smokehouses were below in the canyon (see previous photo). For defensive purposes, the storage pits for this food-rich village were located some distance away from the village site.

© *Canadian Museum of Civilization, No. 49459. Photo: C.M. Barbeau.*

FIGURE 31   Woman cutting salmon beside a Haida-type canoe in front of Glen Vowell, the Salvation Army village located on the Skeena River between Gitanmaax and Kispiox. 1920.

© Canadian Museum of Civilization, No. 49402. Photo: C.M. Barbeau.

FIGURE 32   Lillian Jackson (1896-1927), Wilps Milulek (mother of the late Robert Jackson, Simoogit Xsemgitgigeenix), at the sockeye drying racks in Kisgagas Canyon, summer 1920. According to Simoogit Wii Gaak, Neil Sterritt Sr., when there was sufficient river wind, fish could be dried here without smoke, as is also done along the Fraser River Canyon. Smoke is used to protect the flesh from flies when and wherever there is insufficient wind to keep them at bay.

© Canadian Museum of Civilization, No. 49443. Photo: C.M. Barbeau.

FIGURE 33   Gaffing chinook salmon at Kya Wiget, Moricetown Canyon.
BC Archives, No. I-21865.

FIGURE 34 "The first Hagwilget bridge." Here "first" refers to the earliest bridge over the Hagwilget Canyon observed by Europeans rather than the first in history. Similar cantilevered structures were found crossing many rivers along the trade routes, or "grease trails," of the region and were of construction comparable to fishing platforms in the river canyons. They obviously predate European technology. *BC Archives, No. A-06048.*

FIGURE 35 Arthur Wellington Clah, of Gispaxlo'ots, at Port Simpson 1915. Clah was an avid diarist, and his journals reflect life between the Nass and Skeena Rivers at the turn of the nineteenth century. He was an associate of the powerful Gispaxlo'ots *simoogit* Ligeex, as well as the Tsimshian language teacher of missionary William Duncan (in 1857), and the maternal grandfather of William Beynon, the man who practised Northwest Coast ethnography for half a century, working both on his own and in collaboration with C. Marius Barbeau of the National Museum of Canada.
© *Canadian Museum of Civilization, No. 31056. Photo: C.M. Barbeau.*

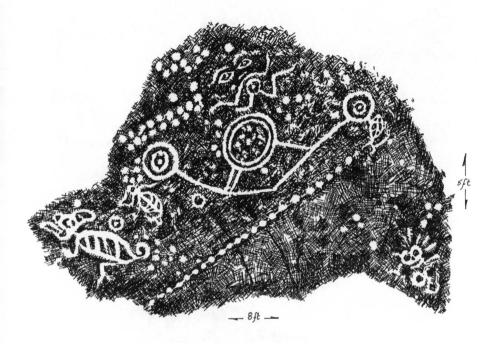

5 ft

— 8 ft —

FIGURE 36 Petroglyph at Anla<u>x</u>sim'de'ex, below Kisgagas Canyon. From a rubbing made by Erica Ball of Hazelton. One August during the mid-1990s, at low water in the Babine River, Brian Muldoe, Rudy Johnson, and George Sampson rescued this petroglyph from mossy obscurity. These images possibly constitute an old psychic boundary marker and a form of protection for the local residents. This one could also be a visual record of an out-of-body power journey experienced at this place. On the riverbank adjacent to these images there are many storage pits. Note the wolf figure at bottom left. Judging by the binary division of villages in this portion of the cordillera (between the Wolves and the Frog/Ravens), this would be an identifying crest of either the mother or father of virtually anyone native to this place. These images probably long predate current Gitksan memories of villages in this vicinity.

Rubbing and reproduced image courtesy of Erica Ball of Two-Mile, Hazelton.

FIGURE 37 Petroglyph found on the riverbank at Kispiox, 1920. A visual record of identity and land occupancy, probably indicating a sense of family or village rootedness, similar in function and social significance to the petroglyph featured in Figure 36.

© *Canadian Museum of Civilization, No. 49533. Photo: C.M. Barbeau.*

FIGURE 38 *Salmon, the Story of Our People,* by Luu Goom'kw (Eric McPherson), of Wilps Wiiget in Kispiox.

FIGURE 39 Simoogit Wii Muk'wilixw (Art Wilson), La<u>x</u> Gibuu, Kispiox Village, surveys what is left of his territory from a slash pile in the middle of a cut-block. This territory, like many others, was clear-cut without permission from the chief and family members of those who own, and are owned by, this piece of Gitksan land.

Photo: Steve Bosch, courtesy the Vancouver Sun.

5
Production Management and Social Hierarchy

A Storage Economy

Two general types of hunter-gatherer societies have been distinguished: "immediate-return" (on-the-spot consumers who forage every few days, year round) and "delayed-return" (people who store the fruits of seasonal foraging and have a fairly complex social organization pertaining to work and distribution). Members of the former uphold an ethic of band-wide egalitarianism, sharing movable property and collective rights to the ethnic territory; they treat all members of society as family. By contrast, the delayed-return type tends towards reciprocal relations that occur in a tribe-oriented society composed of interacting kin groups. Here, social inequality (often acknowledged only *within* the local groupings), and sometimes negative reciprocity, signal a hierarchy of social statuses (Woodburn 1982).

An immediate-consumption hunter-gatherer society usually gathers food on a daily basis, consumes that food immediately, and resumes foraging a day or so later. The precontact coastal Inuit society (Chance 1966) tended towards this type, as did many societies of Aboriginal Australia (Berndt and Berndt 1980; Meggitt 1962; Spencer and Gillen 1927; Strehlow 1947); other classic examples were Khoisan-speaking peoples like the Ju/'hoansi (!Kung San) of the Botswana-Namibia borderlands in the Kalahari Desert (Lee 1979; Lee and DeVore 1976). A hunting society with a storage economy also harvests year-round, yet its distinguishing feature is production and storage in relation to the main growing season, especially in the more seasonal, extreme latitudes.

These distinctions have been further refined in recent years as scholars have pointed out that most hunter-gatherers, even the classically immediate type, also practise some delayed-return activities. Such activities tend to demand trust between people and bind them to one another during the period of delay between expenditure of labour and harvest and consumption (Ingold 1986, 213-17). Bird-David (1994), in arguing for an analytic move away from the ecological and mode-of-production features of such societies, suggests returning to the discourse on the band (Steward 1955; Service 1962; Sahlins 1968) in order to go more deeply into the nature of such social formations. She points out that the strong personal autonomy noted in foraging band societies (hitherto associated with immediate-return activities) does not lead to interpersonal relations of an atomic nature, involving accretion and fragmentation but, rather, that individual identity can be imposed through a hierarchy of influence (such as that imposed by nation-states). However, these forms of association are most profitably viewed as a relational process composed of coalescence and splitting. Bird-David likens this to the behaviour of droplets of oil that flow in and out of one another, with each accretion increasing the individuality of both the whole and its elements. This, she argues, is predicated upon long association and detailed interpersonal knowledge and tradition. She contends that this is determined by long-standing sociological factors associated with small-scale band society rather than being reflective of immediate-return economic practices. Here, individual identity is created through common interaction, whereas in hierarchic modern civil society, individual identity is often considered a condition given prior to interaction. One wonders, however, if both types of interaction – at least conceptually – do not occur in all social formations.[1]

Be that as it may, these refinements do enrich the general distinction made by Woodburn (1982) for understanding the range of possibilities for conducting social relations associated with hunting and gathering activities. If we continue to bear in mind this huge diversity, then we are forced to take account of a multitude of empirical causes and factors to explain foraging phenomena in their processes. We cannot try to locate single causes for phenomena, be they from biology, psychology, ecology, economy, or history.

In small social groupings with some reliance on foraging, the ephemeral appropriation and consumption of goods from nature by autonomous persons capable of flowing into and out of one another's lives, and the structured interdependent relations of super/subordination between people who are linked for finite periods, are polar types of relationship. Such peoples have for long periods of history maintained themselves by exchanging and interacting with surrounding peoples. The balance in any society at a specific point may favour one or the other type.

In the case of the Witsuwit'en and the Gitksan, both immediate consumption and sharing, as well as storage management and reciprocity, are parts of their social and cultural life. This is a reality, despite the fact that Northwest Coast peoples are frequently characterized as complex, hierarchical, affluent slave-taking foragers (Averkieva 1966; Burch and Ellanna 1994, 5-6, 219-21; Hayden 1994). The social construction of the individual suggested above by Bird-David may be conceived as the realizing of identity

through a common form of collective productive activity, where participants learn to become members through their engagement in similar interactive processes. They absorb a habitus that is reproduced in the course of
working together for their daily bread. They also define themselves in relation to the commonality of their work. This reverberates in the working-
class culture that the Gitksan and Witsuwit'en enter in their entrepreneurial
and wage labour lives as well.

Such work-related social learning has been a central feature of certain
schools of pedagogy in industrial society (e.g., those of Vygotsky and Dewey).
Through "workshop learning" the student or apprentice feels more fulfilled
and satisfied in the course of job-related group work and group learning
than in the formal, individual, and competitive scholarly learning tradition
and habitus of the middle class (Mjelde 1995, 1997). It could be that the
dominant form of immediate, individualized relationship discussed by Ingold
and Bird-David is common to the social ordering of many production activities that are not marked by a high degree of labour differentiation and
hierarchy, no matter what the type of society. If this is the case, then my
descriptive emphasis on the generative, identity-creating power of Gitksan
and Witsuwit'en land-based work – parallel with the persisting theme of
material and ecological relations in hunting and gathering studies over the
past three decades – is important for understanding the nature of social
relations and social governance.

Geographical Mobility and Storage

Kinship economies with a marked tendency to storage of foodstuffs are generally associated with tribal structure, sedentary populations with crucial
resources that regularly recur naturally (as the salmon of the Northwest
Coast or sago of Southeast Asia), or populations that have been domesticated. The Gitksan and the Witsuwit'en have stored much of their procured
wild produce without engaging in domestication. At the same time, they
have not lived a totally sedentary life, nor have they been devoid of immediate return activities, nor has the region been immune from shortages and
failures of food sources. Some failures were due to avalanches of boulders
and scree. A major rock fall devastated Witsuwit'en and Nedut'en[2] salmon
supplies in 1820, (referred to in the reports of Trader Brown [Hudson's Bay
Company 1822] and in the fieldnotes of Marius Barbeau [Barbeau and Beynon
1915-57: BF 90.1-29]). Other resource failures were due to occasional shifts
in climatic conditions (Barbeau and Beynon n.d. *[Temlarhlam: The Land of
Plenty]*; Robinson 1962) and failures of the Nass River oolichan runs (Boas
1916, 399).

Protocontact settlements were sedentary to the extent that people lived
in villages with wooden plank or pole frame houses for at least some weeks
of each year (the Witsuwit'en) or to the extent that some persons among

the very young, as well as the old and the chiefs, lived in the village most of the year (Gitksan). The Witsuwit'en had small dwellings on their territories and erected totem poles at some of these "home" locations (e.g., Lhë Tait on a tributary of the upper Bulkley River). These locations were of great importance to the seasonal round and to socioeconomic planning. Relatively fixed houses were used as shelters regularly in certain seasons, but such dwellings did not denote a sedentary population.

A sure indicator of the sedentary life is the ability to have several small children in each family at the same time, as frequently occurs in agricultural societies. Well into the twentieth century, this did not pertain among the Gitksan and Witsuwit'en. Children were spaced out so as to allow for the maximum physical mobility of the family in the course of the seasonal activities. Anxiety about periodic food shortages was not unknown and recurred in the peoples' oral narratives. Even among the most lavish and hierarchic peoples of the Tsimshian family, the Coast Tsimshian, this appears to have been the case. The advent of the oolichan at the end of winter was essential to assuage the hungry season and ensure the survival of village life until the growing season commenced. This is attested to linguistically, with oolichan meaning "our helper," the same term used by missionaries for explaining "our Saviour," Jesus Christ (Daly 1986-87 [Trombley]). As well, the *adaawk'* narratives indicate the crucial nature of this fishery in relation to competition, enmity, war, and diplomacy down through the oral history of the estuary of the Nass River.

The settled village life of the Gitksan, with food secure for the winter months – buried in storage pits or hanging in aerial meat caches (see meat cache in middle distance in Figure 4) – was the product of an economy based on a calendar of activities. This round of activity was centred on summer runs of salmon and supplemented by hunting and gathering pursuits. By contrast, the Witsuwit'en moved out to the hunting territories from salmon fishing sites in the canyons of the Bulkley River, returning to a number of small settlements in the territories during the winter. Witsuwit'en summer fishing settlements on the river, which today have been designated Department of Indian Affairs reserve village sites, are considered by the people to be temporary, seasonal camps into which they have been confined by government decree. Gitksan referred to the short, seasonal use of Kya Wiget (Moricetown) of the Witsuwit'en as Laxilts'ap, "the abandoned place" (Mills 1994, 110). As a result of their massive seasonal migrations between river fishing and the home territories, the Witsuwit'en have had an economy that is somewhat less storage-oriented than that of the Gitksan. Storage was limited to what could be cached for some months, or transported from the summer fishing sites to the winter hunting grounds, and to what could be harvested in the hunting grounds and stored there over the winter. This is a pattern familiar to many Athapaskan- and Algonquian-speaking hunting peoples across the Canadian subarctic. Nevertheless, foodstuffs were likely stored by the Witsuwit'en in greater amounts than among many of their fellow Athapaskan neighbours, and the production of salmon strips, berry cakes, rawhide, furs, and sinews provided the people with a significant quantity of goods for gift-giving and barter. They spent a great amount of energy transporting their stored goods from place to place.[3] The technology of storage was as highly developed among the Witsuwit'en as among the Gitksan.

Today the Gitksan and Witsuwit'en continue to put away stores of supplies for winter use, even if they earn regular wages and live near the supermarkets. They are trained from childhood to understand the importance of preserving and storing salmon, fruit, and other country foods, laying in a good supply of firewood[4] and putting away their money in readiness for funeral and headstone feasts. Unlike the alleged improvidence of immediate-return peoples, who consume what is available today without concern for tomorrow, on the Northwest Coast there is an ethic of locking up valuables and saving for contingencies, emergencies, and inevitable life crises. One has only to enter the homes of House chiefs or other active feast organizers to notice the stockpiling of goods in the spare bedroom, against the living room wall, or in the cellar in readiness for the next ceremonial gathering demanded by lifecycle changes. Storage enables both stable daily nutrition and the fulfillment of kinship obligations between Houses, especially on the occasion of public feasts.

Income derived from sudden profits, such as the high-priced furs during the 1930s, does not have the same feast value as goods or cash obtained from the normal subsistence round of economic activities based on primary resource harvesting (Daly 1986-88 [Joseph]). This evaluation was even stronger in the past; today, wage labour derived from logging, sawmills, construction, and Native administration, as well as pension cheques, is considered to be integral to the annual subsistence round. By contrast, large sums of money from bingo winnings or short-term projects are not regarded in the same light, perhaps because they are less closely related to subsistence and, hence, removed from the status available to the successful management of labour.

Accumulation, Trade, and Hierarchy

In economic anthropology, accumulation is often associated with centralized leadership and redistribution; it is correlated with social inequality, the centripetal force of chiefly redistribution, with its accompanying status hierarchy. This may well have affected the Gitksan and Witsuwit'en prior to the protocontact period, at least at certain points in the lengthy oral history (Marsden 1987, 2001). However, for long periods the degree of inequality, status hierarchy, and centralized authority appears to have been limited by the peoples' preoccupation with the round of subsistence activities. Chiefly persons and elders (often the same people) directed the seasonal round and the flow of labour between the lands and fishing sites of members of House groups closely related to one another.

The density of population at locations where the reliable food staples were harvested (the river fishing stations) may have increased the population's vulnerability to fluctuations and failures in supplementary foodstuffs. The precontact seasonal population aggregations, especially among the Gitksan, demanded considerable planning of land use and storage in order that basic foraged goods, in all their diversity, were available to all families in such a manner that village life could be maintained on a fairly harmonious footing for most of the year. Holocene conditions and a relatively dense population in the Pacific Northwest may have forced people to be less species-selective and more reliant upon kin group division of labour concerning the seasonal round (Schalk 1981; Cohen 1981). On the coast these conditions seem to have created pressure for access to resources controlled by others (e.g., the conflicts noted in the *adaawk*'s between Haida, Tsimshian, and Tlingit groups over access to the Nass River, with its oolichan, its sea mammals, and its salmon fishery). Inland, stability seems to have been sought over the last three millennia at least, through territorial control, management of labour, and resource distribution on the part of the leaders of matrilineal kin groups.

These leaders fulfilled a redistributive role not by calling in goods from across their areas of jurisdiction in order to apportion the produce to members and supporters but by parcelling out usufruct rights to land and controlling the degree of predation thereon. All those within this jurisdiction who had obligations to any specific House, by birth or marriage, were expected to contribute portions of the wealth that they had obtained from the land to support activities necessary to keep up the good name of the House. The emphasis was generally not upon maximizing accumulation and centralizing distribution but, rather, upon ensuring that families within the House, *wil'naat'ahl,* and clan stored enough values to cover contingencies (such as obsequies to the deceased) and simply to get safely through the winter. This of course bound the producers together through the seasons. They held common stores of food and goods by virtue of their kin ties.

As Halpin (1973, 95-6) notes, neither hierarchies nor foraged abundance were carved in stone, even among the more lavish social relations of the Coast Tsimshian: "Rank was obviously an important way of classifying individuals and social groups to the Tsimshian. But it was not an absolute determined by birth, some kind of fixed 'Chain of Being,' as is sometimes implied. Rank was an ideology, a linear pattern used by the Tsimshian to determine priorities in different social contexts. Conceivably, each concrete ranking one might observe might differ from every other, depending upon the context, the population units involved, and the privileges being called forth for the event."

Much of the anthropological literature tends to ascribe a class structure to the northern coastal peoples of the protocontact and contact period, even though these societies lacked paramount leaders like those of Polynesia, although the development of chiefdoms may have been in process at the time of contact. The life stories of nineteenth-century coastal trader chiefs such as Shakes, Tsibasaa, and Ligeex suggest such developments may have been occurring under fur trade conditions (Robinson 1997; Wolf 1982). Nonetheless, as discussed in the next chapter, attempts to expand their authority beyond the limits of their matrilineal kin group were unsuccessful. Dividing the members of one family between aristocrats, commoners, and ne'er-do-well rubbish people is ethnocentric and misleading. Kan (1989), for instance, in his rich and detailed account of nineteenth-century Tlingit feasting, acknowledges that these rankings are all within the local kin group and that the Tlingit did not have a class society. Nonetheless, he refers throughout his book to "the aristocracy" and "the commoners," terms derived from, and evocative of, class societies and, consequently, diverting the reader from the "up-front," face-to-face family medium that expresses social relations across the Northwest Coast region.

Certainly there were/are rankings of Gitksan and Witsuwit'en House groups and families that shifted, that were/are constantly disputed and only partially and severally acknowledged by sections of the local society, as Halpin points out for the Tsimshian in general. There is usually an expression of solidarity vis-à-vis outsiders among House and family members, and this extends across the lines of wealth within the kin group. The process of political life, it seems to me, is more akin to a structure in which "big men" accumulations and expenditures of value can occur (although this term too is problematic – denoting processes more than institutions – as Rosman and Rubel [1971] and Godelier [1986], among others, have noted).

Because members of one Gitksan or Witsuwit'en House group married into several others, crosscutting obligations fanned out widely between villages and territories. In his *Delgamuukw* evidence, Tenimget, Arthur Mathews Jr., described the many consultations that precede the organization of a feast or the taking of a wider decision, such as pursuing a land claim. He explains this practice in terms of the interwoven nature of blood ties, land use, and shared "heritage" through mothers as well as through fathers:

> Like I indicated and tried to show here, we have interests, quite high interest in our own territories, Xsi gwinixst'aat and Ts'ihl gwellii, but our interest far reaches out to other territories through *wilksiwitxw* [patrilateral kin], both your mother and your father's side, and like, relatives from other vil-

lages. This is what we call the helping of each other, a phrase that we have in our language, *nahlimoot*, to help each other. And what is so unique about that, is we have a phrase that my grandparents ... said, the phrase about our Gitksan and Witsuwit'en relations – interconnections of marriage – we are like a *sgano*, a woven fabric, solid. That is the way we look at ourselves, as a woven fabric, together. (Transcript, 4477-8)

Tenimget went on to clarify that what is regarded as *sgano* is not simply relationships but also a web of concern for associated House territories over a region sharing a common culture and, often, a common clan. This is a collective view of local society, but it usually does not include everyone. Sets of extending relations that form relevant collectivities (from any one actor's viewpoint) overlap with one another, thereby weaving the fabric of society. Very rarely, unlike Tsibasaa and Ligeex, who gained control and consensus over whole villages during the height of the maritime fur trade, would any single set of relations extend their reach over the whole society. The result is not a hierarchically structured chiefdom with a paramount leader responsible for the well-being of the whole tribe and capable of enforcing his will with military force (and accompanied by subordinate and segmentary rights devolving from the centre). Nor is it a "private ownership" interest of the sort common in modern market relations between corporations in the nation-state framework of contracts and agreements. Dora Wilson, Yaga'lahl, made a point similar to Mathews' in her evidence (Transcript, 4485).[5] I submit that families are still preoccupied with getting safely through the winter and considering how to use their traditional lands more effectively by utilizing extensive ties of kinship and affinity.[6] This submerged preoccupation with subsistence fortunes contributes to the flux in actual status and authority, and the persistence of both sharing and reciprocity in social relations.

As David Blackwater pointed out (Daly 1986-88) about his life on the trapline with his grandparents in the 1930s: "We only took enough to cover our cost for staples. We weren't in it to get rich. They took the few bucks they got when they sold the furs, and they put it under the pillow. They never trusted banks. Their attitude was to get enough to get by, and always leave enough behind for next year." Always leaving enough behind for next year was integral to survival and to the respect for the natural and social worlds, which, unbalanced by ongoing human actions, demanded counterbalancing in order to ensure future good fortune. Many informants stressed to me that "we are our brother's keeper" and that it was morally impossible to let someone starve so long as there was anything to eat in the village. Elders repeatedly told me, "We never turn anybody away who is hungry, because we know what hunger is." At the same time, accounting was strictly observed, even when the goods involved were dried salmon and berries.

Pearl Trombley, Gwamoon, of the Guldo'o Wolf Clan, explained, "Grandmother pinched my hand, to teach me a lesson. 'It will remind you to pay your debts,' she said. A lady would borrow from neighbouring ladies because the storage pits were only opened at intervals. That pinch was to remind me that all borrowings are repaid" (Daly 1986-88).

While the precontact Gitksan and Witsuwit'en did emphasize storage, as well as an economic life directed by the chiefs and a system of social ranking, all of these features operated within the limits imposed by a subsistence-oriented kinship economy and technology. The chiefs' decisions concerning the amount of goods to be stored have always been informed by the opinions of their elder advisors, senior aunts, uncles, and grandmothers. Arthur Mathews Jr. (Transcript, 4485) described the painstaking preparatory meetings and consultations that occur among a House's relatives, affines, and *wilksilaks/wilksibaksxw* (father's side) before a chief gains the material and political support necessary to hold a successful feast.

With a good stock of produce stored for winter, the House-centric production unit had a firm foundation for its social and political affairs, and for the fulfillment of its role in the credit and debt relations between kin groups. At the same time, the Houses were never islands unto themselves. There was a strong internal exchange of goods between individuals linked through a complex network of House relations.

The storage of goods by many different family groups with many different relationships adhering to them both underwrote and set limits to the authority of the chief. Chiefly authority extended over the deployment of land and labour adhering to that chief's House. Because members of one's House were always resident elsewhere, being sustained by the stored values of the House groups where they happened to be living and contributing their labour, this gave impetus to the inter-House principle of reciprocity through the medium and metaphor of the gift.

The Witsuwit'en and Gitksan constructed internal family hierarchies; yet each House, so long as it worked hard and fulfilled its social responsibilities, was an equal entity, with full rights to cooperate with, or against, other like units. Interacting Houses were conceptualized as like units that engaged democratically in the local political process. Members of a House who worked hard and participated in social affairs could expect to age into leading positions within the extended family, or, if this proved impossible, one could develop influence so as to prepare one's direct descendants' access to these positions. These calculations are made on the basis of both competition/sharing within the House and reciprocal, balancing relations between Houses.[7] Peace-keeping institutions did not extend beyond the reaches of family and clan or *wil'naat'ahl*, except for spiritual congregations like the nineteenth-century winter dance ceremonials. With flexible means for including and excluding personnel according to the issue at hand, Gitksan and Witsuwit'en society exemplifies a subtle intertwining of egalitarian and hierarchic principles.

On occasion, the Gitksan have delegated authority to one individual, or a small group, to represent all. This occurred in relation to retaliatory raids and subsequent diplomacy with other nations; more recently it has been seen in formal dealings with government (including Gitanyow's institution of the office of "president" for dealing with the wider, invasive society). A small number of *simgiget* were appointed by the Gitksan to address local concerns during the McKenna-McBride Royal Commission hearings on the Skeena in the spring of 1915 into the question of establishing reserves (which the chiefs refused to recognize without settlement of the violation of their territorial rights). Similarly, a delegation of Gitksan chiefs were charged by their peers with presenting their plea for government recognition of land title in Ottawa in 1909 (see McKenna-McBride 1915) on behalf of all the Gitksan people. When such tasks have been completed, the chiefs in question are no longer given authority to speak on behalf of anyone beyond their local kin group.

A village could act in unison in response to a sudden and unique external threat to its members, such as armed invasion or natural catastrophe, but there was no indigenous administrative body available to sustain such broad action on a day-to-day basis. Chiefs, as family heads, led by example, building their own prosperity and success by mobilizing their kinspeople. They also married off (or gifted) their House members strategically to Houses in other clans so as to maintain useful and long-standing alliances capable of yielding access to whole watersheds, trade routes, and support in times of hardship or enmity.

The oral histories contain many accounts of groups of Gitksan or Witsuwit'en chiefs acting in unison to retaliate against those outsiders who tried to gain access to one or other of their territories by means of force (see Chapter 4, note 14). The collective retaliation of the Witsuwit'en chiefs against the Haisla, who had raided from Kitimat on the coast, was recounted by Alfred Joseph in his evidence, where the wronged Witsuwit'en chief, Kweese, was assisted by the chiefs of all the clans (Transcript, 1602): "It's – that history of the raid or war party that Kweese formed was by all clans, and that is where all the different clans got most of their crests because it involved every – every clan. So when Kweese went on this raid he, as a reward, gave each clan a crest for their participation." As Lelt, Fred Johnson, explained, a similar collective action was taken by Gitksan chiefs after two Kitwancool/Gitanyow leaders were killed at Meziadin Lake by people from the north (Fred Johnson, Commission I, 60). These events appear to have occurred in protocontact or early contact times as they involve the use of firearms. Lelt explained that after family members had cremated the remains of the deceased, they called on others to assist them in their retaliation. The retaliation resulted in the concluding of a peace settlement with the inter-lopers. The Gitanyow chiefs and warriors were assisted by colleagues from Gitwangax and Gitsegukla. Mary McKenzie, Kyologet, gave a further ex-ample in relation to the ancient battles in the Skeena headwaters country around Gitangasxw when she told the *adaawk'* of Suuwiigos. She recounted the narrative of how Kyologet's chiefs were joined by the leaders and warriors of the Houses of 'Niik'aap, Gwininitxw, Wii Gaak, and Luus (Transcript, 231). These events were also recounted by David Gunanoot, 'Niik'aap (Com-mission I, 58-66).

Marshall Sahlins (1972, 134-5) refers to the tendency of tribal kinship societies to grapple with the development of exploitation. These are situa-tions where "the ideological ambiguity of chiefly office" must at all times be deployed to balance the inequalities wrought by differentials of power, with the necessity of maintaining amicable, face-to-face family and kinship relations. Sahlins's insight is not unlike Bourdieu's account of the function-ing of *méconnaissance*. The chief, as the embodiment of the group, dispenses the fruits of the labour of those living under his/her large roof so that the House may prosper. Often the chief receives all the honour while the House members do most of the actual work. House members and inhabitants give rise to accumulations of goods and services that the chief dispenses to pol-ish the House's name and renown. Sahlins sums up the situation: "The ideo-logical ambiguity is functional. On the one hand, the ethic of chiefly generosity blesses the inequality; on the other, the ideal of reciprocity de-nies that it makes any difference."

This description fits the Gitksan and Witsuwit'en society only with cer-tain qualifications, because here chiefships were not based on centralized assembly and storage of values at the disposal of a hierarchy of chiefs; rather, everybody stored values for their respective family chief and paid them out when asked to share, both in cases of personal need and corporate chiefly need (i.e., to defend House honour). The result was, and remains, an ongoing spreadsheet of intergroup, relatively horizontal reciprocity expressed with both the passions and the tolerance of family life. Sharing and reciprocity coexisted, however imperfectly, and were integral to the negotiation of inter-personal and intergroup relations.

In the feast, when goods are given, the host clearly stands for the whole host House group, and she/he contributes a significant part of the accumu-lated values of his/her immediate family: labour, wealth items, and income. However, all other members of the House and its affiliates must contribute cash and goods and labour, directly and publicly, according to birth, rank, and age. Contributors are all named, and the items and quantities of their contributions are noted and witnessed formally. These "businesses" are an-nounced to the assembled guests, who are expected to store the informa-tion in their minds. The chief is viewed as the major contributor and not as the redistributive provider of everything. Much of his/her "greatness" is derived from the contributions made by House members, and frequently this is publicly acknowledged. The distribution also follows a set of established rules of precedence and etiquette that negatively sanction those who desire to advance by giving extra amounts without already having the status to do so. The chief is assisted by knowledgeable elders, House members, and *wilksilaks/wilksibaksxw* (father's side) and does not make the distribution in a unilateral manner.

A chief's de facto standing is always in a state of flux, although it becomes increasingly consolidated through the proper hosting of feasts. Ideologically, all chiefs are equal, and in practice there tends to be the struggle to "keep up with the Joneses" in order to achieve that equality while neither surpassing it nor falling below it. There is a socially recognized ideal type of standard of giving and collective effort, to which feast-givers aspire, and this, rather than endless competition, provides much of the social dynamism. Chiefs, as the Witsuwit'en in particular stress, are supposed to be modest and not stand out in a crowd. To be arrogantly overbearing or chronically impoverished is to stand out and, thus, to become the target of gossip and unease. Prestige gained from conducting House affairs properly does not build and accumulate beyond the lifetime of the individual chief. The children of chiefs, usually raised in their father's House, do not inherit from him, although the standing of a distinguished woman chief may pass to her children, who, if they do not work hard, will find that their good name quickly begins to oxidize.

The discontinuity in male succession works against intergenerational blocs of personal power. Halpin (1973, chaps. 3 and 4) convincingly argues that Tsimshian chiefs in the nineteenth century tried to overcome this structural hindrance to their consolidation of power by recruiting their own children into the cross-clan and multi-village winter dance societies. They sought to expand their influence beyond the clan to the whole village, and beyond villages to whole tribes, through the control of such spiritual congregations, where status was reaffirmed in ways similar to those employed in the feast without being subject to the limits imposed by the kinship system.

The redistributive use of accumulated goods by chiefly persons in a kinship society is normally limited to the business of the House group and is perhaps extended to those Houses whose ancestors arrived in the homeland with one's own House ancestors.[8] Such local authority and influence by example cannot expand beyond the boundaries of the kinship group. Nineteenth-century attempts to do so were not very successful, as we shall see later.

The individual power of Gitksan and Witsuwit'en chiefs has traditionally been limited by the laws of matrilineal descent and virilocal residence. Power accruing to any particular chief is scrutinized and challenged constantly by other members of the House group who are related through their mothers and are not exclusively dependent upon the chief for their own standing in the House. These members may or may not be closely linked to the high chief, and they possess varying degrees of influence through their non-House kinship links as well.

Since the Gitksan and Witsuwit'en do not possess institutions that reinforce chiefly exploitation of non-chiefly persons, they have never been at ease with enduring hierarchical leaders. Sectional interests make the political life of leaders a constant factional nightmare if they attempt to form political alliances that go beyond the matrilineal House system. Even today, this dislike of long-standing authority beyond the level of the House, *wil'naat'ahl*, or clan is evident in the stormy, often nepotistic political arena of the modern, government-instituted band council system of local government. Sadly, this is not something limited to the Witsuwit'en and Gitksan but is endemic to First Nations band councils across the country.

According to the late Jeff Harris Sr., Simoogit Luus, of the Guldo'o La<u>x</u> Gibuu, the northern Gitksan would make fun of, and look down upon, any chief in their own clan who put on airs, or became preoccupied with his prestige, or issued orders in an imperious manner. They would remind him that he was not, after all, Chief Skat'iin – a La<u>x</u> Gibuu trader chief from the Nass who, in the past, was known to be somewhat despotic and whose own villagers were said to defer to him in ways that the Gitksan found restrictive and undemocratic.[9]

The status hierarchy of the society is based on the individual's age and willingness to take an active role in the feast system. An enumeration of status categories among the Gitksan gives the initial impression of a society that is very hierarchical and undemocratic: there are the chiefs, the *simgiget* ("the very most real people," like the Witsuwit'en *dinïze'yu*, those who are the "head push"). Then there are the followers, who are relatives (workers, warriors, supporters) called the *amgiget*, among whom are the counsellor or wing chiefs. The *la<u>x</u>giget* are "those born to be chiefs" (those in training to inherit chiefly names (*k'ubawilksihlxwt* [pl.], *hlguwilksihlxw* [sing.]); a further category is composed of children, the *sigiget* (Transcripts, 4550-1). There are also poor people who have not fulfilled their feasting obligations, who are *gagweey'*, "so poor," and formerly there were a few *hlihlingit* captives, or slaves (lit. Tlingits). These statuses (with the exception of the last two) are, in most cases, little more than categories of age status. If one works hard, contributes to the honour of the House, and lives long enough, then one will usually become, if not a family chief, then at least an advisory wing chief or consultant on family tradition.

Throughout the seventeenth and eighteenth centuries the Iroquois of upper New York State and, later, of Quebec and the Grand River Valley, Ontario, were known to the British and French as statesmen of great genius.

They were consummate builders of federated political bodies, accumulators of wealth, and artful warriors whose example was said to inspire the political thinking of Benjamin Franklin. Like the history of the Gitksan and Witsuwit'en, that of the Iroquois is marked by periodic indigenous conflict with, and exploitation of, non-Iroquois people. Yet the Iroquois, like the Gitksan and Witsuwit'en, have ensured, through their laws and social institutions, that social inequality and, at times, graphic oppression of one human by another cannot gain a permanent foothold within the society. Such a foothold requires the prior elimination of the matrilineal system of inheritance and succession.

Handsome Lake, the Seneca Iroquois prophet and leader of what came to be called the "Longhouse Movement" at the beginning of the nineteenth century, revealed to his community the contents of his dream prophecies. He used these revelations to construct a syncretic socio-spiritual set of institutions for combining old cultural principles with the new ways of life now confronting the encapsulated Iroquois. This was devised under the political metaphor of the Confederacy's longhouse roof, which is eternally sheltered beneath the boughs of the giant spruce tree, whose white roots of peace are said to run out in all four directions. These conditions emerged in upper New York State shortly after the American Revolution. Handsome Lake's people were beleaguered in eighteenth-century reservations, facing an inflexible invasive government and forcible land cessions.

Handsome Lake and his followers countered the missionizing forces of Anglo-US society with their own highly organized prophetic religious structure. This was composed of the old, pre-Christian theology and ceremony, and a set of rules and principles for dealing with the new conditions under which the people were forced to both resist and bend with the demands of the new governments. The syncretic results risked neither military suppression nor the abandonment of the Iroquois worldview, laws, culture, and languages, which are at the core of their identity (Daly 1985).

Despite the success and esteem achieved by Handsome Lake – he became a statesman in his relations with the federal government in Washington prior to his death in 1815 – he was nonetheless defeated by what Wallace (1972, 296) has called the Iroquois "extreme sensitivity to issues involving personal dominance." Handsome Lake was cut down to size by his own peers' distrust of consolidated power and influence. Wallace's description of the plight of Handsome Lake illuminates the ephemeral nature of the social hierarchy and political influence in matrilineal foraging and foraging/horticultural societies. Both the peoples of the present study and the Iroquois combined hunting with stored accumulation (the cultivation of maize, beans, and squash by the Iroquois and the processing of summer salmon runs and autumn game by the Gitksan and Witsuwit'en). To quote Wallace at length:

In the politics of Chiefs' Council, despite the eminence of his titles, Handsome Lake failed, mired in personal jealousy and tribal factionalism and
was unable to call upon an efficient bureaucracy for the administration of
his policies. *Such a failure was, indeed, in a sense ordained by Iroquois culture,
for a correlate of the theme of freedom was one of extreme sensitivity to issues
involving personal dominance.* Pretenders to greatness, like Logan and Sturgeon, were sometimes assassinated on behalf of an offended community
faction by members of their own family (a procedure which aborted the
revenge process). Leaders like Cornplanter, Red Jacket, and Brant were apt
to suffer rejection or assault. Factionalism was pervasive; and the intense
ambivalence about dominance was traditionally expressed in the polarity
between the politeness of day-to-day encounters and the violence which
erupted in drunken brawls, witchcraft accusations, and, in older times, the
torture rituals. The prophet thus, by his very success in achieving the role of
moral censor guaranteed his own political defeat. (Emphasis added)

Like the Iroquois, the Gitksan and Witsuwit'en have an extreme sensitivity
towards issues involving personal dominance. They retain features of classic
foraging bands, even after adopting a type of tribal organization in which
control over territorial resources, their acquisition, distribution, and consumption, was apportioned between clans and their component House groups.

Expanding Hierarchies beyond Kin Groups
The expansion of status hierarchies beyond the scope of clan and village
issues, which preoccupied big chiefs along the adjacent coast in protocontact
times, was not central to the social and economic processes of the Gitksan
and Witsuwit'en. Their cultural practices appear not to have suffered the
wild swings seen on the coast.[10] Nineteenth-century coastal peoples considered the Gitksan and their "Hagwilget" neighbours to be rather unso-
phisticated "bush people," and, in the subsequent fish cannery period,
they were called "Stick Indians." Yet this inland region was not totally
isolated from events along the coast. The western Gitksan have for a long
time maintained close kinship and affinal ties with the coast – particularly
with the Nisga'a, Tsimshian, and Haida through the oolichan fishery on
the Nass River estuary, and with the Haisla, who fish oolichan at Kitimat
and along the Gardner Canal. The Gitksan of the western villages tend to
regard themselves as having a more elaborate culture than is found among
the eastern Gitksan and the Witsuwit'en.[11] The western Gitksan were indeed in more immediate contact with the cultural elaboration that occurred
in protocontact times along the coast; as well, when white settlement began in the region it was the other Gitksan villages, and the Witsuwit'en
settlements, whose residents bore the brunt of interaction with Europeans.
On the whole, the Gitksan have retained more of their pre-European cul-

tural past than have their coastal neighbours, as the coast has been subject to a greater volume and duration of missionary activity and governmental administration.

On the coast, in the centuries leading to European contact, leaders sought, through trading, raiding, and diplomacy, to expand their accumulation and authority beyond the boundaries of their own matrilineal kin and affines. However, as Halpin (1973, 91) points out, there is no evidence that larger social hierarchies or hegemonies were forming in Gitksan country:

> Unlike the Niska (Nisga'a), whose chiefs vied for superiority over one another, the Gitksan chiefs maintained an egalitarian posture. When the Kitsegukla were invited to a potlatch (feast), for example, "they would call a chief from each clan in turn, otherwise a difference in standing would be implied, and one group would be offended" (Charles Mark [Figure 21]). Similarly, the arrangement of dwellings at both Kitwancool and Kitsegukla placed the two clan chiefs – the *laxk'bu* (*Lax Gibuu*) and *laxse.'l* (*Ganeda*) at Kitwancool, and the *g.anhádə* (*Ganeda*) and *g'isg.a'.st* (*Gisk'aast*) at Kitsegukla – side by side in the middle of the village, with the other houses of their clans ranged out on either side, ideally in descending rank order.[12]

Although structural hierarchies extending beyond the matrilineal kin group did not develop among the Gitksan, some of these expansionary activities did involve Gitksan figures around the time of contact, as attested to by the *adaawk*'s about Nekt (Barbeau and Beynon n.d.; Marsden 1987; MacDonald 1980).

Inequality, status hierarchy, and centralization were even more limited among the Witsuwit'en. While the Gitksan and Witsuwit'en both engaged in material exchanges by means of gift-giving and barter with neighbouring peoples, they did not engage in modern commodity trade of items procured from the land before the establishment of trading posts. Traditionally, however, they produced extra amounts of dried, storable foods and animal pelts that could be exchanged for coveted items produced in other, more distant eco-niches; they also provided craft services in the fields of carving and curing, which were exchanged abroad.

Viewed as a single social phenomenon composed of two linguistic and historical traditions, Gitksan-Witsuwit'en society is a composite, or a blend of both the decentralized and egalitarian social values of the inland Athapaskan lifestyle and the more hierarchical and stratified social values of the north coast. The archaeological record, and the Tsimshianic narratives of origin, indicate that the inland culture moved out, south and west, towards the coast at some point in previous millennia (at least by the last deglaciation). Later, features of the culture that subsequently developed on the coast moved back eastward through the river valleys into the interior in the course of the sweep of trade, gift-giving, reciprocal raiding, religious movements, and diplomacy. These influences moved back and forth across northwest British Columbia and southeast Alaska, ebbing and flowing in cycles through at least the last 3,000 years. MacDonald and Inglis (1981) discuss the latter phase, the historical and cultural spread of coastal influences inland. Focusing upon the development of the coastal culture of the Tsimshian, they tend not to address the question of the earlier, and seminal, inland settlements and the subsequent coastward dispersals, as described in the *adaawk*'s of the region and as supported by linguistic reconstructions (Dyen and Aberle 1974).[13] They are also supported by anthropological inference (Drucker and Heizer 1967; Ives 1990; Rosman and Rubel 1971; Rubel and Rosman 1983)[14] and the archaeological record in general (Borden 1975; de Laguna 1975). This is indicated in particular by continuous habitation for millennia at sites such as Hagwilget (Ames 1979) and Moricetown (Albright 1987), which indicates a long cultural continuity on the upper Skeena and Bulkley Rivers, with their possible coastward diffusion.[15]

The blend of hierarchical/egalitarian and nomadic/sedentary dichotomies appears to have developed during the period of common residence near the confluence of the 'Ksan and Wedzenkwe (Skeena and Bulkley) Rivers, at the fabled settlements of T'imla̱x'aamit/Dizkle. (Features of the material culture at this point in the region's archaeological record are described in Coupland's Paul Mason Phase, Kitselas Canyon [Matson and Coupland 1995, 183ff].) The oral histories speak of a great dispersal from this area long ago. According to the present archaeological evidence, there was a cultural discontinuity in the artifacts from both Hagwilget and Kitselas, which likely occurred at the end of the archaeological period called the Skeena Phase, about 3200 BP (Coupland 1985). As Drucker found (1963, 114-15), the oral record indicates coastward migration of the Tsimshian:

> According to tradition, the ancestors of these people, and of their Gitksan and Niska relatives, came from a legendary site – at Temlaham, "Prairie Town" – somewhere in the interior, very long ago. The tales relating this phase of Tsimshian history have a strong interior flavor. They tell of times when the people were snowbound, and suffered famine; they referred to living in semi-subterranean earth lodges of the interior type. It seems reasonable to accept these tales in a general sense; the Tsimshian had to reach their historic home by moving either from the interior or along the coast, and there is no evidence to support the possibility of coastal migration. After suffering innumerable vicissitudes, the ancestral Tsimshian began to establish themselves in villages below the Skeena River canyon.

Coupland reports that the Kitselas population doubled at 3200 BP, expanding its salmon technology and storage pits, and decreasing slightly the diversity of its hunting tool kit.[16] The *adaawk*'s speak of part of the T'imlax̱'aamit population moving downstream to Kitselas Canyon. As well, there is evidence of warfare (e.g., the existence of the Bulkley River phallic stone clubs [Duff 1975]). As well, the rich range of everyday and luxury artifacts indicates that social ranking, and extensive regional exchange, are determinations that can be made from archaeological sites along the Skeena from Hagwilget (Ames 1979) to Prince Rupert (MacDonald and Inglis 1981).[17]

On the basis of these findings and the sequences of events that occur in the oral histories, one might assume trading and raiding has occupied an important role in the socioeconomic life of the northern Northwest Coast and its cordilleran hinterland for the last 3,000 years. According to local elders and the *adaawk'* records, the externally expansive, highly stratified and generally wealthy Tlingit had once occupied the present-day Tsimshian coastal waters and the lower Skeena. The ancestors of the Tlingit were expelled by the ancestors of the Tsimshian (Drucker 1963; Marsden 2001). (The common Tsimshianic word [including Gitksanimx] for "slaves" – *hlihlingit*[18] – may possibly date from early enmities between the Tlingit and Tsimshian peoples.) In the last 2,000 years the coastal Tlingit and Tsimshian expanded their wealth and physical well-being by means of exchange with interior peoples (Drucker 1963, 37, 41; Oberg 1973, 107-8).

Coastal peoples accumulated foodstuffs for winter consumption and trade, as did their inland neighbours, but they also utilized a wide variety of food sources in the cold months – sea mammals, winter chinook salmon, cod, halibut, herring, clams, winkles, seaweed, and oolichan – not available at inland locations. On the coast, storage and accumulation expanded beyond the subsistence sphere to goods that assumed value for their convertibility. Trade items could be parlayed into a sizable quantity of other goods by means of intercultural differences of evaluation and needs.

Protection of trading routes and partners entailed the expenditure of time and goods on martial preparedness and hospitality to build and renew trust and credit with trade partners or to forge temporary tactical military alliances to defend, or reassert, trading privileges. (According to the *adaawk*'s, Nass chiefs attacked Kispiox and Gitanmaax to eliminate Gitksan middlemen from the trade for furs and hides with the eastward Witsuwit'en and "U'inwit'en." Similarly, there are accounts of the Gispaxlo'ots trader chief Ligeex eliminating competition in relation to trade transport through Kitselas Canyon.) It is likely that there were many political fluctuations over the centuries and that periods of intense feuding and raiding gave rise to the seizure of hostages and captives. In some cases, captives may have helped fill the increasing labour needs when the personnel of the seasonal round were strained by the addition of regular trading, diplomatic, and military activities. Yet most Gitksan and Witsuwit'en say that captives and slaves were items of wealth and were not particularly effective as forces of production.[19] One such spiral of trading and raiding appears to have been in process during protocontact and early contact times.[20]

This protocontact increase in coast-centred trade and, together with it, the necessity for coastal people to protect and control trade routes while maintaining political authority by means of competitive feast-giving, had social repercussions for the inland peoples. Inlanders such as the Tutchone, Tagish, Inland Tlingit, Tahltan, Gitksan, Witsuwit'en, Alkatcho, and Chilcotin were trading partners with coastal peoples. However, by the early 1800s many of these peoples had established alternative access to inland fur trading posts such as those at Bear Lake, Fraser Lake, and further east. The trade practices of the coastal peoples affected the inland social life in the same way that it affected the coast, but to a lesser degree. In terms of pre-European trade, the coastal peoples obviously looked on the inlanders as important but more directly exploitable trading partners, as discussed in Chapter 6. Oberg (1973, 107-10) explains that, before the arrival of Europeans, the Tlingit reserved barter and bargaining for their social and economic relations with non-Tlingit, particularly with Athapaskans of the hinterlands. They did not barter among themselves for fear of destroying their own kin-based social relations. These relationships were predicated upon "family-like" reciprocity and minimizing the outbreak of feuding between blocs of opposed kinspeople.

Trade or barter relations with inland peoples were more to the advantage of the Tlingit than to the Athapaskans, and more to the advantage of the Tsimshian and Nisga'a than to the Gitksan and Witsuwit'en. Yet the hides, pelts, salmon strips, and berries of the interior were of such interest to the Tlingit and Tsimshian that they almost never raided for captives from among their adjacent interior peoples (Oberg 1973). They obtained slaves either in the course of warfare and raiding along the coast or through purchase from the Tsimshian and Haida. The latter obtained slaves from the Kwak̲wak̲'awakw, who in turn purchased or captured them in the south or obtained them from relatives (such as the Le'kwiltoq of the Campbell River region, who raided Halkomélem and other Coast Salish villages in the Gulf of Georgia region) (Daly 1991a).

Women's Status

The position of women is an important indicator of the degree to which economic accumulation and political centralization have changed the reciprocal relations of a kinship society (Etienne and Leacock 1980; Friedl 1975; Leacock 1981; Lee and Daly 1987; Reiter 1975). At the time of contact, Gitksan and Witsuwit'en women's ranking was similar to that of their brothers. No matter what their rank, they maintained control over their household labour, their reproductive rights (in conjunction with their mothers, mothers' brothers, and their own brothers), their annual produce, and their specific rights and responsibilities in the production process through the seasons. No matter where they lived after marrying, women retained status and gained the appropriate authority of age within their own matrilineal House group. They were able to ensure their children's access to names, history, and territory, as inheritance is reckoned through the mother. Male authority, while ascribed and sanctioned in terms of political leadership and military and diplomatic prowess, is somewhat checked by the combining of matrilineal inheritance and virilocal residence. Men inherit from their mother's House of origin rather than from their father's House and territory, where they were raised and gained the specifics of their habitus.

Today, chiefs, even those of a mature age, still consult their descent group, their mothers and mother's siblings, their patrilateral aunts, and their wives before making decisions. Many women are chiefs as well, and female chiefs were not unknown in the past. In many ways it is the women who provide the dynamism and coherence of the feasting system. It is women who keep accounts of the day-to-day credit and debt in the local community, who accumulate goods for feasting, and who know the intricacies of the kinship network and alliances by marriage. In fact, women occupy a leading position in virtually every aspect of contemporary Gitksan and Witsuwit'en life. It is ironic that they only infrequently hold political office today. Kyologet, Antgulilibix, Gwaans, and Dzee were among the first plaintiff witnesses in the *Delgamuukw* land rights case. These are chiefly names held by senior women whose feasting, foraging, and family activities have strongly influenced recent political life.

Matrilineal kinship and succession militate against the formation and entrenchment of social hierarchy and groups of kinspeople capable of consolidating wealth and power generation after generation. Political power accruing to any particular chief is scrutinized and challenged constantly by other members of the House group. A young man raised on his father's land possesses only usufruct rights there. If he seeks to make his mark on history he must associate both with his mother's territories and, in the feast house, with persons to whom he is related through his mother, even if this entails establishing links in a community some distance from his upbringing. Similarly, the tendency to marry into the House or clan of the father creates inheritable possibilities for the children of the man who is using his father's land. This is due to the fact that his own children have rights there that are denied him, yet he is able to teach his own children in situ about their land and its history.[21]

A woman who goes to live in her husband's House's village of origin after marriage retains considerable status and remains active in the feasting arrangements of her own House. Today she may marry outside the region altogether and still retain her rights and standing in her House group, especially if she remains socially and economically active in the home community. So long as she remains active in her culture of origin, she loses none of the rights due to her in her own House after marriage. Today she changes her surname to that of her husband, but she remains the permanent ambassador of her House in the residential group of her husband. She is at all times in a position to defend the interest of her House and her children, who are members of her own House, while contributing to the social, spiritual, economic, and conjugal well-being of the husband.

If a man's House has long-standing marriage ties with that of his wife, then the children are actually living with their own House's father's side *(wilksilaks/bits'ac'elts'it)*. This is the class of people with whom House members interact most frequently and most intensely on formal occasions. (They interact with their own specific father's side as well as with that of their chief.) The intersection of such interest groups tends to thwart the accumulation of power by individual men in a House. Men must remain in close touch with their mother's siblings and with the territories of their mother's brothers in order to prosper legitimately.

It is interesting to note that, for many economies that combine hunting and gathering with some other quite different economic pursuit (such as the Iroquoian hunter-horticulturalists), matrilineal kinship and descent is a frequent option. Like the Gitksan and Witsuwit'en, the Iroquois and Huron of Lake Ontario, the Delaware of the New Jersey and Maryland coast, and the Ashanti of the interior of Ghana in West Africa were able to avail themselves of economic pursuits in pre-European times and for a considerable period thereafter – pursuits that could be combined with hunting (and/or horticulture) and trading. In the North American examples of these hunting combination economies, matrilineal peoples devised a local organization of summer economic activities that was largely under the direction of women and of winter economic activities (hunting, trapping, ice-fishing, and trade pursuits) that was largely under the direction of men. This division of labour necessitated reciprocity between men and women, and between siblings and their in-laws (Stites 1905). These societies accumulated large quantities of foodstuffs for winter use and used a portion of this for trade and diplomatic needs. In both instances, matrilineal inheritance gave great emphasis to local reciprocity, to the "sensitivity to issues of personal dominance" described by Wallace (1972), and militated against enduring power blocs.

6
Gifts, Exchange, and Trade

From Gift-Giving to Barter

Economists, the writers of the Indian Act, and various members of the Canadian juridical community assume that indigenous peoples had no "real" economies, that they simply "ate from the land" like other beasts of the field and, hence, that they had no understanding of or need for exchange and trade. This assumption still remains lamentably under-examined. It holds that trade and commerce were introduced to these indigenous forest-dwellers by Europeans. Gregory (1982, 18) has pointed out that challenging this assumption was one of the fundamental aims of Marcel Mauss in his famous "Essay on the Gift": "One of Mauss' aims was to debunk the prevailing orthodoxy among economists, that economies of the PNG [Papua New Guinea]-type were 'natural' economies which produced for subsistence instead of for exchange." More than three-quarters of a century of research has subsequently accumulated, and yet the same assumptions continue to bolster the thinking of those in power. The debunking process has gone a long way to explaining that kinship societies are also marked by exchange systems, albeit those based on gifting: "The concepts, gifts and commodities, while different, are nevertheless complementary: the concept commodity, which presupposes reciprocal independence and alienability, is a mirror image of the concept gift, which presupposes reciprocal dependence and inalienability" (24).

These advances have been derived from research conducted by anthropologists following the paradigms of political economy (as opposed to that of economics). Since the historical trajectory of the former involves not only Ricardo and Adam Smith, Lévi-Strauss and Sahlins, but also Marx, Engels, and Morgan, I did not feel – given the hegemony of positive empiricist and economistic thinking in the corridors of power – that it would have been wise to go very deeply into these questions when this manuscript was in its "opinion evidence" phase in *Delgamuukw*. I exercised self-censorship and a modicum of discretion in an effort to avoid ideological debates as to whether the plaintiffs' way of producing, consuming, and exchanging followed a "socialistic" or a "capitalistic" road. Now, however, I want quite frankly to admit that I concur with Gregory (1982, 8) when he says gifts and commodities are compatible and together stand opposed to the theory of goods, of economic theory, with its focus on the subjective relationship between consumers and their supposed objects of desire.[1]

Social interaction through the mediation of things and services – whether it be gifts, labour, kindnesses and young people exchanged, gambling, or trade in the form of barter – has long been central to the lives of the Gitksan and Witsuwit'en. In earlier chapters we have seen how these exchanges play out in feasting, in relations with the incarnated land through the seasons, and in relations between kinship groups. This chapter examines more closely that part of the continuum of reciprocal exchanges that occurs, and has long occurred, beyond the local community in the relations between different linguistic groups and ecological zones across the cordillera.

The sharing and the expression of gratitude involved in gift-giving often mask social inequalities and transactions that result in gains for one and losses for another (Bourdieu 1977, 4-6; 1990, 98-111). Gifting itself, as Godelier (1999), like Mauss (1990/1923-4), has noted, is beautifully ambiguous since it can simultaneously produce and ward off subordination and inequality. The gift, in its giving, even if it has been requested or demanded by its recipient (see Peterson's [1993] "demand sharing"), is a discharge of social indebtedness for the giver (whether the recipient registers gratitude or not – usually not). Yet, since the gift is not totally alienated at the time of giving, the transactional relationship remains open and ongoing. In demand sharing the time sequence is quite different in so far as the values are not given and counter-given but, rather, are demanded and counter-demanded. Demand sharing is often treated as internal to a group whose members act like putative family members, generally like siblings. Here credit is not offered by a giver: it is demanded by a taker and is sanctioned by the rules of group membership. The giver, in turn, is expected later to demand a share when he or she feels the need to do so. In this way, indebtedness is minimized. Consistent with Bourdieu's *méconnaissance*, those engaged in generalized reciprocity assume that exchanges balance out in the long run. However, if certain members always demand, and have nothing to give when demanded themselves, they eventually lose membership in the sharing group (e.g., Bodenhorn 2000; Macdonald 2000). Thus the system appears to have an element of compulsion to it, like other "balanced reciprocities" of the gift type (Sahlins 1972). In a demand system, giving up a good upon demand does not alienate it from the owner, or from subsequent obligations, any more than does the freely given gift.

The receiving of a gift results in the immediate creation of another social debt on the part of the giver's former debtor. However, the gifting and response have set up or renewed a long-term relationship between the two actors and their respective family networks.

Annually, the Gitksan and Witsuwit'en receive the gift of foodstuffs, materials, and resources from nature. Each proprietary group, or House, legitimately receives the gifts of nature from its lands and fishing sites. These groups reciprocate respectfully, and show their gratitude, they say, through their participation in the endless spiral of feast-giving. They feel perpetually indebted to the ancestor spirits of all life forms lodged in the land. All they can do by way of recompense is eventually give their lives back to nature and, meanwhile, fulfill their feasting duties to local society. Peoples of the Northwest Coast tradition recall a time when these powers of the land once had human forms, or could transform back and forth at will, as attested by the transformative nature of Northwest Coast art (Anderson 1996). These were the beings that gifted the human world with light and knowledge, giving humans special useful skills and powers, and revealing themselves to the first and founding ancestors of the House groups. These givings are immortalized in the *adaawk*'s and *kungakhs*. They are the source of the peoples' legitimate ownership of inalienable property as well as of their eternal indebtedness. One might consider the periodic opening of the family treasure box to the community, and the revelation of its esoteric powers and ancient history, as a gifting because the knowledge is, during the event, shared out to guests and outsiders, yet without being alienable in the commodity sense. To come up to standard, the guest or outsider must eventually reciprocate in kind since not to do so reveals him or her to be mere driftwood, without roots, pedigree, or citizenship – a vagabond always fed by others.

This "social imaginary," or traditional ideation, gives moral impetus, impelling people to show respect and gratitude to what the Westerner calls the natural world and to what foraging peoples generally call home. Most of this impetus is derived from social pressure to keep up standards and to hold one's family's head above water – in a word, to contribute generously to the feast system. There is also another factor at play, namely, the indeterminacy of the political structure of Gitksan and Witsuwit'en society – a system without a fixed, society-wide hierarchy of paramount chiefs. Instead of this there are many equal units, each internally organized in a hierarchical manner, and here the gift relationship sets up necessary alliances between units. These alliances shift over time and weave, maintain, and rebalance blocs of power (Godelier 1999, 160).

But what happens to these relationships when the Gitksan and Witsuwit'en of, say, 250 years ago, would leave home and head out into the wider world seeking desired goods, materials, and craft items from other regions? How would they do so profitably, with less fear of enmity from interlocutors than they would have felt at home? In other words, how did the switch-over take place, from local gift-giving to more distant trade and barter – the latter with its connotations of winners and losers, of negative reciprocity – in a society without police and standing army?

Sahlins (1972, 185-276) has described a phenomenon he calls "kinship distance," where, as the actors involved in exchange become less and less related by blood and marriage, the things exchanged become less and less gift-like and more and more commodity-like. Gitksan and Witsuwit'en history is consistent with Sahlins's findings.

From the available evidence it appears that the exchange of goods across the region in pre- and early contact times was initiated through a process of mimesis – by holding abbreviated feast ceremonies, and presenting gifts to intended exchange partners, between visiting trader chiefs and their hosts. As Gunther (1972, 102) notes in reference to a Nootkan (Nuu chah nulth) chief that Captain Galiano encountered in the 1780s: "He offered to entertain the visitors if they would come to his village, but he did all his trading under the guise of exchanging presents. This was a frequent practice among the important chiefs, who said they did not want common barter but offered the commanders of expeditions presents, usually of sea otter skins, and in return expected gifts of equal value."

Such ceremonial giving in itself was probably not the arena of major economic exchange and distribution. It was a public ceremonial template, establishing the fraternal diplomatic idiom for subsequent pragmatic trade. Real feast goods, which embody something of the chiefly giver (namely, the emblematic spiritual power, the crest objects that sanction his/her authority), were not given in these feasting encounters, yet the feast format was used to set the tone for subsequent exchanges. In proper feasts, the emphasis was/is on *giving* and topping it off with a little extra. This was usually followed later by gambling (which can also be considered a template for the psychic chance-taking of hunters and fishers), where the expectation was of *receiving* values that included extra value (without having to reciprocate in the course of time).

After an initial welcome feast, the exchange partners would engage in barter. If they were linked by kinship and clanship, the feasting ethic of giving with a little extra might prevail; and if they were not so linked, the expectation of receiving a little extra would prevail. These two types of exchange, ceremonial and secular, usually involved different types of goods and slightly different systems of evaluation – something that became clearer with the advent of greater trading opportunities when first European goods, and later European traders, arrived on the scene.

Barter, from the Contact Record
Oberg (1973, 18) explains the differentiation between goods that represented

feast transactions and economic transactions, at least as this distinction had developed during the nineteenth century – against the lavish backdrop of Tlingit society: "The true potlatch goods, then, are slaves, coppers, blankets, and money. These goods are never used for economic purposes and must be clearly distinguished, on the one hand, from the economic goods in every day use and, on the other, from the totemic crests and emblems to which they give value. Potlatch goods are derived from the surplus of economic goods through exchange, this surplus in turn, arising from an excess of work over that required for purely economic needs."

Oberg stresses the cultural separation between potlatch and economic activities. Goods produced over and beyond subsistence needs and feasting requirements internal to the community were used in barter (externally), even though this was conducted within the feasting format. But do we have to assume that goods produced for feasting were "leftovers" from the subsistence sphere? It is more likely that they were and are consciously planned as part of the annual "subsistence need" of the family. Among the Gitksan, particularly from the women's perspective, there was always a distinction made, regarding the stored foodstuffs, between everyday items for internal use, which were put on one side of the storage pit, and best quality goods for feasting and trading, which were stored on the other side. But both were consciously produced and stored as part of the annual round (Daly 1986-88, Kyologet and G̲wamoon).

Out beyond the local group the potential of enmity arising from the pursuit of negative reciprocity and the acquisition of alienated goods is less important because the exchange partner is now a distant acquaintance or stranger. Investing House surplus in such ways signals the good management of the House leadership and the hard work of its members and affines.

When this form of distribution and exchange occurred between distant peoples, such as between the Chilkat Tlingit of the upper Alaska panhandle and the Athapaskans of the Yukon Valley, or between the Gispaxlo'ots Eagle Clan Tsimshian and the "Hagwilget" (the Witsuwit'en and mixed Witsuwit'en-Gitksan) of the Hazelton vicinity, the initial ceremonial gift exchange would swiftly be replaced with barter, bargaining, and subterfuge. This is graphically described in the *adaawk̲'* wherein the Gispaxlo'ots Eagle chief, Ligeex, tricks and deceives the people of Kispiox with a miraculous new *nax̲nox̲* spirit in the form of an umbrella and then takes deadly vengeance on them for trading with his rivals. Again, Oberg (1973, 110) describes the form that inter-nation bargaining took among the nineteenth-century Tlingit:

Exchanges were made publicly, accompanied by a great deal of haggling. Each side set its prices high and then came down to a level where exchange was possible. Lesser traders and representatives of other house groups bartered on the side. The whole proceedings smacked very much of a market place. When the party was small and the house chief bartered for the group as a whole, his every act was carefully watched by his kinsmen. Quite often a shrewd old woman was taken along who kept a check on exchange values. The two leaders would call out the values of the goods to be exchanged in rotation and, when the price suited the group behind each leader, a shout would go out signifying that exchange was agreeable at that point.

Even the bargaining process followed an old template similar to that of gift-giving. Barter was initiated by gift exchange in order to establish a familiar form for the relationship. Those bartering expected, in relation to their own local scale of values and their limited knowledge of wider trade values, to receive in return goods equal to the value of the goods offered, plus "a little extra." This led to misunderstandings between the early Hudson's Bay Company factors and the indigenous populations. The European traders assessed the furs in terms of the "going rate" across the region and in relation to the London market. On the other hand, the Aboriginal populations expected that they would be recompensed by the fur traders according to local principles of assessing values. They also assumed that this would include the etiquette of repaying a greater value in order to avoid the risk of causing insult.

Probably this conflict accompanied all barter sessions between distant peoples of the region, especially whenever there were no enduring long-term ties between those bartering. William Brown, Hudson's Bay Company factor at Fort Kilmaurs on Lake Babine, noted in his journal the frustration he experienced when he tried to conduct some – profitable to him – negative reciprocity. He operated on the basis of equivalence of value being at the core of gift-giving, and confounded gifting with the Gitksan notion of barter, when he met with a group of Gitksan on 10 March 1826: "From what I have seen of them, their character, manner and customs are much the same as the Carriers – they having the same appearance of generosity in making presents, which is found in the most extreme meanness – for the moment they find the present returned to them is not of more or equal value than what they gave, they make no hesitation in taking it back" (Brown n.d.). Barter was fraught with differences of opinion concerning value and concerning the importance or irrelevance of maintaining the relationship with the trading partner, if not through gifts and diplomacy, then through coercion.

Precontact Barter

A comprehensive view of precontact exchange transactions in the overall Northwest Coast culture area has been summed up by Eric Wolf (1982, 185):

Olachen ran only in restricted areas, such as the Nass and certain rivers and inlets along Queen Charlotte Sound; people came from far away with goods to trade for olachen oil, a monopoly held by groups with rights held over the fishing tracts. Hunting for land animals was especially important in the upriver communities. The northern Tlingit made the Chilkat blankets woven with mountain goat wool and cedar bark ... Copper was brought from the Copper River area to the Chilkat and taken south from there. The Haida and Nootka were especially known for their fine canoes ... The islanders supplied the mainlanders with dried venison, seal oil, dried fish, shellfish, green stone for tools, cedar bark, cedar bark baskets, cedar wood for ceremonial artifacts and yew wood for bows and storage boxes. The mainlanders furnished the islanders with hides and furs, cloth and clothing, olachen and olachen oil, cranberries, horned spoons, baskets of spruce roots, and Chilkat blankets ... The mainlanders also traded with the Athabascan speakers of the interior, bringing cedar bark baskets, fish oil, iron and shell ornaments to them and returning with hides, moccasins, thongs and placer copper.

The Gitksan and Witsuwit'en, by virtue of their location at the overlay of three major North American climatic and biotic zones (Coast, Interior Plateau, and Boreal), and located between the coastal and interior peoples, were in a good position to engage in barter. They would barter for items from the coast and receive items in the form of gifts. In turn they would dispose of a portion of these items among their inland subarctic and plateau neighbours in a manner similar to that by which they had obtained them. The inland neighbours would reciprocate by bartering and giving as gifts inland products, some of which were locally available for harvest by the Gitksan and Witsuwit'en themselves.

These peoples journeyed to the coast, especially in the early spring at the time of the oolichan runs, where they both engaged in the oolichan harvest and bartered their inland products for coast goods. The price of inland goods undoubtedly responded to local coast demand for inland products. Similarly, the price of oolichan grease and dried coast foods increased with the distance it travelled away from the coast and led to profit-taking (negative reciprocity).

This regional overview of trade relations through the area situates the network of exchanges through both gift-giving and barter. When the subject of barter and marketing of foodstuffs is discussed, people do not simply recount the old days of canoeing the river and packing goods in relay on their backs along the grease trails; they also add that, in many ways, this goes on today. Between 1876 and roughly 1960 much of the trade with coastal people took place during the brief summer season when cannery work brought Aboriginal groups together from the greater region. Today highway travel, family ties between coast and interior, and long-distance giving to relatives and in-laws now find local foodstuffs circulating the length and breadth of British Columbia and beyond.

The Grease That Heals Humanity

Oolichan grease has traditionally been in high demand among both coastal and interior peoples (Poudrier 1891; Hart 1973; Drucker 1965; MacDonald 1980). It became the conduit for barter networks all the way from the coast to the Rocky Mountains. The "grease trails" carried oolichan and other sea products inland and inland products coastward. It was by means of the major Chilcotin grease trail that Alexander Mackenzie was directed by local peoples to Bella Coola and the Pacific coast (Drucker 1936, 17).

Traveller George Chismore describes the oolichan trade he witnessed from the Nass in 1870: "By canoe, it travels to Sitka on the north and Puget Sound on the south, as well as up all the navigable rivers. Inland, borne upon the backs of men, it goes, no white man knows how far; certainly to the headwaters of the Frazer River and the Arctic slope, traded from tribe to tribe, and becoming more costly the further it gets from its source" (1885, 451). Chismore goes on to note: "Those who have brought the grease up the river transport it a certain distance on the trail, where they are met by Indians from the interior, who buy it from them to trade it in turn to others at the confines of their territory. Each tribe is exceedingly jealous of its privileges, and it is only on rare occasions that a member of one is allowed to pass through the territory of another" (1885, 455-6).

Although it is unlikely that oolichan grease amounted to more than 5 percent of the annual fat intake of the Gitksan or the Witsuwit'en in precontact times,[2] this product has been in high demand all over the region. This oil becomes available at the end of the winter when other sources of fat are generally not plentiful. Informants suggest that the first half of a residential group's quantity of oolichan grease would be consumed quite rapidly in the spring, due to the scarcity of other fat and vitamin sources in that season, and that the other half would be consumed during the remainder of the year. Oolichan grease can also be used to cure pelts, make babiche (the webbing used for snowshoes and bindings [Alfred Joseph, Transcript, 2113]), and in the preparing of certain carved wooden objects like masks, kerfed boxes, grease dishes, woven and fur garments, and ladles and paddles.

The Gitksan and Witsuwit'en obtained special coast foods, in addition to the oolichan, by exchanging their stores of dried salmon strips and berries. While enough salmon is taken annually to supply most family needs, a number of people have informed me that the quality and quantity of berries fluctuates. Yet rather than eat all of these much-loved and sometimes scarce items themselves, people preferred to use at least part of their annual supply to obtain the grease "that cures all humanity."

When groups of Gitksan went to the Nass River to obtain dried oolichan and oolichan grease each spring (frequently into the 1930s and still widely practised today, as Art Mathews attested, Transcript, 4737-8), they did not simply barter for the finished product with their own produce and crafted goods; rather, they expended their labour in its production as well as conducting barter with the various nations gathered there. It was perhaps the more distant people, such as certain Tlingit groups and interior Athapaskans, whose social relationships, being more tenuous with the Nass people, received grease strictly by barter. Here, among such distant relationships, there was more scope for profit-seeking (or negative reciprocity) and for partisan advantage than in those instances where the hosts and guests both laboured in the production of the oil and dried fish.

When the Gitksan reached the Nass, some of them, through kinship and marriage links, worked, and still work, the same fishing sites each year. They gave/give their home food specialties to their host relatives and received in return certain coast foods. Gitksan without kinship links, and the Witsuwit'en (Jenness 1943) who travelled to the Nass at this time of year, arrived in groups and were formally received by Nisga'a chiefs, who would come out onto the river ice as the inland visitors approached the Nisga'a villages.[3] The Nisga'a took the initiative to welcome the Gitksan to their territory and demonstrate their jurisdiction by offering hospitality, lodging them with allotted (usually same-clan) House groups. As Chismore (1885, 455) noted: "Indians travelling to strange villages go to their own crest, and are received as brothers, though never known before." These guests had no say as to whom they would have as their hosts. This sometimes led to a degree of animosity (*Raven Clan Outlaws on the North Pacific Coast,* Frog/Raven Adaaw<u>k</u>' No. 43, Barbeau and Beynon n.d.; Jenness 1943, 479-80). The inlanders would reciprocate for the use rights to the river and to the grease-rendering sites, cooking stones, and firewood. They gave their hosts foodstuffs, hides, horn spoons, and furs. Thereafter the Gitksan worked together with their hosts to harvest the oolichan. They also engaged in barter with other Nass visitors.

The Witsuwit'en exchanged with the Haisla peoples of Kitimat and the Gardner Canal, and the Bella Coola of Dean Channel. In return for the grease, they gave hides, bags, saskatoon arrow shafts, birchbark containers, moccasins, berries, and dried smoked meat. Usually the Witsuwit'en did not travel all the way to the Nass, although they frequently journeyed down through the mountains to Kitimat or the Kitlope Arm of the Gardner Canal for the actual oolichan harvest in the spring (Alfred Joseph [Daly 1986-88]).

The prominence of the oolichan trade was noted by early BC surveyors, as the following citations indicate. Poudrier explored the Kemano River and its mountain pass. In the course of his survey, he located an established trail from Kemano on the sea to Ootsa Lake inland. At the time he was seeking a route suitable for road and rail communication between coast and interior.

He reported that this trail was taken by the Carrier/Dene (Witsuwit'en) peoples when they went to the coast to obtain oolichan grease (Poudrier 1891, 357): "The Indians of the interior often use it to come down to the sea; as shown by their old camping places, their numerous writings in Tinneh (Dene) characters."[4] Poudrier's description of Gitanyow/Kitwancool allows us to see the importance of the oolichan exchange as late as 1890: "Kitwancool is a market town, where the oolichan grease is taken from the lower Nass and sold to tribes of the interior, who have to pay very dearly for this highly prized luxury. It would be hard to estimate the quantity of that article imported to this spot, but the hundreds of boxes seen by us, show well the great extent of the trade. These boxes are scattered all through the interior, to the foot of the Rockies, and I am told, a long way beyond" (368). About fifteen years earlier Horetzky (1874, 117-8) similarly noted the immensity of the oolichan trade and transport when he recorded meeting Gitsegukla people walking home from a feast at Kitwancool:

> More than one hundred must have passed us, and they were without a single exception, not only the men, but also the women and children, laden with large cedar boxes, of the size and shape of tea chests, which were filled with the rendered grease of the candle fish caught in the Naas [sic] waters ... They passed us in twos and threes ... little children even, of tender years, carried burdens of thirty or forty pounds weight, and tottered along in silence. One savage had, in addition to the usual load of grease, perched on its summit an old and decrepit woman, perhaps his mother. This man could not have had less than two hundred and fifty pounds weight on his back; but they are a tough, hardy set, and great carriers.

These descriptions indicate that the grease was bartered from people to people within their own territories. The more easterly peoples would journey to obtain the product from their western neighbours. The Gitksan (with relations among the Haisla of Kitimat and the Nisga'a of the Nass) and the Witsuwit'en (with relations at Kitimat and Kitlope) found themselves in profitable intermediary positions vis-à-vis the more easterly grease market.

Other Trade Items
Witsuwit'en people and some of the Gitksan obtained obsidian from the volcanic slopes of Mount Anaheim in the Chilcotin country south of Ootsa Lake. The Chilcotin people would sometimes, in return, visit Witsuwit'en territory to obtain flint from a flint place *(bïs k'ët)* and other weapon material called *bulh'ay* (brittle stone) from Bulh'ay C'ikwah (McQuarrie Creek) on the territory of Fireweed/Killer Whale Clan chief Smogelgem. Other items,

such as the special fungus that fixed the red hematite pigment *(tsiyh)* on rock faces within Witsuwit'en territory were similarly used by all the Witsuwit'en (Alfred Joseph, Transcript, 2160-2, and Daly 1986-88). Peoples from other regions would come to Witsuwit'en territory to trade for such items, just as the Witsuwit'en would go south into Chilcotin country to trade for obsidian, passing over the Witsuwit'en frontier south of Ootsa Lake at Lhë nadilh (they're crossing) (Alfred Joseph, Transcript, 2162).

The abundance of reliable, easily preserved salmon and sweet, easily preserved berries; ungulate hides, thongs, and sinew; and furs and dried game has provided the Gitksan and Witsuwit'en with their basic items of barter and gift exchange in their economic relations with coastal people. Their location between the interior and coast has put both peoples into a useful and long-standing trade position. A number of important berries of the northwestern portion of British Columbia were in great demand on the coast: particularly the sweet black huckleberry, the dwarf huckleberry, the saskatoon, and the frothy soapberry. These species were closely tended and maintained by fire clearing until government prohibited this practice. Today many berry patches have been destroyed by cut-block logging practices, or, due to lack of burning, they have changed in such a way that inferior species and subspecies of berries have replaced the quality species of the past (Art Mathews, Transcript, 4695). The Gitksan and Witsuwit'en were proud of the quality of their berries and did their utmost to prepare high-grade produce for exchange on the coast. Their description of berry qualities puts one in mind of the vintner's description of wine vintages. Tenimget, in describing the destruction of the best berry species on his land, tells of an inferior species, which today is the only type of berry growing on the clear-cut sites (Transcript, 4695): "Our berries would never grow in that. It would grow, but it would be a different kind of berries we call in our language *'miigan* – it just means that they are wood berries, they're bush berries. They have no texture. They're too sour and seedy. And if you try to preserve these berries you put tons and tons of sugar there, and it would never sweeten it up very much."

The summer settlement locales of the Gitksan and Witsuwit'en, like those of the neighbouring Tahltan and Carrier-Sekani, are highly favourable for the rapid and efficient drying of foodstuffs that are to be preserved for winter storage and trade, especially for trade with the more moist coastal areas. In contrast, one can cite the weather-related problems of spoilage that attend the preparation of herring, salmon, and game of the southeast Alaskan coast even today (the area north of the Nass River estuary): "For the time being ... weather is still the most important factor in determining whether or not the proper drying of many local game and fish products is possible" (Heller and Scott n.d., 152).

This statement is taken from a discussion of recent spoilage of fish that could not be properly smoke-dried during wet summers. The evapotranspiration rates of the Gitksan-Witsuwit'en territories thus have repercussions for the peoples' long-standing trade in foodstuffs with coastal peoples who, in certain years, had poor drying conditions. Every year, however, coastal people enjoyed the sweet interior berries and dry-smoked salmon from "upriver."

From the Tsimshian *adaawk̲*'s we are able to sketch the following post-contact, nineteenth-century flow of trade items between the lower Skeena and Nass peoples and other regions. These goods flowed in and out of the lower Nass and Metlakatla, with the result that the goods of one area eventually reached all regions. Goods passed through these mainland coastal locations from the Gitksan and "Hagwilget" (with its combination of Gitanmaax Gitksan people, Witsuwit'en, and their kinspeople from the Babine watershed), from the "Tsetsaut," Stikine, Chilkat, Kassaan Haida, Masset Haida, Skidegate Haida, Sitka Tlingit (Barbeau and Beynon n.d., *Raven Clan Outlaws on the North Pacific Coast*, Frog/Raven Adaawk̲' No. 89; *The Gwenhoot of Alaska: In Search of a Bounteous Land*, Eagle Adaawk̲' No. 64; *Wolf Clan Invaders from the Northern Plateaux and among the Tsimsyans*, Wolf Adaawk̲' No. 63).

Many areas in the Skeena system at contact were renowned for their local specialties. Boas (1916, 398) for instance, lists the following Tsimshian villages on the lower Skeena and coast, along with their specialty contributions to feasts in the region: Gitlaen (carved wooden dishes); Gina̲xangiik (carved wooden boxes); Gispaxlo'ots (carved wooden spoons); Gitwiilgo'ots (deep carved wooden dishes); Gitsiis (carved mountain goat horn spoons); Gin'adoiks (dried mountain goat flesh and tallow); Gilots'aw (cranberries and crabapples in grease, sap cakes); Gitsalasxw (Kitselas) (dried blueberries and soapberries, cranberries in grease); Gits'emkalum (cedar-bark mats and dried salmon); Gitxahla (shredded cedar bark, eagle down, local tobacco); Gitx'ada (yellow cedar blankets and burnt clamshell).

The non-local items among the Gitksan artifacts, obtained during the early decades of the twentieth century and located at Canada's Museum of Civilization, reflect both the general flow of produce through the greater region and the abundance and scarcity of products due to variations of climate and ecological niches. The museum collections' accession records[5] contain twenty-four Gitksan items of foreign manufacture, for which there exist fairly complete provenance information. From this list we find that the following goods came into the Gitksan-Witsuwit'en area from the neighbouring peoples: from the Nass River the Gitksan obtained shell goods, painted wooden boxes, smoked clams (and nineteenth-century glass beads, possibly from Fort Simpson). From the Haida they obtained yew-wood paddles, herring eggs on kelp, carved talking sticks, painted bentwood boxes, and one silver brooch. From Edziza in the northern Tahltan country they obtained obsidian; from the Carrier and Sekani they received babiche bags, birchbark containers, dried soapberry flakes, and red ochre (found near Bear Lake). They received trade beads, probably from Fort Connolly on Bear Lake. From the Tsimshian, they received a berry box, a painted bentwood box, a dance apron, an *amhalayt* headdress, and one metal knife, possibly from Fort Simpson.

Transportation Routes

Sinuous trails linked precontact indigenous communities across the breadth of northwest British Columbia and southeast Alaska. These trails formed a conduit for trade and communications between the different Aboriginal villages and settlements. The trails are old. George Chismore spent the summer of 1870, while on furlough from the US Army, exploring the trail up the Nass Valley and across to Kispiox. His observations as to the age of the trail are interesting (Chismore 1885, 457): "In one place the trail leads over the top of a hill denuded of soil, and is worn deeply into the solid granite by the feet of succeeding generations."

In 1870 the Nass-Kispiox trail was much used, even in the summer months, long after the annual oolichan run. Chismore reports: "The trail was a constant source of interest. Daily we passed parties bending under their burdens, or met others hurrying back to seek a load. This highway is broad and clear and very old" (1885, 457). Chismore also indicates the trail-side facilities for the freight packers who would be carrying freight for gold prospectors in the Omineca area as well as produce for local use: "Sweat-houses were built at frequent intervals, where, with a cup of water and a few heated stones, the tired native might assuage his aching limbs by a steam bath. Rude huts of bark afford shelter to him who needs it, and large sheds built of the same material mark the spots where different tribes meet to trade" (1885, 456).

It is appropriate to conclude this description of the grease trail communication, and the general importance of trade in the region, with an understanding of indigenous bridges, of which there were several in Gitksan and Witsuwit'en territories at the time of contact (see Figure 34). Chismore describes the bridge he saw and crossed at the confluence of the Cranberry and Nass Rivers (which was also described by Horetzky in 1872 [Horetzky 1874]). The construction Chismore describes is not unlike that employed by the Gitksan and Witsuwit'en to establish canyon-side fishing platforms, and it conforms to descriptions of the Kisgagas and Hagwilget Canyon bridges, which exhibited a local knowledge of cantilever principles. Chismore describes the bridge he crossed on the Cranberry River when he travelled to Kispiox:

Bridges span the wider streams; one, a suspension crossing the Har-keen, built long ago, replacing a still older one, has a clear span of ninety-two feet. It is located at a point where opposing cliffs form natural abutments, and is thus constructed: From each bank two tapering logs, parallel to each other – some ten feet apart and with points elevated to an angle of ten degrees are pushed out over the stream towards each other as far as their butts will serve as a counterpoise. Then two more are shoved out between the first, but nearer together and almost horizontal. The ends on shore are then secured by piling logs and stones upon them. Then a man crawls out to the end of one of the timbers, and throws a line to another in the same position opposite. A light pole is hauled into place, lashed securely, and that arch completed. The three remaining sets of timbers are treated in the same manner. The upper and lower arches are then fastened together by poles, cross-pieces put in, foot plank laid, and handrail bound in proper position to steady the traveler in crossing the vibrating, swaying structure. No bolt, nail or pin is used from first to last. Strips of bark and tough, flexible roots form all the fastenings. (1885, 456-7)

Commerce between Witsuwit'en and Gitksan

The frontier between Gitksan and Witsuwit'en has been remarkably peaceful over a very long period. In many ways this testifies to the balanced nature of the trade within the region. Both peoples utilize similar ecological niches; both occupy choice positions vis-à-vis coast and inland trade, and while both share the salmon resources of the upper Skeena system, their respective hunting territories fan out from the main-stem rivers in opposite directions. Thus, when the two language groups complete their respective salmon harvest and processing and turn to their hunting grounds, they turn in opposite directions, and the possibility of conflicts developing over access to land are minimized. As we saw in Chapter 3, both have followed similar annual harvest schedules, which required seasonal access to river sites, valleys, and mountaintops for the taking of similar plants, animals, fish, and fowl. Both are blessed with many of the same resources, and those items that happen to be scarce among one or other people have long been the objects of trade and gift-giving between them.

Until the twentieth century (with the establishment of permanent residence at what formerly had been the locations of summer smokehouses for the Witsuwit'en and winter homes for the Gitksan), the annual salmon runs brought the two peoples into the greatest degree of mutual interaction. This social interaction has involved much intermarriage between Houses and clans located adjacent to one another across the cultural frontier.

Dora Wilson, Yaga'lahl (Transcript, 4064ff.), indicated some of the kinship interconnections between her House, Wilps Spookw, and other Houses, both Gitksan and Witsuwit'en. Yaga'lahl's mother, Margaret Austin, holds the chief name of Sanii'hlen in the Gitksan House of Spookw, yet her name is a Witsuwit'en word meaning "looking at the moon." The La̱x Gibuu Wilps Spookw has close ties with the Witsuwit'en Gitdumden (Wolf) House of Gisdaywa (Transcript, 4064-6). Chiefs in the House of Spookw have married into the Gis̱k'aast (Fireweed/Killer Whale) House of Gitludahl in Kispiox (4071), the Laksilyu (Small Frog) House of Wedexget of Moricetown (4073), the Gitsegukla Gis̱k'aast (Firewood/Killer Whale) Clan (4073), as well as the Gis̱k'aast House of Wiiseeks from Kispiox (4085-6), and the Laksilyu (Frog) House of Hagwilneexl (4088, 4095). As well, Spookw has been known to host feasts in Kispiox, Gitanmaax, and Hagwilget (4098).

Transactions and agreements between the two peoples are often conducted by consulting with the counterparts of one's own clan. The following suggests one such agreement. About 1820 the Witsuwit'en Frog Clan chief Sats'aan journeyed from Moricetown together with a Wolf Clan chief to discuss the Bulkley Canyon rockslide with their clan counterparts in the Gitksan village of Gitanmaax. They sought permission for the Witsuwit'en people to fish downstream, within the territories of Gitksan Frog and Wolf chiefs at Hagwilget Canyon in Gitanmaax territory (Barbeau and Beynon n.d., B-F-90.1-29).

Cultural differences provide for a certain amount of exchange of goods between peoples. The Gitksan generally refuse to eat lamprey eels, while the Witsuwit'en smoke them carefully, use their skins in hide-work,[6] and enjoy their flesh. (The Mathews/Matthews family at Wilson Creek south of Gitwangax continues to prepare eels to exchange for Witsuwit'en tanned moosehide [Transcript, 4636].) The Gitksan have long exchanged early spring salmon and smoked eels for the tanned hides and fine hide garments for which the Witsuwit'en and other Athapaskan peoples are widely known. There appears to have been a traditional exchange of those items, which, while indigenous to both regions, are more plentiful in one or other: the Witsuwit'en and Babine would supply soapberries, birchbark, and saskatoon-wood arrows to the Gitksan, who responded with salmon strips, hemlock sap cakes, and cedar bark.

It appears that common clan boundaries and frequent intermarriage made this frontier relatively stable. And since both nations tended to exchange items that were respectively abundant to the seller/giver and were at the same time available in the lands of the buyer/recipient, there were few grounds for major trading disputes (such as both faced with coastal neighbours). At the same time, the village of Hagwilget, where the Witsuwit'en established themselves after the rockslide of 1820, is still regarded by some Gitksan as a temporary arrangement. In the same vein several Witsuwit'en from Hagwilget have told me they are made to feel that they are on foreign territory if they venture into Hazelton/Gitanmaax for an evening's entertainment. The relationship is not unproblematic but has been fundamentally peaceful for hundreds of years.

Protocontact Trade

The new market expectations of Gitksan chiefs in relation to the coastal fur trade of the late eighteenth and early nineteenth century bore little fruit. This was due mainly to the rapid growth of the mercantile power and fire-power of coastal chiefs such as those on the Nass and, in particular, the Gispaxlo'ots Eagle chief, Ligeex, on the Skeena and the adjacent coast. Among the Gitksan, entrepreneurial pretensions may have arisen during the two centuries preceding the actual arrival of Europeans in the region. This is indicated in some of the *adaawk*'s that belong to Gitksan Houses. One such ascendant Gitksan trader chief may have been the Ganeda (Frog/Raven) chief Nekt, in the person of one or more incumbents to that chiefly name, who repulsed attacks by coastal chiefs and went on the offensive against the Haisla at Kitimat (Barbeau and Beynon n.d., *Raven Clan Outlaws on the North Pacific Coast*, Frog/Raven Adaawk's Nos. 47 and 79; MacDonald 1980).

In the eighteenth and early nineteenth centuries, incumbents to the name Ligeex enforced their own trade monopoly on the middle Skeena. These Ligeexs did this by seeking hegemony over Kitselas Canyon, the most strategic transport location on the Skeena River system. The Ligeex of the contact period also accomplished his aims by carrying out murderous raids on Kispiox, Gitanmaaxs, Hagwilget, and Gitsegukla. This was effected so as both to scotch Gitksan overtures to his Nass River rivals and to capture entrepôts to the Athapaskan trade – with the people of Hagwilget, Morice-town, Babine, and eastward (Barbeau and Beynon n.d. *The Gwenhoot of Alaska: In Search of a Bounteous Land*, Eagle Adaawk's Nos. 44 and 50; *Temlaham, The Land of Plenty*, Gisk'aast Adaawk' No. 95; *Raven Clan Outlaws on the North Pacific Coast*, Frog/Raven Adaawk' No. 72).

As far as Gitksan and Witsuwit'en indigenous trade with their neighbours is concerned, a westward flow of berries, furs, and hides was exchanged for an eastward-moving stream of oolichan grease and a trickle of coastal foods and craft goods. The further these goods moved away from their area of origin, the greater was the labour investment devoted to their care and transport, such that the price would increase with both geographical and social distance, just as the quantity of available goods decreased. Here, indeed, there was a degree of commodity trading, with a view to reselling. This was the real negative reciprocity, the real "allocation of scarce resources" for marginal gain, as it occurred throughout the general region in pre-European times, and notably at the margins between First Nations peoples.

The Gitksan, and to some extent the Witsuwit'en, traded large quantities of their dried salmon in both directions. This salmon is said to have a fine balance between sufficient fat for taste but not too much to impede the drying process if there happened to be a humid summer with little wind. They traded this cordillera salmon product towards the coast and towards the Rockies. This contributed greatly to the long-term well-being of the peoples on the upper Skeena River system by adding to the variety of their own diet and their ability to combine fishing with hunting and the regional exchange of goods. Just as Canadians today take for granted the daily use of imported goods like coffee or pepper, so too the peoples of the upper Skeena included oolichan grease in their regular diet (along with other seasonal foods from other ecologies) as well as crafted items like Haida canoes (see Figure 31). Long before the advent of European trade, the Gitksan and Witsuwit'en had a well worked out "mixed economy." Whereas exchange relations at home stressed reciprocity and were couched in the idiom of the gift, in distant places they were much more commercial, with the aim being to secure profitable trade.

Postcontact Trade

As MacDonald has argued (1979, 1980), the trade in European metal goods along the grease trails preceded the European explorers on the Northwest Coast by at least a century. As historical studies of the Pacific coast develop we will also probably find that the protocontact tempo of trade picked up momentum from eastern and southern influences as well. The aggressive transcontinental juggernaut of the Great Lakes and Plains fur trade pushed right across the continent. It threw one nation or people against another and, thereby, created confederacies of tribes joined together for defensive and retaliatory purposes in the context of the scramble to control trade routes and access to furs. Russian traders were working their way down the Alaska panhandle, trading and pillaging. There was similar pressure from the south, by the Spanish, whose horses, guns, and knives, together with the market activity of the westward-rolling fur trade, facilitated the Chinook slave-taking and the increased volume and tempo of trading and raiding all along the Pacific coast (Ruby and Brown 1976).

The Eagle Clan leader of the Coast Tsimshian Gispaxlo'ots, Simoogit Ligeex, came to control coastal trade with the Gitksan and their Witsuwit'en and other Athapaskan neighbours. Usually there were three trading visits a year prior to and during the fur trade period. They were often accompanied by violence (Tomlinson [1875]; see also the *adaawk̲'* accounts by Kispiox and Gitanmaax people). In the spring, in addition to European goods such as blankets and iron products, Ligeex's men brought oolichan grease, dried oolichan, and herring roe, which they exchanged for groundhog and marten pelts as well as caribou and moosehides taken in Gitksan and Witsuwit'en territories over the winter. In the fall they brought marine foodstuffs that they exchanged for upriver dried berries. In the late fall they brought coast foods to barter for berries, groundhog skins, and tanned hides. Similar trade visits were made to the Witsuwit'en at this time, up the Zymoetz/Copper River to McDonnell Lake (Alfred Joseph, Transcript, 2129). From the Gitksan and Witsuwit'en point of view, this trade did not disrupt the normal round of subsistence barter. It did, however, have political and military destabilizing effects in so far as Ligeex sought to maintain his trade monopoly by launching military reprisals on those inland peoples who dared to barter with his rivals.

The first Europeans found the coastal peoples well-practised and highly skilled in barter and diplomacy, and adamantly opposed to losing their go-between status to European traders. The northerly spread of wealth-oriented secret societies appears to have reached the Kitimat and Coast Tsimshian at some point before the advent of Europeans. So too did the spread of standard chiefly regalia, such as copper shields, Chilkat blankets, *amhalayt* headdresses, dance kilts, and "raven" rattles – items that combined fine specialty products assembled, through regional social interaction, from a number of different ecological areas.

In 1774 the first European traders-explorers, on the Spanish ship *Santiago*, appeared on the north coast in Haida waters. Thereafter, the scramble for coastal furs accelerated. By 1797 the Russian state-trading company had established its first post on Kodiak Island in present-day Alaska. The Russian pursuit of sable and marten in Siberia had virtually eliminated these animals by 1750 and impelled the Russian traders to move east to North America via the Kamchatka Peninsula. Here, they began to amass furs, initially sea otter pelts, by using the same technique of feudal expansionism that they had applied in Siberia, trying to subjugate the Aleut and Tlingit and to extract taxes in the form of peltries. Between 1785 and 1825, 330 visits by trading vessels, mainly Russian, Spanish, British, and Bostonian, were recorded on the north coast (Fisher 1977, 13). The ships' captains sold the sea otter pelts for high prices in Canton, and the ships returned to Europe and Boston laden with tea and silk. Then, as quickly as it had begun, the trade in sea otter pelts ended. By 1830 there were virtually no more otters on the coast.

Between 1839 and 1867 the Hudson's Bay Company, hoping to mop up the trade and gain access to the lands across the Coast Range for their conventional custom (e.g., beaver, marten, and muskrat), leased the Alaskan coast from the Russians from Cape Fairweather to the Portland Canal. After 1830 the trade shifted from sea otter pelts on the coast to marten and other forest fur-bearing species, as well as moosehide and caribou hide from the indigenous hunters to the east of the Cascades/Coast Range.

Under these conditions, a number of coastal chiefs gained inordinate power and influence, making alliances with trading firms and missionaries, and collecting hinterland furs, first along the coast, then by controlling access to interior peoples. According to Wolf (1982, 189), the Tlingit at Wrangell, under Chief Shakes, monopolized the trade with the Tahltan and other Athapaskans at the head of the Stikine River. The Tlingit at Taku controlled the trade up and down the Taku River; the Tlingit at Chilkat monopolized the valley of the Chilkat River; and the Tsimshian under Chief Ligeex at Fort Simpson seized control and monopolized the trade on the upper Skeena with the Gitksan and Witsuwit'en, who in turn controlled trade with Carrier peoples and the Sekani.

By the middle of the nineteenth century the Hudson's Bay Company had established two of its most important coastal posts: Fort Rupert, near present-day Port Hardy on the north end of Vancouver Island, and Fort Simpson, near the mouth of the Nass River. The chiefs who moved to the vicinity of these two trading posts with their seemingly endless supplies of exotic foods and durable trade goods (e.g., iron, copper, glass, beads, guns, blankets, and cooking pots) were thrown together in large settlements for the first time. Four groupings among the Fort Rupert Kwakiutl (Kwak̲-wak̲'awakw) and nine among the Fort Simpson Tsimshian began the intricate process of establishing their respective power and ranking under the new conditions. These conditions resulted in an artificially accelerated tempo of gift-giving and the destruction of property, partly in the course of the practice of the winter secret dance societies. Codere (1961, 457-67) notes, for instance, that at Fort Rupert during this time the Kwak̲wak̲'awakw population, due to disease and social chaos, had fallen to one-sixth of what it had been seventy-five years earlier. However, despite this high degree of social disruption, discord, and depopulation, the number of robes and blankets given in a feast at this period rose from about 200 to 30,000.

Depopulation and social dislocation due to the coastal fur trade similarly affected the Coast Tsimshian and their Nass River and inland neighbours. This period saw the competitive giving of vast amounts of commodity wealth between rival trader chiefs, often involving hosts in spectacular challenges to destroy their wealth (which was part of the cost of hosting feasts during those highly inflationary times of social instability). Such destruction, being part of a host's outlay of hospitality, engendered a tacit, unspoken challenge to the host's main rival to repay (either by giving or sacrificing publicly) a greater value on the next encounter. Giving in the form of destroying or sacrificing vast quantities of goods began to occur almost as a matter of honour (see Chapter 1). Bourdieu (1990, 100) has pointed out that honour can be a highly effective medium of exchange between persons of roughly equal status: "The exchange of honour, like every exchange (of gifts, words, etc.) is defined as such – in opposition to the unilateral violence of aggression –

that is, as implying the possibility of a continuation, a reply, a riposte, a return gift, in as much as it contains recognition of the partner (to whom, in the particular case, it accords equality of honour). The challenge, as such, calls for a riposte, and is therefore addressed to a man deemed capable of playing the game of honour, and of playing it well: the challenge confers honour. The converse of this principle of reciprocity is that only a challenge issued by a man equal in honour deserves to be taken up." The early nineteenth century saw the advent of such exchanges of honour between despotic high chiefs, along with aggressive raids with rifles as well as slave-trading (until outlawed by the colonial government) (Cole and Darling 1990).

These developments inflated and expanded traditional relationships along the coast, but they did not undermine the indigenous way of life (Cole and Darling 1990). Undermining occurred later, with the coming of non-Aboriginal settlement, continuing epidemics of European diseases, and government seizure and administration of the land mass of British Columbia, which was justified with the convenient myth of the "hovering sovereign" (Culhane 1998). Certainly for the Tsimshian-speakers in general and the Gitksan in particular, this new economy supplanted neither the old subsistence one nor the customary social institutions that were integral to economic pursuits. It merely bloated and upset the balance of these institutions for a period of time.

Under these conditions, however, stored food and wealth assumed a new function. Formerly they had been associated with the juridical and moral sanctioning of the host's labour force on the land as shown through feasts that involved the fruits of their combined lands and labour. Now, in addition, they became the basis of accumulating ceremonial goods, which were purchased by means of bartering skins, berries, dried salmon, and European trade goods. Most of these items were subsistence items but, due to their increasing use to obtain quantities of ceremonial goods for public gift-giving, they became scarce and gained new but limited convertibility, or commodification (Gregory 1982, 11-28).

Generally, the economic exchange occurring in the local community, where a chief's power was lodged and sanctioned, remained in the sphere of gifting. On the other hand, external exchanges were more market-related in that the same good could function as a gift internally and a commodity externally, as Godelier (1977, 128) pointed out long ago. The hegemony of money in the wider society has not, even today, supplanted the gifting relationships of the local community. The land, designated "Crown land," remains in family hands, and this situation is celebrated publicly with every feast in the local community, even though this proprietorship is not recognized by government. The Witsuwit'en and Gitksan have not become decisively detached from their lands, even though they have been alienated from the market benefits currently being derived from their resources by others.

The inalienability of the land-based crests and narratives that stand behind the things given in the feasts mirror this situation. Whereas dispossessed peasants in Europe had nothing to sell at the advent of industrialization but their labour power, the indigenous peoples of Canada, like land-owning peasants, have largely treated wage labour as target work, something that supplements or coexists with the land-based foraging and gift sector.

Money, the ultimate commodity, has had a restricted passage into these local communities. One reason for this is that the reserve lands now recognized by Government as Aboriginal (approximately 125 square kilometres out of 54,000 square kilometres) are jurally inalienable and cannot serve as collateral in financial ventures, as reserve dwellers find out when they try to obtain a bank loan. Second, the money used for feasting, whether from transfer payments or wage labour, is considered to be part of the subsistence sphere of what researchers call social reproduction. Here, money is used to obtain gifts and to signal recognition of social status within the ethos of giving and counter-giving. These are interfamily exchanges whose explicit aim is to requite the family name and to reproduce relationships for yet another generation. Success here, of course, can lead to political capital that puts the House leaders in a good position to advance sectional interests in political or economic ventures in the wider society.

Recall for a moment Codere's contention (Chapter 1) that, at any point in time, the value of a copper was the value of the goods and services expended in the last feast where it changed hands. This implies that, during the fur trade at least, the copper shield was the gold standard for comparative feasting. Today, the cash expended in gift transactions during feasts serves a similar function.

The English terminology used by the Gitksan and Witsuwit'en to describe exchange transactions is truly mixed. There are people who say that, if one is honest and gives one's work to the whites, then one will be given money in return. Others speak of the feast transactions simply in terms of requiting debts and making payments. These are both aspects of the current habitus concerning the conceptualization of gifting relations. The current, ongoing gift-giving is surrounded by a sea of national and international market relations. Land proprietorship and economic production for these peoples are in a state of flux. We are living through an era of land and Aboriginal rights litigation in Canada that is accompanied by the depletion of such natural resources as wild salmon stocks and timber. By remaining steadfast adherents to feasting and the gift tradition – and their associated symbolic capital – the Gitksan and Witsuwit'en reinforce their social imaginary of a free and independent aristocratic society with its own land and resources, and hold on to this vision as they move into an uncertain future.

Throughout the fur trade period, accumulation continued to be masked by a moral code that extolled giving and disbursing "kindnesses" in the form of wealth. This was necessary because the chiefs had to accumulate commodities from within a local subsistence economy possessing a labour force governed by the concerns and principles of land-based family and kinship rather than by the concerns of maximizing profits obtained from unencumbered labour and resources in the market. While by contrast the entrepreneurial coastal trading chiefs – dependent as they were on the European market – controlled local trade, they did not control production. They had to negotiate with their local Houses and clans to obtain needed goods and produce.

Powerful coastal chiefs like Ligeex, Tsibasaa, Shakes, and Haimas utilized the goods produced by relatives for local use as values to be employed to obtain/buy ceremonial goods. These goods, in turn, were exchanged in the formal giving and receiving between chiefs in a manner that, at first appearance, turned the food and hides into something like market commodities. But this was only a means to an end, a way of quantitatively increasing wealth for feasting and for winter dance "potlatching." As Cole and Darling (1990, 122-3) point out, Aboriginal traders sought out goods to be used in their feasting cycles: "The pattern in trade exchange indicates that the Indians, like any set of consumers, exercised a strong discrimination in their selection of items. If traders could not offer the type or quality of articles Indians demanded, there could be no trade." However, engaging in the fur trade, raiding and intimidating neighbouring peoples to obtain their trade goods, also put extra pressure on local kin and affines. Externally, the scope of economic activity by these trader chiefs now surpassed the subsistence round of their individual Houses and clans. They were tempted to ignore many of the constraints that a House normally places on the power and authority of a chief. Slaves of the Stikine Tlingit, for example, were sold by chiefs for around ten dollars in 1840, and Chilkat Tlingit rented out their slave labour to whites in the 1890s in order to obtain money for purchasing potlatch wealth (Hays 1975, 96; Oberg 1973, 111-12).

Drucker (1963, 137) stressed that at Fort Rupert in Kwakwak'awakw territory on Vancouver Island, and at Port Simpson in Metlakatla Pass in Tsimshian territory, the new missionary and trading post conditions had created new social configurations where enduring social statuses had yet to be solidified. Here agonistic gifting was used to settle the issues of social status among candidates for chiefly position, and Boas's accounts of these competitive feastings became the sine qua non of "the potlatch" for anthropologists and, in the form of the Potlatch Law, led to legislation against Aboriginal ceremonial activity. Across the region massive feasts and *nuhlim* dance society gatherings became openly competitive. They were no longer staged merely to repay the debts accruing from day-to-day living. Psychic or spiritual powers, too, including charges and counter-charges of bad medicine, were at this time integrated into overall competition and accumulation, often by means of sorcery and witchcraft accusations.

At that point in time, trader chiefs engaged in market relations through trade networks and barter that was facilitated by a mixture of feasting and violent coercion, but they did not possess appropriate social institutions that would allow them to free themselves from the demands of kinship. Thus they were unable to become modern traders of fully alienated goods that they could buy and sell for profit, free of obligation in the local gift sphere. They were not able to transcend and move beyond the kinship system of their indigenous society, with its annual subsistence round of harvesting game and fish, and paying respect to one another, and to nature, according to principles of matrilineal gift exchange.

Eric Wolf (1982), in surveying the effects of European trade and colonialism on indigenous societies, makes the following observation on kinship limits to economic and political consolidation. He specifically discusses the new trader chiefs in different countries who build power through accumulation of trade goods and the monopolization of trade routes and trade networks: "The fact that leaders can rise to prominence in this way constitutes one of the Achilles' heels of the kinship mode, one of its diagnostic points of stress. For as a chief or other leader draws a following through the judicious management of alliances and redistributive action, he reaches a limit that can only be surpassed by breaking through the bounds of the kinship order" (94).

A succession of nineteenth-century incumbents to the name Ligeex were unable to break through the bounds of the kinship order of the Tsimshian. They milked it and manipulated it; they showed no modesty of demeanor as chiefs, no deference to elders or to tradition. Their kinspeople – their *wil'naat'ahl* – were urged by law to support them, or at least not to oppose them publicly.

In earlier times a captive, when his or her true identity became known, would generally be kept as a political hostage between nations or villages. The captive would live as a member of the chief's retinue. Being persona non grata, the slave of a Gitksan or Witsuwit'en chiefly family was frequently the closest confidant of the members of the household.[7] During the late eighteenth and nineteenth centuries captives seized along the Northwest Coast became increasingly important as labour power, or they were simply sought after by rival chiefs as newly prized possessions. They became a new type of wealth object – one that could be employed as an exchangeable commodity; sacrificed, with the full emotive power of spiritual and ceremonial connotations; or otherwise disposed of in potlatch competition.[8]

For the most part, the fur trade was a supplement to, and not a replacement for, the normal seasonal round (Fisher 1977; Wolf 1982, 193). The hinterland regions of the Gitksan and Witsuwit'en seem to have remained peripheral to competitive feasting in the nineteenth century, particularly in the eastern portions of the region. The upper Skeena area did not become a central area of presettlement European trade. An adjacent area that did, however, was the Nass River estuary, and another, as already mentioned, was the Fort Rupert region on northern Vancouver Island. At these locations a number of formerly disparate chiefs were drawn into competition and interaction. Gitksan and Witsuwit'en oral history indicates that, to some extent, this form of competition occurred, though on a minor scale, in the vicinity of the Hudson's Bay Company trading posts at Bear Lake and Stuart Lake.

As frequently happens in such historical situations, the coastal trader chiefs, unable and unwilling to expend the forces needed to produce goods for the market, scrambled to control access to other producers, raided rivals, took captives, burned villages, and seized one another's trading parties. They used armed force to secure hegemony over lucrative routes, and they sought to legitimize this behaviour by silencing potential protest through the agonistic giving of a massive over-abundance of wealth to potential rivals and protesters. This, of course, violated the laws of feasting and shifted relationships from those associated with gifting to those associated with a form of negative reciprocity played out through the medium of honour (see above).

All these negative reciprocity activities consequently spelled the eventual socio-political downfall of the trader chiefs, who, by their actions, had torn and tattered the fabric of normal kinship relations. When such trader chiefs lost status and approval in the communities, they lost their links to the goods demanded by the trade and the hands that would produce and transport them. The chief could maintain his status or increase it only if he leavened his competitive gift-giving with expansionary military prowess. The tendency towards competitive overpayment of gifts was risky, but the trader chiefs had no alternative course of action if they were to assume and maintain the paramount position in the market. One of missionary William Duncan's early converts and lay preachers, Arthur Wellington Clah (Figure 35), was said to have defended the missionary from physical attack by Ligeex, but shortly thereafter this once-powerful trader chief changed his modus operandi. When he reached the limit of expansion with the HBC (he married his daughter to the factor and became chief trader), he converted to Christianity and became chief trader for William Duncan, and later sought his fortunes through the commercial fishery and government agencies (Usher 1974). For his part, Clah went on to keep a diary of Port Simpson events, which is now lodged at the Wellcome Institute in London. His daughter gave birth to a son who grew up to be William Beynon, who, for over forty years, was the main provider of detailed Nass River and Skeena River ethnographic materials to the National Museum of Canada.[9] As Michael

Robinson (1997 [1978], 69) has pointed out, trading families of the past swiftly joined the new world order:

> Interestingly enough, those men and women of prominence who had held hereditary family titles in Fort Simpson soon rose to positions of prominence in the Christian community. Paul Legaik became chief of the village police force, and his constables were men who had once been house chiefs. When the Bishop of Columbia paid a visit to Metlakatla in 1863, Legaik 3, aged about 40, spoke the following words: "We must put away all our evil ways. I want to take hold of God. I believe in God the Father, my sins are too heavy. I think we have not strength of ourselves."

Along the coast, the territorial base of the chiefs was lost with the onset of European settlement, the establishment of reserves, and the involvement in wage labour. To a limited degree, persons of little hereditary standing were able to buy their way into prominence and use newly found cash from wage labour to mount feasts. This was more prevalent on the coast than in the mountains; as the Witsuwit'en chiefs attest, no amount of cash can buy a hereditary title. As well, missionaries strove to end the millennia-long tradition of feasts and gift-giving (cf. Usher 1974). Inland, however, "back in the bush," among the mountains, where the Gitksan and Witsuwit'en live, the market economy and the development of trade had not been able to supplant the traditional network of jural and moral obligations associated with foraging and feasting between Houses.

The post-*Delgamuukw* years have seen vibrant support for the feasting system, and this is due, in part at least, to the increasing possibilities of the Gitksan and the Witsuwit'en House groups to get back to again using their territories. This is not to suggest, as did counsel for the government defendants in *Delgamuukw*, that feasting had ever become a dead jalopy in the front yard, cranked up expressly so that it could roll down the land claim road as a "living relic of the past." The *Delgamuukw* plaintiffs are gaining recognition of the justice of their claim to landownership in Canadian society. What is slower, and more grudgingly given, is recognition by governments of First Nations' proprietorship. Government continues to cling to the legal metonym of Crown ownership of these lands, but it is beginning to take cognizance of recent court decisions that call for consultation and negotiation between indigenous owners, governments, and private-sector entrepreneurs before further resource extraction occurs. To the extent that these peoples utilize, inventory, and manage their traditional lands and fishing sites, they are gradually able to make plans that should allow them to re-enter the wider world of exchange and trade – that aspect of Aboriginal life that has always been denied by colonial powers. Indeed, if Aboriginal groups can show that they have always relied upon exchange relations

(whether of the gift or barter type) for substantial parts of their social reproduction, then governments will have to stop treating them as creatures of
the forest and regard them as *real* human societies with extensive economic,
family, and cultural ties to other peoples. As one of the Gitksan political
leaders says, "We want to show the world that there has always been more
to our way of life than berry-picking."

7
Owners and Stewards

[A kinship system] is a way of thinking about rights and usages
with respect to land.

– E.R. Leach (1961, 146)

The foregoing chapters have examined the workings of reciprocal gifting
and trade among the Gitksan and Witsuwit'en over the last two centuries.
We have viewed a pole-raising feast as a gifting paradigm and looked at the
seasonal round of land use organized according to overlapping family ties
that are acknowledged and reciprocated in day-to-day exchanges and in the
feast system. I then discussed storage, hierarchy, and the continuum between gift and commodity in regional trade and barter. Chapter 7 explores
the system of territorial entitlement, without which an economy cannot
function – unless, of course, its practitioners occupied the land of the so-
called New World by force of arms (as did, for example, the Viking economy
a millennium ago, and industrial Europe more recently).

The way a society sanctions its form of proprietorship varies according to
the specific history and cultural ethos involved. Yet, whatever the form,
land title and land rights are essential to a people's material well-being and
self-governance. The colonial power denied the indigenous sense of place,
home, and customary system of landholding, and based its notion of rights
in land on the concept of traditional usufruct. This has always been hotly
contested by those alienated from their lands. It was integral to the Gitksan
chiefs' presentation of what they called "the land question" when they appeared before the Royal Commission into Indian land reserves (McKenna-
McBride Commission 1915).

I heard what the white men said today, that if there is any reservation too
big for his Band then the Government is going to cut it off and divide the
money. Since I heard this I was pretty near crying. It's because this land

belongs to our old forefathers that have died and I feel awful sore when I heard that. (Mool'xan, to Royal Commission, Gitsegukla, 20 April 1915)

We are not mistaken when we ask for our own. We are born citizens in this country. We were born in this place – we were born here and we own this land, and we want to get it back. (William Holland, father of the present Kyologet, Mary McKenzie, to Royal Commission, Gitanmaax, 21 April 1915)

This was not the first time claims to ownership had assailed the ears of the colonial officials. The question arose as British sovereignty was declared over Vancouver Island. In 1849 Archibald Barclay, secretary of the Hudson's Bay Company, wrote to the HBC governor for the Island, James Douglas: "With respect to the rights of the natives, you will have to confer with the chiefs of the tribes on that subject, and in your negotiations with them you are to consider the natives as the rightful possessors of such lands only as they are occupied by cultivation, or had houses built on, at the time when the island came under the undivided sovereignty of Great Britain in 1846. All other land is to be regarded as waste, and applicable to the purposes of colonisation" (Tennant 1990, 18). And some years later, in 1865, British Columbia's colonial land commissioner, Joseph Trutch, reported:

the claims of Indians over tracts of land, on which they assume to exercise ownership, but of which they make no real use, operate very materially to prevent settlement and cultivation beside that to which attention has been directed by Mr. Nind, and I should advise that these claims be as soon as practicable inquired into and defined. (Joseph Trutch, chief commissioner, Lands and Works of British Columbia, 20 September 1865 [Fisher 1977, 162-3])

Commissioner Trutch dismisses Aboriginal ownership on the grounds that Aboriginal British Columbians did not utilize their territories for industry or agriculture. This still-prevalent Eurocentric assumption considers ownership to be in direct ratio to the technological sophistication of the societies under inquiry. It assumes bona fide owners are they who "develop" the environment in radical ways easily observable by modern eyes. All others merely roam the land and possess no more – and often less – than usufruct rights. As Arnett (1999, 32) has pointed out: "Part of the problem was British acceptance of the social theory developed by Vattel, an eighteenth-century French legalist, who argued that cultivation alone gave the right to hold title to land. Hunting and food-gathering were considered 'idle' forms of existence. 'Those who yet hold to the idle mode of life,' wrote Vattel, 'usurp more land than they would require with honest labour, and cannot complain if other nations, more laborious and too much pent-up, come

and occupy a portion of it.'" In 1802, in the course of defending the punitive raids by the cavalry against Aboriginal resistance to land cessions in the
United States, John Quincy Adams rationalized the seizure of Aboriginal
lands in the same terms: "But what is the right of a huntsman to the forest
of a thousand miles over which he accidentally ranged in quest of prey?
Shall the liberal bounties of Providence to the race of man be monopolized
by one of ten thousand for whom they were created? Shall the exuberant
bosom of the common mother, amply adequate to the nourishment of millions, be claimed exclusively by a few hundreds of her offspring?" (Clark
1947, 221-2).

Exposing this line of reasoning, Anthony Wallace (1957) explained that
North American indigenous peoples possessed a clear sense of territorial
boundaries based upon natural features like waterways and heights of land,
and traditional social systems of tenure. Unfortunately, it was not in the
interests of land-hungry Europeans to understand this:

> It is by no means certain that the concepts entertained by those Europeans
> with whom Indians had most contact – i.e., soldiers, traders, government
> officials, hunters and frontier settlers – would have emphasized the bounded
> territory principle. One needs to consider that to many Europeans, the bulk
> of a tribe's territory was hunting ground; and lands used or usable for the
> hunt have a special status in European and American real estate custom and
> law. Even today, unposted private lands in this country may be hunted over
> by persons having no ownership title to the land itself. To the frontiers-
> man, and to some traders, interest and cultural expectation alike might
> well coincide in minimizing tribal rights to bounded tracts largely used for
> hunting and trapping: they were "only hunting grounds." (Wallace 1947,
> 311-12)

At European contact, the Gitksan and Witsuwit'en were noted to have
been led by "men of property" and to have possessed an elaborate system
of owning and defending parcels of corporately held land. Despite these
men of property, their lands were considered by the newcomers to be
"merely hunting grounds" whose assumed usufruct tenure was ultimately
overridden by the Crown's declaration of underlying title to the "Dominion of Canada."

Yet early on the federal government of Canada took legal cognizance of
the provisions of the Royal Proclamation of 1763, and the rulings of Chief
Justice Marshall of the United States in the 1820s, to recognize Aboriginal
title cases pertaining to lands taken for colonization as well as to conclude
land treaties. British Columbia did not follow suit, however. Australian Aboriginal jurist Noel Pearson points out that this treaty-type of recognition is
half of Aboriginal title, governing "external" relations between the tribal,

or indigenous, group and the newcomer nation-state. He says that the internal land tenure system (inter se rights of members of the community) is the other half. Pearson highlights the former and argues that dwelling on the latter (as anthropologists in land title work tend to do) often lays an unfair burden of proof on Aboriginal groups, while downplaying and diverting attention from the recognition of Aboriginal land rights that already exists under English common law: "The correct concept was established when the first native title cases in the English common law tradition were decided in the United States in the 1820s. The Supreme Court accorded the 'Indians' the right to possession, based upon their occupation of the land – consistent with the common law. The only relevance that the traditional laws and customs of the 'Indians' had was in governing the allocation of rights, interests and duties within their tribe" (Pearson 2002, n.p.). In other words, the land rights adjudication accorded Aboriginal peoples in colonial locations under English common law are a very important part of the current land rights litigation. Yet the mindset of Archibald Barclay, Joseph Trutch, and John Quincy Adams remains well entrenched in the administrative world. I therefore find it of value, despite Pearson's criticism of this anthropological trend, to lay out an explication of traditional land rights and duties. I do so in the hope that this might show those who dwell in the halls of justice and administration that indigenous populations in colonized lands, who conducted external relations with the colonizing powers, also did so upon a solid foundation of proprietary rights and duties.

Property

Objects that are possessed and defended by, or exchanged between, interacting persons are forms of property. The rights and duties that these objects are invested with differ greatly from culture to culture. This makes difficult the task of finding a satisfactory cross-cultural definition of property and ownership, even within the realm of state societies, let alone in societies where there is no state.

> When located in the context of nation states, "property" is used: ... popularly to refer to a thing owned by a person, but used more accurately in law to refer to a scheme of relationships, recognized or established by government, by individuals with respect to an object. The object may be tangible, such as land, or completely the creature of law, such as a patent or copyright. Since the objects of property and the protected relationships vary among societies and over time, it is difficult to find a least common denominator of property. "My property" probably means, at a minimum that government will help me exclude others from the use or enjoyment of an object without my consent, which I may withhold except at a price. (*Encyclopedia Britannica* 1970)

Any inquiry into property-holding and ownership must consider the subject's basic relevant features. First, ownership implies the concept of exclusive possession. In relation to land this entails the delineation of boundaries. While exclusive possession is a dominant feature of ownership, it does not preclude the existence of property over which there are common or joint rights. Second, ownership entails rules to govern the conveyance of rights from person to person, and generation to generation. In some societies the conveyance of land is limited to inheritance; in others, it can be forfeited, bought, sold, traded, or auctioned. Third, ownership entails property management. Fourth, it involves social recognition of ownership with attendant rights and duties.

Landownership implies the managerial rights of owners to direct and control activities concerning the property in question, be they activities of production, marketing, or property maintenance. Depending upon the actual society this usually involves the maintenance of the best possible annual returns from the land over the generations and/or the security and defence of the property. In hunter-gatherer kinship societies (whose members, prior to colonial expansion, acted without recourse to a state), this defence means direct action, with policing by the owning person or group and the recognition by others of this policing as an act of law. In such instances, trespassers and other transgressors are subject to the self-help of customary law. Scrupulous attention to the law is paid, as any perceived illegality of action on the part of property owners may be cause for disruptive enmity, feud, or war with the kin group and political constituency of the alleged offender.

Other societies administer an indirect defence of property rights through institutions of a hierarchical nature, including sanctions enforced by police and army. In both systems property-holders must make payments to society for the right to have their ownership claims validated and publicly recognized. In nation-states (where the state is not the owner) these payments take the form of taxes and/or public endowments and charity by property-holders.[1] In hunter-gatherer kinship societies such as those of the Gitksan and Witsuwit'en, corporate property-holding groups consider they are paying for the right of ownership when, as an extended group of matrikin, they discharge kindnesses and feast-related obligations "to the father's side" or to their moiety-like counterparts.

As we saw in Chapter 2, the public, sumptuary, and ceremonial announcement of personnel changes and reaffirmations of matters pertaining to property is an integral part of the oral recording and retrieval of local history. Property relations, as an affair recorded in the mind and complemented by iconic clan images and land-based narratives, require the local community to bear witness to changes of status and rights to property.

These procedures are not unique to the Gitksan and Witsuwit'en. Among the Delaware, neighbours of the Iroquois in the seventeenth century, all matters pertaining to landownership, and to the transfer of land to the English colonialist William Penn, were necessarily witnessed by fellow chiefs: "Even in cases where the sale is apparently a private arrangement between Penn and a single Indian, there is evidence to suggest that the Indian was not acting as a free agent with exclusive rights of disposal of his land. Israel Acrelius remarked that in order for a sale to be valid in Indian eyes, the sachems concerned had to sign the deed in the presence of representatives of their community. The individual sales were invariably witnessed by other Indians, and these Indian 'witnesses' often were men of consequence" (Wallace 1947, 5). Wallace's conclusion is that the ultimate decision and approval of the disposition of the individual territory was up to the community. Witnesses in Delaware landownership affairs were recompensed for fulfilling their role as mental recorders of the decisions, just as Gitksan and Witsuwit'en feast-goers are paid under similar circumstances to the present day.

Cadwallader Colden, His Majesty's Surveyor General for New York in 1747, wrote a history of the treaties made between the Iroquois nations and the colonial powers of the eastern seaboard. In it he alluded to the system of validating and conforming to agreements regarding public affairs: "They have certain Customs, which they observe in their publick Transactions with other Nations, and in their private Affairs among themselves; which it is scandalous for any one among them not to observe, and these always draw after them either publick or private Resentment, whenever they are broke" (Colden 1922, 2).

Exclusive Possession

> Why not ask if you can use it? I said to them. They said, but their grandmother used it. Yes, I said, lots of people have used it, but we own it. If you just ask me, you can use it. I will even tell you where you can set your net.
>
> By marrying into our House they had the right to use it in the past. But those marriage ties died out long ago, and they were told, right in the feast, that they could not use it any more.
>
> – Xhliimlaxha, the late Martha Brown (Daly 1986-88 [08/86, Glen Vowell]).

In all societies the property owner can, by socially recognized law and custom, withhold consent and permission from certain others who may wish to use and enjoy her/his property. This social recognition of the owner's rights to benefit from that parcel of land, to the exclusion of others, entails a certain cost to the owner(s). Owners must make appropriate contributions to the well-being of the wider collectivity in which they are enmeshed.

Among the Gitksan and Witsuwit'en, ownership is predicated not upon parliamentary and administrative sanction but, rather, upon a system of negotiated, consensual kinship and affinal relations. Here, the system of decision taking and enforcement is worked out between Houses, *wil'naat'ahl*, and clans according to established rules and laws that ensure a form of social control and public order. When these rules are violated, the offenders are met with socially approved negative sanctions, such as, formerly, the House's legitimate right to warn trespassers and, if warnings are not heeded, the right to use force. (Today people warn trespassers in the community, publicly exerting pressure on them in the feast hall to acknowledge their violation and to conform to the law so as to avoid an escalation of community criticism and ostracism.)

Among the Gitksan and Witsuwit'en the owner of landed property is the whole House group, the *wilp* (Git.), or *yikh* (Wit.). While use rights can be allocated to the House group's separate members and their relatives, the rights entailed in ownership can be allocated only by means of succession to chiefly names and consultation with seniors. Ownership is vested in the persons of the *simgiget* (Gitksan) or *diniize'yu* (Witsuwit'en), the high chiefs (singular: *simoogit/diniize'*). Each territory has a House chief designation and a geographical name. Map 5 (Gitksan) and Map 6 (Witsuwit'en) indicate territories according to House chief.

The Witsuwit'en sometimes refer to the chiefs collectively as "the head push" (*hu tuh yë'*: Emma Michell, Lilloos),[2] the ones upon whose advice people will act. The Gitksan have the same concept of vesting group ownership and management rights in the person of a chief who exercises ownership in consultation with his or her counsellor chiefs, who are known as "wings" or "branches."

The *simoogit* or *diniize'* represents the House group's right to exclusive possession of land and resources, and he/she has responsibility for securing and directing the House's production components: the fruits of land, labour, knowledge, and skills necessary to produce an appropriate standard of living. He or she ought to behave as the embodiment of the House, its activities, and its proprietorship.

Exclusivity and the Crest System

The control of the flow of information between Houses over the Northwest Coast region has long been related to chiefly training, especially with regard to House crests and territory. The crests of each House or group of Houses are a mnemonic script that can be read by the appropriately trained chiefs whose ancient historical narratives (see Duff n.d.; Halpin 1973) overlap to

MAP 5 Gitksan House territories, including Gitanyow. Maps 5 and 6 are diagrammatic and not intended to indicate actual boundaries. *Source:* Gitksan and Wet'suwet'en Chiefs (1988).

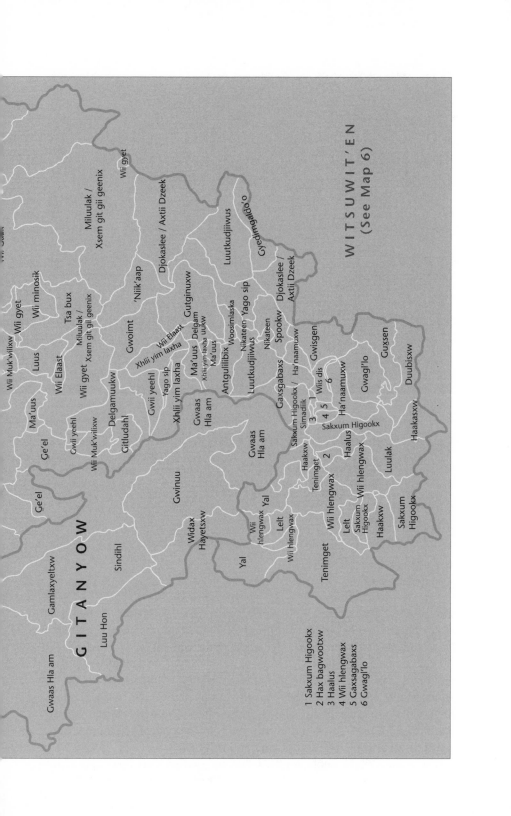

GITANYOW

Gwaas Hla am

Gamlaxyeltxw

Luu Hon

Ge'el

Ge'el

Ma'uus

Sindihl

Wii Muk'wilixw

Luus

Wii gyet

Wii minosik

Tsa bux

Wii Elaast

Gwii yeehl

Wii gyet
Miluulak /
Xsem git gii geenix

Wii Muk'wilixw

Delgamuukw

Gitludahl

Gwoimt

'Niik'aap

Miluulak /
Xsem git gii geenix

Wii gyet

Wii Elaast
Xhlii yim laxha

Gwii yeehl

Yago sip

Xhlii yim laxha

Wii Elaast
Xhlii yim laxha

Delgam
Ma'uus

Ma'uus
Xhlii yim laxha uukw

Gutginuxw

Woosimlaska

Antgulilibix

Nikateen
Luutkudjiiwus

Nikateen Yago sip

Djokaslee / Axtii Dzeek

Luutkudjiiwus

Gyedimgaldo'o

WITSUWIT'EN
(See Map 6)

Gwinuu

Widax
Hayetsxw

Yal

Wii
hlengwax

Yal

Lelt

Wii hlengwax

Teninget

Gwaas
Hla am

Gwaas
Hla am

Sakxum Higookx /
Simadiik

Gaxsgabaxs

Haakxw

Teninget

Wii hlengwax

Lelt

Sakxum
Higookx

Haakxw

Spookw

Djokaslee /
Axtii Dzeek

Ha'naamuxw

Gwisgen

Wiis dis

Sakxum Higookx

Haalus

Wii hlengwax

Sakxum
Higookx

Haalus

Ha'naamuxw

Gwagl'lo

Luulak

Guxsen

Duubisxw

Haakasxw

Sakxum
Higookx

1 Sakxum Higookx
2 Hax bagwootxw
3 Haalus
4 Wii hlengwax
5 Gaxsgabaxs
6 Gwagl'lo

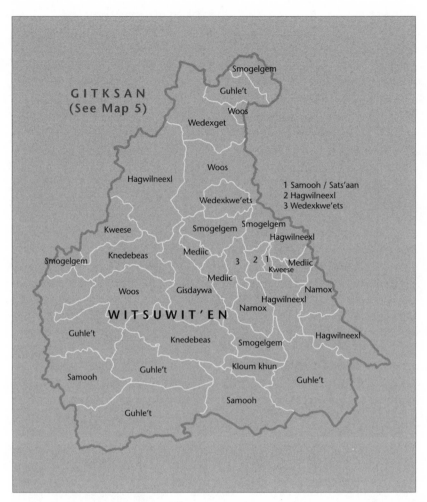

MAP 6 Witsuwit'en House territories
Source: Gitksan and Wet'suwet'en Chiefs (1988).

some degree. Oral cultures utilize many such memory devices. A chief has long-standing ties of history and proximity with a number of other chiefs. He or she has only to look into the face of these familiar fellow chiefs, or at their crest insignia, or hear their ancient names, songs, and narratives, to be reminded of the boundaries of their lands in relation to his/her own. Gitksan and Witsuwit'en chiefs regularly make such associations. By "reading into" the familiar faces, crests, and crest histories their territorial location, chiefs reaffirm the relationships enmeshing them in the system of House group rights to exclusive possession of land and fishing sites.

Gisdaywa, Alfred Joseph, testified that the Witsuwit'en used to put up their crests as boundary markers on the territories (Transcript, 2127;

Blackstock 2001).[3] In the same passage Joseph alludes to the aide-memoire function of crests and their relationship to events on the land and in the feast hall:

> There is the crests. Like the boundary would have a marking, a carving on a boundary, and then you have the totem poles and songs, and their personal crests relate to the land or some – whatever happened in the land. So there is always some reminder of different feasts that have happened ... I personally know how these were kept alive. If an elder is – if two or three of them are visiting and they would sing these songs, and when one quits they say ... "Do you remember where this came from?" If they don't, well they say – they tell them this was that feast when this chief died, or when this chief erected his totem pole. And that was going on at every community, discussions going on and how names, songs and crests were acquired.

The late Mary Johnson, Antgulilibix, demonstrated the chiefly ability to read the crests of those linked to her own family through the ancient narratives. She identified the House and clan crests of various *gyedimgan* (lit. people carved on poles) in Kispiox and the general territories from which they emanated. She was familiar with the crests of, above all, the other *simgiget* in her own Gisk̲'aast (Fireweed) Clan, such as the *Midiigim Ts'a'wi'aks*, "Grizzly in the water" (Transcript, 690); the wolf, snake, and black whale (Transcript, 693), which are all crests of Simoogit G̲e'el; the owl crest of Wilps Gutgwinuxs (Transcript, 694); the sea bear of Gwiiyeehl (Transcript, 695). Mary Johnson also knew the crests of Delgamuukw, Axgiigii, and Haaxw, closely related Lax̲ Se'el (Frog/Raven) Clan chiefs with the ancient crest of the small eagle, *gwax̲sgiik* (Transcript, 696), and with the raiding wolf crest *(gitwaaltxum gibuu)* of the Kispiox Wolf Clan House of X̲hliimlax̲ha (Transcript, 695), with whom Mary Johnson's House has frequently intermarried over the generations.

The late James Morrison, Tx̲awok̲, said that, on official occasions, each chief of an area is supposed to reveal the crests of his/her robe, talking stick, rattle, and *amhalayt* headdress, as well as the crest presentation on poles and other possessions. In so doing, this chief – usually as host – reminds the other chiefs of his/her crest history as well as of their own. When the chief stands, or dances, in his/her blanket robe with its chief's crest, this evokes, in the chiefly minds of guests, the House history, which has some common features with the histories of other guest chiefs or guests' fathers, grandfathers, or spouses. The guests witness and vet the hosts' conduct in relation to traditional narratives of legitimacy. The chiefs visualize this specific crest history in relation to natural landmarks, to a distinct alpine glaciated cirque or particular river rapids.[4] They also bring to mind the established seating order of the chiefs: a certain crest traditionally belongs beside or in front of a specific other crest on the basis of a related history of origin, migration, or divine experience.

Txawok said that the creeks and the mountains described in the *adaawk's* "still flow and still stand." The areas where crests originated are denoted in the histories, and the witnesses know them and the specific land features because their families have been harvesting species in these places for a very long time. These places are known by the human activities and unique events peculiar to them. The telling of a crest story, Txawok explained, might call to mind a region the people have regularly hunted. Such a spot might be a steep alpine meadow where groundhog snares swing the catch away from the game track (An hagostxwn'gwiikw, or An luuxw'ot'iitsxw [place of the swinging snare]), or a flat alpine meadow (Ust'aan [place of the level ground snare]), or the area where you use a deadfall trap weighted with a stone (An t'iapxw).[5]

The minds of the chiefs, visualizing the land of the host, say, in a feast, visit these places mentally, following lines of kinship, territorial proximity, and memories of family seasonal activity. The seasonal history, in turn, activates profound knowledge of the life habits of the species living there, the game trails and shelters of the animals, and the rock features around which morally instructive stories *(ant'imahlasxw)* developed. These associations well up in the minds of the listeners when an *adaawk'* or *kungakh* (our trail of song [Mills 1994, 122]) is revealed and performed.

Both James Morrison and Neil J. Sterritt[6] explained this system in the feast hosted by the Carrier-Sekani Tribal Council at Burns Lake on 4-5 April 1987.[7] Morrison pointed out that this is quite different from the system of territoriality imposed by government administration under the Indian Act and generally adopted by recent tribal council organizations. He says that if First Nations in the region look into their roots, by talking to their elders, then they would find that ownership, and areas of jurisdiction, emerge not from governmental administrative districts but, rather, from crest histories on the land. He said that each House group in Kisgagas used to have a crest pole whose images symbolized, evoked, and communicated the House's history and territories. (Figure 30 shows one of these poles in the village as it stood in 1920.)

On the afternoon of 4 April 1987 the late David Gunanoot, Lax Gibuu (Wolf) Simoogit 'Niik'aap, stood at the front of the hall at the second intertribal all-clans feast at Burns Lake. He stood still in his robe while the Gitksan northern chiefs made their presentation. They asked 'Niik'aap if he would tell the part of his *adaawk'* that explained the origin of his territory in the headwaters of the Skeena, near the Sustut River.[8] Then James Morrison, who grew up, hunted, and fished on his father's Kisgagas territories and knew the whole region well (and had been asked to act as 'Niik'aap's spokesperson), explained to the Carrier-Sekani hosts the 'Niik'aap crest's legitimate claim to that territory.

Later, outside during a break, Morrison explained to me that the crest on 'Niik'aap's button blanket robe, the Split Bear, Haymaa'dim, was taken by 'Niik'aap after an ancient battle with northern peoples. (See also David Gunanoot, Commission Evidence I, 66.) Txawok̲ explained that the patch of white feathers at the shoulders of 'Niik'aap's robe signifies the snow of certain peaks in the territory belonging to the House of 'Niik'aap at the headwaters of the Skeena. It was here that the events occurred that led to 'Niik'aap taking the Haymaa'dim as his crest. These specific snowy peaks are called to mind by neighbouring House chiefs because the actual feathers on the robe are taken from a white-tailed species of ptarmigan that is peculiar to those mountains. There are two species of ptarmigan native to the mountains of the northern 'Niik'aap territory. The feathers on the blanket denote the unique area where only the high-elevation ptarmigan live.

James Morrison also reiterated that white feathers and down generally denote a peace settlement and are used to welcome visiting chiefs. In the "split-bear" narrative, a *xsiisxw*, or peace settlement and feast, were integral features of this particular crest's origin.

The all-important crests, together with the songs and narratives that situate and explain them, are performed as reaffirmation of a heritage both genealogical and geographical. The crests, on bodies, house fronts, interior house screens, talking sticks, house posts, and totem poles, legitimate property-holding and constantly stand for human roots in the land. They are cultural capital and, as such, are affairs of the mind, integral to the much practised art of visualization.[9] They are found in tattoos, on ladles, bentwood boxes, robes, and blankets. In the words of Lelt, Fred Johnson (Commission Evidence II, 108): "*Ayuks* [one's crest] is something you always wore, just like my jacket."

There is archaeological evidence of the inscription of crests on material objects along the Skeena system for at least the last two and a half millennia: "Northwest Coast peoples of the historic period decorated and embellished almost everything they made in order to display the crests and status symbols of noble families and to illustrate personal spirit power. The prevalence of art and ornaments suggests that they were well established in the prehistoric cultures 3500-2500 years ago" (Fladmark 1986, 74).

Among the Gitksan the carved crest poles of each House chief were formerly located in the village along the river in front of the *simoogit*'s house. They would stand before the house, facing the flow of the traffic on the river, from whence travellers and visitors arrived (Figures 1, 2, 13, 14, and 27). Today they tend to face the road, which has replaced the river as the main conduit of traffic. The crests, or *ayuks*, on the pole display the history of the events whereby the crest was first adopted. They stand for the pedigree of the House, as do the names of river sites and features of the land and the songs. Each crest pole legitimates rights to specific fishing sites and hunting grounds. Olive Ryan, Gwaans, said in her evidence that the crest pole holds everything in the House and functions like a white man's map, except that the map is in the head of the chief. Its crests and figures, not unlike a drawing made with pencil and paper, help the family visualize relationships (Transcript, 1067 [13-20]). Gwaans elaborated (1078 [17-24]): "the pole holds everything. They hold the fishing site and they hold the hunting ground and they hold the House ... It tells like a map, when you look at the map, and you can see the road and the number on that map." Ryan suggests in her evidence that, by periodically renewing the presentation of House crests (by means of totem pole raisings, the telling of the *adaawk*'s, and the witnessing of these actions by other House groups and their leaders), the legitimacy of ownership and standing – the legitimate power/energy *(daxget)* of the House and clan *(pdeek)* – are also renewed and invigorated. Guédon (1984, 149) says that *pdeek* also used to denote the animal or thing that became the standard crest for the clan. Ryan explained that this was the reasoning behind her House's decision to raise a new pole and to re-establish the old pole, which had been removed from its site at Gitsegukla in a manner that had violated Gitksan legality and traditional sense of respect (Transcript, 1050ff.).

In the course of her evidence Ryan closed her eyes and took the court on a tour of the consecutive fishing sites, starting from her village, Gitsegukla, and continuing all the way down the Skeena to the Gitksan-Tsimshian boundary (see Map 4B and 4C). She described each site location, named it, and explained its owning House and clan. She knew where each chief sat in relation to the others in the feasts; she knew where they fished; and she had some knowledge of the narratives by which their fishing sites came to be owned. She could visualize their arrangement down the river by virtue of the structure of the relationships in her feast-going society.[10]

Tenimget elaborated on this point when he explained that not only the crests of the chief of a House but also the specific spirit power, which originally revealed itself in specific locations – the *naxnox* – is also briefly shown to the guests. House regalia is taken from the family treasure box, is animated by being donned by a House member, and is then displayed before the guests gathered at the feast. This is to suffuse them with the unique powers said to be inherent in a specific territory. This enactment is a sewing up of the power, or *daxget*, of the House chief across the generations and stands as an existential token of ownership (Transcript [Tenimget], 4608): "The actual name of showing your *naxnox* is in our language, *Luu hetxwhl halayt* [the shaman stands inside] ... which means you are going to show the power which I described as daxget – is going to be transferred to another person, to exact its rightful line of that name, so therefore this had to take place."

The crests and the story of their acquisition give legitimacy to landownership. They are mental maps, aide-memoires (the Iroquois similarly use a "memory cane," not unlike the Gitksan talking stick, when recalling the detailed oral history of their Longhouse League [Fenton 1950]). The existence of the crests on blankets, poles, house fronts, and elsewhere refreshes the *adaawk'/kungakh* in the minds of the chiefs. As Mary McKenzie, Kyologet, has testified (Transcript, 228 [23ff.]), the taking of the crest was a component of the House history: "Now this is the way that the Gitksan people get their crests – it's anything unique that they've come across or they've seen, they've taken it as their crests." The crests call up the history and the legitimacy of ownership and authority of the chief and his House. Kyologet explained (236 [2-12]): "Adaawk' in Gitksan language is a powerful word for describing what the House stands for, what the chief stands for, what the territory stands for, is the adaawk'. It's not a story, it's just how people travelled is the adaawk'. And it's the most important thing in Gitksan is to have an adaawk'. Without an adaawk' you can't very well say you are a chief or you own a territory. Without the adaawk' – it has to come first, the adaawk' – names come after, songs come after, crests come after it, and the territory that's held, fishing places – all those come into one, and that's the adaawk'."

In this explanation of the Gitksan narrative (and the "trail of song," which plays a similar role among the Witsuwit'en), the ancient liminal journeys across the land gave rise to the chiefs' songs and crests. There are resonances here of the Australian Aboriginal songlines recently introduced to the popular imagination by Bruce Chatwin (Ignatieff 1987, 30-1): "Aboriginal creation myths tell of the legendary totemic ancestors – part animal, part man – who create themselves and then set out on immense journeys across the continent, singing the name of everything that crosses their path, and so singing the world into existence. In fact, there's hardly a rock or a creek or a stand of eucalyptus that isn't an 'event' on one or other of the songlines."[11]

The ownership rights to long sections of these songlines are defined by reference to kinship, economy, and the surge of energy and power said to activate the natural world. Aboriginal Australian rights to property ownership are validated in ways similar to those found among the Gitksan and Witsuwit'en: through crests, narratives, and songs that have to do with the way the ancestors came to walk the land. In Australia these ancestors walked in sinuous lines across the length and breadth of the continent. In the Gitksan areas the travels were journeys through or retreats from catastrophes to either the northern interior or the adjacent coast and, ultimately, to their descendants' present territorial locations. The *adaawk*'s and *kungakhs*[12] tell of migrations and dispersals that were the peoples' responses to a combination of factors, including the settlement patterns of other human groups, climatic changes, and the importance of trying to remain within seasonal reach of the phenomenal salmon runs.

Access to Territory

The right to grant or withhold usufruct rights to House territory is closely linked to the owner's public responsibility to see that the land is well used, its general fertility maintained, and the people's basic subsistence requirements fulfilled. Among those who are not members of the owning House, there are two categories that may legitimately seek permission to use hunting and fishing territories. First are members of the father's House group (the actual scope of inclusion involved depends upon the person who is the point of reference in the kinship system). This category includes the children of male members of the House. These people may be granted rights to use the territory. Their use rights are called *amnigwootxw* (Git.), *nec'idilt'ës* (just cooking something there [Wit.]). Second are members of the spouses' kin groups, *ant'im'nak* (Git.), *indimenik* (Wit.). The *ant'im'nak* or *ant'im'hanak'* territorial usufruct came to light in Olive Ryan's evidence (Transcript, 1168). Land use through marriage is a major factor in the extensive Alfred Mitchell example given in Chapter 4. Kyologet, Mary McKenzie, explained the rights given her husband to use territory belonging to her House and his subsequent obligation to contribute to the feasting costs of her House (Transcript, 321-2):

> When the name was put upon me, my mother spoke that being married to a trapper, that she had given permission to go and trap to our territory ... there are other territories that he has to go through to get to our territory. So this has to be explained in the feasting, that the people up there, my neighbours ... if they see him they know where his destination is, where he is going to go and trap ... So this is why it's announced in the feasting house, and him being my husband and he has to support me with money which I may use in another feasting.

On page 1,288, Ryan, Gwaans, gives an example of someone using Ha'naamuxw land who is in Category A. Johnny David (Commission IV, 44) was in Category B – *nec'idilt'ës* – when he used and cared for his father's House territory. Alfred Joseph, Gisdaywa, used Gisdaywa territory at Owen Lake with his father, who of course was only married into the House (Transcript, 1539; laws pertaining to this are discussed by Joseph on 1597).

Those accorded use rights by the House of Tenimget/Axti Hiix show the intermingling of blood and marriage. Tenimget explains these rights: "Privileged *amnigwootxw* right is you don't have a name from our House but you're privileged to come on our territory through your father's side" (4557).

Tenimget's mother, Paxheldiseet, explained that the House only allows her grandfather's son, Henry Wilson, on her father's side to use one of the Axti Hiix/Tenimget fishing sites. Everyone else who uses the sites and the land is either kin, spouse, or one of Wallace Morgan's sons, who use the land for hunting and trapping because they are children of male members of the House (using their *amnigwootxw* rights as well).

Persons not in these relationships to the House in question may also be granted permission to use House lands and fishing sites. Such grants are usually of short duration and will be extinguished publicly by the House in the course of a feast, as is apparent in the statement by X̱hliimlax̱ha, Martha Brown (see p. 242).

(see p. 242)

Whether the user is linked to the House through his or her father or spouse, or whether she/he has a more distant association, use rights ought to be extinguished by the death of the person to whom these rights were granted (Olive Ryan, Transcript, 1168). Due to pressures on the territories by outsiders over the past century, people often find it difficult to leave their father's territory after his death, especially with the patrilineal succession that is integral to provincial trapline registrations (Alfred Joseph, Transcript, 1598). Gisdaywa also suggests that other pressures work against people returning to their own House lands, particularly the massive use of Witsuwit'en land by outsiders (2221).

Emma Michell, Lilloos, states that people living to the east of the Witsuwit'en, especially relatives from Babine Lake, would ask permission to use her House's fishing site at Moricetown Canyon. She recounts that these people were granted the right to fish because "fish belong here on earth; they are not raised by the people" and no persons should be left in destitution when one is able to feed them. At the same time, Michell continued, the sites from which the salmon are caught are indeed subject to the laws of society: distant Carrier neighbours would be given use rights for a day or half a day during the salmon runs. For the right to fish there, they would make public payments during one of the evening summer feasts. Lilloos's daughter still lets Babine people use the House of Namox fishing site, and the speaker said that the Babine repay her later, usually with jars of salmon.

The user of a fishing site customarily makes an on-the-spot payment for short-term use rights to fishing locations. When today's elders were young, the payment usually consisted of a sum of approximately three to five dollars in cash, clothes, blankets, or moosehide. These items are not for the receiver's personal consumption. As payments to the House, they were saved for future gifts at the next feast in which the House was involved. Even the children of the male members of the House who use the House fishing sites are expected to make some form of payment. Formerly they went off in the fall to the hunting territories and returned with dried game and hides (caribou and mountain goat) and berry cakes from their own House territories, which would be presented to the *dinïze'* of their father's House as payment for use of the salmon sites.

All of these payments are utilized by the House to settle its obligations to creditors, to provide for the aged and sick, and as contributions to feasts. In these ways, the Houses, the territory-owning groups, gain recognition of their ownership from users (who must ask permission to use the land and fishing sites) and themselves pay for that right.

Trapline Registration

Today, particularly as a result of trapline registration early in the twentieth century, there is considerable pressure upon the Gitksan and Witsuwit'en to convert matrilineal exclusive ownership and inheritance into a system where property passes from father to son. However, the property rights of the matrilineal owners are still recognized in the communities, even over lands that have been in use for considerable periods of time by people whose predecessors were in father-son relationship to the owning House. Elderly persons stress adherence to the long-standing rules of succession and the attendant system of exclusive matrilineal ownership rights. As Alfred Joseph has testified (Transcript, 1598), the elders carry out public education in the feasts, striving to undo the confusion caused by patrilineal inheritance of traplines (1599).

To an outsider it may look as though the Gitksan and Witsuwit'en pass land from father to son. But this impression is incorrect because the apparent father-to-son succession to land is frequently made legitimate when the sons practise cross-cousin marriage or are adopted into the owning House. Cross-cousin marriage (which occurs when a House member marries her/his father's sister's child or a mother's brother's child) or, more generally, the significant incidence of marriage between two Houses over time, establishes a seemingly perpetual relationship between the House to which a certain child belongs and the House to which the father belongs. These interacting Houses and clans will be "feeding each other's children" from their own respective territories in alternate generations. This system of enduring reciprocal relations knits the respective kinship units together and helps perpetuate long-standing control of joint territories or complete watersheds. Together, such intermarrying groups make up "the family" whose relations are mediated by gift exchange between Houses.

Such current adoptions and marriage alliances can also be viewed as a striving to reassert the matrilineal inheritance principle and set right the confusions wrought by modern trapline inheritance. The principle of matrilineal inheritance may conflict with the residential pattern wherein a wife moves to her husband's territory. (This used to occur following a period of bride service, during which a new husband lived and worked among his wife's people. He would work and hunt on their behalf for a seasonal round before gaining permission to take his wife to live on his House territory. This was the personal experience of, among others, Johnny David [Commission III, 28].) When the wife moves to live among her husband's people, she loses none of her rights of inheritance, but her sons, who are subsequently raised on their father's land, have no rights of ownership there. This situation provides a dynamic tension to family and social life and is intrinsic to the system of residence and inheritance where the child grows up on its father's land and yet inherits through its mother.

If the maternal uncle is geographically close enough to be involved in his sister's sons' upbringing, then the boys can be coached in the knowledge of the land to which their mother belongs and which one day their own generation of House members will inherit. If these boys are not in a position to learn from their mother's brother, then they will usually not come to know their own territories until later in life.

If, for instance, a young man raised among his father's people decides to establish himself there, instead of returning to his mother's people, he may intermarry with one of the Houses to which his father's people are linked through the generations. This allows him to enjoy land use rights that are already well established between two regularly marrying groups. This is what the late Alfred Mitchell (Chapter 4) did in Moricetown. Such a person could also return to his own House group among his mother's people and take up rights and responsibilities. (In point of fact, Alfred Mitchell had a seat in the Tsayu Beaver Clan section of the Witsuwit'en feast hall – that is, an adopted place in the House of his de facto adopted mother, Emma Michell. He also had a chiefly name in the Gisk̲'aast Clan[13] of his birth in the Gitksan village of Kispiox [Transcript, 3166-7].)

Over the years, "companies," usually groups of matrilineal kin from within the House, have registered traplines, both out of fear of losing their territories to the government and out of a desire to gain a degree of government recognition of their ownership and their right to be on the lands where their traplines have been located. They believed that they had, by this means, obtained at least a practical form of government recognition of their authority over their own lands. In the face of considerable pressure from outsiders they wanted to have their ownership on the official government record: "what did you believe you were registering when you signed this? A – First it is for transferring the registration over to me, and to my belief is that to protect that territory from somebody else taking it."

This is Dan Michell, Wigetimschol, responding to a question from Stuart Rush (counsel for the plaintiffs) pertaining to trapline registration, (Transcript, 3667). Alfred Joseph testified similarly. Tenimget described the initial Gitksan and Witsuwit'en response to trapline registrations as follows: "And they were told that if they registered these particular areas that were quite dear to them, that that was a sign of approval by the governments that no one could – it was as if they referred it back to the law that nobody could get on there or trespass if they had registered these traplines with their names, and that appears that ain't true" (4741).

Children of the original trapline companies hunted and trapped on these lands together with their parents, and inherited them, for the first time, from their fathers or from both parents. The former system of access to lands by reference to matrilineal ownership began to erode as a consequence of pressure exerted by the father-to-son trapline registration procedure. A formerly flexible, reciprocal system rapidly became quite rigid because the names of children were fixed to one trapping company in the official records. Under British Columbia law, the Gitksan and Witsuwit'en were faced with either inheriting traplines from their fathers or losing them altogether. Over the years, this clash between the imposed trapline registration system and their own has led to much acrimony. Among the Witsuwit'en, those who were from the father's side in relation to the land they used were unable to inherit ownership over trapping and hunting lands in the normal manner (i.e., from their mother's brother or grandfather). As a result, today some remain on the land of others, not owning the land in the feast-sanctioned sense yet officially registered there. The community does not accept their claims to ownership, although in a limited way the province does. The community regards them as caretakers for the rightful owners.[14]

Gisdaywa explained that, before the days of the regulations of the British Columbia Fish and Wildlife Ministry, there would be a feast where long-term users of a father's House territory would speak up. They would say that, as their father had been dead for some time, they were now turning this land back to its rightful owners (1597-8), but now "the Fish and Wildlife people say that the territory has to go to the son, and that is against the Witsuwit'en law."

The flexibility of movement between territories linked by House, affinal, and spousal connections, and the duration of the use rights to a father's House territories, have been affected by trapline registration, with its patrilineal bias. Nevertheless, Gitksan and Witsuwit'en ownership has not been eclipsed by the inheritance system instituted by the province. The integrity of House ownership and exclusive rights to possess and enjoy territories continues to be reiterated in the feasts. As well, marriage continues to be contracted between House groups with long-standing intergenerational ties.

The Fish and Wildlife regulations sought to convert what, under Gitksan and Witsuwit'en law, was a privilege to use land into a right to use it. However, such is the strength and tenacity of the indigenous legal order that the original system of ownership has been maintained and retains enough flexibility to flow around the obstacle created by provincial regulations and, thereby, to reassert itself.

Among the Witsuwit'en, the long-term interactions between Houses can be seen in the relationship between the House of Namox, Tsayu Clan, and the Houses of Hagwilneexl and Wedexkw'ets, Laksilyu Clan. John and Pat Namox of the House of Wedexkw'ets, Laksilyu Clan, were raised on the Sam Goosley Lake territory of the House of Namox, Tsayu Clan, by their Tsayu father, Alfred Namox. Sometimes, however, they would hunt on their own matrilineal land, west of Telkwa in the Dennis Lake area. On the other hand, Emma Michell, Lilloos, of the House of Namox – her mother's brother was Alfred Namox – was raised in the area west of Telkwa on the Laksilyu territory called Kilwoneetz, the territory of her father, Jimmy Mitchell, who held the name Maxlaxlex in the House of Hagwilneghl. This territory was adjacent to that of Pat Namox, K'askibus, and John Namox, Wedexkw'ets. Emma spent much of her active life on this Laksilyu land as she married Tommy Michell, Skokum Wasas, of the Laksilyu House of Hagwilneghl. However, Emma would also go with her family to hunt, especially in the beaver season, on her own House territory at Sam Goosley Lake. Thus, these two areas – Goosley, south of Houston, and the Telkwa lands – were used and owned in such a way that the respective owners tended to spend more time on their affines' land than on their own. In other words, Alfred Namox's Laksilyu sons grew up on Alfred and Emma's Tsayu territory while Emma Michell (Tsayu) spent much of her working life on the Laksilyu land adjacent to the territory belonging to Alfred Namox's Laksilyu sons.

Despite this apparent switch of landholdings, formal title to the two areas has been retained in the customary manner. This ownership has been acknowledged in the feasts and by the appropriate elders of the two sides. The same system pertains among the Gitksan, although it is my impression that long-term use rights (such as several chiefs hunting jointly on their combined territories) are granted less frequently to those who are not members of the land-owning House (or for shorter duration than is the case among the Witsuwit'en). Frequently, however, when children behave properly towards their father or mother's father, and fulfill their obligations to ensure that the father or mother's father (or father-in-law) is buried properly, they will be awarded rights to use and care for the territory of the deceased. Lax Gibuu chief, 'Niik'aap, David Gunanoot, in his evidence (Commission II,

126) explained that his mother's father, with the La̲x Se'el chief name of Haimas, had bequeathed his territory, Tsiltsila, to David's mother. She was to use it during her lifetime, with her children, but after her death, the old man instructed David and his brothers, "You boys are not to go there." David's mother felt justified in using this mountain for the rest of her life-time, David said, because she had looked after her father's funeral feast ex-penses while her father's nephew and heir had not. Among the Gitksan, these *amnigwootxw* use rights often terminate after one generation. Among the Witsuwit'en they tend to be treated more flexibly, sometimes prolonged for subsequent generations by means of strategic cousin marriages or adop-tions, such that the children of temporary users become members of the House of the owner and, hence, part of the proprietary group.

With Respect

Gitksan and Witsuwit'en chiefs do not speak about the House property of other chiefs unless given specific permission to do so. Olive Ryan (Tran-script, 1490) obtained permission from Gitsegukla and Gitwangax chiefs to give evidence to the court about the location of their fishing sites. Not only the land and fishing sites but also all verbal references to them are consid-ered to be exclusive property. Similarly, other incorporeal possessions and experiences of the House are owned exclusively. Narratives, too, are owned (e.g., the history of disputes in which a House has been involved [Olive Ryan, 1366]), and the "House names" that members hold are also subject to exclusive possession, as are songs, crests, *kungakhs,* and *adaaw̲k*'s. Mary McKenzie explained that crests are the property of the House and cannot be used by others without permission (Transcript, 228). Alfred Joseph gave evi-dence that, while generally the events of a House chief's *kungakh* are exclu-sive, some of the crest origins among the Witsuwit'en can indeed be talked about by all Witsuwit'en because each clan participated in historical events that gave rise to these crests (Transcript, 1602).

Trespass

Tenimget, speaking of his House, says that all (other than close kin or affines) who would like to use Tenimget land are required to carry an emblem of permission when they are on his House territory. Otherwise they run the risk of running afoul of House members who may consider them trespass-ers. Women wanting to use Tenimget/Axti Hiix berry patches would be given woven tumplines (of specific colours) called *dee̲x'iiyasxw* for their berry boxes; these tumplines denoted that they had obtained permission to be on the House's land. Similarly, men who had permission to hunt on the House's territories were given a special cane called *k̲'aat'*, which was dyed blue with the mud of a certain lake in Tenimget territory (4720, 4722-3). In order to control foreign access to the territories, those chiefs who lived downstream near the frontier with the coastal peoples required all river travellers to check in at the respective chiefs' lookout sites, called *anjok* (4634).

The Witsuwit'en maintained the same scrupulous attention to trespass. Alfred Joseph lists a number of Witsuwit'en terms that describe aspects of territorial trespass (1572-3). Madeline Alfred (2726-7) explained that long ago a Nutsenï trespasser and poacher was warned to leave Wedexget territory near Moricetown at a bear watering hole noted by the Wedexget people as a regular location for setting snares. After the Nutsenï man had ignored the warning, he was strangled at this spot on Wedexget territory, and a song was composed about this. This song is part of the chiefly property of Wedexget; it is performed, to dramatic pedagogical effect, in feasts. Emma Michell, in her Commission Evidence, states that in the past the penalty for trespass on a House chief's land was death. She said that crossing the land was permissible but trapping there, or camping on that land, was deemed to be trespass (Commission III, 78).

When a Witsuwit'en had caught someone in the act of trespassing more than once or twice he was within his rights to kill the offender. Thereafter, he would wear a braided cedar-bark bracelet for one year to indicate that a trespasser had been killed and that there were no grounds for retribution. The family of the deceased trespasser could not recover his remains until they had acknowledged the trespass and a settlement had been reached. Making peace after an instance of trespass followed a pattern similar to the *xsiisxw*, the peace settlement between different villages or peoples.

When following recognized trails across the territories of other Houses, travellers had the right to hunt to feed themselves, even without obtaining permission from the owners of the land through which they were passing (Alfred Joseph, Transcript, 2254). This right pertained only to the taking of small game for immediate consumption. Usually the chiefs knew who was travelling across their land and when this travel was likely to occur. Most long-distance travel occurred seasonally, on the way to the fall hunt, the winter settlement, the winter fishing, the spring beaver hunt, or the summer fishing (Alfred Joseph, Transcript, 2153). As well, regular users of a territory are announced publicly in the feast hall, which informs the local people as to whom legal passage has been granted (Mary McKenzie, Transcript, 321-2).

In the past 150 years the punitive systems of most peoples and nations have undergone great changes. The Gitksan and Witsuwit'en no longer kill trespassers on their lands, just as the destitute of Europe are no longer executed for the theft of a loaf of bread. The general climate of punitive law enforcement has been leavened internationally by social reform. Sanctions once considered appropriate among the Gitksan and Witsuwit'en, as among the people of any civilized society, are no longer deemed proper. Today, proportionate punishment tends to have supplanted ultimate punishment.

Public opinion mobilized against trespassers, including warnings and social ostracism, was and remains a forceful sanction against those who violate the laws of ownership. The actions taken to combat trespass involve the warning, isolation, and ostracism of offenders; sometimes the issue spills into the feast hall.

Johnny David testified in his Commission Evidence (IV, 2-3) that one who is untrustworthy and uses land without permission is referred to in the community as a sneak, a *ninil'li'y'*. Social pressure is applied to such a person in the hope that he will mend his ways.[15] He is denied the use of any territory and denied entry into the feast hall. This transgressor may be called to a feast known as a *so'nini dlandïnlhi*. Alfred Joseph explained this process: "If it's continued, that person will have to be invited to a feast, and it is taken up at that – in that place ... then the chief would say why the feast is held, and he would be told that he is – he or she – is not supposed to be at a certain place, not supposed to be taking food out of, or food or animals, off that territory, in front of witnesses" (Transcript, 1845).

A further means of asserting exclusive rights to land involves a belief in the protection of House lands by psychic means. Misfortunes and illnesses suffered by trespassers and their close relations are ascribed, first, to the protective power of the owners' crests and legitimacy, and second, to the trespasser's dishonourable actions – to his or her anti-social, anti-reciprocal, anti-respectful behaviour. The powers of the owners to call down misfortune on trespassers by tapping into the life force of the land and projecting it outward against incursions by the unauthorized are frequently manifested in the form of carvings (arboroglyphs) or drawings (arborographs) on trees in boundary areas, as has been so elegantly recorded by Blackstock (2001). This is an almost intangible feature of societies without central government, but it has a social reality bolstered by many anecdotes, and it affects local behaviour regarding territorial boundaries (Daly 1986-88 [Charlie Austin]).

When a new incumbent is "being blanketed" with a robe and a name – usually at the headstone or pole-raising feast for the previous holder, one of the older personalities addresses both the incumbent and the guests, telling the history of the incumbent's name, crest, and the boundaries of his territories (Alfred Joseph, 1781): "He's told that he is responsible for the House that he's the head of, and he's told of the boundaries and what area the territory is. And it is repeated by all the head chiefs, the subchiefs of that clan are giving their support to this – to a new chief, and they're asking the guests at that time to speak to what happened."

In these instructive speeches the creeks, the fishing places, the mountains where they go for goats and groundhog are all listed. Often the hosts will emphasize the territory and its resources by mentioning that they gave the guest chiefs, at dinner, meat and berries from specific locations, as occurred when Henry Alfred received the name of Wedexget (Madeline Alfred,

Transcript, 2714). Late one evening at the Gitksan-Witsuwit'en office in Vancouver during the trial stage of *Delgamuukw*, I observed the following. The family of the current witness entered bearing boxes of Kentucky Fried Chicken and soft drinks over their heads. Someone began to beat on a door and sing the *hawaal* song. Grinning widely, they invited the staff to share with them the "grouse and berry juice" from their territory.

Exclusivity and "Common Lands"

The right to exclude non-members from the enjoyment of matrilineal family land and resources was qualified by certain common use rights. By virtue of the presence of unique resources, certain places in the territories have traditionally been treated as "common land." This term warrants couching in quotation marks because generally the land in question does not lack ownership. The point is that under certain conditions these locations are open to all members of the local community. The village itself is shared land, yet the chiefs are aware of the fact that the settlements are located within the territory of one or other chief. Thus, Kya Wiget (Moricetown) is on the "Frog" land of Wedexget; Hagwilget is on the "Wolf" land of Spookw; and Gitwangax is on the "Eagle" land of Sakxum Higookx and Simadiik.

Common access in such an otherwise highly structured land tenure system reflects the hunting and gathering ethic of not hoarding and not denying food to either those in need or those who request help. Gitksan and Witsuwit'en tell instructive stories of the consequences of starvation and hoarding, of occasions when, due to lack of human humility and respect, the salmon runs failed or summer did not follow winter. Sharing in the form of generalized reciprocity, in relation to small game and gathered foods, was integral to Gitksan and Witsuwit'en land tenure and use.

Typical examples of common use land are large berry patches found near villages and the occasional fishing place in a village. Alfred Joseph gave evidence that "common berry sites" existed in the past around Moricetown, especially within the territory of Wah Tah K'eght (2158). These common use rights still pertain in relation to some sites, as Johnny David explained regarding a particularly good berry ground on the territory of Wah Tah K'eght (Commission III, 66): "That area belonged to Mrs. Peter Alfred, who's known as Dzee, and when the berries would ripen she would invite all people from the village to go pick berries ... Madeline's [Mrs. Alfred's] predecessors, they did the same thing as she had done. It went quite a ways back."

Obviously this is not really common use as the senior woman of the owning House invites the village to pick berries, but it is a resource upon which there are notably few constraints concerning access by non-members of the owning group. Johnny David (ibid.) also mentions that Babine people would come to use berry sites around Moricetown. Gwaans, Olive Ryan, gave evidence that the berry sites on the lands of the House of Ha'naamuxw were open to use by other House groups while at the same time the village recognized Ha'naamuxw's ownership (Transcript, 1137).

Common access also pertained, at different times, to one or two fishing places near villages. For the most part, this common use has been limited to villagers and their close kin by the consent of the community. Due to pressure from non-Aboriginal sports fishers, some modern-day villages have allotted one area or another for outsiders to fish with rod and reel, for example, "Idiot Rock" downstream from Moricetown Canyon, where outsiders must seek village permission. Another such site is a place called Lax Anixw at the mouth of Kitwanga River, on the right bank of the Skeena (Olive Ryan, Transcript, 1222, 1414). Emma Michell recounts that her family used to fish at a location on the Bulkley River that was "open." This was a gill-net site that had not been used before the adoption of modern nets. It was located downstream from Moricetown Canyon and was considered open to all villagers. It is probable that in each village a convenient fishing site is held "open" for villagers and their relatives to obtain fish for immediate consumption.

Alfred Joseph told about two alpine regions in Witsuwit'en territory and another in Gitksan territory that were, in effect, public domain (Transcript, 2165-6). In one instance this included "people from over there" (U'inwit'en), from Babine. These areas are surrounded by House territories but, traditionally, they did not come under the direct authority of the chief or chiefs of the surrounding area. The surrounding chiefs, however, expect to be asked for permission to cross their territories to reach such locations (Transcript, 2168).

Called *wë'së'ht*, or common land, such places were available for use on a first-come, first-served basis. The use and users of these areas were discussed among the hunters of each clan with the result that everyone knew the degree of harvesting that was currently being carried out in that particular region. The first person to get up into this alpine zone could take the best part of the mountain for his/her own harvest needs, but she/he was held responsible for conducting the hunt (2167) properly and maintaining the overall well-being of the species for those who would use the place the following year.

One such location is in the region of Mount Cronin in the headwaters of Driftwood Creek, in the Silver King Basin east of Smithers (2165), which was noted for its wealth in groundhog as well as being the home of mountain goats. The place, Widiltl'its Bït (it's green inside), is situated between the Laksilyu territory of Chief Wedexget and the Gitdumden territory of Chiefs Wos and Gyologet. The other remembered site is on Mount Loring, at Morice Lake (2167), which was a common area hunted for caribou and mountain goat by groups of hunters in the fall.

The Gitksan and Witsuwit'en consider that, if an area of exceptional productivity is available in their territories, then it must be opened to the benefit of others. The species hunted in these two locations were not available in all House territories. These were known to be particularly productive areas, with exceptional resources needed by the people not only for their consumable flesh but also for clothing and trade. A. Joseph (2248) listed groundhog (both the fatty flesh and the pelts), mountain goat (fat, flesh, hides, horn, hair for blankets, and skin for drums), and caribou (fat, hides for clothing and footwear). The chiefs encouraged hunting parties in such common areas, saying this contributed to the maintenance of a certain re-production level.[16]

Access to certain other needed resources, particularly minerals, was open to all groups. At the same time, each of these materials was located within definite and acknowledged House territories. The Nadina flint beds *(bïs k'ët)* were one location in Witsuwit'en territory that was open to non-House members. These rights did not extend to foreigners (2161) as the flint (and other items, like ochre) possessed an important exchange value. The access to flint was controlled for purposes of trade (2161). There is a similar com-mon resource east of Houston where another arrow stone was obtained – a substance called *its*. This place is called Bulh'ay C'ikwah (2160) and is lo-cated at McQuarrie Creek, Smogelgem territory.

Red ochre *(tsiyh)* was another common resource found at "red ochre places," south and east of Mount Evelyn and west of Hudson Bay Mountain (2161). Also found here was a special fungus used to mix and spread the ochre pigment for rock painting. (This substance was said to have the prop-erty of preserving the pigment on rock faces.) The ochre and the fungus were found in swampy land on Laksilyu territory. Rock salt extruded from the ground on Noostel's land west of Smoke Mountain, south of Newcombe Lake. This too was used commonly by all Witsuwit'en.

The Witsuwit'en also obtained obsidian from the south, from the Chilcotin people at Mount Anaheim. Prior to the Aluminum Company of Canada's vast hydroelectric inundation, this highly prized volcanic glass entered Witsuwit'en territory at a point on Ootsa Lake known as "Witsuwit'en Crossing."

I would further suggest that Figure 36 and Figure 37, petroglyphs located in the river in front of village sites at, respectively, Anlaxsim'de'ex (below Kisgagas) and Kispiox, were once markers indicating collective, village-wide proprietorship. They probably signified the spiritual protection of the in-habitants against uninvited incursions by outsiders, as such images are fre-quently located at questing or dreaming locations near running water (York, Daly, and Arnett 1993) and are linked to family origin narratives that re-count ancestral rights to the land. This hypothesis is based on the assump-tion that the people who made these petroglyphs were ancestral to the Gitksan and had the same need to interweave the village's landholding kin groups by means of local marriage and kinship links, and to defend these links against outsiders.

Conveyance of Property Rights

Gitksan and Witsuwit'en territories and fishing sites do not easily change hands. Territory is not "for sale" in the modern market economy sense; nor can it normally be alienated according to the principles of reciprocity. The alienation of land is rare; its ongoing, collective ownership is an important feature of House group activities. The jural relations governing the ownership of land include provisions for granting use rights; they do not facilitate ultimate alienation, nor do they allow the owner to destroy the land so that it is rendered unfit for customary use.[17] A House may occasionally lose its land due to a peace settlement or when the population of a House became so reduced due to disease and social crises (especially in postcontact times) that members were sometimes unable to pay back the funeral expenses of a deceased chief. In this way land could default to the hands of the House or clan that paid for the burial of the deceased chief or line of chiefs.

When confronted by the terms "ownership" and "property," Gitksan and Witsuwit'en have little difficulty applying these European concepts to movable property and its conveyance from person to person; but when the objects involved are immovable property, then the nature of the conveyance is not cut and dried. *The elders say that the land belongs to the people, and, at the same time, the people belong to the land.* Here, clearly, the land cannot be alienated as can a carved box or a dance apron, buckskin leggings or a pair of snowshoes. The nature of the relationship between proprietor and land is similar to a reciprocal interaction between equal partners, not unlike the long-standing ties between father's side and mother's side in social life. This view of the land stems from a general attitude towards nature as a whole – the great giver to whom all are eternally indebted. Whereas foodstuffs, tools, and luxury items can be conveyed from one proprietor to another through feast contributions, gift exchange, gambling, or barter (and today through buying and selling), the conveyance of hunting grounds and fishing sites, freighted as they are with both sacred and profane history, lacks this convertibility.

Inheritance

Property rights over territory and fishing sites are viewed as organic extensions of genealogical lifecycles and all the social reciprocation that these cycles entail. Upon the death of a chief, the House requires a new incumbent to take the chiefly name. An upward readjustment of name-holding is made by those from whose ranks the new chief has been selected. Its necessity is apparent not only to the House in question but also to all others enmeshed in the House system. Social stability demands public recognition of the identity of a certain House with a certain territory, as this configuration of ownership affects the fortunes of all members of the community through networks of kinship and affinity.

In any society marked by a strong market economy, parcels of land are viewed as commodities that can be bought and sold. Here, they are possessions that stand for, or that can be realized in terms of, other commodities. In a kinship economy, however, land conveyance shifts the managerial and custodial rights and duties from one member of the proprietary group to another not by resorting to a market but by publicly sanctioning generational inheritance. The proprietary rights to the land are vested in the owning kinship group and, specifically, in the person of the chief (who is expected to act consultatively).

Under the present-day mixed economy, Gitksan and Witsuwit'en people have engaged in a certain amount of land purchase, preemption, and the setting up of enterprises like sawmills within the territories. These ventures, while conforming to the Canadian legal and economic systems, have been regarded by the people as economic activities necessary to the continuance of use and enjoyment of their territories and resources – when these territories are under pressure from alternative, and often non-Aboriginal, users and harvesters. Land transactions associated with these ventures are not seen as having supplanted the Gitksan and Witsuwit'en system of chiefly inheritance of territory, history, regalia, and fishing sites but, rather, are regarded as a necessary and temporary defensive adaptation to the economic and political conditions of the times.

When the members of House groups see the old-growth trees being removed from their territories by strangers earning high wages, and then sold on the market, they have tried to make the best of a bad situation. This has entailed participating in the raw-material market relations so that at least a small portion of the wealth of their lands remains within their communities. Pete Muldoe, Simoogit Gitludahl, explains in his evidence (Transcript, 6126) how he operated a sawmill just west of Kispiox until forced out of business by large-scale enterprises. This venture was set up in an era when many small logging and sawmill operations contracted to the larger forestry concerns. These firms proliferated in the Kispiox and Hazelton region. Hence Muldoe and his brothers-in-law decided to start their own enterprise and participate in the harvest of Kispiox logs to provide winter work for the unemployed of Kispiox village (6126ff.). While this logging entailed the removal of some cedar and mature spruce from the territories of Kispiox chiefs, it did not denude the forests as does present-day logging. It provided work for members of several Houses and generated a portion of the modern-day wealth that circulates in the local community, both in the commercial sector and through the institution of the feast.

Among the Gitksan and Witsuwit'en the conveyance of rights to landed property is played out in the arena of succession to office within the House group or within the broader scope of otherwise distant kin united since ancient times by a strong sense of common history and association. The matrilineal kinship principle of succession, together with clan exogamy, helps organize the exchange of people between groups and territories. Marriage becomes a political alliance between definite matrilineal kinship groups – in this case, Houses and clans. This quality of inter-House and interclan alliance can be seen in a feast when a chief announces some of the persons s/he is delegating to use and care for parts of the House territory. As Art Mathews Jr., Tenimget, explained to me:

> The head chief presides at the feast. Say his nephew is getting married. The nephew's bride is from a different clan and she is welcomed into the wilp by the simoogit. He puts his blanket, *gwila*, around her, and names the places on wilp land where she can fish and pick berries. This is called *sigwilamsxw* from the blanketting the chief does in the feast. If the spouse of the wilp member is a man, the simoogit stands up and says to him, "You are welcome here, and here and here." He names some of the places on the wilp land and says, "you will use them to provide for the children which you will have with our daughter, for our House." (Daly 1986-88)

When members of a Gitksan or Witsuwit'en House vie for chiefly names and the managerial authority associated with these names, they can seek the support of members of other related Houses. While this process may tend to broaden disputes to include a number of families and Houses, it tends to diffuse power and authority. Incumbents to names are chosen on the basis of their inherent position in the kinship structure and, at the same time, on the basis of their interest, industriousness, demonstrated responsibility, and leadership potential. Selection is by no means a matter of simple ascription to office. It can be highly contested. The struggle for succession weakens the formation of enduring nodes of power.

An incumbent is chosen privately, in a House meeting.[18] Thereafter the decision is taken to the public feast hall for validation. This public registry of title before witnesses affirms in the minds of the whole community the legitimacy of succession to the name and transmission of property rights. Because marriages articulate two or more House groups there are standard rules, as we have seen, for the additional right to use the territories of the father's side. This provides a degree of flexibility in land use within a quite inflexible system of ownership. Lifetime use rights have sometimes been given to non-House members by a chief without this constituting an alienation of the land. Lifetime *nec'idilt'ës* was granted to Bazil Michell, Hattakumex, of the House of Hagwilneexl, by the House of Wedexget after

Hattakumex helped pay the funeral costs of the deceased chief Wedexget (Madeline Alfred, Transcript, 2667).

Indebtedness and Forfeiture of House Property
The deceased's father's side helps to wipe away the tears at the bereavement and finances the funeral, for which it is recompensed in the funeral feast and the headstone feast a year later. If the repayment of these expenses is not forthcoming, then the father's House, or any other House that assumed the burden of paying the funeral costs, may fall into a situation where, in time, it can take possession of the land.

Those father's side persons – the *wilksilaks/wilksibaksxw* (Git.) or *bits'ac'-elts'it* (Wit.) – expect repayment for their services in the subsequent funeral feast and/or the headstone feast that follows about a year later. In lieu of repayment these creditors may be paid off with a portion of House property (regalia, a song, or some land) if proper repayment is not forthcoming. If we drop the *méconnaissance* of the ceremonial gifting procedure for a moment and look at the material and jural aspect of this relationship, then such a transfer of a House's property is a form of default penalty paid by the other side for not having redeemed its pledge.

Olive Ryan gave an example of an unredeemed pledge resulting in the transfer of ownership of land (Transcript, 1274). The late Jessie Sterritt, Wii Goob'l of the Lax̲ Se'el (Frog/Raven) House of Gyedimgaldo'o, explained to me that, years ago, while she was working at Port Edward near Prince Rupert, the Witsuwit'en chief, Knedebeas, died. Knedebeas, a high chief in the Witsuwit'en Gilserhyu Frog Clan, was of the same clan although of a different nation and language, the Gilserhyu being considered roughly kin to Jessie Sterritt's eastern Gitksan Lax̲ Se'el Clan. When Jessie returned from the coast at the end of the cannery season her maternal uncle, Daniel Skawil, informed her that he had contributed significantly to the funeral expenses for Knedebeas and that, in the subsequent funeral feast, the Knedebeas House had presented him with the deceased's trapline west of Houston.[19]

Another example of this type of forfeiture, involving not land but a chiefly name, is cited by William Beynon from the lower Skeena Tsimshian village of Gin'adoiks (Barbeau and Beynon n.d., *Temlaham – The Land of Plenty*, Gisk̲'aast Adaaw̲k' No. 57: "A Controversy among the Gin'adoiks"). Beynon notes that a chiefly name can be taken publicly in a feast from a debtor who has steadfastly refused to discharge his debts. By way of example he cites the Frog/Raven Clan name of Sa'edzan, which became a Wolf name as a result of non-payment of a long-standing debt by the Ginadoiks Frog/Ravens. The Wolf Clan subsequently threatened to give the name back to the Frog/Ravens, thereby doubling both their shame and their indebtedness. The threat was intended to coerce the Frog/Ravens to hold a feast and to redeem their name, their crest, and the honour of the Ganeda (Frog/Raven) Clan as a whole.

The House that, on such a rare occasion, would make such a seizure is required to announce publicly, in a feast, what action it has taken. If the defaulting House is to redeem its land, then it must discharge its indebtedness and show its gratitude "with a little extra" in a feast. Normally this is done swiftly. If the debt is not paid it might indicate that the House is waning in strength and influence and does not have the membership necessary to clear its name. Outstanding funeral debts undermine a House's claims to ownership and respect. It was concern for this loss of respect and authority – not due to unpaid debts but, rather, to the fact that the House was sparsely represented in its home village – that inspired Olive Ryan to move back to Gitsegukla and hold a proper headstone feast for her deceased uncle, Jeffrey Johnson. Furthermore, this prompted her, some years later, together with her whole House, to prepare for the reinstallment of the old Ha'naamuxw crest pole and the raising of a new one (Transcript, 1054-6, 1060-1).[20]

The loss of such a name or crest, or even land, is the penalty to be paid for non-reciprocation in the unending cycle of gift-giving and repayment. The recipient usually prefers that the relinquisher redeem the debt and "clear the slate," so to speak, rather than forfeit the property. Property forfeiture is considered to be temporary, as it undermines the system of reciprocal giving and repayment that is at the heart of feasting. At the same time, I suspect that such forfeiture did occur historically.

War, Homicide, and Accidental Death Compensation
Land may also change hands in conjunction with peace settlements (*xsiisxw* [Git.] and *lhëne c'a dït cis* [Wit.]). Compensation for homicide or the accidental death of a person while on the land of another House, or reparations arising from wars and feuds, have to be paid to the offended group so as to avoid, or end, hostilities. These peace settlements frequently involve the transfer of property and/or House members as well as a peace ceremony that includes the spreading of eagle or swansdown (*mix̱k'aax* [Git.], *cis* [Wit.]), which signifies the binding law of peace. Peace agreements are legally validated when they have been witnessed in the feast house (Mills 1994).

Olive Ryan explained that the House of Ha'naamuxw had obtained a fishing site called An Sibilaa from the House of Luutkudjiiwus due to a homicide committed against a member of Ha'naamuxw's House. Now that much time has gone by, Ha'naamuxw was ready to return it and planned to do so formally when the pole-raising feast took place (1249-51).[21]

Some peace settlements resulting in the conveyance of property from one House to another are very old. Mary Johnson, Antgulilibix, testified that her House obtained a mountain hunting area called Where-the-Moon-Shines-On as compensation after Yal, of her *wil'naat'ahl*, had been killed on the ice of the river "in the ancient times" (Transcript, 800-3).

On the other hand, some peace settlements are recent. Olive Ryan attended one such *xsiisxw* settlement in 1957 or 1958 when a dispute was settled between Guxsen of Gitsegukla, part of her *wil'naat'ahl,* and the Lax Xskiik (Eagles) of Gitwangax. The latter were responsible for the death of a member of Guxsen's House, and they compensated with a hunting territory below Gitwangax on the bank of the Skeena, at a place called Xsi k'alii gajit (1251-2). In her Commission Evidence, Martha Brown similarly recounted the warfare and subsequent *xsiisxw* that resulted in the Tahltan Wolf chief, Malii, giving his name and his territory to one of Martha's predecessors, the Kispiox Gitksan Wolf chief, Xhliimlaxha. This occurred at the headwaters of the Nass and Skeena (Commission II, 22-3).

Olive Ryan added that *xsiisxw* sometimes entailed a transfer of persons – a young man and/or a young woman would be given to the other side (1252-3). In this way, members of the offender House might be married to members of the victim House by way of compensation and replacement of lost personnel. Wii Goob'l, the late Jessie Sterritt, told me that such marriages were for life. Yet Jenness's informant in 1924, the Kispiox woman who had been married to a Long Grass Sekani as part of the *xsiisxw* that was held to settle the last of the northern wars, had been allowed to return home in her old age after her husband had died (Jenness 1937, Preface).

If land is given in settlement of hostilities, then it is expected that when the hurt has worn off, no matter how many generations this might take, the land should eventually be given back. Olive Ryan explained that Ha'naamuxw was now ready to return the fishing site of An Sibilaa to the House of Luutkudjiiwus (1251):

Q - Why will you return it to them?
A - Well, that's settled. All the family will settle down and they not mad and not angry any more.
Q - So this settlement of giving this fishing site was temporary?
A - Yes.

Olive Ryan explained that peace settlements were arranged in a feast and ceremony called *gawagani* (1251). Some people say that *gawagani* originated in the course of ending a battle in which the Gitksan were involved.[22] It is said that when the two sides drew apart after their hostilities, the down and feathers from a flock of white birds floated over the battlefield. That is why, once *mixk'aax* is "put out," there can be no further animosity and a peace settlement must be concluded. According to Ryan, "The spreading of eagle down is the chief's law." Kyologet, Mary McKenzie, and Pearl Trombley, Gwamoon, explained to me that, at the end of the *gawagani,* when it is done properly, the down should be floated over the protagonists. As it floats, suspended in the air, the speaker tells the chiefs from both sides to think over the history of their people and to put the dispute and the bitter feelings behind them forever. While the feathery down settles around them, the speaker exhorts them. "Waa, simgiget! Walk softly on the breath of your ancestors."

Wii Goob'l explained *xsiisxw* in relation to a fishing site associated with her Lax Se'el House, Wilps Gyedimgaldo'o. She said that one of Gyedimgaldo'o's sites in Hagwilget Canyon was owned by the Gisk'aast. One member of Gyedimgaldo'o's House fell into the rapids and drowned while fishing at the Gisk'aast site. As a result, the Gisk'aast compensated Gyedimgaldo'o by giving the fishing site that had been theirs. I asked Jessie Sterritt if the law of returning such territory to the owners eventually applied in this case. She indicated that it did, and that it would be up to the House of Gyedimgaldo'o to decide when to return it.

Marius Barbeau's novel, *The Downfall of Temlaham*, follows real events that occurred in 1888 and involved people of Gitanyow and Gitsegukla (Barbeau and Beynon n.d., B-F-68-2 through 68-7 and 204.5). One man known to the new colonial Canadian world as "Kiwancool Jim" had caused the death of a man by the name of Neetuh. Kitwancool Jim was subsequently shot in the back and killed by the constable sent to arrest him for murder. This outraged the Gitksan community, particularly in Gitanyow, where the matter had been resolved according to Gitksan law before the Canadians came gunning for their man. Kitwancool Jim had been the husband of Gwaans's (Olive Ryan's) maternal grandmother, Fanny Johnson, the "Sunbeams" in Barbeau's book (see Figure 20). I tried to get Gwaans to tell the story, but all she would say was that evil had been done by the Canadians and a proper *xsiisxw* had been held. She said once it was settled and the *mixk'aax* had been put out – the eagle down of peace had been spread over the two parties involved – it was forbidden to talk about it or open the subject again. Unless, that is, it was something very, very ancient and there was no more hurt in it for either side. And besides, it was not for her, of Gitsegukla, to say: it was a matter for the people of Gitanyow to consider. I also asked one of Olive Ryan's grandsons about these events and he said that his granny had told him the same thing she told me.

Stewardship and Management

Management is used here to refer to the directing and implementing of activities that are part of the rights of ownership of territory. Management entails the direction of human activities and relationships vis-à-vis the property in question. Many of these relations and activities possess economic features. Stewardship, on the other hand, is used to refer to the managers' responsibility, to the fact that they are not free agents but, rather, must answer for their actions to their own social group and to the ecological and spiritual authority of the territories they manage.

Dan Michell, Wigetimschol, explained in his evidence that the Witsuwit'en do not simply fish, hunt, and trap on the land; rather, they are themselves integral to those lands (Transcript, 3756): "They live on those lands. Like I explained before, they are part of that land ... They belong to it and they return back there."

The relationship between the land and its owners is marked by a conceptual gift exchange. The land sustains the generations. The ashes and dust of each generation are returned to the land to refreshen its history and productivity. Earlier in his evidence, Dan Michell explained the authority of the Witsuwit'en chiefs in relation to their territories (3647): "It was handed down to us by our forefathers. And we are brought up in those territory where we know that we belong to the land and the land belong to us. That is one way of putting it, and all the resources in it we are entitled to it. And that is why we are taught to respect the land and everything that's in it."

Dan outlined some of the management responsibilities of the chief who both owns and is owned by the land: "He don't clean it out and get it empty. He always took care of it and just use so much of it, and leave the rest for like safe-keeping. You look after it, eh? You don't kill off all the moose or all the other animals. You always took just what you need off the land. And the same thing with the berry patches. They really protect that."

Given the scope of the Gitksan and Witsuwit'en technology at the time of contact, the people were unable to regard nature as conquerable. The relationship was one of relative equivalence, a reciprocal psychic consciousness between human populations and the forces of nature. By contrast, in a state-organized social system, the energy and technology ratio favours the human society with its tools and weapons directed against nature. In a non-state system, the ratio favours neither nature nor human society.

The worldviews of those living in nature in a foraging, kinship society reflect the basic reciprocal principle that governs day-to-day social relations in the society itself. On the one hand, nature's life force is seen to nurture the people; on the other, nature exacts its price from the people, its life force feeding upon them and their society, consuming them, causing death, and nurturing rebirth.

The House group's proprietary representative, its leader or chief, exercises a reciprocal stewardship vis-à-vis the land and all the life and spiritual energies it contains. At the same time, this representative holds a proprietary right towards the same land vis-à-vis the claims of other groups or nations. In the latter instance, the land is dealt with as a property object between two potentially competitive groups. As such it is subject to ownership. In the former instance, the land is non-property when it is viewed in terms of the people's relationship to the life force in the natural world.[23]

Joan Ryan, Chief Ha'naamuxw, expressed this duality that is implicit in the Gitksan and Witsuwit'en concept of landownership when she explained what is inherited with the name of a high chief (Transcript, 5006-8): "You are the one that has been selected to take the land that was your inheritance, to hold it and to take care of it ... It is not your personal property, but rather, you are designated as the person to manage that property not just for yourself, but for all the members of your House."

Ownership rights to land entail competition and conflict management in relation to people: we must remember that it is the *rights* and social relations, not the *land* itself, that are protected and conveyed. At the same time, ownership in such societies entails a responsibility to nurture the fruitfulness of the property. Management and stewardship require a blend of ownership and stewardship, aggressive control (vis-à-vis other groups) and careful respect and gentle intervention (vis-à-vis the ecology). The resultant interweave of competitiveness and rights to ownership, with respectful reciprocation, leaves its stamp throughout Gitksan and Witsuwit'en society.

Centralized social systems view the question of directing and managing the transformation of nature's energy into human energy as a process whereby human beings subordinate, transform, and dominate nature. By contrast, societies abhorring highly centralized structures look on this relationship as a dynamic gift exchange between two relatively equal actors involved in a spiral of death and rebirth, of taking life, making peace, consuming, and giving birth to new life and energy.

Tenimget explained the control and management of the territories and resources (Daly 1986-88, n.p.):

We look after our land by using it. If you don't hunt and fish your territories the salmon, the mountain goats, the beaver and groundhog won't stay around. If you're not active they just go away. We've always taken just what we needed, and then we protect the life cycle of the rest. We have always limited our hunting to the fall and winter, when the young are no longer dependent on their mothers. We guarded the spawning beds, we burned the berry patches to keep them healthy and productive. We even used controlled burning to get rid of the insects that kill off the trees. It was more effective than insecticides – at least we did until 1936 when they started charging us with being arsonists on our own land.

The Gitksan philosophy of conservation is based upon active pursuit and harvest of the useful species. Without the regular pursuit of these species at a sustained intensity, they say, the species will either abandon an area or its numbers will fall to such an extent that the remaining population would not remain viable if any hunting were to be carried out. Such a conservation ethic is based upon the need to maintain long-term relationships with many species: many different species are harvested, yet within limits that allow for regenerative balances in the ecological system.

Sesatxw/Halh'ala

The most respected chiefs have fulfilled their proprietary and management duties by means of example, in the way they lead their own lives. Here moral standards and the jural overlap. A chief, not unlike a member of the bench in our judicial system, is expected to lead a stable life, guided by the accumulated wisdom of those who preceded him or her. Chiefs also ask users of the House lands to observe rules of respect, which have developed over the centuries to ensure both successful harvests and a healthy, continuing ecosystem. In the Gitksan tongue, this body of observances and practices is called *sesatxw;* in Witsuwit'en it is called *halh'ala*. Properly observed, *sesatxw/halh'ala* is said to empower the hunter to succeed in his mission, especially in the winter-long task of obtaining fish and game. Today, among families whose members actively harvest the resources of their territories, at least some of these features are observed, although this aspect of the two cultures is not readily revealed to outsiders. A significant number of younger members of House groups are tutored in *sesatxw/halh'ala* as part of their training by their fathers or older members of their own House.[24] The reluctance to explain these practices is reflected, for example, in Gwaans's evidence, where she hesitated when asked about the cleansing medicine, *malgwasxw* (Transcript, 1254), and in Tenimget's explanation that the spiritual and *sesatxw* components of the *adaawk*'s of his House are not revealed to outsiders (4561).

These procedures, viewed as practical preparations for success in all major, serious endeavours, are composed of both objective and subjective practices. The objective features include technical skills, practical workmanship, knowledge of the terrain, of the lifecycles and habits of the target species, and a regimen of creative visualization and personal discipline considered essential for achieving success. Part of the discipline involves sexual abstinence and the physical and mental cleansing of the hunter. The subjective features are equally involved with self-discipline and knowledge of the terrain. They include the elimination from the mind of thoughts that can divert attention and psychic focus from the task at hand. They may involve excursions into altered states of consciousness, journeys to that portion of the mind where the human and natural life forces come closest to fusing with one another.[25] By combining these objective and subjective preparations, the hunter consolidates his skill and power and focuses his forces upon his goal without violating the basic principles of respect, sharing, and gifting.

To the uninformed outsider these purification procedures may appear to be "magical and superstitious," as nineteenth-century missionaries and administrators charged. However, my field experience has revealed that these peoples are very practical and down-to-earth in their relations with the natural world: both the physical and psychic practices are pursued for their technical and social efficacy. Over the centuries the peoples' detailed knowledge of the movement of animals across the territories became so finely honed that good hunters developed the ability to divine the whereabouts of animals by combining experience, intense focus, mental deduction, and meditation.

This power of divination was possible only for those who could divest themselves of all their everyday preoccupations and flow with the currents of energy said to unite the natural species. In the Gitksan and Witsuwit'en cultures the people believe that this almost liminal state of being can be achieved only by consciously putting into abeyance all other concerns and interests, bathing and purifying, and focusing upon the whereabouts of the animals. Certain patterns of sexual activity used to be practised before the hunting season, though this is generally no longer followed. For the specialists even today, however, it is said that during the hunting season sexual abstinence is to be observed. Not only do the hunters refrain from sexual relations during the hunting season but their wives and lovers are expected to remain chaste at hunting times as well, the idea being that the immediate family unit should focus on the hunt. The oral tradition includes many stories of the woman who defied the taboo and endangered the men or destroyed their luck. There are also stories of hunters being diverted from their hunting by a shape-shifting otter-woman. In general, discipline and focus are impressed on the whole family in hunting season. This included the discipline imposed by the culture upon the young women at the time of first menstruation (Madeline Alfred, Transcript, 2762-3, Mary Johnson, 696-9). It was considered that the first menses constituted such a powerful life force that they could damage the growth cycles in nature if they were not governed and restrained by society.

According to the body of procedures governing the hunt, once the animal was located, its demise became a matter of technological skill; however, at the same time, its death was to be treated seriously and with respect and the type of gratitude expressed in the death obsequies of a relative. Those who go hunting without focusing all their powers upon the animals, their movements, habits, and habitat are said to be unlikely to succeed.

Until the will of missionaries was imposed upon the Witsuwit'en, *halh'ala* practices were part of daily life. It began each year when the fish-drying racks, or *dziwhgï*, were put away in late August. *Halh'ala* would be observed through the winter for approximately six months. This was the spiritual season, the season of discipline and sensitivity to the natural world. The Oblate Fathers were aghast at the winter preparations, particularly at the sexual abstinence. Gisdaywa said: "We told them that this was a necessary part of our lives but they said it was superstition and had to stop. They told the ladies it wasn't necessary" (Daly 1986-88, n.p.).

Gisdaywa explained that, when the people acquiesced and no longer observed the winter abstinence, miscarriages became a frequent occurrence, whereas before this time they were extremely rare: "In winter," he said, "the hunting grounds can be tough. It's not a good place to start a pregnancy" (ibid.).

Among the Gitksan, *sesatxw* was much the same institution, although the degree of sexual abstinence varied considerably, depending partly upon the individual family's winter residential pattern: whether the family hunted from the central village or wintered regularly and extensively on the hunting ground. In the past, the chiefs acquainted the young men with the many laws governing the hunt. These laws would tell the hunter what he must and must not do to be successful on a certain territory; they instructed him to study the terrain, the plant life, the game trails, and the seasonal, annual, and biennial movements of the animals.[26] There are rules for finding the animals, for killing and butchering them, for venerating them, for asking forgiveness for taking their lives, for showing respect to their spirits, for utilizing the whole carcass, for distributing it to fellow villagers, and for disposing of waste portions. There are laws governing the preparation of the state of mind and the body of the hunter. Today the instruction of the youth continues but with varying degrees of intensity (see James Morrison, Transcript, 5124-7; Richard Benson, Commission, 65).

The preparations involve undergoing sexual abstinence, medicinal and sweat bath cleansing, and special sleeping postures (Thomas Wright, Commission, 86-7). Finally, the preparation is complete and the hunter is clean and clear of the vestiges of his non-hunting life. At this point the spirit of the game animals is said to sense the hunter's need.

The laws of *sesatxw* constitute one facet of management: he who follows the rules demonstrates how the territory is to be properly used and cared for.[27] This view is expressed by Txawok, the late James Morrison: "They followed the law. That's why Indian people always knew what was deep inside the animals, where they came from, where they were going when they were killed. These hunting laws are all about your ownership."[28]

Conservation

Increasingly, research into management and conservation practices of hunting societies indicates that foragers have long conserved species important to them in ways that approach domestication, with the result being that their forest lands are partially domesticated and may be considered "cultural," or "anthropogenic," lands. In some regions, foragers' interventions have resulted in the alteration of natural cycles of growth for thousands of years (Balée 1989, 1992, 1993; Chase 1989; Harris 1989, 1990; Posey 1983; Yen 1989). Hunting peoples engage in a process of culling some of the biological populations and actively studying the habits of the animals they hunt, trap, and snare. They also work on the face of the land to make the vegetation cycles sustain the productivity of species in which they are particularly interested, something Masgaak alludes to in his Afterword below.

Some Australian foragers controlled the ecology of the Australian outback in ethnographic times, and probably much longer, by means of their "firestick" practices. Similar practices have been reported among Kalahari foragers. Regular burning facilitated the perpetuation of the seral vegetation that most benefitted the people economically. In semi-desert conditions, controlled burning creates firebreaks that efficiently contain bush fires. The natural vegetation and prevailing stage of ecological maturity found by Europeans upon their arrival in many colonial parts of the world is now considered by scholars to have been the result of planned, purposive human intervention (Gamble 1986; B. Mills 1986; Balée 1989; Rival 1999, 2002; Turner 1999; Turner and Peacock, forthcoming).[29]

The Gitksan and Witsuwit'en frequently discuss the importance of burning for ensuring prolonged good berry yields. Thomas Wright was of the opinion that lightning fires were best because they burned a larger area than could a human-made fire (Commission, 78). Of course sometimes lightning fires were too big and the people would try to contain them. Tenimget adds that burning, which is now outlawed by the Ministry of Forests, had been used by his ancestors not only for berry patches but also to control insect infestations and to create suitable habitat for deer and other seral forest ungulates.[30] Botanist Sybille Haeussler (1986, 21) notes the long-term fire-altered appearance of the vegetation in the Skeena-Bulkley corridor between Gitsegukla, Hazelton, and Moricetown: "there are areas of open scrub and grass in sunny, dry locales. This vegetation has developed as a result of frequent, repeated fires and appears to be at least partly a product of prolonged human activity within the valley corridors."

The chiefly management of ecological relations in the territories was a function of the rules of respect that the chief and elders instilled in House members and insisted that they apply when dealing with the biological species upon which the people relied. The First Salmon Ceremony exhibits this respect, wherein the early spring salmon is caught and sprinkled with eagle down, as is an honoured guest at one's feast, and the broiled flesh is then cut into small pieces, skewered, and given ceremonially to as many people in the village as possible (Olive Ryan, Transcript, 1242-3). According to Madeline Alfred: "When you're handling fish, you always put down a bed of leaves and you always take care of the handling. You make sure you don't mishandle them at all at any time."

She explained that this is done to ensure good fishing and good relations with the fish. The Witsuwit'en have stories about the fish returning, but avoiding those who had not treated them with respect. Richard Benson explains the First Salmon Ceremony as follows (Commission, 14):

In the spring when the first fish that comes along, they caught like what I said, you know, they put it in that feather. We call it miixk̲'aax ... That's the respect, and they talk to the fish, the first one that comes up. And after that, when they dress the fish, and they start cutting it up because it's the only one. And each person, each House, get a piece ...

Q - Was this a special kind of down feather?

A - Yeah. That's really down feather from that eagle. We called that miixḵ'aax. That's what the Indian use when they respect somebody.

Richard Benson spoke of the strictness with which his grandfather, a chief of Gitanyow, enforced the rules among the children (Commission, 13): "I was surprised because my grandfather, the boss of that thing, is really got a strict rules about it. Because you see, when the fish are spawning, because they [the children] are going to ruin all those eggs that spawned in there, because if you do, it wouldn't have very much fish."

Conservation is closely linked to respect and reciprocal interaction between the people and the animal world. This is clearly delineated in the Gitksan *adaawḵ'* of the one-horned mountain goat and the retribution of the goats when the hunters did not show them respect, allowing their uncultured children to tease and torment a captive young goat (David Gunanoot, Commission, 77-81). The same ethic is stressed in the *adaawḵ'* told by Antgulilibix, Mary Johnson, about how the spirits took revenge when the people did not respect the salmon, the mountain goats, and groundhogs off which they were living (Transcript, 665-9). According to Antgulilibix, "That's why the wise elders told the young people not to play around with fish or meat or anything, because the ... sun god gave them food to eat. They should just take enough to eat and not to play with it, that's why this tragedy happens to them ... they believed that it's the revenge of those trouts, because they played around with their bones."

The harvesting was carried out under the chief's direction according to a sustained yield policy. Madeline Alfred explained the present-day rotation system used on the trapline (2652). In terms of the written record, this concern for the close husbandry of fur-bearing animals, and the practice of sustained yield harvesting, was noted by the earliest Europeans. Collective control of resources and labour, and their use to validate the authority of the House group, was described by trading post factor William Brown. Brown wrote that "chiefs and men of property" among the Babine Carrier, the Bulkley Carrier (the Witsuwit'en), and the Gitksan strictly controlled their peoples' access to beaver harvesting. He noted, from the perspective of his own partisan interests, that the chiefs allowed only twenty or thirty beavers to be taken each year and that these would frequently be husbanded for gambling, gift-giving, and feast consumption (HBC 1822, B11/e/1-2, 107-112).

Yerbury (1975, 117-31) has argued that a severe over-harvesting of furs caused many Western Carrier to abandon the centuries-old seasonal round and integrate into the general Canadian economy. This hypothesis does not seem to hold among the Witsuwit'en "Western Carrier." Undoubtedly, in many other Athapaskan areas the fur trade devastated the fauna due to competition for pelts, but among the Witsuwit'en it appears that the chiefs resisted the market-driven thrust to deplete the animals. They generally husbanded and conserved them for both cash needs and, particularly (as traders Brown, Daniel Harmon, and Peter Ogden lamented in the early nineteenth century), for feasting purposes (HBC 1822; Lamb 1957; Ogden 1853). They protected their territories from early contact fur trapping invaders as well. This is recorded in the *adaawk̲'s*, particularly those of the northern and eastern House groups.

Organization of Production
The chiefs, in consultation with the senior matrons and wing chiefs, would plan and organize the annual production calendar. X̲hliimlax̲ha, Martha Brown, explained (Daly 1986-88 [April 1987]) that when she was a child the House chief directed the seasonal round of economic activities for his matrikin. Each spring the chief discussed with the family the plan for the summer season. The plan might be announced at a small feast. He would say that certain people were going to work with certain others at the smokehouse. The youths would be told to put in the *t'iin*, or fish weir.

Martha said that the chief divided his labour force in order to be properly organized for the hectic summer season. She said her predecessor, Simoogit X̲liimlax̲ha, would direct operations out on the land as well. She recalls being told not to go beyond a certain hill because that was the boundary line. If she were to shoot a game animal that, once wounded, strayed across the boundary and died, then she was not allowed to cross over to get it. If this happened, then she was expected to tell the chief, who would negotiate with the owners of the adjacent land for the return of at least part of the animal.

For the summer season the chief made bentwood (kerfed) boxes for cooking and drying racks, called *sk̲'eex̲sin*, and the women made baskets. He saw to it that nobody rested until all the food was in, and by then it was time to go hunting and trapping. In the months between fall and spring the chief would ensure that the young men and boys hauled firewood every day for all those in need. The chiefs were expected to be aware of the needs of the community at all times. It was also the chief's duty to know the territories she was responsible for, to know them intimately, and to be able to sense the movements of the animals. (Johnny David recalls a chief who claimed to be able to feel on his skin and in his body the movements of the animals across his territory.)

The chief, or the senior person allotted to use a section of House land in Witsuwit'en territory, directed the harvesting of animals on a sustained yield basis. The Gitksan followed the same practice. Persons from different territories might hunt and trap together, basing their harvest on the game trails and cyclical movement of fur-bearers from one territory to the next. In this system, persons from proximate territories would hunt and trap together, gradually harvesting one territory then moving to another so that two or three owners' lands would be hunted selectively, in conjunction with periods of fallow time. (This is amply explained in the evidence of Alfred Mitchell [Transcript, 3270-323]; Chapter 4 above.)

The chief had to know the fertility and the population growth rate of different species in different regions and different elevations. Harvesting methods were adjusted to the carrying capacity of these varying conditions. As the Gitksan and Witsuwit'en participated increasingly in market relations associated with furs, the authority of the chief over harvesting methods appears (from all oral accounts by the people) not to have been overrun by the entrepreneurial spirit of trappers but, rather, to have intensified. Survival, based on the resources of the land, depended on this close husbandry of both marketable and food species. Evidence of this concern is found in the testimony of several chiefs; see, for example, James Morrison (Transcript, 5119-24).

Resource Management and Feasting

A significant part of House management involves the calculation of goods and services potentially available to the House if it is to fulfill its obligations to host, or contribute to the hosting of, a major feast. Planning, holding, and account-keeping for feasts make up a significant part of the managerial duties of the House chief, matrons, and wives in the annual round of economic activities and harvest calculations. Until quite recently the chief, as coordinator, had to know what each senior matron had put by for the winter in storage pits, root cellars, and meat caches.

In the pits they stored boxes of oolichan grease, cooking oil rendered from salmon heads and game animals, berry cakes, hemlock sap cakes, berries preserved in oil, bulbs, and nuts. In raised cache houses they kept most of the smoke-dried strips of salmon, steelhead, and game. In both types of storage the items of top quality were piled on one side for feast use, and the items for everyday use were piled on the other side (Book Builders of 'Ksan 1980). Today, when the medium of exchange is cash and is no longer limited to tanned hides, salmon strips, and berry cakes, many dwellings continue to stock feast gifts. Many homes have at least a wall, if not several chests or a whole room or basement, devoted to the accumulation of goods to be used in future feasts. The chief has to assess these piles of commodities in the homes of his or her House members and know the general state of the domestic economy. Before a feast the chief must ask about the amount of preserved berries and fruit, as well as the bank balances of House members, so as to be able to assess the House's ability to acquit itself well when called upon to support a relative's feast. In her evidence, Kyologet, Mary McKenzie, gave an example of what a chief is expected to contribute to a typical head-stone feast that one's own clan is hosting. In addition to moose meat, deer, beaver, or beef, a chief contributes a four-gallon pot of soup (Transcript, 292): "Well, one head chief would bring about half a dozen boxes of or-anges and apples and about two hundred loaves of bread, crackers by the boxes – might be one hundred – and with the glassware, china area, women would bring in three or four dozens, each woman, and the same way with towels, we distribute them by the dozens."

The chief must also oversee the storage of gifts and payments he/she has received, such as those given for allowing others to borrow a net or a fishing site. As we saw in Chapter 2, most of these items are expended later in the course of feasting.

The key to wealth and social approval lies in this endeavour. Chiefs are rich if they have lots of heirs, if they have lots of nieces and nephews to contribute their efforts to the prosperity of the House and to its history and traditions. They are even richer if they acquit themselves well with feasting and participate in the creation and discharge of social indebtedness. At the same time, as Mary McKenzie, Pearl Trombley, Mary Johnson, So-lomon Marsden, and others have pointed out, today's poverty and under-employment puts an ever-greater feasting burden on the shoulders of the chief, as does the present practice of inviting whole families to attend. Tra-ditionally, only the chiefs and their heirs would feast, and the gifts received would be taken home, where food, anecdotes, and political information received would be given to those assembled under the chief's roof.

By their industriousness, chiefs and elders can be the role model for the young and, as a living example, show the philosophy and values of the culture. In the Witsuwit'en language, the chief is expected to be *ama'andzï,* "a good example," and maintain the honour of the House and its ability to be a good provider to all in need, no matter what the season might be. When Gitksan or Witsuwit'en of the nineteenth century were scouting for spouses for a nephew or niece, son or daughter, they looked for clues to industriousness. Were there new aromatic evergreen boughs on the floor of the winter lodge or were they old, with the needles falling off? Was there a good stack of firewood outside? Were a young man's thumbs properly cal-loused with hard work?

In the Witsuwit'en language a lazy person is referred to as *nits'ezdi'a:* "go-ing around used up, of no consequence." The lazy are dependent upon others; they are not free. The lazy person is always talked about. They say she/he is *biligg'idetsat:* "always being fed"; while the hard worker, the plan-ner, is *dïlhdzu:* "nice, beautiful" "with all the best qualities" and hence not subject to attention. The community can depend upon her/him. The guiding ethic of management, as well as with most other social pursuits, is the ability to feed others. When this ethic is implemented and reciprocated, the whole community benefits.

The public display of foodstuffs from the land is an integral part of the House leaders' active validation of their authority and jurisdiction over specific territory (Mary McKenzie, Transcript, 291). Madeline Alfred, Dzee, testified that, at a family headstone feast in 1981, meat and berries were brought in from Wedexget territory, their origin was announced, and they were distributed to the guests (2710). Alfred said that when her son, Henry, took the name Wedexget he had been hunting on the territory for a year to get the meat and berries necessary for distribution at his feast (2714). Art Mathews says that even the modern foods presented to the guests are related, metaphorically, to the territories of the hosts as it is essential to the unity of chief, property, and authority. This is one of the ways in which the territory is affirmed in the feast hall through a holy communion with specific territories (4607): "and they were announced when you bring your soup, your tea, your bread, whatever. They are announced, and said so and so, this meat comes from – and they specify each mountain or its territory where it comes from. Each creek is mentioned. So in our rule and laws we say that if you eat and digest the words, it's within your very soul."

"You eat and digest the words, it's within your very soul." Land, family, and proprietorship are summed up in this sentence, which speaks to the unity of the heart and the brain. It illustrates the nature of the symbolic capital by which the relationship (stewardship towards the living land and proprietorship towards other families) is sanctioned and maintained down through the generations. Long ago, under protocontact conditions, the primary importance of this same relationship between land, resources, and House ownership among the Witsuwit'en and the Gitksan was documented in the journals of fur trader Daniel Harmon. In 1811 Harmon said of a Fort Fraser Carrier chief who was hosting a feast: "he takes up a whole bear, and with a raised voice, relates how and where he killed it, that all present may know that it came from his own land" (Lamb 1957, 253). In these ways, then, Gitksan and Witsuwit'en land proprietorship is manifested.

8
Epilogue

Two decades have passed since the *Delgamuukw* litigation process began. The Gitksan and the Witsuwit'en now, like the Nisga'a before them, have experienced long years of unproductive treaty talks. Their lands continue to be clear-cut for their market value in wood-fibre products, usually without consultation and almost always without their permission. This industrial predation of the forests opens the door to further raw material extraction by non-Aboriginal interests. As Chief Wigetimschol, Dan Michel, told the court in *Delgamuukw*, white people come and go. They plunder the land for a while, then leave. Then others come and repeat the pattern. It is the Witsuwit'en who stay put and have been rooted to the spot for millennia. Chief Wigetimschol was describing his local experiences with the classic imperial seizure of resources that marks much of human history.

Just as the Romans denuded the forests of the Mediterranean over 2,000 years ago, and Great Britain denuded much of the timber of northern Europe during its mercantile and colonial expansion, international corporations and global marketeering are, to the detriment of climate and ecology, following suit in the remainder of the world today. The removal of wealth from the traditional lands of the Gitksan and Witsuwit'en continues even during the current downturn in the global economy. Moreover, the Gitksan and Witsuwit'en are not currently working in tandem towards their political goals. There is considerable internal dissent within each community, village, and clan.

All the same, life goes on. People continue to fish the rivers during the salmon runs and fight for the right to trade in fish. They catch trout in winter and spring. They negotiate with coastal neighbours for oolichan at the end of winter and for herring eggs on kelp or hemlock. They hunt in fall and winter, and pick mushrooms for the Japanese market in September and October. They also pursue whatever wage labour options are available in the faltering regional economy.

They interact and intermarry with immigrant Canadians, many of whom become adopted into the local matrilineal society. They mount feasts to commemorate their dead and pass on the ancient names that legitimate their identity and their proprietorship. They show their gratitude to the spirits of the land, and they also continue to resist the exploitation of their lands, as Don Ryan indicates below.

Our Box Was Full is an attempt to present different but overlapping situated knowledges that came together in the context of a vast Aboriginal rights case at a specific point in Canadian history. The work has been based on my recording of experiences and research, as well as views about what I have learned from these situated knowledges, and, indeed, is itself part of the discourse surrounding this case and the subject communities. My point of entry was as a participant in the "land claim process" – as someone mandated to translate what he learned of, and from, the plaintiff communities for consideration by the positivistic discipline of law. As I suggested in Chapter 1, I was gifted with the opportunity to be involved with this process and hope this book will be seen as a giving in return.

Indigenous gift exchange is central to the colonial history of Canada. Initially, Europeans were fitted into Aboriginal cultures by being adopted as "brothers" and given a place in local kin-based citizenship. They in turn sought to adopt Aboriginals, not as family but, rather, as "kin under the eyes of [one or other Christian] god." Early Europeans in North America quickly learned the importance of gifting to solidify relationships in the kinship idiom. They began to give presents that their hosts reciprocated in terms of alliances and temporary fealty in the ongoing conflicts with other European powers for control of North America. These processes were central to social interaction between Aboriginals and Europeans from the time of Jacques Cartier onward (Bailey 1969). After the Treaty of Paris, which followed the end of the Seven Years War in 1763, major factors contributing to the Pontiac Rebellion were the termination of gift-giving by the British to their "Indian and Métis allies" together with the latter's loss of their intermediary role between distant tribes and Europeans in the fur trade. The Pontiac Rebellion, in turn, contributed to the creation of the subsequent Royal Proclamation of 1763 (Jennings 1975; Wallace 1972).

The British resumed gift-giving to former allies, at least until the cessation of hostilities with their former American colonists after the War of 1812; then, at the end of the nineteenth century, although the semiotics of the gift were still part of Aboriginal-colonial relations, the relationship changed. The former indigenous peoples who had been allies of the French or the British had now become colonial subjects.

Of course gift-giving between persons of different social standing invariably turns sour. No longer in legal possession of their lands, First Nations peoples were in no political or economic position to reciprocate, and they probably lacked a sense of gratitude towards the new European state-organized way of life. Gratitude is implicit in gifting, but under the new conditions the need for the *méconnaissance* of gift-giving as a form of inter-nation intercourse waned, although the form was retained when the Canadian government began concluding treaties across much of the country in the nineteenth century. Arnett (1999, 33-8) describes how the Douglas treaties on southern Vancouver Island were considered by peoples such as the Songhees, Cowichan, and Nanaimo to be peace treaties, not land cessions. They considered the payments received from Douglas on behalf of the Hudson's Bay Company to be prestations akin to gifts received in feasts for witnessing the hosts' transactions. Little did they know that the treaties were not unique to the immediate relationship between Douglas and the local indigenous population; rather, they were a standard British form of land cession agreement developed for dispossessing peoples across the im-perium (including the Maori in the colony of New Zealand).

In central and prairie Canada treaties were accompanied by government representatives giving small annual gifts to seal these land cessions – an act that made evident the impotency of the First Nations of the day, their in-ability to reciprocate, and their inferior status within the new world order and its armed campaign against local "terrorism." By the time these treaties were offered, the recipients had neither the means nor the taste for recipro-cation. This is not to imply that some treating chiefs did not observe mini-mal etiquette in order to maintain a semblance of nation-to-nation relations in their dealings with government and to retain some vestige of First Nations identity.

It is ironic that today official gifts from the Canadian government – gifts embodying the essence of Canada – that are presented to foreign heads of state are often Aboriginal works of art and that quintessentially Canadian tourist T-shirts and coffee mugs are frequently stamped with Aboriginal ico-nography. Northwest Coast works of art, formerly among the splendid wealth items given at potlatch feasts, have been appropriated as the symbols of Canada itself. In terms of iconography, Canada is represented at its embassy on Pennsylvania Avenue, Washington, DC, by Bill Reid's monumental sculp-ture *The Black Canoe,* a version of which *(The Jade Canoe)* greets visitors to the international terminal of Vancouver's airport. Northwest Coast archi-tecture, sculpture, and design are featured in the main atrium of the Cana-dian Museum of Civilization in Ottawa, presumably as a prominent feature of Canadian heritage.

Is there not some faulty logic at work when Canada identifies itself with the art that was formerly part of local internal gift-giving among such peoples as the speakers of Inuqtituk, Haida, Tsimshian, Wakashan, Salishan, Atha-paskan, Algonquian, and Iroquoian language families, while at the same time refusing to identify with, or even recognize, the tradition of Aboriginal landholding and self-governance? In other words, it would certainly make for a more just society if Canada, before appropriating the gifts and talents of Aboriginal peoples as state presents and as emblems of national identity, would have acknowledged and respected Aboriginal cultures and life forms. We have seen in earlier parts of this book that a real gift or talent is defined not only by what is given but also by the sense of proprietary right and identity that is retained after the gift has gone out and embarked upon its social journey.

The Gitksan and Witsuwit'en have regulated and organized their everyday life for well over the past two centuries through the modality of giving and counter-giving. I have demonstrated the workings of a reciprocity of gifting that are evident in various aspects of these peoples' life on the land: their feasting, their seasonal rounds, their family relations, their social structure, their relations with more distant peoples, and their local system of proprietorship. What I have not yet described are some of the changes evident in the local plaintiff communities in the post-*Delgamuukw* period.

Colonized communities tend to reflect the structural contradictions of class, gender, and ethnic distinctions of the society in which they are encapsulated. This was certainly the case when Gitksan and Witsuwit'en elders and political leaders of the 1980s decided to take the Governments of British Columbia and Canada to court to seek official recognition of Aboriginal rights under Canada's Constitution. They sought recognition of their proprietorship and the general contours of their social structure. However, this does not mean that these communities were of one mind in the matter. Much of the local social dynamism has always been provided by the tensions between different points of view and statuses – tensions that are normally leavened by the intergenerational reciprocities between Houses, clans, and villages, and the moral discipline exerted by elders.

For the past 150 years many of these contradictions have unfolded in an idiom provided by the colonial context. In addition to colonialism's opponents within such communities, one also finds subaltern segments reconciled to their diminished position within the nation-state. The subalterns take to heart the rationale – the road to power and influence – provided by the colonizer (Fanon 1963, 1986; Guha and Spivak 1987; Spivak 1988). They become petty political and economic entrepreneurs, as described by Barth (1967), trading at the interface between their own and the colonial culture so as to maximize their personal well-being in the colonial context. During much of the twentieth century in Gitksan and Witsuwit'en territories, such subaltern activities took the form of lay preaching for various Christian denominations and controlling the band council political process instituted by Canada when it set up the system of Indian reserves. These activities were never carved in stone, and people changed their attitudes, alliances, and practices concerning their Aboriginality according to the trajectories of disputes and of changing conditions of life.

Of course there are people in the communities who are neither entrepreneurial subalterns, nor radical innovators, nor politicized "traditionalists" demanding title recognition to their lands. Many do their best to harness whatever aspect of their own culture, and that of Canada's mainstream, they can to their own specific daily requirements. However, in the late twentieth century, litigation became a new field for subaltern entrepreneurial activity. The zeitgeist that accompanied this development did not suddenly blow over the territories. It had been learned over recent decades from Aboriginal land rights cases in Canada, Australia, and New Zealand as well as from the earlier US experience. In the Gitksan and Witsuwit'en territories, the greatest pedagogical tool has been the *Delgamuukw* case itself (Daly and Napoleon 2003).

The Supreme Court of Canada found that the *Delgamuukw* plaintiff House chiefs must, on behalf of their members, be consulted prior to the implementation of resource extraction on the traditional lands claimed by these chiefs. In some cases this has resulted in more ecologically friendly resource extraction; in others, chiefly acquiescence has been gained in exchange for jobs and other perks on the resource frontier.

Similarly, at the trial level, the plaintiff communities experienced the cold contempt to which their identity, ontology, heritage, chiefs, and elders were treated in the judge's ruling. They also learned of the respect and influence enjoyed by the legal system and its practitioners. It was a stark lesson in where power lies in the wider world. Today many Houses are sending young people to law school, and not always with a view to fighting more effectively for self-governance. More and more families are turning to the dyadic, contractual relationship between the individual and the state to settle conflicts. They call the police and they take one another to court instead of seeking consensus through negotiations and the subtle, nuanced one-upping common to ceremonial inter-House relations. Today they engage in naked adversarial games of winning and losing, while continuing to live with a high level of local enmity in cramped reserve conditions marked by high unemployment, social violence, and substance abuse.

At the same time there has been little movement in treaty negotiations. The Government of British Columbia refuses to consider the hereditary system of social organization as a viable form of society. It insists upon the governmental structure of non-hereditary elected band councils. At the same time, the higher courts find that hereditary leaders must be consulted prior to resource extraction on disputed Crown lands. In their offerings to First Nations, the provincial government seems to be seeking a hybrid system of Aboriginal governance. For instance, in its initiatives to further "privatize" the forests and thus shift its negotiating position with the US government over softwood lumber tariffs, the BC government is offering the public a five-year limited forest tenure over a portion of the province's trees considered ready for cutting. A small portion of this is being offered to First Nations. To be eligible, the Aboriginal nation must constitute itself according to federal Department of Indian Affairs band membership lists rather than according to bloodline and marriage. However, hereditary chiefs (governed by bloodline and marriage) are expected to ratify this arrangement on behalf of their (bureaucratically organized and government band-numbered) members as a hybrid response to the findings of the Supreme Court in *Delgamuukw* concerning consultation regarding land development or exploitation. For peoples such as the Gitksan, this does not address the crucial question of the forest industry suffering from severe over-cutting, nor does it address the question of recognizing and identifying Aboriginal rights to land and governance. To date, this scheme has been spectacularly successful in creating many additional disputes within the local communities. And these disputes are not being settled by chiefs and elders concerned with the future of the whole community but, rather, by litigation and the courts.

Another problem arising from the land claims process is the way the filing of evidence has tended to encode what is a living social process into a documented custom or law. Once immured in juridical archives, these customs and laws tend to acquire a legitimating mystique within the eyes of members of their communities of origin. A society, like the phenomena studied by subatomic physicists, consists of both entities and processes, or particles and waves. The process of litigation has given an excess of legitimacy to the particles, or entities, at the expense of the ongoing waves, or processes of social interaction, which are so central to the daily life of any society. This has had problematic effects on family relations with regard to House groups being equated with petty corporations, as discussed below, and in some cases with ascribing territories to Houses other than those to whom they belong. The latter issue is an ongoing concern particularly among the Witsuwit'en. Here the practice of a man using his wife's territory, according to the principle of *nec'idilt'ës* (just cooking something there), was particularly distorted with patrilineal trapline registration. Many men worked the territories of their wives and had their names on the government registry for these lands. Others worked their own matrilineal territories, and their children subsequently hunted and fished there according to the use rights for the children's father's side, which sometimes also got registered patrilineally. This was not of such importance before the court case, as acknowledgment of *nec'idilt'ës*, the confirming of ownership, the arranging of marriages, and the occasional adoption kept the society-wide reciprocal relations of landownership and use functioning according to collective matrilineal principles. The insistence on individual House rights that emerged from *Delgamuukw,* however, has changed this dynamic and the former cooperative and consultative management of land and land use.

This situation of owners using wives' and fathers' House territories more often than their own did not bother the actual collective, interactive, reciprocal use of the territories, even in the recent past, as attested to in Chapter 4 by the late Alfred Mitchell, Txemsin. Witsuwit'en hunters managed their territories by sharing them extensively in seasonal and annual cycles. Moreover, the Witsuwit'en, like many Athapaskan-speaking peoples, have always worked closely together and caucused about important matters affecting the whole community. On this point they view themselves as quite distinct from the Gitksan, who more frequently break into factions when faced with important decisions and then work towards negotiated agreements that try to conciliate the various different points of view. With the Supreme Court of Canada decision in *Delgamuukw,* and the potential for land development and consultation with corporations and government departments regarding resource extraction, the local communities find that the question of House territorial title, as a thing in itself, has moved to the foreground. Among the Witsuwit'en this has awakened the need for further unravelling of the complex use and ownership rights over specific territories where members of certain Houses may have lived, even though some of these territories are actually owned by others. The process of unravelling actual proprietorship appears not to have been thoroughly completed (and such completion is always suspect for it stops an ongoing negotiating process). In the instance of some territories before the *Delgamuukw* case went to trial, incomplete information is now locally perceived to have distorted the boundary-setting research carried out by the plaintiffs. Witsuwit'en chiefs assumed the litigation would be on behalf of their whole nation. Consequently, they assumed that the remaining boundary disputes could be worked out later. They did not envisage the courts treating their community as a set of discrete socioeconomic units based on Houses that acted like petty businesses rather than like interwoven entities that reinforced one another through generations of multi-functional social interaction.

The litigation process changed perceptions: what were once seen as fluid, ongoing social relationships were now being seen as immutable truths. The names of chiefs entered on the territorial maps and submitted to the court, and that appear in books like this one (Maps 5 and 6), take on an immutability that does not readily admit to further discussion and adjustment. In fact, such discussion more often leads to animosities and a sense of injustice. Further clarification of ownership is extremely difficult and has led to an increase in disputes over proprietorship. Briefly, the processes of daily life on the land have always been fluid but structured by history, House identity, and interlinked leaders who reiterated their legitimacy with one another through feasting. With the massive litigation of *Delgamuukw* this fluidity has coagulated into metes and bounds, creating new social and economic divisions at the local level.

Let us return for a moment to the zeitgeist. The current worldwide emphasis on human rights can function as a Trojan horse that reinforces hegemonic relationships, particularly the contractual relationship between individuals backed by the power of the state. Viewed differently, human rights usually presuppose a personal relationship between the individual (usually the rational person of consumer choice models) and the state. The promotion of human rights is predicated upon litigation and the constitutional sanctions that have been perfected under the aegis of the nation-state. It becomes an alternative to kinship forms of establishing and negotiating rights and conflicts between claimants. Human rights can certainly be a powerful weapon for alleviating human suffering when applied in state-to-state relations with regard to national minorities, but they are the creation of nation-states. For millennia, other forms of establishing rights held sway. Kinship societies, for instance, used to rely much more on their own traditions in dispute settlement than they do today. Nowadays, in Gitksan communities, the question of human rights is even raised in internal litigation at the level of the rights of the individual, over and above his or her rights as a member of a family in a system of interacting clans and Houses.

One of the negative features of the *Delgamuukw* process was the deconstruction of the *sgano,* or interweaving of local kin relations, and the reification of the House into something akin to a corporation or a petty enterprise. This has resulted in inter-House disputes being removed from crosscutting family relationships and submitted instead to litigation for redress. Formerly, the notion and ceremonial expression of Household provided the armature for reciprocal relations between a large group of people related by matriline and articulated through marriage and collateral kinship ties. Disputes were internal family affairs that disrupted the whole community if they were not settled, normally through the idiom of reciprocal gift exchange, which is implicitly (and sometimes explicitly) based on respect and gratitude. In serious disputes the whole community got busy to see that a just solution was reached, thus ensuring that all won and lost something and so could re-establish a relative state of peace.

This form of dispute settlement involved both subtle rivalry and delicate diplomacy, such as we found in gift exchange, which simultaneously created new social indebtedness while it discharged an old one. It also entailed respect for elders and for all the generations that went before. I am not suggesting that the feast system of the Gitksan and the Wisuwit'en, the paradigm for this region's gift-centred societies, has died and gone to the museum of antiquities as a result of *Delgamuukw;* rather, since the collective litigation, feasts have become a medium for new challenges in a rapidly changing world, as the following instance shows.

I was at the village of Gitanmaax in eastern Gitksan territory on 17 October 2002 when a mortuary feast was held to honour Art Ridsdale, the holder of the chiefly name Luutkudjiiwus in Wilps Luutkudjiiwus-Xsimits'iin, of the Frog/Raven Lax̱ Se'el Clan. This is a very large House with two *simgiget* names and two territories. (Some Houses, of course, have three or four territories.) It is closely related to other *huwilp* (Houses) of the clan, such as Gyedimgaldo'o, Skawil, and Wii Goob'l, who all lived in one Big House on the riverbank during the childhood of the late Wii Goob'l, Jessie Sterritt. In terms of size and internal contradictions, this *wilp* seems due for fissioning into two *huwilp*, each with its own *simoogit* and territory, but this is not a desirable solution in the eyes of the most energetic House members. This House is unusual in that it has a braided *sto'owilp* structure as, in a dispute over the chiefship early in the twentieth century, the chiefs of the local Frog/Raven Clan decided to award the two chief names to the opposite "sides" of the House. Accordingly, Luutkudjiiwus went to the Xsimits'iin side and vice versa. This was a practice designed to slow down the tempo of internal disputes, but the subsequent problem has been that the families on each side of the House feel called upon to control both the names and both the territories. I learned that in the past, when the enmities became so great that normal everyday life was disrupted, the chiefs of the local villages would meet and propose a fissioning of the *wilp*. The name Xsimits'iin was traditionally linked to a territory in the Suskwa Valley on the border with the Witsuwit'en, and Luutkudjiiwus was associated with a territory on the right bank of the Skeena River across from Hazelton and downstream towards Gitsegukla. There are four or five lineage segments within the House, but one of these segments has been much more active than the others in pursuing wing chief names and *wilp* decision taking.

The deceased was said to have indicated that the Luutkudjiiwus name should be taken by the son of a strand from the opposite side of this *sto'owilp* House, but it appears that after further consideration he left a written testament favouring the son of a different strand in the House. This person is a prominent political figure in treaty negotiations and the Gitksan watershed protection system. These were both pursuits that the deceased vigorously supported. Neither side would acquiesce to the desires of the other. This led to acrimony at the smoke feast on 15 October 2002 and flared up again in the mortuary feast itself.

According to the current state of the law, the territories of this House, like other Gitksan and Witsuwit'en territories, are still conceived of as Crown land, owned by Queen Elizabeth II on behalf of the people of her Dominion of Canada. Recent decisions by the Supreme Court of Canada, such as *Sparrow* and *Delgamuukw*, call on government and private industry to consult with traditional owners before commencing resource extraction. This gives new stature and voice to House chiefs, as well as some jobs and cash benefits that they can dispense at their pleasure. In this way, chiefship has become separated from the interwoven relationships of the past and more closely linked to contemporary economic possibilities.

On the morning of 17 October 2002 the chiefs gathered at the home of the deceased, said their farewells, and sent him on his journey to the afterworld, telling him, "Hawil'yiin, hawil'yiin, lax hlan'aahlx xsinaahlxwhl G̲a'Nii ye'etxwm" [Walk softly, walk softly, on the breath of Our Grandfathers]. The funeral was held at the Roman Catholic church's hall in Hagwilget. The choir wanted to honour the deceased with a few of his favourite dance tunes, but the priest instructed them to stick to the hymns. The burial ceremony took place at the Gitanmaax cemetery high above the confluence of the 'Ksan (Skeena) and Wedzenkwe (Bulkley), from where there is a transcendent view of Stikyoo'denhl – "home of the mountain goats" – and further off, the Seven Sisters, Mean'skanist. The mortuary feast began at six in the evening. The seating proceeded rapidly and I was placed at the missionary table with my back to the proceedings, which occasioned a set of traumatized neck muscles for the next few days.

The Gisk̲'aast (Fireweed/Killer Whale) chiefs of the village of Gitsegukla did not enter individually as is normally the case for all the guest chiefs. They entered en bloc, wearing headbands and singing a peace song. They were protesting, taking collective action, working as a unit, as the *nidilx*, or opposite side to the hosts, the role they fulfilled whenever the Frog/Ravens hold a feast in their own home village of Gitsegukla. This action was intended to signal their displeasure at the fact that the hosts had decided to use the feast as a public arena in which to push conflicting claims to the Luutkudjiiwus name rather than resolving the issue beforehand, behind closed doors.

The feast started up quickly and those who came late were turned away by a group of large young men at the main entrance. This was a highly insulting gesture towards guest chiefs, something I had never witnessed before. I later learned that most of those turned away were supporters of the political candidate for the name and not of the candidate for the Xsimits'iin strand of the House. The Xsimits'iin people assumed the role of the hosts on behalf of the House's population of several hundred members, and the other faction was not pleased by this de facto leading role. However, the Xsimits'iin people are very knowledgeable, adept in the language, culture, and protocol of the feast system, and the other faction somewhat less so.

Xsimits'iin welcomed the guests in chiefly robe and *amhalayt* headdress. He explained how his family was within its rights to appoint a successor to the name of Luutkudjiiwus. He called upon the *wilp*'s *nidilx*, or *nidinsxwit* (chief witness and acknowledger from the main opposite clan in the village),

Wilps Spookw, to stand up. Wilps Spookw stood but did not know why they had been requested to do so. The members of Xsimits'iin's strand of the House also got to their feet. Now, in front of those chosen to acknowledge his choice, Xsimits'iin announced the person who would inherit the title of Luutkudjiiwus, and those standing were expected to acknowledge this choice. Wilps Spookw sat down in surprise. Xsimits'iin's brother, a graduating law student, now proceeded to call out the names of guest chiefs whom his family expected would follow protocol and acknowledge the choice. This is done by calling out an acknowledgment sentence, the *ayesxw,* of the person to whom the name is floated *(uxwshedint),* as explained in Chapter 2. Only one chief responded with his *ayesxw;* the others whose names were called remained silent.

There was now muttering in the hall and much signalling with body language from table to table. The *ant'im'nak* of the deceased's brother (who had also held the name Luutkudjiiwus) hired another clansperson to speak on their behalf. They were responding to an allegation that, at the funeral feast of the previous Luutkudjiiwus (their husband and father), a member of their *wilp* had physically attacked the person of Xsimits'iin. The speaker for this *wilp* proceeded to make several significant cash payments to chiefs who might feel that their own honour had been sullied by this accusation.

The spokesperson for the above-mentioned Gisk'aast Clan of Gitsegukla stood up, suggesting that the chiefs he represented had come to honour the deceased and not to witness a battle over succession. They called on the hosts "to take care not to put spring before winter," counselling that the wise and proper course would be to proceed in the proper order, by commemorating the deceased with solemnity and cooperation. An emergency meeting of the Frog/Raven Clan was now held in a back room of the hall in an attempt to quell the conflict before it became more aggravated. The meeting was inconclusive.

The food was served and the *batsa'a* distribution began. Xsimits'iin again took the floor. He reiterated his family's rights under Gitksan law to appoint the successor and conduct the funeral feast as his family saw fit. He did not take kindly to dissent and disagreement under his roof beams. The feast would go ahead on the terms laid down by him and his family. Supporters of the other potential candidate for the *wam simoogit* name of Luutkudjiiwus would do as he said; they would cease their disruption and behave themselves.

Xsimits'iin's brother now spoke at length, in Gitksanimx and then in English. He supported their matriline's claim to the names and the territories, and said the community had maligned their family long enough. He said that since this feast had begun, a member of their immediate matriline had been threatened in the washroom by a member of the opposing faction. He spoke of the effects of residential schooling on him, on his brother, on charges of sexual abuse, on their lifestyle and their family. He called on the rival candidate to accept Xsimits'iin's decision about the succession and to apologize for disrupting the feast. By way of punishment, Xsimits'iin decreed that the other faction of House members would not be allowed to send the deceased on his way. In other words, they would not be allowed to contribute to the *tsek*, to the wealth being collected to honour the passing of Art Ridsdale, holder of Luutkudjiiwus, which would be used as gifts of gratitude *(xdaala)* to the guests for witnessing the *wilps'* feast business.

The other incumbent, together with a chiefly Frog/Raven ally from the village of Gitwangax, now went up to the front of the hall bearing their own *tsek*. There were now two *tseks* and two incumbents at the front. Xsimits'iin's brother had begun to call in the family to contribute to their *tsek*, even before the guests had finished eating. The Xsimits'iin *sto'owilp* side had reached the sum of approximately $9,000 when word went around the hall, from chief to chief and then to all the guests seated at each table according to the rank of their names, "Put on your coats and stand up. If things go so far as we all walk out, do not take any of the gift food with you when you leave." The guests, over 400 of us, got to our feet and pulled on our coats. We stood facing the two factions at the front of the hall. The Xsimits'iin *sto'owilp* people were conferring with their *sigidim hanaak*, or elderly matron. It appeared to me that we would soon be leaving the hall and that this would precipitate the long-expected splitting of this *wilp* into two.

Neil Sterritt Jr., who had been tribal council president at the beginning of the *Delgamuukw* process, now spoke up. He said that he, for one, had not come here to witness a brawl about a name. He had come to honour the deceased and to console the bereaved. Since there was such disagreement over the name, he suggested that Luutkudjiiwus be "hung up," or retired, for a year or so and that the incumbent could be chosen later, when passions had cooled.

A wild burst of applause broke out, something totally foreign to the usual good-natured but solemn feast atmosphere. Another ten minutes passed while Xsimitis'iin and his family conferred. Neil Sterritt then said he expected a response or he would leave. Xsimits'iin's brother asked him for patience and a little more time. We continued to stand in our coats and hats. Some minutes later the hosts announced that, yes, they would hang up the name for a year and would now proceed with the feast to honour the deceased.

In the end, at 5:30 the next morning, over $40,000, including $12,000 from the deceased and his wife, had been collected, given out, and acknowledged, making this an inconclusive but respectable feast. Later, certain culturally well-versed guests told me that, had we walked out, a division in the *wilp* would have been insisted upon by the other chiefs and elders and that, as a result of this, the local political situation would have been decisively resolved. Elderly chiefs say that, in the past, chiefs and elders consulted about everything that happened in the communities. They complain today, in the time-honoured pedagogy of the old, that the young chiefs should slow down and discuss their collective vision for the future.

In the year that followed this agonistic feast the community continued to be riven with conflicts without resolution, including that of the succession to Luutkudjiiwus, which affects the future of treaty negotiations and collective land management talks with government agencies. There are slanders, threats of violence, internal picket lines against one another, and increasing amounts of litigation between community members. Since then, a further year has passed and it appears that the House is indeed bowing to community pressure. It is moving towards a division of powers and territories.

The feast system and its underlying spirit of the gift is not dying, but it is facing new and challenging times. Time-honoured consensus decision taking, where a dispute might take several generations of feasting and intermarriage to resolve completely, is increasingly being circumvented due to the impatience of a world where time is measured in money. Agonistic giving in the form of the classic potlatch has not reappeared either. Today people have at least a toehold in the mainstream culture and society. They resort to the police and litigation to redress what they perceive to be injustices within the local community. At the same time, however, the territories, the fishing sites along the rivers, and family histories and narratives remain central elements of proprietorship, of political, economic, and symbolic capital. The force of community (such as the chiefs' implied readiness to intervene and enforce a division in Wilps Luutkudjiiwus-Xsimits'iin, and the threatened exodus from the feast hall when there was no unanimity or possibility of witnessing a proper chiefly installation) appears to have considerable strength, vibrancy, and elasticity. This is still a community where social relations are profoundly based on kinship rooted in territory.

Such feasts as that of 17 October 2002 have occurred before and have been sorted out collectively by local hereditary leaders. An elderly *sigidim hanaak* of Wilps Spookw explained to me how, almost a century ago, around the time when Johnson Alexander was Simoogit Spookw, there was a feast where the *wilp* members had been unable to decide on the succession prior to the mortuary ceremonies. Two candidates had come to the front of the feast hall with their respective piles of gifts. They stood beside their goods while their spokespeople justified their respective claims to the deceased's name. The feast could not proceed; the guests left and went home. Later the collective chiefs of Gitanmaax, Hagwilget, and Gitsegukla gathered to sort out the succession. Both men were told to share the name, with it remaining on the shoulders of he who lived the longer.

Such violations of protocol as I witnessed on 17 October 2002 break frame with the more serviceable *méconnaissance* of dignity, gratitude, and kindness, and the sharing of self and sorrow at the passing of the deceased, which are central to mortuary feast-giving. They reveal overt conflict and naked partisan interests, with threats of violence, enmity in everyday life, and endless litigation. They are highly disruptive to the community, and just as, in the past, such disruptions were collectively resolved at a supraclan level, so could they be today. This would re-establish the masked dance of the gift, where, despite the pressures from the surrounding socioeconomic world, local obligations do not and cannot end with a contract, at least not without calling into question the whole indigenous system of proprietorship. Among the Gitksan and their Witsuwit'en neighbours the legitimacy of ownership is bound up with nature's gift to the ancestors. The descendants are bound to a system of perpetual obligatory reciprocity. The next gift is always a new overture to the other.

Even the contractual world of the nation-state tends not to be ultimately carved in marble: it can bend to the public will. The balance between social rights and duties is always shifting, as is the balance between overlays of generations, classes, genders, and ethnicities. One current feature of the ephemeral rights offered by the state today – namely, cutbacks in social transfer payments – shows that the state can be as processual in nature as can the social systems of non-state peoples. Currently in rural Canada, as in many other corners of the world, there are concerted efforts to concentrate the population in larger and larger centres to make the provision of services more cost-effective. Such processes free up the land for massive corporate raiding of raw materials, whether it be agribusiness, aquaculture, mining, or forestry, and turn rural communities into ghost towns. In the Gitksan and Witsuwit'en region, social services are being curtailed, welfare limited, post offices and schools closed, and hospital beds eliminated, along with care for the chronically ill and aged. In such situations retail services naturally move away as well. Chief Wigetimschol's observation, cited at the beginning of this epilogue – that white people come and go and that the Witsuwit'en are the ones who stay – now applies at a corporate level to the exploitation of the resource frontier. Immigrants to these territories, who arrived in times of high economic conjunctures, have not been noticeably fighting this policy politically; rather, they are voting with their feet – leaving in droves due to the lack of jobs, severe over-cutting of forests, and subsequent downturns in retail trade and cuts in social services, health, and education.

How the First Nations of this frontier respond to the fact that the state is reneging on its responsibilities to the citizenry of the region has yet to be analyzed. But the economic situation that underlies current local discord

and litigation also reveals that shifting from negotiated flexible kinship institutions to the apparently inflexible rights and duties of the nation-state
system does not necessarily provide long-term social security. Rights and
duties may be adjudicated by courts of law, but even these decisions are
ultimately coloured by the political arena, where sections of the population
fight for their interests and against those of others. Even the courts themselves are not immune from the effects of the changing zeitgeist, especially
regarding the issue of Aboriginal rights, as we see, for instance in the judgment in *Sparrow* (1990, 177):

> By the late 1960s, aboriginal claims were not even recognized by the federal
> government as having any legal status. Thus the Statement of the Govern-
> ment of Canada on Indian Policy (1969), although well-meaning, contained
> the assertion (at p. 11) that "aboriginal claims to land ... are so general and
> undefined that it is not realistic to think of them as specific claims capable
> of remedy except through a policy and program that will end injustice to
> the Indians as members of the Canadian society." ... It took a number of
> judicial decisions and notably the Calder case in this Court (1973) to prompt
> a reassessment of the position being taken by government.

While the higher courts might consider that they have been the torch-
bearers for enlightening government over Aboriginal rights, the social sciences would put much of this flexibility and enlightenment down to pressure
exerted on Canada and its institutions by its First Nations communities
themselves.

Given the current flux and insecurity at the national level, there is still
great scope for waging flexible and nuanced political campaigns, and negotiating outcomes for another generation – even by means of kinship
structures and the gifting phenomenon. Decision making on the basis of
contractual agreements is not historically inevitable. The Aboriginal communities, experts in gift exchange, have much to teach us newcomers about
negotiating for our rights, creating and recreating obligations, and actually
practising a local-level democracy in the process of doing so.

Finally, whether actors in any society exchange by means of contracts
and markets, or by gift-giving, in order for there to be movement, there
have to be things that are kept out of circulation, that are not exchanged.
No matter how we exchange people, goods, and services, we need stable
points around which other items can revolve, circulate, and achieve a standard of evaluation.

For the Gitksan and Witsuwit'en the point of stability is the land itself,
with its histories of gift exchange between the life forces of nature and the
ancestors, between the living generations and the spirits of all things lodged
there. Gifting and the kinship organization of local society continue to seize

the lives and passions of these two peoples today, more than two centuries after the first apocryphal white man stumbled over the mountains, as the late Mary Johnson, Antgulilibix, recounted with great verve and drama. This tattered newcomer, with no pedigree, no territory, and no family, staggered into the people's midst with gaping holes in his pants and hunger in his belly. They took him into one of the big houses, where they washed and fed and clothed him with the gifts given by the land to the people and by the people to him.

We all know that the way to a man's heart is through his stomach. This apocryphal white man's hunger was great not only for food but also for land and golden riches. His descendants have inherited his appetite. Gitksan and Witsuwit'en lands have now assuaged the newcomers' hunger for more than two centuries. Has this caused the heart to grow fonder? I would like to think so, but the onus of proof remains with our newcomer population and its nation-state way of life. We still suffer from the legacy of descriptions of New World peoples made by Renaissance Europeans who judged the social worlds they discovered in terms of all the things these worlds lacked. Thomas Hobbes, whose sensibilities were coloured by the civil war in England of the 1640s, wrote in *Leviathan* of those lacking the nation-state. He maintained they lived in a state of "warre, as is of every man against every man," and indeed, he found that those in this condition lacked much: "In such condition there is no place for Industry; because the fruit thereof is uncertain, and consequently no Culture of the Earth; no Navigation, nor use of the commodities that may be imported by Sea; no commodious Building, no Instruments of moving and removing such things as require much force; no Knowledge of the face of the earth, no account of Time; no Arts; no Letters; No Society, and which is worst of all, continuall feare, and danger of violent Death; and the life of man, solitary, nasty, brutish and short" (Hobbes 1651, 62). Cultural historian Olive Dickason (1984, 52), who has gleaned from the Renaissance record a lengthy list of negative features of Aboriginal life in Europe's overseas colonies, presents this list so that we are able to see the genesis of colonial thinking that has yet to be transcended: "The negative list at times became a bit strained: Amerindians, besides being without wine, were also without bread. Neither did they possess ports, firearms, or swords; they were without 'polite conversation,' and so ignorant that they were not even aware of their deprived state. Without morals, vagabonds without homes, they were without possessions, and without a country."

Our settler society has yet to recognize that these peoples all had their countries and will not readily relinquish them. Such recognition, were it to come even at this late date, would show our gratitude for having had our ancestors welcomed here with practical assistance and hospitality, and having had their transgressions tolerated so patiently by the local inhabitants of this non-state – and non-India – that they had reached. There are still deep colonial wounds to heal. Reciprocating with First Nations as equals is part of this healing process. For Canada, and for the non-Aboriginal world, recognition of Aboriginal rights to land and self-government would be a good beginning to the postcolonial healing process. It would demonstrate gratitude and constitute an overture to a common future in which First Nations peoples would have the right to live not without a country but, rather, without intolerance and without injustice.

Afterword:
Back to the Future

Don Ryan, Masgaak, Wilps Ha'naamuxw,
Gitxsan Treaty Office

This book is based on research that Richard Daly undertook for the Gitksan and Witsuwit'en peoples in relation to our litigation in the Canadian courts. The case is known as *Delgamuukw,* named for the first of our hereditary chiefs to sign the original Statement of Claim against the Province of British Columbia in 1984. The claim was filed with the Supreme Court of British Columbia on behalf of Simoogit Delgamuukw and his *wilp,* his House members, and on behalf of the other hereditary chiefs and members of the other Gitksan and Witsuwit'en Houses. I am happy to respond to Richard Daly's suggestion that I "add on," as we Gitksan say, to this book by letting readers know what the plaintiffs have been up to since the Supreme Court of Canada decision in December 1997. What follows are my views about what is going on among the Gitksan.

Since the Supreme Court of Canada decision on *Delgamuukw* we have been trying to build up a general reconciliation process to strengthen our people and take us into the future. We see the reconciliation process as having both internal and external components. Internal processes and initiatives are being taken to deal with the lack of unity in inter-*wilp* (house) politics, and on such questions as territory boundaries. Each *wilp* has to go through such a process to heal its wounds and consolidate. Some of this work is going on at the present time. External reconciliation, by contrast, has to do with our relationship to the Crown at both federal and provincial levels of government. Both levels of government have a large number of statutory decision makers who make decisions and judgments on behalf of the Crown without having the jurisdictional authority to do so – such as the awarding of cutting contracts and the establishment of cut levels carried out provincially through the Department of Forests. They put all forest disputes and public issues before something called a Forest Appeals Board.

We consider this wrong. The Province of British Columbia does not possess the jurisdictional rights to do this. I think we ourselves could do this through an Aboriginal rights appeal board, where our rights and those of the two levels of government are worked out.

The reconciliation model that I have put forward is really simple. It just follows the existing constitutional arrangement in the country. You have section 91 of the Canadian Constitution, which gives powers to the federal government. Then you drop down a level to section 92, which deals with the powers of the provincial government. In our model for Confederation and reconciliation, the Gitksan jurisdiction, based on our pre-existing rights, fits right in between them.

This gives a picture of overlapping rights and allows us to see who is doing what, and to see what the House groups have to do to exercise their authority. The Supreme Court decision was clear that the House groups too have their jurisdictional rights, at least in so far as the court said that the title and the rights of the Gitksan were created by two things. One, the occupation of the land by our people, and two, the ancient laws that the Gitksan had developed over time. The Crown never, ever created these things. So that is the power base that the Gitksan are coming from. What we have to do is reconcile what our ancient family authority, our *ayuks eyetxw*, has to say and what all of these legislative objectives that the two levels of the Crown say they are doing: these have to be reconciled.

At the end of the day, what would happen in this model is that you would end up with a co-management regime with this process of interaction between these jurisdictional levels. I do not think we need a treaty to do that. I don't think we need a formal agreement on that at this point. It is simply an exercise in reconciling each other's higher level of authority and operational plans.

This is what I was advocating before we went into the Supreme Court of Canada, and those attempts were frustrated. After the Supreme Court decision in *Delgamuukw* we put this forward again, instead of a treaty. The whole thing fell apart. The only one to accept this was the former premier of British Columbia, Glen Clark. I went there personally and spoke with him. He could understand what I was getting at.

Now, once again, we are having another go at the same kind of approach, with the same constitutional arrangements. You have Canada and British Columbia, and Canada has the jurisdiction to develop higher-level planning. In Canada's case it is the Department of the Environment, Natural Resources Canada, Oil and Gas Canada – those are the higher-level planning entities in the country under the terms of the Constitution. They do all these different things, and at the British Columbia level you have the Ministry of Sustainable Resource Management and the land, water, and air protection ministry – the big ministries into higher-level planning.

In response to this, we are getting into our own higher-level planning, and everybody is reacting to this. All our people are saying, "We don't need their consent. We don't need their support to do high-level planning for the Gitksan." So we are working on fish sustainability plans and *wilp*-based sustainability plans. All those things that the Crown continues to ignore.

Part of this process is getting our watershed administrative tables established. If we can get them off the ground, I think it is a good start for this higher-level planning and the exertion of our jurisdiction and other rights. Some of us began this years ago, probably the same year as McEachern's decision (1991). We have called it the Gitksan Watershed Authorities. This was to send a signal out to our people that we have this legal authority and that we can do this.

We have been consolidating administrative units in recent years: the upper Skeena, the upper Nass, the Suui'gas, the Kispiox, the Suskwa, the Gitsegukla, and the Gitwangax. All of those tables are now established administrative units. Inside each of those watersheds there are the *huwilp,* the House territories, as subunits. We already have a planning model that has been in place for a long time. What the internal exercise is now, is partially to "ground-truth" all the things that our people have been doing in those watersheds.

We have compiled all of the data that the Gitksan have put together over the years. They are now going to be put into binders for the use of the people with territories in each of the watersheds. All the maps, the transcripts from all Aboriginal rights cases – on fishing, forestry, or whatever – commission evidence, supporting affidavits, so that we are developing some pretty sophisticated cultural layer maps for the Gitksan. We have completed the profiles for some of the watersheds, and in there is a cultural layer map that goes with it. The two of these are linked. We will continue to work on this.

All we want to do is show the world that the Gitksan have their own management regimes. Our people always knew what they were doing in the forest. Up the Babine there, we have thousands of hectares of trees bearing the scars that show they were used for food purposes. Really big zones. Big zones for other species too. It was not just hemlock for the nutritious *tso'o* but Jack pine and even birch.

We are looking at the forests in a completely different way from what the province's standard view is. All the province wants is to take the best logs off our territories. We are saying, "No, you can't continue to do that because you have destroyed all the things that each of the watersheds had. All the interconnections." We are carrying out inventories of all the species useful to our economy over the centuries. We have the capacity upstairs here at the treaty office to consolidate all this information. We have obtained all the databases from Canada and British Columbia. There are some new sensory data inventories they are doing now, but I'm sure we will get our hands on them too.

What I see is that we will be able to carry out these plans and then begin our own harvesting. We are in trouble in terms of the forest as it is today. All of the prime areas have been logged already. There are several places on the map where we will have pitched battles over this. One is the Babine Table and the other is just north of Guldo, up the Sincintine. There is another very good timber valley up in the Swingoola. That territory – the whole valley was burned over by the Gitksan. And when you go in there now it is spectacular timber. It is the territory of Wilps Gwininitxw. You can go from the mouth at the Skeena and right to the back of the valley and it is just beautiful old trees.

If you take a look at the work that will come out of this, we can put together our higher-level plans, our harvest plans, and plans for rebuilding the forests. We can interact with the Crown. We are into modelling for these administrative tables. I want to show people that they can do things themselves. They don't need anybody else. One of the things we are seeing with the cut-blocks and plantations is that some of the plantations are in trouble. There is a pathogen problem and the tree becomes spindly, the needle growth is retarded, and they just turn red and they die. It is not just the pine, but the same thing is happening to the spruce as well. All they tell us is that it is a pathogen. What we have said in response is that we want to do more research into this and find out what went wrong, and what is the solution to it. We invited all the senior managers for a field trip out to Kisgagas last summer, in August. We asked their professional opinion as to the solution. All the foresters said the solution was to burn it. We have all the old oral history data from our people about how they burned whole areas to reduce disease, to create berry grounds and stuff. If you look at our cultural air map we have for the Babine, it shows all that. We can go from area to area and show you this information.

What I see the province does is this. They know all this is out there, but they do not want to acknowledge it, and they do not want to research it. We are researching it, and, for example, we can tell you exactly when the burns took place. Coring the trees and the stumps we can say, for instance, well, in 1650 this was burned. This was done in 1740, and this in 1792. So we are bringing forward the real forest management in our territories. What we are telling these arrogant forestry officials is that where these corporations have made the most money is where burning was carried out under Gitksan forest management. You can directly link it by examining the historical record where the first Europeans came through and what they reported.

So all the material you were doing in relation to *Delgamuukw* – the cultural stuff and the work of the historians is all very useful. All the surveyors and traders and geologists. Even those guys from the Ministry of Forests must realize this because they were trying to suppress all those reports and fieldnotes.

The whole forest has changed due to fire suppression under provincial jurisdiction. What we have to do now is come back and start to take over again. I am telling these officials we don't care what you say, we have justice and science on our side. Sybille Hauessler, remember her? [Dr. Hauessler is a forest ecologist who testified as an expert witness for the Gitksan and Witsuwit'en in *Delgamuukw.*] She has done a burn, down on Gitsegukla territory, down along the Copper River. We want to catch up with her and find out what she has learned from that process. We have been managing the territories and using burns for thousands of years, but the officials do not want to see the evidence of this.

All I am saying to the senior managers is this: Here we have an opportunity. You destroyed it in the Gitsegukla area, you destroyed it in the Suskwa, you destroyed it at Gitwangax, and you destroyed it up the Kispiox. And so, all the little pieces that are left, you should leave them alone and use them as a demonstration for the rest of the world, so the world can see what the local population was doing to manage things. I am saying, "You should research it and learn from it." People can come and see it. Come up to Kisgagas and you can see hectare after hectare where the trees were being harvested for food. And that, as history goes, is just recent. There are a few families who are still doing it. What I would like to see is for all the families to go back there and start doing it again. It is a lucrative business. The sweet cambium of immature tree trunks can be harvested and marketed. If we set up the recipes properly, the Seventh Day Adventists at least will be receptive to it. It is very healthy food and has medicinal strength too.

It is the same for the fishing. We are now focusing on the habitat and trying to get going on a fish sustainability plan so we can outflank Canada and the province in terms of modern restoration projects. These are very lucrative sectors of the regional economy. These are going to lead to more fighting on the ground with the different levels of government because the issues here involve basic resources.

The feast system is all connected up in this road to the future. What goes on in the feast involves the connections of the different families with each other, and their identity is tied into the topography of their territories. I saw our experiments with the inland fishery really set the stage for us, occupying the crucial riparian zones along the rivers and creeks. We are now doing research into other areas along the main rivers too.

We have ecological zone mapping going on, and we can go into the tributaries and creeks and do the same, and then the mid-elevation and high-elevation areas and resources. That's the plan, and we want to keep the momentum going and start to do business. We have all the watershed trusts up and started. Every one of the nine tables will have a trust vehicle they can use. Each of these tables signs an agreement called an inter-*wilp* agreement, and the trusts are being set up to hold the land and protect its use for the future generations.

We always have individuals who try to act on their own. Some get taken in by corporations and others want to get their hands on the resources. That is why we are thinking along the lines of trusts. I think every *wilp* should do a trust. The individualism is a problem, and we can work a lot more effectively as collective forces. There is a strong push in society towards individualism. The *simgiget* have a responsibility to keep their members in the collective loop, and, on the other hand, the *wilp* members have the responsibility to make sure they track their chief. There is no excuse now. We have shown everybody how we can make money and assert our own jurisdiction. We can make money on fish, on mushrooms, on wood, on tourism, and on land-based craft-related ventures.

Even with our experience running an inland fishery a few years ago, we had a glimpse of these possibilities. Through it all there is the reality that the Gitksan have always been selling and trading their wealth and produce, and not just eating from the land. They are still selling household items, consumables. They sell *hlo'ots* now for up to fifty dollars, and half-smoked salmon. The Gitksan keep selling their fish cheap, but the possibilities for marketing are good.

We have also been doing stuff on thermal history, the oil and gas potential on the territory. We are using one of the best technologies. We are testing, and we found that oil and gas had formed on our lands sixty million years ago but broke up with the clash of the tectonic plates. We are now trying to track where it has collected. Canada says that there is potential here, and it is not unrelated to the finds in Dixon Entrance. The big problem is to contain and control this future resource collectively.

So there you have it. These are some of the things taking the Gitksan into the future.

Notes

Preface

1 Due to his workload, Professor Lee did not continue with the project, and thus none of whatever errors and omissions occur in what follows can in any way be attributed to him. I remain deeply grateful for his practical encouragement in both this and my earlier doctoral project.

2 The word "clan," used here to refer to exogamic group, and in general use among the contemporary plaintiff peoples, was somewhat confusingly referred to as "phratry" in earlier literature, and what today are called Houses used to be called clans. A phratry (rarely used today) usually refers to a group of clans whose members claim a common origin. Here it is a set of matrilineal Houses within one clan who consider they have a common origin. In some clans there is more than one such grouping of Houses with common origin. Such relatives of common origin among the Gitksan are *wil'naat'ahl*. To add to the complexity, elderly indigenous people of the area frequently use the English word "tribe" to refer to what today are called clans – the Wolves, Eagles, Frog/Ravens, and Fireweed/Killer Whales of the Gitksan, and the Wolves, Small Frogs, Big Frogs, Killer Whales, and Beavers of the Witsuwit'en.

Chapter 1: Introduction

1 "A field may be defined as a network or a configuration of objective relations between positions. These positions are objectively defined ... by their present and potential situation *(situs)* in the structure of the distribution of species of power (or capital) whose possession commands access to the specific profits that are at stake in the field" (Bourdieu and Wacquant 1992, 97).

"A field is a patterned system of objective forces (much in the manner of a magnetic field), a *relational configuration endowed with a specific gravity* which it imposes on the objects and agents which enter it ... A field is simultaneously a *space of conflict and competition*, the analogy here being with a battlefield, in which participants vie to establish monopoly over the species of capital effective in it" (ibid., 17-18).

"Habitus is ... the strategy generating principle enabling agents to cope with unforeseen and everchanging situations ... a system of lasting and transposable dispositions which, integrating past experiences, functions at every moment as a matrix of perceptions, appreciations and actions and makes possible the achievement of infinitely diversified tasks" (ibid., 18).

"The relation between habitus and field operates in two ways. On one side, it is a relation of *conditioning:* the field structures the habitus, which is the product of the embodiment of the immanent necessity of a field (or a set of intersecting fields, the extent of their intersection or discrepancy being at the root of a divided or even torn habitus). On the other side, it is a relation of knowledge or *cognitive construction*" (ibid., 127-8).

2 While Bourdieu (1992 [1977], 82) distinguishes between social space and material space, in this situation, they overlap to a high degree.

3 The Supreme Court of Canada, however, in *Delgamuukw* (S.C.C. file 23799), found that oral history must be accorded greater weight and reliability as evidence vis-à-vis documentary sources.

4 The Supreme Court of Canada ruling on *Delgamuukw* makes a considerable effort to engage in twentieth-century discourse regarding anthropological research, even though it holds fast to the hegemony of British sovereignty and acknowledges no injustices in the assertion of this hegemony. Aboriginal title, for example, remains "a burden on the underlying title of the Crown."

5 The textual adherence to knowledge abstracted from the actual observable world – an often unreflexive practice assumed to be executed out of time and space – is an integral part of scholastic tradition: "The four-fold Stoic qualities of *ataraxia* (imperturbability), *adiophoria* (tolerance), *apatheia* (dispassion) and *epokhe* (suspension of judgement) are the historical roots of this objectivity which has become the characteristic of our social science as a profession ... They have become a means of training in the West, and in the East, and in the end to be sought in professional training which has as its goal the quasi-objective value of judicial, and more generally, judicious neutrality, impartiality, tolerance or indifference and, in the literal sense, balance or suspension of judgement. These qualities are attributed by Hegel to the executive branch of the state, the bureaucrat being exemplary of the Stoic virtues of equanimity, integrity and moderation" (Krader 1980, 27).

6 This statement is not intended to include the competence of the provincial defendants' star "anthropologist," an underwater archaeological geographer who was more akin to a stage-actress playing a dispassionate professor than she was to the real thing. Called by Culhane (1998, 155) "Her Majesty's loyal anthropologist," Sheila Patricia Robinson provided academic arguments in many cases through the 1980s and 1990s to support law firms hired either to prosecute First Nations peoples or to defend government from First Nations plaintiffs. She was a professional witness and not a practising scholar or academic.

7 The judge's Reasons for Judgment incorporates several bodies of data directly from the "anthropological" documents submitted by the provincial defendants. See, for example, Schedule 4 on the purportedly postcontact features of Gitksan *adaawk'* oral histories (McEachern 1991, 315-30).

8 Countervailing views and alternative positions are found in Solway and Lee (1990); Lee and Guenther (1991); Lee (1992); Kent (1992); and Headland (1997). Bird-David (1992a, 1992b, 1994) has suggested shifting hunter-gatherer studies away from the centrality of ecology and subsistence and towards social relational questions. More Olympian overviews of developments in this discourse include Barnard (1983); Myers (1988); Burch and Ellanna (1994); Burch (1994); and Ingold (1986, 1999).

9 As far back as the 1830s, Lewis Henry Morgan was predicting the end of the seminal Midwinter Ceremonies of the horticultural/hunter/trader Iroquois due to the rapid changes that followed the American War of Independence. Fenton (1936, 1941) made similar statements about the same institution a century later. The rumours of the death of the Midwinter Ceremonies are still somewhat exaggerated.

10 Bourdieu (1990, 99) urges social science to opt for such risk-oriented, temporal approaches to social institutions: "To reintroduce uncertainty is to reintroduce time, with its rhythm, its orientation and its irreversibility, substituting the dialectic of strategies for the mechanics of the model, but without falling over into the imaginary anthropology of 'rational actor' theories."

11 Houses have great scope for expanding the status of certain House names, such that entrepreneurial political activity percolates through internal House affairs within the system of ascriptive statuses. There are quite a few examples of the names held by a large personality in one House in the 1920s being superseded decades later by another name held by another strong personality.

12 Gitksan maintain that they wove their own tapestry-weave Chilkat blankets and did not import them. I, as the token male, participated in a Chilkat weaving course in 1991 given by an Interior Tlingit woman who had received training from Cheryl Samuel, Chilkat weaver and author of the lavish book on that art (Samuel 1982).

13 Bill Reid himself contributed artwork to help the Gitksan and Witsuwit'en land rights case, *Delgamuukw.*

Chapter 2: The Reciprocities of a Pole-Raising Feast

1 The information assembled here comes from a number of elderly Gitksan women experienced in feast organizing. I had asked them to teach me by recreating a virtual (ideal type) pole-raising feast. I peppered them with questions based upon queries that had come to me while attending three or four pole-raisings, and they themselves frequently called me back to give further clarification. There is more emphasis here on the procedures used in the eastern villages, although the contours are the same in the western villages.

2 "Potlatch" was a nineteenth-century Chinook trade jargon word for "give," yet, in the literature it has become associated primarily with the competitive giving of escalating amounts of value, the destruction of property, and the material impoverishment of the hosts; second, its use frequently confounds feasting activities with winter dance ceremonies, and third, it is associated publicly with "the excesses of Aboriginal culture" and with the consequent suppression of Aboriginal ceremonial life under the Potlatch Law from 1885 to 1952. The broader institution from which potlatching grew is what practitioners call "the feast," or, occasionally, *baahlats.*

3 Such as Adams (1973); Barnett (1938, 1968); Benedict (1934); Beynon (n.d.); Boas (1897, 1966 [Codere, ed.], 1966 [McFeat, ed.]); Boelscher (1988); Codere (1950); Clutesi (1950); Drucker (1963, 1965); Drucker and Heizer (1967); Garfield (1966); Goldman (1975); Halpin (1973); Jenness (1943); Kan (1989); Krause (1956); Lévi-Strauss (1969); Mauss (1990); Mills (1994); Nash (1964); Oberg (1973); Piddocke (1965); Rosman and Rubel (1971); Rubel and Rosman (1983); Seguin (1984, 1985); Suttles (1960, 1962, 1968); Vayda (1961); and Walens (1981).

4 Government has decreed that Gitksan and Witsuwit'en lands belong to the Crown; these peoples dispute this ownership and are currently setting up watershed authorities to protect dwindling forest resources and to assert their respective management rights (see Afterword).

5 Current genealogies do not, in general, extend back very far into colonial history.

6 Some *adaawk*'s recount names of leaders from sections of two different clans sharing common events of in-migration and the overcoming of crisis. This recalled affinity is marked by cooperation in relation to feasting, especially in confirming each other's histories, names, and crests.

7 Wilps Spookw, for example, holds in dormancy the chiefly names of other Houses in their *wil'naat'ahl,* and Wilps Luutkudjiiwus has recently revitalized one of the names in its safekeeping. See note 10, below.

8 After their families' long experience of vehemently negative missionary pronouncements on the rich hermeneutics of Tsimshianic culture, many current feast leaders are reticent about discussing the spiritual, symbolic, and shamanic features of the proceedings.

9 Leading chiefs speak at the feast's end on the basis of their kinship and geographical distance from the hosts. The opposite side of the host village, the host's *'nidinsxwit,* or *'nidilx,* speaks first, and the most distant villages speak last.

10 In recent years, for instance, in the Gitanmaax Lax̱ Se'el (Frog/Raven) Clan, Simoogit Xsimits'iin has reasserted his independence as a House chief, which formerly came under the roof of the House of Luutkudjiiwus. Guu Hat'akxw, a Gitanmaax Wolf chief name, has been held by the House of Spookw since the death of the most recent incumbent.

11 A major *glok* was held by a Nisga'a chief on the Nass River as recently as October 2002, after a hiatus of many years. The host spoke of his transgressions. Those who had suffered from his transgressions spoke as well. He was then disrobed by his father's side, and his garments were burned. He was washed and ritually redressed. The witnesses were paid and a lavish feast followed (Val Napoleon, personal communication).

12 "Phratry" is the term frequently used in the literature to refer to *pdeek̲,* but phratry is properly a term referring to two or more clans who claim common descent from a purported ancestor and, hence, is misleading in Tsimshian culture. The *wil'naat'ahl* principle is more flexible and relates people to narratives of origin – the *adaawk̲'.* *Pdeek̲* is commonly referred to by these peoples as "clan."

13 Judge McEachern made much of the complaints by elders that the young people do not follow the old ways. In my estimation this is part of the pedagogical arsenal of the old who try to discipline the young. Kathleen Matthews, the mother of the present Tenimget, catches herself saying such nihilistic things to her grandchildren. "I call them rotten kids who aren't interested in any of the old ways, then I laugh, because Grannie used to say exactly the same thing to us." Trigger (1976) found the same response among the elderly of the seventeenth-century Huron, as reported in *The Jesuit Relations*, regarding youths who defied the wishes and agendas of their elders, and received warning that they too would come to a no-good end (often for threatening diplomatic relations with other nations for raiding without the permission or blessing of their elders).

14 The sources for the substantive material in the following account are my interview notes, the transcripts of evidence by Kyologet (Mary McKenzie), Antgulilibix (Mary Johnson), Gwaans (Olive Ryan), Gisdaywa (Alfred Joseph), discussions and interview material with Ha'naamuxw (Joan Ryan), Gamlaxyeltxw (Solomon Marsden), Tenimget (Art Mathews Jr.), (Gwamoon) Pearl Trombley, Wii Goob'l (Jessie Sterritt), Gwisgen (Stanley Williams), Lilloos (Emma Michel), and Yaga'lahl (Dora Wilson). I have learned much from my experience as feast guest among both Witsuwit'en and Gitksan peoples, the pole-raising of Guxsen in Gitsegukla in 1986, the pole invocation ceremony of Ha'naamuxw (which was held beside the pole in the garden of the carver, Earl Muldon, who is the current Simoogit Delgamuukw, in April 1987, and later the Ha'naamuxw pole-raising. (Since this period I have attended several more pole-raisings in Gitsegukla and Gitanyow.) The documentary sources of most utility have been the William Beynon notebooks of the 1945 Gitsegukla pole-raisings (Barbeau and Beynon 1915-57, B-F-425-428; Anderson and Halpin 2000), which were also described by Gwaans in her evidence and "updated" a few years later when the Ha'naamuxw poles were raised.

15 LaViolette (1972) and Titley (1986).

16 Cultural change is not always cultural genocide. Often features of the system of meaning and value lie fallow or are actively suppressed, only to reappear, as needed, under subsequent social conditions, especially in cultures that pay attention to, and organize socially and politically from, dream prophecies (Daly 1985).

17 The *adaawk*'s suggest that, long ago, the dedication of the House structure, covered with crest figures externally and containing posts covered with the same figures, served as a *daxget* conduit similar to that of the totem pole. House dedication probably fulfilled the role that subsequently came to be associated with pole-raising.

18 Modern technology aims to extend the longevity of poles with preservatives and concrete footings, but people say the continuity of the crests derives not from the actual pole but from an imprint on the mind, which springs from the ancestors who first walked the land.

19 Although I am aware of powerful contributions of non-Natives like Duane Pasco, Bill Holm, Wilson Duff, Polly Sargent, George MacDonald, and others to the "Northwest Coast Renaissance" in Hazelton and other areas over the last quarter century, the old aesthetics and craftsmanship were not entirely dead. Young carvers were learning from old ones, from old artifacts, from each other, as well as from the practical and documentary efforts of those like Holm (1965) and Pasco. The material culture had reached a low ebb, but it had not expired. In recent decades a cross-cultural team effort has brought it to ever-wider attention.

20 The late Mrs. Polly Sargent of Hazelton was instrumental in this effort through the Skeena Totem Pole Restoration Society. The process is documented in Dawn (1981).

21 The old Ha'naamuxw pole, raised in 1991 for the third time, was also carved by the "father's side," by Tom Campbell, Luutkudjiiwus of the Gitanmaax Frog/Raven Pdeek (Barbeau 1929, 184). It was raised for the second time after the poles of the village had washed away in a river flood. This occurred in 1945 during the potlatch ban (see Anderson and Halpin 2000). It was subsequently taken down by the band council without the owners' consent. Wilps Ha'naamuxw raised this same pole for the third time in 1991, together with a new pole commemorating the current Ha'naamuxw's predecessors and her father's side.

22 The eighty-one-foot pole of the Nisga'a chief Mountain, which is now in the stairwell of the Royal Ontario Museum, holds many crests belonging to other clans, as the pole

appears to have been raised in the spirit of fur trade competition, probably in the 1860s (Barbeau 1950). In Gitksan eyes, the use of more than one or two non-*wil'naat'ahl* crests is not considered appropriate as it signals the pole-raiser's feeling of "crest-poverty" in his own family. It can also indicate, in a not so subtle manner, the chief's intentions to appropriate the crests of others.

23 Informants reported having witnessed such an action in Kispiox prior to the Second World War.

24 The "mattress" and "blanket" can also be construed as contributions to the proper preparations for the repose of the deceased.

25 This is suggestive of Weiner's (1992) contention that, on the weavings of women, stand the grand gift-givings that make and reinforce men's status.

26 The western Gitksan of Gitanyow, Gitwangax, and Gitsegukla call the Frog/Raven Clan, the Ganeda, while the eastern villages refer to it as Lax̱ Se'el.

27 Bone fragments from earlier cremations of former *wilp simgiget* were sometimes attached to the pole. The canoe resting in the arms of a crest figure on one of Delgamuukw's poles in Kispiox once contained the ash and bones of the deceased (Antgulilibix, personal communication). In this sense the pole-raising is the final touch of the double obsequies of the Northwest Coast mortuary ceremony.

28 See note 11 above for recent variation among the neighbouring Nisga'a.

29 In *Delgamuukw* the defence counsel expended much effort reducing the feast complex to a postcontact ceremonial excrescence of the fur trade. They utilized Barbeau's (1929, 1950) contention that pole-raising was postcontact in origin. This was based on the fact that early explorers made few reports of poles being raised and on the difficulty of carving cedar without iron, both points adequately refuted in some detail by Drucker (1948) and Duff (1964). Obviously poles are ephemeral objects in the climates of the Northwest Coast, and they, like all social phenomena, have histories of development. Certainly they became bigger, more elaborate, and more sculptural in postcontact times. Contemporary carvers assume that, if their ancestors could make stone sculptures such as those assembled by Duff (1975), then they could sculpt wood as well. They also believe that iron has found its way across/around the North Pacific for a very long time. In what appear to be the most ancient portions of the *adaawk'* narratives, there is generally no mention of poles, though one gets the impression of carved house posts and other regalia plus the exhibition of narrative crests woven into the tapestry-weave Chilkat blankets (MacDonald 1984). Important feasting seems to have occurred to validate newly built houses, occasions used for commemorating a generation of deceased kin and the centuries of ancestors. Some informants say that the veneration of the ancestor through poles was preceded by the "talking stick," which has a chiefly name and "wears" the family's crests, and reminds the owners of their stories and songs of exquisite mourning. I attended an invocation feast for the talking stick of Simoogit G̱amlax̱yeltxw of Gitanyow/Kitwancool in late September 1993, which, in abbreviated form, followed the procedures described above for pole-raising. In my opinion, whatever the plastic art form associated with the ceremonies, the structure of reciprocal social credit and debt relations has been functioning for a very long time.

Chapter 3: A Giving Environment

1 A leading precedent for limited rights to Aboriginal land due to usufruct was the case known as *St. Catherines Milling and Lumber Co. v. the Queen* (1887). A century later, this case was still being cited as reason for limiting claims to ownership by McEachern, C.J., in *Delgamuukw*. The Supreme Court of Canada ruling on *Delgamuukw* replaced the organized society test used in cases like *St. Catherines Milling* and *Baker Lake* for a title test based on occupancy and ownership. Nowadays, First Nations asserting title must ensure that the land has been occupied prior to British sovereignty, that if present occupancy is argued there must be continuity with pre-British sovereignty occupancy, and that at sovereignty occupancy must have been exclusive.

2 Barbeau and Beynon n.d. (reprinted 1989, National Museums of Canada). These include *adaawk*'s 1-2, 4-6, 8, 12, 16-17, 20, 27-8, 30-3, 35-7, 40, 43-4, 46-50, 52, 55-8, 61, 64, 66, 70, 75, 76, 79, 81, 83. Similar references abound in the other clan *adaawk*'s.

3 In reviewing the allegedly diffused modernisms noted by Sheila Robinson (researcher for the provincial defendants in *Delgamuukw*) in the *adaawk*'s and appended to Chief Justice McEachern's Reasons for Judgment, one can only say that it was an exercise in decontextualized "essentialism." According to Robinson, the possession of any item of technology at variance with the popular image of the "traditional Indian" negates the identity of the people and their right to live like anyone else: namely, in a state of cultural flux AND continuity. Most of Robinson's alleged modernisms are indeed from recent *adaawk*'s and have been acknowledged as such by the indigenous tellers and/or scholars such as Wilson Duff; the indigenous nature of other features, such as "red hair," the two-storey house mentioned in the *adaawk*'s of the Gitsegukla Gisk'aast Clan, the use of copper, the presence of moose, and so on are still debatable open-ended questions. The thinking that draws up such lists and appends them to reports is clouded by hubris, the notion that Aboriginal peoples have a past without history, and a belief in the set-in-amber type of small primitive society, ticking away in perpetuum and lacking all contact with the outside world. Jurists who hold these views subscribe to the outdated notion that aboriginality of culture must have been pristine and uncontaminated by social intercourse with other peoples or even with the prevailing, and changing, ideas of different epochs. If John Donne maintained that "no man is an island, entire of itself," then the colonial corollary might be "unless he or she happens to be an Aboriginal person."

4 There seems to be no consensus about standardizing the spelling of this fish, which has swum into our world from oral cultures of the North Pacific. "Oolichan," "ooligan," "eulachon," and "olachen" are some of the most common forms; others use the term "candlefish," which derives from this fish's burning properties.

5 Since the trial years (1987-1991), both peoples have slightly changed the orthography of their names (from Gitksan to Gitxsan and now, to a degree, back to Gitksan or Gitksen, and from Wet'suwet'en to Witsuwit'en).

6 The limit of red cedar habitat is just down-river from Moricetown.

7 This is suggested in the evidence of Alfred Joseph and in my interviews with him; Olive Ryan, Don Ryan (personal communication), and others indicated that women were more directly conscious of their fertility cycles prior to the arrival of missionaries.

8 The two generations spell their surname slightly differently.

9 Counsel for the provincial defendants were fascinated by the "Little Ice Age" and argued throughout the case that human life would have been impossible until climate abatement in the early nineteenth century. Thus voila! – the plaintiffs become recent immigrants "just like everybody else."

10 It was also a staple of soups served on political blockades against logging operations in the territories during my time in the region.

11 Data for this section taken from elderly plaintiffs' evidence in *Delgamuukw* (Transcripts and Commission Evidence). Many of these persons were raised at the beginning of the twentieth century and were acculturated on the land during the seasonal round. They were instructed by elders who, in turn, experienced the seasonal round of the early nineteenth century. Other data were taken from written records and the experiences of younger Gitksan and Witsuwit'en.

12 Kenneth Muldoe, who was Simoogit Delgamuukw, passed away 8 April 1990, and his funeral feast was held on 12 April 1990 in his home village of Kispiox. Albert Tait, the previous Delgamuukw, who filed the Statement of Claim to take the two peoples' claim to court also died in the course of events, shortly before the trial opened in 1987. The present Delgamuukw is Kenneth Muldoe's brother, the artist Earl Muldon.

13 Sources: Daly Interviews (1986-88); Book Builders (1980); Transcripts (Olive Ryan, Mary Johnson); commission (Martha Brown); archaeological record; Barbeau and Beynon *adaawk*'s; and ethnohistorical sources cited for Witsuwit'en.

14 Charlotte Sullivan now holds the chief name Wii Goob'l. This "hearsay" evidence was bolstered in court with photo exhibits of the cabin in question.

15 This level of predation is said to have produced a relatively high marmot population. When certain areas were no longer regularly harvested/hunted, subsequent hunters reported a marked fall in the number of marmot in the region (Daly 1986-88 [A. Joseph interviews]).

16 Daly (1986-88) (David Blackwater).
17 Snowshoes were also part of the traditional material culture of this region. Mr. Blackwater said that a person without snowshoes could keep the trails open if he was not lazy and walked the line, checking the traps constantly, especially during snowstorms.

Chapter 4: A Kinship Economy

1 All those whose daily lives are shared with – or who are married to, descended from, or adopted by – House members are part of the necessary relations of social reproduction, which are essential to the ontological functioning of the Houses.
2 Even today, House-member clustering on reserves, around matriarchs, or in the vicinity of a chief and his sisters is a significant residential feature.
3 Some clans have several other crests that define them as well (Jenness 1943; Duff n.d.).
4 The orthography used in *Delgamuukw* is retained here for clan and House names, although the Witsuwit'en are now shifting to a standard Revised Hildebrandt orthography.
5 Kitwancool, the Gitksan village closest to the Nisga'a Nation, decided not to participate in *Delgamuukw*. They have recently changed their village name back to its earlier designation, Gitanyow.
6 See Marsden (1987) and her oral history reconstruction and analysis in Sterritt et al. (1998), as well as in Cybulski (2001).
7 I recall the sotto voce objections made by defence counsel when this evidence on affinal and consanguineal legitimacy of land use was adduced. Counsel muttered in a clearly audible voice, "So everybody is related to everybody. So what? That's not social organization, it's chaos." But it was too structured and logical for chaos: Shortly after my court testimony, Alfred Mitchell died in an industrial accident at Moricetown. His funeral feast was hosted jointly by the Gitludahl (Gitksan) Gisk̲'aast and the Namox (Witsuwit'en) Tsayu in the Kya Wiget community hall. All those (and their direct descendants) described in court by Mr. Mitchell as his closest hunting associates and relations were the dominant figures in the feasting that marked his passing.
8 Carrying the remains of the deceased to the home place for obsequies is said to have given rise to the Europeans' name for the Witsuwit'en and their eastern neighbours: namely, Carrier. This has been graphically represented by Witsuwit'en artist Robert Sebastian.
9 Informants, *adaawk̲'* narratives, and the archaeological record of regional non-perishable items (e.g., Boas 1916; Barbeau and Beynon 1915-57; Drucker 1963, 1965; MacDonald 1979, 1980).
10 See Cole and Darling (1990), who found that, for a long period of time, trade with Europeans failed to transform the indigenous economy and that First Nations dictated to the foreigners which goods they were willing to accept (i.e., goods that conformed to their traditional needs). This article appeared subsequent to my report. Similar points of view have been made by many others, such as Wike (1951); Suttles (1951); Ruby and Brown (1976); and Fisher (1977).
11 Book Builders of 'Ksan (1980) and Franz Boas's introduction to *Tsimshian Mythology* (Boaz 1916).
12 This was written prior to the high unemployment in the region's forest industry during the late 1990s.
13 McEachern took to heart the statements by elderly Gitksan and Witsuwit'en that the young people do not obey, do not follow the old ways, and he used this as evidence that the young have, for the most part, given up on Native ways. Were he familiar with the pedagogical methods of elders in most "anthropological societies," he would realize that their lamentation regarding change and lack of respect from the young is a near universal phenomenon – a point that I belaboured in my introductory chapter of the original opinion evidence report in relation to my experience with similar accounts of intergenerational complaints, recorded by the Jesuits, who were doing "fieldwork" among the recently discovered Huron and Iroquois in the early 1600s.
14 First, from the archaeological record: George MacDonald (1979, 37-8) found that the trade routes into Gitksan country were extremely old and, as major trading corridors, became important between 2,000 and 3,000 years ago. Foreign trade goods, especially obsidian for

arrow points and flake tools, have been found in archaeological sites at Moricetown, Hagwilget, and Kitselas, some of these items dating back several millennia (Albright 1987; Ames 1979; Coupland 1988). Jewellery, labrets, and lip pins – status items at contact – appear in archaeological sites along the Skeena River and suggest time depth to interior-coastal trade and exchange, as well as enmity and social status (MacDonald and Inglis 1976; Ames 1981). In relation to the oral histories that describe the protocontact period, there are numerous accounts of raids/territorial trespass wherein new weapons are mentioned and, in one instance, a green frothing at the mouth among those who invaded the Kisgagas country. The Gitksan explained this as spiritual *halayt* power (Raven/Frog Adaaw<u>k</u>' 83), but it could well have been a case of cholera. Such incidents can be ascribed to competition and territorial invasion, which swept ahead of the fur trade both westward from the Rocky Mountains and eastward from the Pacific coast. Contemporary elders also told the stories that their elders had witnessed in which recent skirmishes occurred with northern peoples. See La<u>x</u> Gibuu chief, Guuhada<u>k</u>xw (Thomas Wright, Commission Evidence II, 118 [ll.36-67], p.120 [ll.20-6]). 'Niik'aap told of the Nass River people invading Guldo'o with steel knives, which caused the villagers to move downstream to Kisgagas (David Gunanoot, Commission Evidence, 55-6), and Ganeda chief Lelt told of peace negotiations at Meziadin Lake, where the two sides put down their guns (Fred Johnson, Commission Evidence, 57-60). Lelt's account is similar to that collected from his predecessors (Barbeau and Beynon n.d., *Wolf Clan Invaders* No. 63-5), and David Gunanoot's account was very similar to that collected from David's father, the famous fugitive Simon Gunanoot, in 1923 by Beynon (Barbeau and Beynon n.d., No. 66) and in Barbeau's Frog/Raven Adaaw<u>k</u>' No. 81, recorded at Kispiox in 1920 (Barbeau and Beynon 1915-57). The events recounted by Thomas Wright for the *Delgamuukw* trial were recorded in Beynon's fieldnotes of 1923, from one "Abraham Gaidax<u>k</u>et," who said that the man who arranged the peace was, in 1923, still living. These events are further corroborated by Jenness in his 1924 fieldnotes from a visit to the Sekani, wherein a young woman of the Long Grass Sekani had been married to a boy from Kispiox as part of the peace agreement. Jenness (1937, 11, 17-8) stated that the Sekani had been pushed west by the fur trade, by the Beaver and the Cree east of the Rockies. Much older enmities and migrations are told with equal detail (e.g., the testimony of Tenimget, Art Mathews [Transcripts, 4730-3, 4778]).

15 Archaeological confirmation has not advanced very far on this matter, as the acid soils and long-term changes to the course of the river confluence would have radically disturbed residential sites.

16 Such feasts generally have incurred additional expenses of several tens of thousands of dollars, over and above the public exchanges witnessed in the feast hall.

17 The Moricetown political leaders felt that their land had been misused, the tree cover damaged, and the jobs subsequently created unattainable by their constituents, who are the ancient owners of these territories. Thus they decided to start their own sawmill and apply for a cutting licence, even though the cut-block method of harvesting contradicted all their own feelings about how to treat the forest. They were between the proverbial rock and a hard place.

18 Perhaps their highest value accrued when they were broken and distributed, either to the ancestors of all things (by being cast into the river or sea) or to the assembled guests. Even today, the feast term for the person counting the contributions is translated as "the one who breaks the coppers."

Chapter 5: Production Management and Social Hierarchy

1 Bird-David writes that, over the last thirty years, the term hunter-gatherer has acquired a broad set of meanings that include engagement with nature, a mode of sociality, and an environmental perception and ideology. "The pursuit of hunting and gathering in and of itself – let alone its pursuit in exclusion of other activities – must not and cannot any longer be the crucial criterion for membership in the category of classification" (Bird-David 1999, 235).

2 Babine people are known formally as Nedut'en, though in common Witsuwit'en speech they are known as "the people over there," or U'inwit'en (Sharon Hargus, personal communication).

3 This is an additional feature of their earlier appellation by Europeans: Carriers. They carried the elderly with them when they moved between summer and winter camps. They carried the deceased to the home territories for proper death obsequies; and they carried goods and supplies, even transporting boxes of oolichan oil up the steep trail from Haisla country on the Gardner Canal.

4 Elderly people, evaluating candidates for bridegroom to their granddaughters, note the size and quality of firewood stacked outside the candidate's dwelling as an indicator of his industriousness. In the past, potential brides were similarly assessed in relation to freshness and aromatic quality of the spruce boughs spread across the floors of dwellings. Old boughs losing needles and turning brown suggested laziness, the deadliest of sins in a world of cold winters and seasonal resources.

5 While these sentiments were made in the context of a court action against government jurisdiction over "First Nations" rights, they are an honest reflection of social interdependence: the tolerance, concern, and respect that the Gitksan and Witsuwit'en exhibit locally, and that coexists with local conflicts and competitions. People compete but realize that there are limits to competition among those who come face to face almost daily.

6 Government transfer payments are considered a right and are integral to today's subsistence. Gitksan and Witsuwit'en see pensions, welfare, and housing grants as a small payment that government makes to acknowledge its unjust appropriation of House lands. At the same time, these "handouts" do much to reduce local self-esteem, and they increase the elders' and political leaders' determination to press for recognition of land title as a basis for engaging in land-based, self-supporting enterprises.

7 One of the families I came to know quite well had recently become the matrilineal segment to hold the House's highest chiefly name. The chief's mother decided that the high office should be shared with the opposing matrilineal fraction "to balance things out" and minimize bad feelings. I asked why her immediate descendants did not retire or rest one of the chiefly names so as to give her son a free run as head of the House. Her reply revealed a concern for the heritage and well-being of the whole House. She stressed that too much wealth had been raised and expended in defending the heritage of the House and its names to jeopardize this by not sharing power and compromising personal prestige for the well-being of the corporate unit to which she and her children belonged. Discussions with elders in other Houses reflected a similar concern for a balance to competition. With this outlook among participants, many disagreements unfold very slowly, often over several generations. Each new incumbent to feast names advances his or her claims, but carefully, so as not to cause an irreparable division in House solidarity.

8 This common migration legitimacy has parallels among the Maori, who discuss their potential links with one another on the basis of arriving in the homeland in the same canoe, or the same migration. This applies only to the Gitksan *wil'naat'ahl*, as the Witsuwit'en *pdeek̲* say they have always been in their current territories.

9 *Delgamuukw* interview material gathered by researcher Susan Marsden (personal communication).

10 Kan (1989, 235), speaking of the waxing and waning of competition and potlatching among the Tlingit, concludes: "in general, social differentiation increased from the middle to the end of the nineteenth century and then decreased again in the twentieth."

11 Conversely, the eastern Gitksan and Witsuwit'en tend to feel that their social relations have traditionally been more philosophically subtle, civilized, and spiritual than have those of the more westerly peoples, whom they view as aggressive and ostentatious. A similar local perception between coastal and inland peoples (as relating particularly to winter dance procedures) pertains among the Halkomélem peoples of the lower Fraser River regarding their sea-going neighbours (Siemches, Chief Frank Malloway, Culture/Heritage Officer, Sto:lo Nation, personal communication).

12 The descending order mentioned here is somewhat deceptive for those who hail from a state society in which all individuals theoretically have a clear view of the extent and configuration of society. In Gitksan society, by contrast, nobody is much concerned by the overall, structural whole. Ranking is viewed as somewhat piecemeal, with the greatest attention to detail paid to the immediate villagers and region. Ordering of the Houses is enthusiastically affirmed by some and almost denied by others. The descending order is

that seen from the perspective of the two ritual leading chiefs, who rank their clan Houses according to their distance from their own respective adaaw<u>k</u>'s and crests of origin (which Houses are descendants of first arrivals in the region and which are not). Those not so highly ordered validate their own potential status with other oral narratives and with polite comments on the failings of the more highly ranked to live up to their claimed status. In a word, levelling factors occur constantly during the course of social interaction.

13 David Aberle in Dyen and Aberle (1974), and personal communication, posits (from a comparison of the relative economy with which regional kinship terminology evolved) that the centre of the Proto-Athapaskan language was a salmon-eating matrilineal culture located in the region between northern British Columbia and the Copper River area of Alaska. Earlier, scholars assumed that Proto-Athapaskan culture was bilateral and centred in the Great Bear Lake area of the central subarctic, but this is not indicated by Aberle's compilations. Aberle indicates the matrilineal Proto-Athapaskan region may have been a factor in the development of matrilineal kinship and exogamous clans in the cordillera region, although he is of the opinion that social hierarchy and the elaboration of feasting later diffused inland from the adjacent coast.

14 The acknowledgment of an inland, cordilleran social structure providing the basis of later coastal elaborations is also found in Kan (1989, chap. 10) in the conclusion to his reconstruction of nineteenth-century Tlingit mortuary rituals (the elaborate double obsequies and the associated system of meanings central to potlatch procedure). Kan stresses a matrilineal moiety division associated with commemoration of the dead among the western subarctic Athapaskans, a division that was probably the basis for the more complex moiety, clan, and House relations along the adjacent north coast. Others, like de Laguna and Aberle, have related rudimentary matriliny in this region to partial sedentarization due to the regular salmon runs that appear to have begun in the late Holocene.

15 Of course more archaeological work is needed before such hypotheses can be tested. Archer (2001), for example, has reported evidence of ranked society in Prince Rupert Harbour almost 2,000 years ago.

16 Citing the artifact record in Kitselas Canyon, Prince Rupert Harbour, weir sites in southeast Alaska, and changes at sites on the Queen Charlotte Islands, Matson and Coupland (1995, 183) have recently said: "This period [3200 to 2700 BP] on the north coast witnesses the introduction of permanent villages of multifamily houses, intensive exploitation of fish resources, especially salmon, and large-scale storage, all core elements of the Developed Northwest Coast Pattern."

17 In time we might have sufficient archaeological data to determine which features of the regional culture moved down the rivers to the coast and which diffused back upriver. The *adaaw<u>k</u>'* histories indicate that cultural elaboration was not all one way.

18 Hindle and Rigsby (1973) and Halpin and Seguin (1990, 276). This is asserted today by the Gitksan, especially when joking with Tlingit visitors.

19 Gitksan tend to put a good spin on slaves. They suggest that, generally, slaves were not labourers so much as young companions and helpmates to the children of their wealthy masters. They claim that the presence of slaves was occasional and that their proportion of the population was negligible.

20 Circa AD 1500 to 1800, a period noted for population decrease due to epidemics that frequently preceded the Europeans. It was also the period of Ne<u>k</u>t, the warrior with whom MacDonald (1980) has long been fascinated, and of the appearance of Russian iron goods from the north.

21 Such marriage arrangements do occur. The late Arthur Matthews Sr. was raised on the land of his father's side, and he subsequently married one of the women whose children would legally inherit that land. In this way his immediate family became consolidated on the legitimate land of the children, where the Frog Clan father, Art Matthews Sr., was able to teach his own Wolf Clan children their land-based skills, their history, crests, songs, and dances, and to do so precisely where these family emblems are said to have come into being.

Chapter 6: Gifts, Exchange, and Trade

1 This is a glaring example of the sort of damage done to the advance of social theory and its empirical backing, which seems to be endemic in consultative anthropology. As contract

workers rather than tenured members of the academic establishment we lose the privilege of independent thought and the luxury of following the path down which logic takes us, especially if this is an ideologically contentious path. We have to be objective and careful in our work, yes, but at the same time most of us feel a commitment and responsibility towards those who employ us. Perhaps such problems should be made an explicit part of our research (Daly 2003).

2 Oolichan consumption: Using the figures supplied by Kuhnlein (1984) and Kuhnlein et al. (1982), and the fact that a substance like oolichan oil, which is 99 percent fat, contains approximately nine calories per gram (Richard Lee, personal communication), the following calculations were made. If one litre of water, which has a slightly greater specific gravity than fish oil, weighs 1,000 grams, then one litre of oolichan oil will weigh approximately one kilogram and contain 9,000 calories. An oolichan grease box used for freighting the grease into the upper Skeena area averaged, very conservatively, twenty-five kilograms. Assuming fifty persons on average resident in each of the Houses said to exist in protocontact times, or at least in times before European-introduced epidemics, then there was a population of approximately 10,000. Kuhnlein found that, under modern conditions, one family of five consumed five million calories of grease in a year at Nuxalk in the Bella Coola region, in order to gain 6.8 percent of their annual caloric needs. To obtain 6.8 percent of caloric needs per family of five would require twenty-two boxes of grease being packed over the trails from the spawning grounds, solely for local consumption.

Gitksan and Witsuwit'en consumption was thus probably considerably less than that 6.8 percent consumed by modern Nuxalk people, with their ready access to the fish. With a Gitksan-Witsuwit'en population of 10,000 and double or triple relay loads along the trails, with dogs carrying an additional ten to twenty kilograms, the people could feasibly have transported enough grease to supply each family of five with the equivalent of five to six gallons (approximately twenty-five litres), and distributed approximately the same amount in local gifts and barter with inland neighbours. This would have entailed about 4,000 boxes of grease moving inland each spring and increasing in value as it moved further from its sources. The amount of grease people like to have on hand today is about a gallon. This is kept in the refrigerator and used for special occasions. That is approximately 20 percent of the contents of one grease box.

3 Jenness (1943, 478) suggests that the Gitksan may have discouraged the Witsuwit'en from travelling to the Nass River source of grease in order to protect their own intermediary role with Athapaskan-speaking peoples further east.

4 These rock writings were said by the Witsuwit'en to be trail messages written in red ochre but using Father Morice's syllabic script (Andrew George, Alfred Joseph, personal communication).

5 Artifact registration/accession files, Canadian Museum of Civilization, Ottawa.

6 The late Mary George and Christine Holland spoke of combining eel skin and strips of rabbit hide to weave "rabbit blankets" the way they did "in the old times" (Moricetown Elders n.d.).

7 This explanation of hostages/slaves was given by the elderly to the young. Some of my elderly informants learned this nineteenth-century point of view in their own childhood early in the twentieth century and related it to the ethnographer late in the twentieth century.

8 Here are the words of Rena Bolton, a craftswoman and keeper of the Salish *sxwaixwe* who is resident on Tsimshian land at Kitsumkalum: "Human sacrifice was practiced at that time by some of our coastal tribes. Slaves were forced to enter the open post-hole which was to be the foundation for a new totem pole. The slave would be made to sit with the knees bent and chin on knees. His arms would be wrapped around his legs. The huge totem pole would then be erected on top of him. The result was a very gory death" (Daly fieldnotes 1988-2002).

9 Before becoming a Christian, Ligeex, according to Arctander (1909, 133), had threatened the missionary William Duncan, who was defended at gunpoint by Clah.

Chapter 7: Owners and Stewards

1 The paradox is that the largest proprietors today, whose holdings often span many nation-states, have the power to avoid paying requisite national taxes. Historically, such disparities

tend to contribute to social unrest as they violate the popular belief that the privilege of ownership ought to be seen to be paid for through tax, philanthropy, and so on.

2 From an interview kindly shown me by Antonia Mills.

3 During the *Delgamuukw* trial, one such crest marker was found in the course of a logging cut-block operation at one of the boundaries of Simoogit Ge'el's land in the Kispiox Valley (photo in Monet and Skanu'u 1992, 210).

4 Descriptions are often graphic. The Witsuwit'en refer to Hudson Bay Mountain (Smithers), where the glacier is framed between the peaks, as "Her knees are open."

5 Orthography of these snare locations has not been vetted by linguists.

6 President of the Gitksan-Wet'suwet'en Tribal Council at that time.

7 The second All Clans Feast concerning systems of territorial reckoning used between the Witsuwit'en and Gitksan on one side, and the Carrier-Sekani Tribal Council on the other. See Mills's (1994, 44-55) description of the first feast, a year earlier, on 6 April 1986.

8 Located at the top of Gitksan chiefs' territorial map, and on the boundary with peoples now located under the administrative jurisdiction of the Carrier-Sekani Tribal Council. See Map 5.

9 Tenimget told me on numerous occasions that visualizing one's aims is essential to hunting and any other goal-oriented enterprise. Jeff Harris Sr. said that people who were most effective in society did *sesatxw,* which he described as almost a form of meditation. 'Ksan artists also tell me of their visual adventures conceptualizing formlines and ovoids when they seek the form that a new work is to have.

10 An elderly woman linked to the same tradition and region, and who was sitting in the courtroom that day, recalled what the recitation of fishing-site names had evoked in her. The naming evoked history and a divine sanctioning of the Gitksan rights to land and fishing sites (Daly 6 August 1993): "And that day I was sitting there alone in the courtroom and a voice came to me. The voice came from God and it said, 'Yes, this is what our people have always done. They have looked after the land. It's a good thing. It's powerful.' The voice said, 'When God made the world there were vast grounds, and grounds of places all over. He made a man. He grabbed a handful of earth and he breathed life into it. Then he made the woman from the man's rib. Those first people, a man and a woman, he put them on this territory which was going to be their own. He put on berries there, and animals, for them to eat, and fish in all the rivers. He gave those first people names. The name he gave your ancestor, as he gave him his territory. Its name was____. It was your name and your territory. Then he told all the first people what was on the Bible, what to do and what not to do. Then he told them to pass on that knowledge that's on that Bible, from generation to generation, together with the name and the land, right down through time to you, ____, who have the name today.' The voice was still telling me about this when it was noon and the judge sent everybody out for lunch. I walked out of there in wonder. It was a *powerful* experience."

11 There are, of course, "more anthropological" descriptions of The Dreaming and its importance to spiritual and land tenure aspects of life, but during the *Delgamuukw* trial, the Chatwin version was part of the local zeitgeist. Compare, for example, "Land was/is the object of 'ownership' anchored to places created by mythological figures from The Dreaming. The owning group controls use of stories, objects and ritual pertaining to local figures in The Dreaming. Descending kindreds belong to these sites, either conceived there in relation to The Dreaming, or having inherited legitimacy from ascending generations" (Fred Myers, "Pintupi," in Lee and Daly 1999, 350). See also Françoise Dussart's "Warlpiri": "Jukurrpa (Dreamings) itineraries of Ancestral Beings are reenacted by those claiming descent from them. All Warlpiri are linked to specific locations from whence Ancestral Beings, like Honey Ant, Emu, Fire and Water, emerged. Each Warlpiri 'owns' one or more Dreamings" (Lee and Daly 1999, 365).

12 The Witsuwit'en assert that they have been in situ since Creation, but the *kungakhs* still record movement and both sacred and profane events on the land.

13 Witsuwit'en Laksamshu/Tsayu and Gitksan Gisḵ'aast are closely linked clans with a number of overlapping crests.

14 The recent severe reduction of fur trapping in the economy seems to be accompanied by a stronger assertion of orthodox matrilineal landholding as well as House land-use mapping and planning for future economic activity.

15 On different occasions I was shown the sites where young European "back to the landers" have tried, in recent decades, to establish themselves. Ignorant of Aboriginal ownership, they were expelled from Aboriginal land by having their cabins burned. Similarly, where Gitksan trapping cabins had been taken over by latter-day prospectors who have not sought permission to do so, the traditional owners left large signs and messages asserting their ownership and demanding that the interlopers leave.

16 Hunters and fishers of the area claim that both excessive and insufficient levels of predation lead to the fall of species productivity.

17 This was one of the reasons the trial judge in *Calder* rejected Nisga'a claims to landownership: owners did not have the right to destroy the land, something guaranteed in "civilized" society.

18 At the funeral feast of Art Ridsdale, Simoogit Luutkudjiiwus, 17 October 2002, the family was unable to reach a unanimous decision (see Epilogue of this book). This indicates the large size of what earlier was an amalgamated *wilp*, its need for fission into two independent units, and the high stakes with which the land is associated in people's minds today.

19 Jessie Sterritt left instructions about this matter, which were carried out, in the writer's presence, at her funeral feast in 1993. The Wii Goob'l/Gyedimgaldo'o family announced that they were renouncing claims to this trapline in the spirit of good relations with the Witsuwit'en and that the deceased Wii Goob'l wanted everyone to know that this matter would now be buried. While such arrangements are a matter of strict accounting among the Gitksan, in Witsuwit'en eyes such payments in usufruct rights for unredeemed funeral expenses, particularly by chiefs from the members of one's own clan (whether local or distant clanspeople), automatically revert to the rightful owners after the death of the person who paid the funeral expense.

20 On 19 October 1991 Jeffrey Johnson's Ha'naamuxw pole was raised for the third time. (Long after its first raising it had been washed away in the flood of 1936; subsequently, it was one of three re-raised in 1945, in defiance of the Potlatch Law, in the presence of William Beynon, who recorded the event [Barbeau-Beynon 1915-57]). On its third raising, it was accompanied by the pole of the next generation of the present Ha'namuxw, Joan Ryan, daughter of Gwaans, in memory of Jeffrey Johnson's generation as well as of the previous ancestral generations. New names were given, various business conducted, a xsiisxw fishing site was returned, and the spiritual powers of the wilp were revealed. In the course of the ceremonies, the House of Ha'naamuxw revealed a new *naxnox* wild monster spirit, which chased the guests and menaced the children from behind half-frame spectacles, a black robe, white bib, and a face possessing a remarkable resemblance to Chief Justice McEachern.

21 See note 19, above.

22 *Gawagani* is derived from the Tahltan word for deer. Bruce Rigsby, personal communication.

23 This is the passage cited by McEachern (1991, 51) as an example of my obtuseness, what he saw as my being "detached from what happens on the ground." I would submit that this description of the social reality of Gitksan and Witsuwit'en cosmology is quite consistent with contemporary environmental studies and their holistic approach to human ecology.

24 This is often referred to as "working on your luck," and some of the observances are said to be effective for winning at bingo games. (See *R. v. Jim*, Transcript, BC Provincial Court, Smithers Registry.) Young hunters, in my presence, have ascribed their ill-luck to not having bothered to purify themselves before hunting.

25 Alfred Joseph learned from the old people of Hagwilget, usually while resting between trips up the canyon wall with loads of salmon for processing in the village above, that before humans were fully formed they and all other beings on earth had a common language as well as common human characteristics and that they communicated constantly. Later, human beings grew more sophisticated and, apart from dream occurrences, they had to learn various techniques in order to achieve interspecies conversation (personal communication).

26 The late Louie Phillips, elder of the 'Nlaka'pamux people of the Lytton area, in relating to me the training procedures in his culture in the early years of the twentieth century, said, "They would send you out to train. They told you to listen to the land" (York, Daly, and Arnett 1993, xvii). Stanley Williams, Gwisgen, a leading hunter, a Gitksan chief of a Gitsegukla *wilp*, also underwent such training, and Solomon Marsden, Gamlaxyeltxw of the Gitanyow Ganeda Clan, confirmed that he had received similar training out on the winter trapline when he was a youth.

27 See Sider's (1980) argument for the common etymology of "property" and "propriety."

28 During my giving of evidence in *Delgamuukw* I described these procedures and Chief Justice McEachern commented that I ought to have conducted a controlled experiment. His own uncle always went out and got a deer whenever he pleased. Later, members of the plaintiff community commented that obviously the uncle and the uncle's wife were not having much of a sex life.

29 The effects of controlled burning on hunting, and on the close, almost cooperative relations between lions and hunter-gatherer humans in the Kalahari, are discussed by Elizabeth Marshall Thomas (1990, 1994).

30 Lutz (1995) shows how the Garry oak parkland vegetation around the city of Victoria, British Columbia, is the creation of Straits Salish people who regularly burned the area and disturbed the ground extensively in the extraction of camas bulbs. Now, after a century without this regular human intervention, the landscape is changing from the seral meadow lands that had been in stasis due to burning and digging.

References

Adams, J. 1973. *The Gitksan potlatch: Population flux, resource ownership and reciprocity.* Toronto and New York: Holt, Rinehart and Winston.

Adlam, R.G. 1985. The structural basis of Tahltan Indian society. Ph.D. diss., University of Toronto.

Albright, S. 1987. Archaeological evidence of Gitksan and Wet'suwet'en prehistory. Opinion evidence for the plaintiffs in *Delgamuukw et al. v. The Queen.* On file Supreme Court of British Columbia, Vancouver, and Gitksan Treaty Office, Hazelton, BC.

Allaire, L. 1979. The cultural sequence at Gitaus: A case of prehistoric acculturation. In R.I. Inglis and G.F. MacDonald, eds., *Skeena River prehistory,* 18-52. Archaeological Survey of Canada, Paper 87. Ottawa: National Museums of Canada.

Ames, K.M. 1979. Report of excavations at GhSv 2, Hagwilget Canyon. In R.I. Inglis and G.F. MacDonald, eds., *Skeena River prehistory,* 181-218. Archaeological Survey of Canada Paper 87. Ottawa: National Museums of Canada.

–. 1981. The evolution of social ranking on the Northwest Coast of North America. *American Antiquity* 46 (4): 789-805.

Anderson, E.N., ed. 1996. *Bird of paradox: The unpublished writings of Wilson Duff.* Surrey, BC: Hancock House.

Anderson, M., and M. Halpin, eds. 2000. *Potlatch at Gitsegukla: William Beynon's 1945 field notes.* Vancouver: UBC Press.

Archer, D. 2001. Village patterns and the emergence of ranked society in the Prince Rupert area. In J.S. Cybulski, ed., *Perspectives on northern Northwest Coast prehistory,* 203-22. Mercury Series, Archaeological Survey of Canada, Paper 160. Ottawa: Canadian Museum of Civilization.

Arctander, J.W. 1909. *The apostle of Alaska: The story of William Duncan of Metlakahtla.* New York: Fleming Revell.

Arnett, C. 1999. *The terror of the coast: Land alienation and colonial war on Vancouver Island and the Gulf Islands 1849-1863.* Vancouver: Talonbooks.

Asch, M. 1992. Errors in *Delgamuukw:* An anthropological perspective. In F. Cassidy, ed., *Aboriginal title in British Columbia: Delgamuukw v. The Queen,* 221-43. Lantzville, BC: Oolichan Books and the Institute for Research on Public Policy.

Averkieva, Y.P. 1966 [1941]. *Slavery among the Indians of North America.* G.R. Elliott, trans. Victoria: Victoria College.

Bailey, A.G. 1969 [1937]. *The conflict of European and eastern Algonkian cultures 1504-1700: A study in Canadian civilization.* Toronto: University of Toronto Press.

Bailey, G.N. 1980. Holocene Australia. In A. Sherratt, ed., *The Cambridge encyclopedia of archaeology,* 333-41. Cambridge: Cambridge University Press.

Balée, W. 1989. The culture of Amazonian forests. In D.A. Posey and W. Balée, eds., Resource management in Amazonia: Indigenous and folk strategies. *Advances in Economic Botany* 7: 1-21.

–. 1992. People of the fallow: An historical ecology of foraging in lowland South America. In K.H. Redford and C. Padoch, eds., *Conservation in neotropical forests: Building on traditional resource use,* 35-57. New York: Columbia University Press.

–. 1993. Indigenous transformation of Amazonian forests: An example from Maranhão, Brazil. LeRemontée de l'Amazone. *L'Homme* 126-8: 231-54.

Ball, G. 1985. The monopoly system of wildlife management of the Indians and the Hudson's Bay Company in the early history of British Columbia. *BC Studies* (66): 37-58.

Barbeau, M. 1928. [1973 fac. reprint.] *The downfall of Temlaham.* Edmonton: Hurtig Publishers.

–. 1929. [1973 fac. reprint.] Totem poles of the Gitksan, upper Skeena River, British Columbia. National Museum of Canada, Bulletin 61, Anthropological Series, No. 12. Ottawa.

–. 1950. Totem poles. National Museum of Canada, Bulletin 119, Anthropological Series No. 30. 2 vols. Ottawa.

Barbeau, M., and W. Beynon. N.d. Adaorh of the Tsimshian speakers (Tsimshian, Nishga, Gitksan). National Archives of Canada. 4 vols. (1. Wolf clan invaders of the northern plateaux among the Tsimsyans [Wolf]; 2. Raven clan outlaws on the north Pacific coast [Frog/Raven]; 3. Temlarhlam, the land of plenty on the north Pacific coast [Killer Whale/Fireweed]; 4. The Gwenhoot of Alaska, in search of a bounteous land [Eagle]).

–. 1915-57. Tsimshian papers. Ottawa: Public Archives of Canada. Unpublished. (Index to these papers published in 1985. See Cove 1985.)

Barnard, A. 1983. Contemporary hunter-gatherers: Current theoretical issues in ecology and social organization. *Annual Review of Anthropology* 12: 193-214.

Barnett, H. 1938. The nature of the potlatch. *American Anthropologist* 40: 349-58.

–. 1968. *The nature and function of the potlatch.* Eugene: University of Oregon, Department of Anthropology.

Barth, F. 1967. Economic spheres in Darfur. In R. Firth, ed., *Themes in economic anthropology,* 149-74. London: Tavistock.

Baudrillard, J. 1997. The "laying off" of desire. In P. Lopate, ed., *Best of 1997: The Anchor essay annual,* 135-40. New York: Anchor/Doubleday.

Benedict, R. 1934. *Patterns of culture.* New York: Houghton Mifflin.

Berger, T. 1991. *A long and terrible shadow: White values, native rights in the Americas, 1492-1992.* Vancouver: Douglas and McIntyre.

Berkes, F. 1986. Common property resources and hunting territories. In C.A. Bishop and T. Morantz, eds., *Who owns the beaver? Northern Algonquian land tenure reconsidered. Anthropologica* (special issue) n.s. 28 (1-2): 145-62.

Berndt, R.M., and C.H. Berndt, eds. 1980. *Aborigines of the west: Their past and their present.* Nedlands: University of Western Australia.

Beynon, W. N.d. Notebooks, Skeena Crossing/Gidzagukla. B-F-425/428 (vol. 1-4). Ottawa: National Archives of Canada.

Biesele, M., and P. Weinberg. 1990. *Shaken roots: The Bushmen of Namibia.* Johannesburg: EDA Publications.

Bird-David, N. 1990. The giving environment: Another perspective on the economic system of gatherer-hunters. *Current Anthropology* 31: 183-96.

–. 1992a. Beyond "the original affluent society": A cultural formulation. *Current Anthropology* 33: 25-47.

–. 1992b. Beyond "the hunting and gathering mode of subsistence": Culture-sensitive observations on the Nayaka and other modern hunter-gatherers. *Man* 27: 19-44.

–. 1994. Sociality and immediacy: Or, past and present conversations on bands. *Man* 29: 583-603.

–. 1999. Introduction: South Asia. In R.B. Lee and R.H. Daly, eds., *The Cambridge encyclopedia of hunters and gatherers,* 231-7. Cambridge: Cambridge University Press.

Birdsell, J. 1953. Some environmental and cultural factors influencing the structuring of Australian Aboriginal populations. *American Naturalist* 87: 171-201.

–. 1958. On population structure in generalized hunting and collecting populations. *Evolution* 12 (2): 189-205.

–. 1968. Some predictions for the Pleistocene based on equilibrium systems among recent hunters. In R.B. Lee and I. DeVore, eds., *Man the hunter,* 229-40. Chicago: Aldine.

–. 1972. *Human evolution: An introduction to the new physical anthropology.* Chicago: Rand-McNally.

Birket-Smith, K. 1929. *The Caribou Eskimos: Material and social life, and their position,* Pts. 1 and 2. Report of the fifth Thule expedition, 1921-24, vol. 5. Copenhagen: Gyldendal.

Bishop, C.A. 1986. Territoriality among northeastern Algonquians. In C.A. Bishop and T. Morantz, eds., *Who owns the beaver? Northern Algonquian land tenure reconsidered. Anthropologica* (special issue) n.s. 28 (1-2): 37-63.

–. 1987. Coast-Interior exchange: The origins of stratification in northwestern North America. *Arctic Anthropology* 24 (l): 72-83.

Bishop, C.A., and A.J. Ray. 1976. Ethnohistoric research in the central sub-Arctic: Some conceptual and methodological problems. *Western Canadian Journal of Anthropology* 6 (1): 116-44.

Blackstock, M.D. 2001. *Faces in the forest: First Nations art created on living trees.* Montreal: McGill-Queen's University Press.

Boas, F. 1890. First general report on the Indians of British Columbia. 59th Report of the British Association for the Advancement of Science for 1889, 801-93. London.

–. 1897. The social organization and the secret societies of the Kwakiutl Indians. Report of the US National Museums for 1895, 311-738. Washington, DC.

–. 1899. Summary of the work of the committee in British Columbia. 68th Report of the British Association for the Advancement of Science for 1898, 667-82. London.

–. 1916. *Tsimshian mythology.* Bureau of American Ethnology Annual Report 31. Washington, DC: Smithsonian Institution.

–. 1932. *Bella Bella tales.* New York: G.E. Stechert, for the American Folklore Society.

Bodenhorn, B. 2000. It's good to know who your relatives are. *Senri Ethnological Studies* 53: 27-59.

Boelscher, M. 1988. *The curtain within: Haida social and mythical discourse.* Vancouver: UBC Press.

Bohannan, P., and G. Dalton, eds. 1962. *Markets in Africa: Eight subsistence economies in transition.* Evanston, IL: Northwestern University Press.

Book Builders of 'Ksan. 1980. *Gathering what the great nature provided.* Vancouver: Douglas and McIntyre.

Borden, C.E. 1975. *Origins and development of early Northwest Coast culture to about 3000 B.C.* Archaeological Survey of Canada Paper 45. Ottawa: National Museums of Canada.

Bourdieu, P. 1990a. *In other words: Essays towards a reflective sociology.* Oxford: Polity Press.

–. 1990b. *The logic of practice.* Oxford: Polity Press.

–. 1992 [1977]. *Outline of a theory of practice.* Cambridge: Cambridge University Press.

–. 1993. *Sociology in question.* London: Sage.

–. 1999. *Homo academicus.* Oxford: Polity Press.

Bourdieu, P., and L.J.D. Wacquant. 1992. *An invitation to reflexive sociology.* Cambridge: Polity Press.

Boyd, J.P., ed. 1938. *Indian treaties printed by Benjamin Franklin, 1736-1762.* Philadelphia: Historical Society of Pennsylvania.

Bridge, K. 1998. *By snowshoe, buckboard and steamer: Women of the frontier.* Victoria, BC: Sono Nis Press.

Briggs, J. 1997. From trait to emblem and back: Living and representing culture in everyday Inuit life. *Arctic Anthropology* 34 (1): 227-35.

Brody, H. 1986. *Maps and dreams: Indians and the British Columbia frontier.* 2nd ed. London: Faber and Faber.

Brown, W. N.d. Untitled journal of a trip from Fort Kilmaurs to the forks of the Babine and Skeena rivers in 1826. Public Archives of Canada, MG-19, D8.

Burch, E.S., Jr. 1986. The Caribou Inuit. In R.B. Morrison and C.R. Wilson, eds., *Native peoples: The Canadian experience,* 106-33. Toronto: McClelland and Stewart.

–. 1994. The future of hunter-gatherer research. In E.S. Burch Jr. and L.J. Ellanna, eds., *Key issues in hunter-gatherer research*, 441-55. Oxford and Providence: Berg Publishers.

Burch, E.S., Jr., and L.J. Ellanna. 1994. Introduction. In E.S. Burch Jr. and L.J. Ellanna, eds., *Key issues in hunter-gatherer research*, 1-8. Oxford and Providence: Berg Publishers.

Campbell, M., and A. Manicom, eds. 1995. *Knowledge, experience and ruling relations: Studies in the social organization of knowledge.* Toronto: University of Toronto Press.

Carlson, R.L. 1979. The early period on the central coast of British Columbia. *Canadian Journal of Archaeology* 3: 211-28.

–. 1983. Prehistory of the Northwest Coast. In R.L. Carlson, ed., *Indian art traditions of the Northwest Coast,* 13-32. Burnaby: Simon Fraser University.

Cassidy, F., ed. 1992. *Aboriginal title in British Columbia: Delgamuukw v. The Queen.* Lantzville, BC: Oolichan Books and the Institute for Research on Public Policy.

Chance, N.A. 1966. *The Eskimo of north Alaska.* New York: Holt, Rinehart, and Winston.

–. 1990. *The Inupiat and arctic Alaska: An ethnography of development.* Forth Worth: Holt, Rinehart, and Winston.

Chase, A.K. 1989. Domestication and domiculture in northern Australia: A social perspective. In D. Harris and G. Hillman, eds., *Foraging and farming: The evolution of plant exploitation,* 42-54. London: Unwin-Hyman.

Chilton, R. 1987. Opinion evidence report on climatology of northwestern British Columbia, for the plaintiffs, *Delgamuukw et al.* v. *The Queen,* in the Supreme Court of British Columbia. On file at the Gitksan Treaty Office library, Hazelton, BC.

Chismore, G. 1885. From the Nass to the Skeena. The Overland Monthly Devoted to the Development of the Country, 6 (2nd ser.), November 1885, No. 35.

Clark, D.E. 1947. *The west in American history.* New York: Thomas Y. Crowell Co.

Clutesi, G. 1969. *Potlatch.* Sidney, BC: Gray's Publishing.

Codere, H. 1950. *Fighting with property.* American Ethnological Society Monograph 18. Seattle: University of Washington Press.

–. 1961. Kwakiutl. In E.H. Spicer, ed., *Perspectives in American Indian culture change,* 431-516. Chicago: University of Chicago Press.

–. 1966. *The Kwakiutl ethnography of Franz Boas.* Chicago: University of Chicago Press.

–. 1990. Kwakiutl: Traditional culture. In W. Suttles, gen. ed., *Handbook of North American Indians.* Vol. 7: *Northwest Coast,* 359-77. Washington, DC: Smithsonian Institution.

Cohen, M.N. 1981. Pacific coast foragers: Affluent or overcrowded? *Senri Ethnological Studies* 9: 275-95.

Colden, C. 1922 [1823]. *History of the five Indian nations of Canada.* 2 vols. New York: Allerton Books.

Cole, D., and D. Darling. 1990. History of the early period. In W. Suttles, gen. ed., *Handbook of North American Indians.* Vol. 7: *Northwest Coast,* 119-34. Washington, DC: Smithsonian Institution.

Collman, J. 1988. *Fringe-dwellers and welfare.* St. Lucia: University of Queensland Press.

Comaroff, J. 1985. *Body of power, spirit of resistance: The culture and history of a South African people.* Chicago: University of Chicago Press.

Commission Evidence. 1985-88. Transcript of evidence given by Gitksan and Witsuwit'en elders in their homes in the presence of counsel, court recorders, and video camera, pertaining to *Delgamuukw et al.* (No. 0834, Smithers Registry). On file, by elders' names, Gitksan Treaty Office library, Hazelton, BC.

Coupland, G. 1985. Prehistoric cultural change of Kitselas Canyon. Ph.D. diss., University of British Columbia, Vancouver.

–. 1988. *The prehistoric cultural sequence at Kitselas Canyon: Evidence for social and economic change.* Canadian Museum of Civilization Mercury Series. Archaeological Survey of Canada Paper 138. Ottawa.

Cove, J.J. 1985. *A detailed inventory of the Barbeau Northwest Coast files.* Canadian Centre for Folk Studies, Paper 54. Ottawa: National Museums of Canada.

Croes, D.R. 1989a. Prehistoric ethnicity on the Northwest Coast of North America: An evaluation of style in basketry and lithics. *Journal of Anthropological Archaeology* 8: 101-30.

–. 1989b. Lachane basketry and cordage: A technical, comparative and functional study. *Canadian Journal of Archaeology* 13: 165-205.

Cruikshank, J. 1992. Oral tradition and material culture, multiplying meanings of "words" and "things." *Anthropology Today* 8 (3): 5-9.

Csonka, Y. 1995. *Les Ahiarmiut*. Neuchâtel: Editions Victor Attinger.

Culhane, D. 1992. Adding insult to injury: Her Majesty's loyal anthropologist. *BC Studies* (95): 66-92.

–. 1998. *The pleasure of the Crown: Anthropology, law and First Nations*. Vancouver: Talonbooks.

Cybulski, J.S., ed. 2001. *Perspectives on northern Northwest Coast prehistory*. Mercury Series, Archaeological Survey of Canada, Paper 160. Ottawa: Canadian Museum of Civilization.

Daly, R. 1985. Housing metaphors: A study of the role of the longhouse in the persistence of Iroquois culture. Ph.D. diss., University of Toronto.

–. 1986-88. Notes and transcripts of interviews with Gitksan and Witsuwit'en people, in preparation for *Delgamuukw*. On file at Supreme Court of British Columbia and Gitksan Treaty Office, Hazelton, BC.

–. 1988-90. Unpublished fieldnotes for the Alliance of Tribal Councils, to be used as background to a case against the Canadian railways and their plans to double track both sides of the Fraser River Canyon.

–. 1991a. The river people: An anthropological opinion on the nature of the Sto:lo people of British Columbia at the time of European contact. 3 vols. Unpublished, on archive at the Alliance of Tribal Councils, Vancouver.

–. 1991b. The sound of one hand clapping: Narratives of resistance in an Aboriginal rights case. Paper delivered at CASCA Annual Meetings, University of Western Ontario, London, ON, 9-12 May 1991.

–. 1993. Those born at Andimaul. Transcribed oral history and notes requested by elder chiefs of Gitsegukla. Recorded and produced September 1993. Unpublished.

–. 1994a. Multiple realities in a Canadian land claims court room. Lecture delivered at the Institute of Social Science, University of Tromsø, Norway, 3 November 1994.

–. 1994b. Cultural hegemony and cultural dialectics in a Canadian land claims case. Lecture presented at the Institute of Social Science, University of Tromsø, 4 November 1994.

–. 1999. Proprietary narratives: Land conflicts in northern British Columbia. Paper presented at Land Rights Conference, Free University of Berlin, February 1999.

–. 2002. Pure gifts and impure thoughts. Paper presented at Conference on Hunters and Gatherers 9, Heriot-Watt University, Edinburgh, September 2002.

–. 2003. Anthropological consultancy and the crisis of globalization. *Social Analysis* 47 (1): 106-10.

Daly, R., and A. Mills. 1993. Ethics and objectivity: American Anthropological Association principles of responsibility discredit testimony. *Anthropology Newsletter* 34 (8): 1, 6.

Daly, R., and L. Mjelde. 1990. Urbefolkningsrettigheter i Canada: Stillheten er full av mening [Aboriginal rights in Canada: Silence is full of meaning]. *Populærvitenskapelig Magasin* 9/90: 13-18. Oslo.

Daly, R., and V. Napoleon. 2003. A dialogue on the effects of Aboriginal rights litigation and activism on Aboriginal communities in northwestern British Columbia. *Social Analysis* 47 (3): 108-29.

Dauenhauer, N.M., and R. Dauenhauer, eds. 1990. *Haa tuwunáagu yis – For healing our spirit: Tlingit oratory*. Seattle: University of Washington Press and Juneau Sealaska Heritage.

Davidson, D.S. 1928. *Family hunting territories in northwestern North America*. New York: Museum of the American Indian.

Dawn, L. 1981. 'Ksan: Museum, cultural and artistic activity among the Gitksan Indians of the upper Skeena, 1920-1973. Master's thesis, University of Victoria, Victoria, BC.

Dawson, G. 1881. Report on an exploration from Port Simpson on the Pacific to Edmonton on the Saskatchewan River. Geological and Natural History Survey of Canada, Report of Progress for 1879-80, Part B. Ottawa.

de Laguna, F. 1975. *The archaeology of Cook Inlet*. New York: AMS Press.

Dickason, O.P. 1984. *The myth of the savage and the beginnings of French colonialism in the Americas*. Edmonton: University of Alberta Press.

Donahue, P.F. 1974. Closed loops and prehistory: A questionable union. *Arctic Anthropology* 11 (Supplement): 104-11.

Draper, H.H. 1977. The Aboriginal Eskimo diet in modern perspective. *American Anthropologist* 79: 309-16.

Drucker, P. 1936. Diffusion in Northwest Coast culture growth in the light of some distributions. PhD diss., Washington, DC: Smithsonian Institution – Smithsonian #4516 (47). Reprinted in Human Relations Area Files.

–. 1948. The antiquity of the Northwest Coast totem pole. *Journal of the Washington Academy of Sciences* 38 (12): 389-97.

–. 1958. The Native brotherhoods: Modern intertribal organizations on the Northwest Coast. *Bureau of American Ethnology Bulletin 168*. Washington.

–. 1963. *Indians of the Northwest Coast*. Garden City, New York: Natural History Press.

–. 1965. *Cultures of the north Pacific coast*. New York: Harper Row.

–. 1983. Ecology and political organization on the Northwest Coast of America. In E. Tooker, ed., *The development of political organization in Native North America*, 86-96. New York: J.J. Augustin.

Drucker, P., and R.F. Heizer. 1967. *To make my name good: A reexamination of the southern Kwakiutl potlatch*. Berkeley: University of California Press.

Duff, W., ed. 1959. *Histories, territories and laws of the Kitwancool*. Anthropology in British Columbia 4. Victoria, BC: British Columbia Provincial Museum.

–. 1964. Contributions of Marius Barbeau to west coast ethnology. *Anthropologica* n.s. 6 (1): 63-96.

–. 1975. *Images: Stone: BC: Thirty centuries of Northwest Coast Indian sculpture*. Seattle: University of Washington Press.

–. N.d. Handwritten summaries of Barbeau-Beynon Tsimshian material pertinent to the Gitksan. Ottawa: Public Archives of Canada. *Delgamuukw* plaintiffs' document #3271. 2 vols.

Dumond, D.E. 1969. Toward a prehistory of the Na-Dene, with a general comment on population movements among nomadic hunters. *American Anthropologist* 71: 851-63.

Dussart, F. 1999. Warlpiri. In R.B. Lee and R.H. Daly, eds., *The Cambridge encyclopedia of hunters and gatherers*, 363-6. Cambridge: Cambridge University Press.

Dyen, I., and D. Aberle. 1974. *Lexical reconstruction: The case of the Proto-Athabaskan kinship system*. Cambridge: Cambridge University Press.

Elias, P.D. 1993. Anthropology and Aboriginal claims research. In N. Dyck and J. Waldram, eds., *Anthropology, public policy and Native Peoples in Canada*, 233-370. Montreal: McGill-Queen's University Press.

Ellen, R.F. 1988. Foraging, starch extraction and the sedentary lifestyle in the lowland rainforest of central Seram. In T. Ingold, D. Riches, and J. Woodburn, eds., *Hunters and gatherers*. Vol. 1: *Evolution and social change*, 117-34. Oxford: Berg.

Ellen, R.F., and F. Fukai, eds. 1996. *Redefining nature: Ecology, culture and domestication*. Oxford: Berg.

Emmons, G.T. 1911. *The Tahltan Indians*. Anthropological Publications 4 (1). Philadelphia: University of Pennsylvania Museum.

–. 1912. Tahltan. In F.W. Hodge, ed. *Handbook of Indians in Canada*. Appendix to the tenth report of the Geographical Board of Canada, Sessional Paper 21a, 444-5. Ottawa: Geographical Board of Canada.

Etienne, M., and E.B. Leacock, eds. 1980. *Women and colonization: Anthropological perspectives*. New York: Praeger.

Fanon, F. 1963. *The wretched of the earth*. New York: Grove Press.

–. 1986. *Black skin, white masks*. London: Pluto Press.

Feit, H.A. 1969. Misstassini hunters of the boreal forest: Ecosystem dynamics and multiple subsistence patterns. Master's thesis, McGill University, Montreal.

–. 1973. The ethno-ecology of the Waswanipi Cree: Or how hunters can manage their resources. In B. Cox, ed., *Cultural ecology: Readings on the Canadian Indians and Eskimos*, 115-25. Toronto: McClelland and Stewart.

–. 1994. The enduring pursuit: Land, time and social relationships in anthropological models of hunter-gatherers and in subarctic hunters' images. In E.S. Burch Jr. and L.J. Ellanna, eds., *Key issues in hunter-gatherer research*, 421-40. Oxford and Providence: Berg Publishers.

Fenton, W.N. 1936. *An outline of Seneca ceremonies at Coldspring longhouse*. Yale University Publications in Anthropology 9. New Haven: Yale University.

–. 1941. Tonawanda longhouse ceremonies: Ninety years after Lewis Henry Morgan. *Bureau of American Ethnology Bulletin* 128 (15): 140-66. Washington, DC.

–. 1946. An Iroquois condolence council for installing Cayuga chiefs in 1945. *Journal of Washington Academy of Sciences* 36 (4): 110-27. Washington, DC.

–. 1950. The roll call of the Iroquois chiefs: A study of a mnemonic cane from the Six Nations Reserve. *Smithsonian Miscellaneous Collections* 111 (15): 1-73. Washington, DC.

Fenton, W.N., and E. Moore, eds. 1974-77 [1724]. *Customs of the American Indians*. Toronto: Champlain Society. Originally entitled *Moeurs des sauvages ameriquains, comparées aux moeurs des premiers temps*.

Firth, R.W. 1939. *Primitive Polynesian economy*. London: George Routledge.

–. 1967. Themes in economic anthropology, a general comment. In R.W. Firth, ed., *Themes in economic anthropology*, 1-28. London: Tavistock Publications.

Fisher, R. 1977. *Contact and conflict: Indian-European relations in British Columbia, 1774-1890*. Vancouver: UBC Press.

–. 1992. Judging history: Reflections on the reasons for judgment in *Delgamuukw v. British Columbia*. *BC Studies* (95): 43-54.

Fladmark, K. 1986. *British Columbia prehistory*. Ottawa: National Museums of Canada.

Fladmark, K.R., K.M. Ames, and P.D. Sutherland. 1990. Prehistory of the northern coast of British Columbia. In W. Suttles, gen. ed., *Handbook of North American Indians*. Vol. 7: *Northwest Coast*, 229-39. Washington, DC: Smithsonian Institution.

Fortes, M. 1953. The structure of unilineal descent groups. *American Anthropologist* 55: 17-41.

Foster, H., and A. Grove. 1993. Looking behind the masks: A land claims discussion paper for researchers, lawyers and their employers. *University of British Columbia Law Review* 27: 213-55.

Foucault, M. 1970. *The order of things: An archaeology of the human sciences*. London: Tavistock.

–. 1972. *The archaeology of knowledge*. London: Tavistock.

–. 1981. The order of discourse. In R. Young, ed., *Untying the text: A post-structuralist reader*, 51-78. London: Routledge.

Fowler, C.S. 1996. Historical perspectives on Timbisha Shoshone land management practices, Death Valley, California. In E.J. Reitz, L.A. Newson, and S.J. Scudder, eds., *Case studies in environmental archeology*, 87-101. New York: Plenum Press.

Fox, R.G. 1969. Professional primitives: Hunter-gatherers of nuclear south Asia. *Man in India* 49: 139-60.

Francis, D. 1992. *The imaginary Indian*. Vancouver: Arsenal Pulp Press.

Friedl, E. 1975. *Women and men: An anthropologist's view*. New York: Holt, Rinehart, and Winston.

Galois, R. 1986. Gitksan-Wet'suwet'en history, 1850-1870. Opinion evidence report for *Delgamuukw* plaintiffs. On file in the Gitksan Treaty Office, Hazelton, BC.

Gamble, C. 1986. The artificial wilderness. *New Scientist*, 10 April 1986.

Garfield, V.E. 1939. Tsimshian clan and society. *University of Washington Publications in Anthropology* 7: 167-340.

–. 1966. The Tsimshian and their neighbors. In V.E. Garfield and P.S. Wingert, eds., *The Tsimshian Indians and their arts*, 3-70. Seattle: University of Washington Press.

Geertz, C. 1967. Ritual and social change: A Javanese example. In N.J. Nemerath III and R.A. Patterson, eds., *System, change and conflict*, 231-50. New York: Free Press.

Gitksan and Wet'suwet'en Chiefs. 1988. *Territorial map atlas*. Hazelton, BC, Gitksan Treaty Office Library.

Gitxsan Strategic Analysis Team. 1999. *The Gitxsan model: An alternative to the destruction of forests, salmon and Gitxsan land*. Victoria: Eco-Research Chair of Environmental Law and Policy, University of Victoria.

Godelier, M. 1965. Objet et methodes de l'anthropologie economique. *L'Homme* 5 (avril-juin): 32-91.

–. 1966. *Rationalité et irrationalité en économie*. Paris: Maspero.

–. 1969. La monnaie de sel des Baruya de Nouvelle-Guinée. *L'Homme* 9 (2): 5-37.

–. 1977. *Perspectives in Marxist anthropology*. Cambridge: Cambridge University Press.

–. 1986. *The making of great men: Male domination and power among the New Guinea Baruya*. R. Swyer, trans. Cambridge: Cambridge University Press.

–. 1999. *The Enigma of the gift*. N. Scott, trans. Cambridge: Polity Press.

Goffman, I. 1959. *The presentation of self in everyday life*. Garden City, New York: Doubleday Anchor Books.

–. 1961. *Asylums: Essays on the social situation of mental patients and other inmates*. Garden City, New York: Doubleday Anchor Books.

Goldman, I. 1975. *The mouth of heaven: An introduction to Kwakiutl religious thought*. New York: John Wiley and Sons.

Gottesfeld, L.M. 1994. Aboriginal burning for vegetation management in northwest British Columbia. *Human Ecology* 22 (2): 171-88.

Gottesfeld, L.M., and B. Anderson. 1988. Gitksan traditional medicine: Herbs and healing. *Journal of Ethnobotany* 8 (1): 13-33.

Gregory, C.A. 1982. *Gifts and commodities*. London and New York: Academic Press.

Guedon, M.-F. 1984. An introduction to Tsimshian worldview and its practioners. In M. Seguin, ed., *The Tsimshian: Images of the past: Views for the present*, 137-59. Vancouver: UBC Press.

Guha, R., and G.C. Spivak, eds. 1987. *Selected subaltern studies*. New York: Oxford University Press.

Gunther, E. 1972. *Indian life on the Northwest Coast of North America: As seen by the early explorers and fur traders during the last decades of the eighteenth century*. Chicago: University of Chicago Press.

Haeussler, S. 1986. Ecology and berry chemistry of some food plant species used by northwest British Columbia Indians. Opinion evidence for the plaintiffs in *Delgamuukw*. On file at the Gitksan Treaty Office, Hazelton, BC.

Hall, Justice E. 1973. Judgement. In *Calder*, before the Supreme Court of Canada. 34 D.L.R. (3d), 145.

Hallowell, I. 1943. The nature and function of property as a social institution. *Journal of Legal and Political Sociology* 1 (3-4): 115-38.

Halpin, M. 1973. The Tsimshian crest system. Ph.D. diss., University of British Columbia, Department of Anthropology and Sociology, Vancouver.

Halpin, M.M., and M. Seguin. 1990. Tsimshian peoples: Southern Tsimshian, Coast Tsimshian, Nishga and Gitksan. In W. Suttles, gen. ed., *Handbook of North American Indians*. Vol. 7: *Northwest Coast*, 267-84. Washington, DC: Smithsonian Institution.

Hamell, G.R. 1983. Trading in metaphors: The magic of beads. In *Proceedings of the 1982 glass trade bead conference, Rochester Museum and Science Center Research Records* 16: 5-28. Rochester, NY.

Haraway, D. 1988. Situated knowledges: "The science question in feminism" and the privilege of partial perspective. *Feminist Studies* 14 (3): 575-99.

Hardesty, D.L. 1977. *Ecological anthropology*. New York: John Wiley and Sons.

Harding, S. 1986. *The science question in feminism*. Ithaca and London: Cornell University Press.

–. 1991. *Whose science? Whose knowledge? Thinking from women's lives*. Milton Keynes: Open University Press.

Harris, D. 1989. An evolutionary continuum of people-plant interaction. In D. Harris and G. Hillman, eds., *Foraging and farming: The evolution of plant exploitation*, 11-26. London: Unwin-Hyman.

–. 1990. Settling down and breaking ground: Rethinking the Neolithic revolution. *Twaalfde Kroon-Voordracht*. Amsterdam: Stichting Nederlands Museum voor Anthropologie en Praehistorie.

Hart, J.L. 1973. *Pacific fishes of Canada*. Fisheries Research Board of Canada, Bulletin 180. Ottawa: Fisheries Research Board.

Hatler, D. 1987. History and zoogeography of some selected mammals in northern British Columbia. Opinion evidence for the plaintiffs in the Supreme Court of British Columbia, No. 0834, Smithers Registry, *Delgamuukw et al* v. *The Queen*. On file at Gitksan Treaty Office, Hazelton, BC.

Hayden, B. 1994. Competition, labor, and complex hunter-gatherers. In E.S. Burch Jr. and L.J. Ellanna, eds., *Key issues in hunter-gatherer research*, 223-42. Oxford and Providence: Berg.

Hays, H.R. 1975. *Children of the raven: The seven Indian nations of the Northwest Coast*. New York: McGraw-Hill.

Headland, T.N. 1997. Revisionism in ecological anthropology. *Current Anthropology* 38 (4): 605-30.

Headland, T.N., and L.A. Read. 1989. Hunter-gatherers and their neighbors from prehistory to the present. *Current Anthropology* 30 (1): 43-66.

Heller, C., and E.M. Scott. N.d. The Alaska dietary survey, 1956-1961. Public Health Service Publication 999-AH-2. Anchorage: US Department of Health, Education and Welfare.

Herskovits, M.J. 1952. *Economic anthropology: A study in comparative economics*. New York: Alfred A. Knopf.

Hindle, L., and B. Rigsby. 1973. A short practical dictionary of the Gitksan language. *Northwest Anthropological Research Notes* 7 (1): 1-60. Moscow, Idaho.

Hoare, Q., and G.N. Smith, eds. and trans. 1971. *Selections from the prison notebooks of Antonio Gramsci*. New York: International Publishers.

Hobbes, T. 1651. *The Leviathan, or the matter, forme and power of a commonwealth, ecclesiasticall and civill*. London: Andrew Crook.

Holm, B. 1965. *Northwest Coast Indian art: An analysis of form*. Thomas Burke Memorial Washington State Museum Monographs 1. Seattle: University of Washington Press.

Horetzky, C. 1874. *Canada on the Pacific*. Montreal: Dawson Bros.

Hudson's Bay Company. 1822. Babine Fort (Fort Kilmaurs) district report, HBCAPAM B11-e-1-2, 107-112. Also HBC 188/a/1. Winnipeg: Public Archives of Manitoba.

Hyde, L. 1999 [1979]. *The gift: Imagination and the erotic life of property*. London: Vintage.

Ichikawa, M. 1978. The residential groups of the Mbuti Pygmies. *Senri Ethnological Studies* 1: 131-88.

–. 1996. The coexistence of man and nature in the central African rainforest. In R.F. Ellen and F. Fukai, eds., *Redefining nature*, 467-92. Oxford: Berg.

–. 1999. Mbuti. In R.B. Lee and R.H. Daly, eds., *The Cambridge encyclopedia of hunters and gatherers*, 210-14. Cambridge: Cambridge University Press.

Ignatieff, M. 1987. An interview with Bruce Chatwin. *Granta* 21: 29-38.

Inglis, R.I., and G.F. MacDonald, eds. 1979. *Skeena River prehistory*. Archaeological Survey of Canada Paper 87. Ottawa: National Museums of Canada.

Ingold, T. 1986. *The appropriation of nature: Essays on human ecology and social relations*. Manchester: Manchester University Press.

–. 1993. From trust to domination: An alternative history of human-animal relations. In A. Manning and J. Serpell, eds., *Animals and human society*, 1-22. London: Routledge.

–. 1996. *Key debates in anthropology*. London: Routledge.

–. 1999. On the social relations of the hunter-gatherer band. In R.B. Lee and R.H. Daly, eds., *The Cambridge encyclopedia of hunters and gatherers*, 399-410. Cambridge: Cambridge University Press.

Ives, J.W. 1990. *A theory of northern Athapaskan prehistory*. Boulder: Westview Press.

Jenness, D. 1932. *The Indians of Canada*. Ottawa: National Museum of Canada.

–. 1937. *The Sekani Indians of British Columbia*. Bulletin 84, Anthropological Series, No. 20. Ottawa: Department of Mines and Resources.

–. 1943. The Carrier Indians of the Bulkley River: Their social and religious life. *Bureau of American Ethnology* 133 (25): 469-586.

Jennings, F. 1975. *The invasion of America: Indians, colonialism and the cant of conquest*. Chapel Hill: University of North Carolina Press for the Institute of Early American History and Culture.

Jolly, P. 1996. Symbiotic interaction between black farmers and south-eastern San: Implications for southern African rock art studies, ethnographic analogy and hunter-gatherer cultural identity. *Current Anthropology* 37 (2): 277-305.

Jopling, C. 1968. The coppers of the Northwest Coast Indians: Their origin, development and possible antecedents. *Transactions of the American Philosophical Society* 79 (1). Philadelphia.

Kan, S. 1989. *Symbolic immortality: The Tlingit potlatch of the nineteenth century.* Washington, DC: Smithsonian Institution Press.

Kelly, R.L., J-F. Rabedimy, and L. Poyer. 1999. Mikea. In R.B. Lee and R.H. Daly, eds., *The Cambridge encyclopedia of hunters and gatherers,* 215-19. Cambridge: Cambridge University Press.

Kent, S. 1992. The current forager controversy: Real versus ideal views of hunter-gatherers. *Man* 27 (1): 25-70.

Knight, R. 1968. Ecological factors in changing economy and social organization among the Rupert House Cree. *National Museum of Canada Anthropology Paper* 15. Ottawa.

Kolb, D. 1986. *Critique of pure modernity: Hegel, Heidegger and after.* Chicago: University of Chicago Press.

Koyama, S., and D.H. Thomas, eds. 1981. Affluent foragers: Pacific coasts east and west. *Senri Ethnological Studies* 9.

Krader, L. 1980. Anthropological traditions: Their relationship as a dialectic. In S. Diamond, ed., *Anthropology: Ancestors and heirs,* 19-34. The Hague: Mouton.

Krause, A. 1956. *The Tlingit Indians: Results of a trip to the Northwest Coast of America and Bering Straits.* E. Gunther, trans. Monographs of the American Ethnological Society. Seattle: University of Washington Press.

Krause, M. 1973. Na-Dene. In T.A. Sebeok, ed., *Linguistics in North America: Current trends in linguistics,* 903-78. Paris: Mouton.

Kuhnlein, H.V. 1984. Traditional and contemporary Nuxalk foods. *Nutrition Research* 4: 789-809.

Kuhnlein, H.V., A.C. Chan, J.N. Thompson, and S. Nakai. 1982. Ooligan grease: A nutritious fat used by Native people of coastal British Columbia. *Journal of Ethnobiology* 2 (2): 154-61.

Laghi, B. 1997. Getting into the spirit of things. *Globe and Mail* (Toronto), 9 August.

Lamb, W.K., ed. 1957. *Sixteen years in the Indian country: The journal of Daniel William Harmon (1800-1816).* Toronto: Macmillan of Canada.

Lappé, F.M. 1982. *Diet for a small planet* (rev. ed.). New York: Ballantine Books.

LaViolette, F. 1961. *The struggle for survival: Indian cultures and the Protestant ethic in British Columbia.* Toronto: University of Toronto Press.

Leach, E.R. 1961. *Pul Eliya: A village in Ceylon.* Cambridge: Cambridge University Press.

Leacock, E.B. 1954. The Montagnais "hunting territory" and the fur trade. *American Anthropological Association Memoir 78.* Menasha, WI: American Anthropological Association.

–. 1981. *Myths of male dominance: Collected articles on women cross-culturally.* New York: Monthly Review Press.

LeClair, E.E., and H.K. Schneider. 1968. *Economic anthropology: Readings in theory and analysis.* New York: Holt, Rinehart, and Winston.

Lee, R.B. 1976. !Kung spatial organization: An ecological and historical perspective. In R.B. Lee and I. DeVore, eds., *Kalahari hunter-gatherers: Studies of the !Kung San and their neighbors,* 73-97. Cambridge, MA: Harvard University Press.

–. 1979. *The !Kung San: Men, women and work in a foraging society.* Cambridge: Cambridge University Press.

–. 1984. *The Dobe !Kung.* New York: Holt, Rinehart, and Winston.

–. 1990. Primitive communism and the origin of social inequality. In S. Upman, ed., *The evolution of political systems: Sociopolitics in small-scale sedentary societies,* 225-46. Cambridge: Cambridge University Press.

–. 1992. Art, science or politics? The crisis in hunter-gatherer studies. *American Anthropologist* 94 (1): 31-54.

Lee, R.B., and R.H. Daly, eds. 1999. *The Cambridge encyclopedia of hunters and gatherers.* Cambridge: Cambridge University Press.

Lee, R.B., and I. DeVore, eds. 1976. *Kalahari hunter-gatherers: Studies of the !Kung San and their neighbors.* Cambridge, MA: Harvard University Press.

Lee, R.B., and M. Guenther. 1991. Oxen or onions: The search for trade (and truth) in the Kalahari. *Current Anthropology* 32 (5): 592-601.

LeRoy Ladurie, E. 1971. *Times of feast, times of famine: History of climate since the year 1000.* Garden City, New York: Doubleday.

Lévi-Strauss, C. 1967. The story of Asdiwal. In E. Leach, ed., *The structural study of myth and totemism,* 1-47. London: Tavistock.

–. 1969. *The elementary structures of kinship.* Boston: Beacon Press.

–. 1987. *Introduction to the work of Marcel Mauss.* F. Baker, trans. London: Routledge and Kegan Paul.

Lothrop, S.K. 1928. *The Indians of Tierra del Fuego.* Contributions of the Museum of the American Indian. New York: Heye Foundation.

Lowie, R.H. 1936. Lewis Henry Morgan in historical perspective. In R.H. Lowie, ed., *Essays in anthropology presented to Alfred L. Kroeber,* 169-81. Berkeley: University of California Press.

Lutz, J. 1995. Preparing Eden: Aboriginal land use and European settlement. Paper presented at 1995 Annual Meetings of the Canadian Historical Association, Victoria, BC.

Macdonald, G. 2000. Economies and personhood: Demand-sharing among the Wiradjuri. *Senri Ethnological Studies* 53: 87-111.

MacDonald, G.F. 1979. Kitwanga Fort National Historic Site, Skeena River, British Columbia. Parks Canada Manuscript Report, No. 341.

–. 1980. The epic of Nekt: The archaeology of metaphor. Banquet address at the 13th Annual Meeting of the Canadian Archaeological Association, Saskatoon, 24-7 April 1980.

–. 1983. Prehistoric art of the northern Northwest Coast. In R. Carlson, ed., *Indian art traditions of the Northwest Coast,* 99-120. Burnaby: Simon Fraser University, Archaeology Press.

–. 1984. Painted houses and woven blankets: Symbols of wealth in Tsimshian art and myth. In J. Miller and C.M. Eastman, eds., *The Tsimshian and their neighbors of the north Pacific coast,* 109-36. Seattle: University of Washington Press.

–. 1986. Marginalia, In a draft of Coupland, 1986. On file at the Gitksan Treaty Office, Hazelton, BC.

MacDonald, G.F., and R.I. Inglis. 1976. The north coast archaeological research project: A ten-year reevaluation. Archaeological Survey of Canada, National Museum of Man Manuscript.

–. 1981. An overview of the north coast prehistory project, 1966-80. *BC Studies* (48): 37-63.

MacLachlan, B.B. 1981. Tahltan. In J. Helm, gen. ed., *Handbook of North American Indians.* Vol. 6: *Subarctic,* 458-68. Washington, DC: Smithsonian Institution.

MacNeish, R.S. 1960. The Colliston site in the light of the archaeological survey of southwest Yukon. National Museum of Canada Bulletin 162, Contributions to Anthropology, 1957, pp.1-51.

–. 1964. Investigations of southwest Yukon. Papers of R.S. Peabody Foundation for Archeology 6 (2): 199-488. Andover, MA.

Mailhot, J. 1986. Territorial mobility among the Montagnais-Naskapi of Labrador. In C.A. Bishop and T. Morantz, eds., *Who owns the beaver? Northern Algonquian land tenure reconsidered. Anthropologica* (special issue), n.s. 28 (1-2): 92-107.

–. 1999. Innu. In R.B. Lee and R.H. Daly, eds., *The Cambridge encyclopedia of hunters and gatherers,* 51-5. Cambridge: Cambridge University Press.

Malinowski, B. 1922. *Argonauts of the western Pacific.* London: George Routledge and Sons.

Marsden, S. 1987. A history of the Gitksan. Opinion evidence for the plaintiffs in *Delgamuukw.* On file at the Supreme Court of British Columbia and the Gitksan Treaty Office, Hazelton, BC.

–. 2001. Defending the mouth of the Skeena: Perspectives on Tlingit Tsimshian relations. In J.S. Cybulski, ed., *Perspectives on northern Northwest Coast prehistory,* 61-106. Mercury Series, Archaeological Survey of Canada, Paper 160. Ottawa: Canadian Museum of Civilization.

Marshall, L. 1976. *The !Kung of Nyae Nyae.* Cambridge, MA: Harvard University Press.

Martin, C. 1978. *The keepers of the game: Indian-animal relationships and the fur trade*. Berkeley: University of California Press.

Matson, R.G., and G. Coupland. 1995. *The prehistory of the Northwest Coast*. New York and London: Academic Press.

Mauss, M. 1923-24 [1954]. Essai sur le don. *L'Année sociologique* 1 (i): 30-186.

–. 1990. *The gift: The form and reason for exchange in archaic societies*. W.D. Halls, trans., and M. Douglas, introduction. London: Routledge.

McClelland, C. 1981a. Inland Tlingit. In J. Helm, gen. ed., *Handbook of North American Indians*. Vol. 6: *Subarctic*, 469-80. Washington, DC: Smithsonian Institution.

–. 1981b. Tagish. In J. Helms, gen. ed., *Handbook of North American Indians*. Vol. 6: *Subarctic*, 481-92. Washington, DC: Smithsonian Institution.

–. 1981c. Tutchone. In J. Helms, gen. ed., *Handbook of North American Indians*. Vol. 6: *Subarctic*, 493-505. Washington, DC: Smithsonian Institution.

McDonald, J.A., and J. Joseph. 2000. Key events in the Gitksan encounter with the colonial world. In M. Anderson and M. Halpin, eds., *Potlatch at Gitsegukla: William Beynon's 1945 field notebooks*, 193-214. Vancouver: UBC Press.

McEachern, Hon. Chief Justice A. 1991. Reasons for judgment in the Supreme Court of British Columbia, No.0843, Smithers Registry, in *Delgamuukw et al. v. Her Majesty the Queen* in Right of the Province of British Columbia and the Attorney General of Canada. Vancouver: Supreme Court of British Columbia.

McFeat, T., ed. 1966. *Indians of the north Pacific coast*. Toronto: McClelland and Stewart.

McKenna-McBride Commission. 1915. Transcripts of commission meetings, Babine Agency, April 1915. (From *Report of the Royal Commission on Indian Affairs for the Province of British Columbia*. 4 vols. Victoria: Acme, 1916.)

Mead, G.H., ed. 1947. *Mind, self and society: From the standpoint of a social behaviorist*. Chicago: University of Chicago Press.

Meggitt, M. 1962. *Desert people: A study of the Warlbiri aborigines of Central Australia*. Sydney: August Robertson.

Miller, B., ed. 1992. *BC Studies*, special issue on the *Delgamuukw* case, 95 (Autumn).

Miller, J. 1997. *Tsimshian culture: A light through the ages*. Lincoln: University of Nebraska Press.

Mills, A. 1988a. A preliminary investigation of reincarnation among the Beaver and Gitksan Indians. *Anthropologica* 30 (1): 23-59.

–. 1988b. A comparison of Wet'suwet'en cases of the reincarnation type with Gitksan and Beaver. *Journal of Anthropological Research* 44 (4): 385-415.

–. 1994. *Eagle down is our law: Witsuwit'en laws, feasts, and land claims*. Vancouver: UBC Press.

Mills, A., and R. Slobodin, eds. 1994. *Amerindian rebirth: Reincarnation belief among North American Indians and Inuit*. Toronto: University of Toronto Press.

Mills, B. 1986. Prescribed burning and hunter-gatherer subsistence systems, Hailiksa'i. *UNM Contributions to Anthropology* 5: 1-26.

Misra, V.N. 1973. Bagar: A late mesolithic settlement in northwest India. *World Archaeology* 5 (1): 92-110.

Mjelde, L. 1995. Activity pedagogy: How does it really work? In A. Heikkinen, ed., *Vocational education and culture: European prospects from theory and practice*, 131-54. Hämeenlinna: Tampereen yliopiston opettajan koulutuslaitos.

–. 1997. The promise of alternative pedagogies: The case of workshop learning. In K. Watson, C. Modgil, and Y.S. Modgil, eds., *Educational dilemmas: Debate and diversity*. Vol. 4: *Quality and education*, 331-40. London: Cassell.

Monet, D., and Skanu'u (A. Wilson). 1992. *Colonialism on trial: Indigenous land rights and the Gitksan and Wetsuwet'en sovereignty case*. Philadelphia and Gabriola Island, BC: New Society Publishers.

Morantz, T. 1986. Historical perspectives on family hunting territories in eastern James Bay. In C.A. Bishop and T. Morantz, eds., *Who owns the beaver? Northern Algonquian land tenure reconsidered. Anthropologica* (special issue) n.s. 28 (1-2): 62-91.

Morgan, L.H. 1965 [1881]. *Houses and house-life of the American aborigines*. Chicago: University of Chicago Press.

Morice, A.G. 1888-89. The western Denes: Their manners and customs. Proceedings of the Canadian Institute, 3rd Series, vol. 7. Toronto.

–. 1892-93. Notes on the western Denes. Transactions of the Canadian Institute. Vol. 4.

–. 1895. Notes archaeological, industrial and sociological on the western Denes with an ethnological sketch of the same. Transactions of the Canadian Institute 4: 1-222.

–. 1905. *The History of the northern interior of British Columbia (formerly New Caledonia), 1660-1880*. 3rd ed. Toronto: William Briggs.

–. 1928. The fur trader in anthropology: A few related questions. *American Anthropologist* 30 (1): 60-84.

Moricetown Elders. N.d. Carrier legends and history. Typescript of recollections by Witsuwit'en elders. Smithers, BC: Smithers Indian Friendship Centre.

Morrell, M. 1987. Gitksan and Wet'suwet'en Fishery Management. Report commissioned by the Gitksan-Wet'suwet'en Tribal Council. On file at the Gitksan Treaty Office, Hazelton, BC.

Morrison, K. 1999. Archaeology in south Asia. In R.B. Lee and R.H. Daly, eds., *The Cambridge encyclopedia of hunters and gatherers*, 238-42. Cambridge: Cambridge University Press.

Murphy, R.F., and J.H. Steward. 1968 [1956]. Tappers and trappers: Parallel process in acculturation. In Y. Cohen, ed., *Man in adaptation: The cultural present*, 216-33. Chicago: Aldine.

Myers, F. 1986. *Pintupi country, Pintupi self: Sentiment, place and politics among Western Desert Aborigines*. Washington, DC: Smithsonian Institution Press.

–. 1988. Locating ethnographic practice: Romance, reality and politics in the outback. *American Ethnologist* 90: 609-24.

–. 1999. Pintupi. In R.B. Lee and R.H. Daly, eds., *The Cambridge encyclopedia of hunters and gatherers*, 348-52. Cambridge: Cambridge University Press.

Nash, M. 1964. The organization of economic life. In S. Tax, ed., *Horizons of anthropology*, 171-80. Chicago: Aldine.

National Museums of Canada. 1972. *'Ksan, the breath of our ancestors: An exhibition of 'Ksan art*. Ottawa: National Museums of Canada.

Oberg, K. 1973. *The social economy of the Tlingit Indians*. American Ethnological Society, Monograph No. 55. Seattle: University of Washington Press.

Ogden, P.S. 1853. *Traits of American Indian life*. London: Smith, Elder and Co.

Paine, R. 1985. Ethnodrama and the "fourth world": The Saami action group in Norway, 1979-1981. In N. Dyck, ed., *Indigenous peoples and the nation state*, 190-235. St. John's, NF: Institute of Social and Economic Research, Memorial University of Newfoundland.

–. N.d. In Chief Justice McEachern's shoes: Anthropology's failure in court. Paper delivered at the Annual Meetings of the Canadian Anthropology Society/Societé canadienne d'anthropologie, Montreal, May 1995.

Pasco. Pasco v. Canadian Railway Co. [1989] 1 C.N.L.R. 35.

Pearson, N. 2002. Native title's days in the sun are over. *The Age*, <http//:www.theage.com.au/articles/2002/08/27/1030053058615.html>, 28 August 2002.

Peterson, N. 1993. Demand sharing: Reciprocity and the pressure for generosity among foragers. *American Anthropologist* 95 (4): 860-74.

Phillips, D.B., ed. 2000. *Going public: The changing face of New Zealand history*. Auckland: Auckland University Press.

Piddocke, S. 1965. The potlatch system of the southern Kwakiutl: A new perspective. *Southwestern Journal of Anthropology* 21: 244-64.

Posey, D. 1983. Indigenous ecological knowledge and development of the Amazon. In E. Moran, ed., *The dilemma of Amazonian development*, 225-57. Boulder, CO: Westview Press.

Possehl, G.L., and P. Rissman. 1992. The chronology of prehistoric India: From earliest times to the Iron Age. In R.W. Erlich, ed., *Chronologies in old world archeology*, vol. 1, 465-90. Chicago: University of Chicago Press.

Poudrier, A.L. 1891. Exploration survey of New Caledonia. *British Columbia Department of Lands, Crown Lands, Surveys, B.C.S.P.*, Part 1: 354-70.

Price, J.A. 1975. Sharing: The integration of intimate economies. *Anthropologica* 17: 3-27.

Price, T.D., and J.A. Brown. 1985. Aspects of hunter-gatherer complexity. In T.D. Price and J.A. Brown, eds., *Prehistoric hunters and gatherers: The emergence of social complexity*, 3-20. Orlando: Academic Press.

Pryce, P. 1992. Manipulation of culture and history: A critique of two expert witnesses. *Nature Studies Review* 8 (1): 35-46.

Raunet, D. 1984. *Without surrender, without consent: A history of the Nishga land claims*. Vancouver: Douglas and McIntyre.

Ray, A.J. 2003. Native history on trial: Confessions of an expert witness. *Canadian Historical Review* 84 (2): 253-73.

Regina v. *Jim*. 1993. British Columbia Provincial Court, Smithers. Transcript.

Reid, B. 1971. *Out of the silence*. Photos: A. de Menil. New York: Outerbridge and Dienstfrey, for Amon Carter Museum, Fort Worth, TX.

Reiter, R.R., ed. 1975. *Toward an anthropology of women*. New York: Monthly Review Press.

Rigsby, B. 2001. Representations of culture and expert knowledge and opinions of anthropologists. Paper presented at the Adelaide Native Title Conference, 6-7 July.

Rigsby, B., and J. Kari. 1987. Gitksan and Wet'suwet'en linguistic relations. Opinion evidence for the plaintiffs, *Delgamuukw et al.* v. *Her Majesty the Queen*. On file at the Gitksan Treaty Office, Hazelton, BC.

Rival, L.M. 1999. Hunters and gatherers of South America. In R.B. Lee and R.H. Daly, eds., *The Cambridge encyclopedia of hunters and gatherers*, 77-85. Cambridge: Cambridge University Press.

–. 2002. *Trekking through history: The Huaorani of Amazonian Ecuador*. New York: Columbia University Press.

Robinson, M. 1997 [1978]. *Sea otter chiefs*. Calgary: Bayeux Arts.

Robinson, S. 1987. Proto-historic developments in Gitksan and Wet'suwet'en territories. Opinion evidence for the defendants in *Delgamuukw et al.* On file at the Gitksan Treaty Office, Hazelton, BC.

Robinson, W. 1962. *Men of Medeek, as told by Walter Wright*. Terrace: Northern Sentinel Press, and Part 2, typescript on file at the Gitksan Treaty Office, Hazelton, BC.

Rosman, A., and P. Rubel. 1971. *Feasting with mine enemy: Rank and exchange among Northwest Coast societies*. New York: Columbia University Press.

Roth, Christopher. 2002. Goods, names and selves: Rethinking the Tsimshian potlatch. *American Ethnologist* 29 (1): 123-50.

Rubel, P., and A. Rosman. 1983. The evolution of exchange structures and ranking: Some Northwest Coast and Athapaskan examples. *Journal of Anthropological Research* 39 (1): 1-25.

Ruby, R.H., and J.A. Brown. 1976. *The Chinook Indians: Traders of the lower Columbia River*. Norman, OK: University of Oklahoma Press.

Russell, B. 1985. The greatness of Albert Einstein. In M. Gardner, ed., *The sacred beetle and other great essays in science*, 408-12. Buffalo, NY: Prometheus Books.

Sahlins, M.D. 1965. On the sociology of primitive exchange. In M. Banton, ed., *The relevance of models for social anthropology*, 139-236. Association of Social Anthropology Series No. 1. London: Tavistock Publications.

–. 1968. *Tribesmen*. Englewood Cliffs, NJ: Prentice-Hall.

–. 1972. *Stone Age economics*. Chicago: Aldine-Atherton.

Samuel, C. 1982. *The Chilkat dancing blanket*. Seattle: Pacific Search Press.

Sapir, E. 1915a. The social organization of the west coast tribes. Proceedings and Transactions of the Royal Society of Canada, sec. 2, ser. 3, vol. 9. Ottawa.

–. 1915b. A sketch of the social organization of the Nass River Indians. *Museum Bulletin 19, Anthropological Series* 7. Ottawa: Canadian Geological Survey, Department of Mines.

Schalk, R.F. 1981. Land use and organizational complexity among foragers of northwestern North America. In S. Koyama and D.H. Thomas, eds., *Affluent foragers: Pacific coasts east and west*, 53-75. Osaka: Senri Ethnological Studies 9.

Schrire, C. 1984. *Past and present in hunter-gatherer studies*. Orlando, FL: Academic Press.

Schutz, A. 1964. *Collected papers II: Studies in social theory*, A. Brodersen, ed. The Hague: Martinus Nijhoff.

Scott, C. 1986. Hunting territories, hunting bosses and communal production among coastal James Bay Cree. In C.A. Bishop and T. Morantz, eds., *Who owns the beaver? Northern Algonquian land tenure reconsidered. Anthropologica* (special issue) n.s. 28 (1-2): 163-74.

Seguin, M. 1984. Lest there be no salmon: Symbols in the traditional Tsimshian potlatch. In M. Seguin, ed., *The Tsimshian: Images of the past, views for the present*, 99-109. Vancouver: UBC Press.

–. 1985. *Interpretive contexts for traditional and current Coast Tsimshian feasts*. National Museum of Man, Mercury Series, Ethnology Service Paper 98. Ottawa.

Service, E.R. 1962. *Primitive social organization: An evolutionary perspective*. New York: Random House.

–. 1966. *The hunters*. Englewood Cliffs, NJ: Prentice-Hall.

Sider, G. 1980. The ties that bind: Culture and agriculture, property and propriety in the Newfoundland village fishery. *Social History* 5 (1): 1-40.

Sieciechowicz, K. 1986. Northern Ojibwa land tenure. In C.A. Bishop and T. Morantz, eds., *Who owns the beaver? Northern Algonquian land tenure reconsidered. Anthropologica* (special issue) n.s. 28 (1-2): 187-202.

Smith, D.B. 1984. Textually mediated social organization. *International Social Science Journal* 36: 59-75.

–. 1987. *The everyday world as problematic: A feminist sociology*. Boston: Northwestern University Press.

–. 1990a. *The conceptual practices of power: A feminist sociology of knowledge*. Toronto: University of Toronto Press.

–. 1990b. *Texts, facts and femininity: Exploring the relations of ruling*. London: Routledge and Kegan Paul.

–. 1996. Telling the truth after postmodernism. *Symbolic Interaction* 19 (3): 171-202.

Smith, M.W. 1945. Seabird Island fieldnotes, summer 1945. London: Royal Anthropological Institute. Unpublished.

Solway, J., and R.B. Lee. 1990. Foragers, genuine or spurious? Situating the Kalahari San in history. *Current Anthropology* 31 (2): 109-46.

Sparrow. Regina v. Sparrow [1990] 3 C.N.L.R. 160.

Speck, F. 1926. Land ownership among hunting peoples in primitive America and the world's marginal areas. *International Congress of Americanists, 22nd session*, 2: 323-32. Rome.

Speck, F., and L. Eiseley. 1942. Montagnais-Naskapi bands and family hunting districts of the central and southeastern Labrador peninsula. *American Philosophical Society* 85: 215-42.

Spencer, B., and F.J. Gillen. 1927. *The Arunta: The study of a Stone Age people*. New York: Harper and Row.

Speth, J.D., and K.A. Spielman. 1983. Energy source, protein metabolism, and hunter-gatherers. *Journal of Anthropological Archaeology* 2: 1-31.

Spivak, G.C. 1988. *In other worlds: Essays in cultural politics*. New York: Routledge.

Sponsel, L. 1989. Farming and foraging: A necessary complementarity in Amazonia? In S. Kent, ed., *Farmers as hunters: The implications of sedentism*, 37-45. Cambridge: Cambridge University Press.

Stefansson, V. 1945. *Arctic manual*. New York: Macmillan.

–. 1946. *Not by bread alone*. New York: Macmillan.

Sterritt, N.J., S. Marsden, P.R. Grant, R. Galois, and R. Overstall. 1998. *Tribal boundaries in the Nass Watershed*. Vancouver: UBC Press.

Steward, J. 1955. *Theory of culture change: An evolutionary perspective*. New York: Random House.

–. 1969. Postscript to bands: On taxonomy, processes and causes. In D. Dames, ed., *Contributions to anthropology: Band societies*. National Museum of Canada Bulletin 228, 290-1. Ottawa.

Stites, S.H. 1905. *Economics of the Iroquois*. Lancaster, PA: New Era Printing Co.

Strehlow, T.G.H. 1947. *Aranda traditions*. Melbourne: Melbourne University Press.

Supreme Court of Canada (SCC). 1997. *Delgamuukw et al. v. The Queen, on appeal from the Court of Appeal for British Columbia*, before Lamer, C.J., LaForest, L'Heureux-Dubé, Sopinka, Cory, McLachlin and Major, J.J. File No. 23799, 11 December, Ottawa.

[Susman, A., V.E. Garfield, and W. Beynon?] N.d. Process of change from matrilineal to patrilineal inheritance as illustrated in building, ownership and transmission of houses and house sites in a Tsimshian village. *Volkerkundliche Arbeitsgemeinschaft, Anthropology Study Groups Abhandlungen*, vol. 26. Reprint 1976, Nortorf (copy at Northwest Community College, Hazelton; author identity uncertain).

Suttles, W. 1951. The early diffusion of the potato among the Coast Salish. *Southwestern Journal of Anthropology* 7 (3): 72-88.

–. 1960. Affinal ties, subsistence and prestige among the Coast Salish. *American Anthropologist* 62: 296-305.

–. 1962. Variation in habitat and culture in the Northwest Coast. *Akten des 34 Internationalen Amerikannishen Kongresses, Wein, 1960*: 522-37.

–. 1966 [1956]. Private knowledge, morality and social classes among the Coast Salish. In T. McFeat, ed., *Indians of the north Pacific coast*, 166-79. Toronto: McClelland and Stewart.

–. 1968. Coping with abundance: Subsistence on the Northwest Coast. In R.B. Lee and I. DeVore, eds., *Man the hunter*, 56-68. Chicago: Aldine.

–. 1990a. General ed. *Handbook of North American Indians*. Vol. 7: *Northwest Coast*. Washington, DC: Smithsonian Institution. 1984.

–. 1990b. History of research: Early sources. In W. Suttles, gen. ed., *Handbook of North American Indians*. Vol. 7: *Northwest Coast*, 70-2. Washington, DC: Smithsonian Institution.

Suttles, W., and A. Jonaitis. 1990. History of research in ethnology. In W. Suttles, gen. ed., *Handbook of North American Indians*. Vol. 7: *Northwest Coast*, 73-87. Washington, DC: Smithsonian Institution.

Swanton, J.R. 1905. *Contributions to the ethnology of the Haida*. American Museum of Natural History Memoirs, Vol. 8, Part 1: 1-300. New York.

Tanaka, J. 1980. *The San hunter-gatherers of the Kalahari: A study in ecological anthropology*. Tokyo: University of Tokyo Press. 1984.

Tanner, A. 1979. *Bringing home animals: Religious ideology and mode of production of the Mistassini Cree hunters*. Montreal: McGill-Queen's University Press.

–. 1991. Canadian Aboriginal resistance to fur trade mercantilism. Paper presented at the symposium "Narratives of resistance," Canadian Anthropological Society, London, Ontario, May.

Teit, J.A. 1912-15. Report on Tahltan fieldwork among the Tahltan, Kaska and Bear Lake Indians. National Museum of Canada, Canadian Ethnology Service, 210.4c: B121. 1984.

Tennant, P. 1990. *Aboriginal peoples and politics: The Indian land question in British Columbia, 1849-1989*. Vancouver: UBC Press.

Thomas, E.M. 1990. The old way. *New Yorker*, 15 October.

–. 1994. *The tribe of tiger*. New York: Simon and Schuster.

Thuen, T. 1992. Juridiske og politiske aspekter ved utviklingen av urbefolkningsrettigheter i Canada [Jural and political aspects of the development of Aboriginal rights in Canada]. *Norsk Antropologisk Tidsskrift* 2/1992.

–. 1995. *Quest for equity: Norway and the Saami challenge*. St. John's, NF: Institute of Social and Economic Research, Memorial University of Newfoundland.

Titley, B. 1986. *A narrow vision: Duncan Campbell Scott and the administration of Indian Affairs in Canada*. Vancouver: UBC Press.

Tobey, M. 1981. Carrier. In J. Helm, gen. ed., *Handbook of North American Indians*. Vol. 6: *Subarctic*, 413-32. Washington, DC: Smithsonian Institution.

Tomlinson, Rev. R. 1875. A journey up the Skeena River, British Columbia. *Church Missionary Intelligencer* 25l-6, 281-8.

Transcripts. 1987-1989. Official transcripts of proceedings at trial, in the Supreme Court of British Columbia, before the Honourable Chief Justice, no. 0834, Smithers Registry, between: *Delgamuukw*, suing on his own behalf and on behalf of all other members of the *House of Delgamuukw*, and others, Plaintiffs, and: *Her Majesty the Queen in Right of the*

Province of British Columbia and *The Attorney-General of Canada*, Defendants. Vancouver. Supreme Court of British Columbia.

Trigger, B.G. 1962. The historic location of the Hurons. *Ontario History* 54 (2): 137-48.

–. 1963. Settlement as an aspect of Iroquoian adaptation at the time of contact. *American Anthropologist* 65 (1): 86-101.

–. 1972. Hochelaga: History and ethnohistory. In J.F. Pendergast and B.G. Trigger, eds., *Cartier's Hochelaga and the Dawson site*. Montreal: McGill-Queen's University Press.

–. 1976. *The children of Aataentsic: A history of the Huron people to 1660*. Montreal: McGill-Queen's University Press.

Tringham, R. 1971. *Hunters, fishers, and farmers of eastern Europe, 6000 to 3000 BC*. London: Hutchinson University Library.

Turnbull, C.J. 1966. Report on Moricetown and Babine Lake. Manuscript 72, Archives of the Archaeological Survey of Canada. Ottawa.

Turnbull, C.M. 1961. *The forest people*. New York: Natural History Press.

–. 1965. *Wayward servants: Two worlds of the African Pygmies*. New York: Natural History Press.

–. 1968. The importance of flux in two hunting societies. In R.B. Lee and I. DeVore, eds., *Man the hunter*, 132-7. Chicago: Aldine.

Turner, N.J. 1999. "Time to burn": Traditional use of fire to enhance resource production by Aboriginal peoples in British Columbia. In R. Boyd, ed., *Indians, fire and the land*, 185-218. Corvallis, OR: Oregon State University.

Turner, N.J., and S.L. Peacock. Forthcoming. Solving the perennial paradox: Evidence for plant resource management on the Northwest Coast. In D.E. Deur and N.J. Turner, eds., *Keeping it living: Traditions of plant use and cultivation on the Northwest Coast*. Seattle: University of Washington Press.

Usher, J. 1974. *William Duncan of Metlakatla: A Victorian missionary in British Columbia*. National Museums of Canada, Publications in History, No. 5. Ottawa: National Museum of Man.

Vayda, A.P. 1961. A re-examination of Northwest Coast economic systems. *Transactions of the New York Academy of Sciences, Series 2*, 23: 618-24.

Walens, S. 1981. *Feasting with cannibals: An essay on Kwakiutl cosmology*. Princeton: Princeton University Press.

Wallace, A.F.C. 1947. Woman, land, and society: Three aspects of Aboriginal Delaware life. *Pennsylvania Archeologist* 27 (1-4): 1-35.

–. 1957. Political organization and land tenure among the northeastern Indians, 1600-1830. *Southwestern Journal of Anthropology* 13: 301-21.

–. 1972. *The death and rebirth of the Seneca*. New York: Vintage Books.

Weiner, A. 1976. *Women of value, men of renown: New perspectives in Trobriand exchange*. Austin: University of Texas Press.

–. 1985. Inalienable wealth. *American Ethnologist* 12 (2): 210-27.

–. 1992. *Inalienable possessions: The paradox of keeping-while-giving*. Berkeley: University of California Press.

Widmer, R.J. 1988. *The evolution of the Calusa*. Tuscaloosa and London: University of Alabama Press.

Wike, J.A. 1951. The effect of the maritime fur trade on Northwest Coast Indian society. Ph.D. diss., Columbia University, New York.

Williams, S.C. 1921. William Tatham Wataugan. *Tennessee Historical Magazine* 7 (3): 154-79.

Wilmsen, E.N. 1983. The ecology of illusion: Anthropological foraging in the Kalahari. *Reviews in Anthropology* 10 (1): 9-20.

Wilmsen, E.N., and J. Denbow. 1990. Paradigmatic history of San-speaking peoples and current attempts at revision. *Current Anthropology* 31 (5): 489-524.

Wirsing, R.L. 1985. The health of traditional societies and the effects of acculturation. *Current Anthropology* 26 (3): 303-22.

Wolf, E. 1982. *Europe and the peoples without history*. Berkeley and Los Angeles: University of California Press.

Woodburn, J. 1968. An introduction to Hadza ecology. In R.B. Lee and I. DeVore, eds., *Man the hunter,* 103-10. Chicago: Aldine.

–. 1970. *Hunters and gatherers: The material culture of the nomadic Hadza.* London: British Museum.

–. 1979. Minimal politics: The political organization of the Hadza of Tanzania. In P. Cohen and W. Shack, eds., *Politics in leadership: A comparative perspective,* 244-6. Oxford: Clarendon Press.

–. 1980. Hunters and gatherers today and reconstruction of the past. In E. Gellner, ed., *Soviet and western anthropology,* 95-117. London: Duckworth.

–. 1982. Egalitarian societies. *Man* 17: 431-51.

Woodward, A.E. 1973. *Aboriginal Rights Commission first report.* Canberra: Australian Government Printing Service.

–. 1974. *Aboriginal Rights Commission second report.* Canberra: Australian Government Printing Service.

Worl, R., and C.W. Smythe. 1986. *Barrow: A decade of modernization.* Anchorage: Minerals Management Service, Alaska OCS Region, Alaska OCS Economic Studies Program.

Wright, R. 1992. *Stolen continents: The Indian story.* New York and London: Random House.

Yen, D.E. 1989. The domestication of the environment. In D. Harris and G. Hillman, eds., *Foraging and farming: The evolution of plant exploitation,* 55-75. London: Unwin-Hyman.

Yerbury, J.C. 1975. An ethnohistorical reconstruction of the social oganization of Athabascan Indians in the Alaskan subarctic and Pacific drainage. Master's thesis, Simon Fraser University, Burnaby, BC.

York, A., R. Daly, and C. Arnett. 1993. *They write their dreams on the rock forever: Rock writing in the Stein River valley of British Columbia.* Vancouver: Talonbooks.

Zvelebil, M. 1986. Postglacial foraging in the forests of Europe. *Scientific American,* May.

Index